Cambridge Studies in French

THE ORDER OF MIMESIS

Cambridge Studies in French

General editor: MALCOLM BOWIE

THE ORDER OF MIMESIS

BALZAC, STENDHAL, NERVAL, FLAUBERT

CHRISTOPHER PRENDERGAST

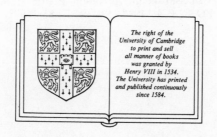

The right of the
University of Cambridge
to print and sell
all manner of books
was granted by
Henry VIII in 1534.
The University has printed
and published continuously
since 1584.

CAMBRIDGE UNIVERSITY PRESS

CAMBRIDGE

LONDON   NEW YORK   NEW ROCHELLE

MELBOURNE   SYDNEY

Published by the Press Syndicate of the University of Cambridge
The Pitt Building, Trumpington Street, Cambridge CB2 1RP
32 East 57th Street, New York, NY 10022, USA
10 Stamford Road, Oakleigh, Melbourne 3166, Australia

© Cambridge University Press 1986

First published 1986

Printed in Great Britain at
the University Press, Cambridge

British Library cataloguing in publication data
Prendergast, Christopher
The Order of Mimesis: Balzac, Stendhal, Nerval, Flaubert. –
(Cambridge studies in French)
1. French fiction – 19th century – History and criticism
2. Mimesis in literature
I. Title
843'7   PQ653

Library of Congress cataloguing in publication data
Prendergast, Christopher.
The Order of Mimesis.
(Cambridge Studies in French)
Bibliography: p.
Includes index.
1. French literature – 19th century – History and criticism.
2. Mimesis in literature. 3. Balzac, Honoré de, 1799–1850 –
Criticism and interpretation. 4. Stendhal, 1783–1842 –
Criticism and interpretation. 5. Nerval, Gérard de, 1808–1855
– Criticism and interpretation. 6. Flaubert, Gustave, 1821–
1880 – Criticism and interpretation. I. Title. II. Series.
PQ382.P74   1986   840'.9÷1   85–18998

ISBN 0 521 23789 0

CONTENTS

GENERAL EDITOR'S PREFACE

This series aims at providing a new forum for the discussion of major critical or scholarly topics within the field of French studies. It differs from most similar-seeming ventures in the degree of freedom which contributing authors are allowed and in the range of subjects covered. For the series is not concerned to promote any single area of academic specialisation or any single theoretical approach. Authors are invited to address themselves to *problems*, and to argue their solutions in whatever terms seem best able to produce an incisive and cogent account of the matter in hand. The search for such terms will sometimes involve the crossing of boundaries between familiar academic disciplines, or the calling of those boundaries into dispute. Most of the studies will be written especially for the series, although from time to time it will also provide new editions of outstanding works which were previously out of print, or originally published in languages other than English or French.

ACKNOWLEDGEMENTS

Two sections of this book have appeared, in modified form, in the following journals: *French Studies* and *Paragraph*. I am grateful to the respective editors for permission to reprint here. I should also like to express my thanks to the various people who have helped with the preparation of the final typescript: Joanne Griffith, Carolyn Featherstone, Sandra Kendall and Frances Pink. I am particularly grateful to Heather Pratt for her unstinting help with the proofs; without her vigilant eye the final product would have been considerably messier. Special thanks go to Malcolm Bowie who, as both friend and general editor, was immensely generous in giving support and guidance at a particularly difficult moment. I should also like to record my gratitude to all those friends and colleagues who, on a variety of matters and in a variety of ways, have helped with information, advice and encouragement: John Barrell, Geoff Bennington, Norman Bryson, Terence Cave, John Forrester, Ross Harrison, Leslie Hill, Geoffrey Lloyd, Andy Martin. My greatest debt (although he himself would repudiate that notion) is to Tony Tanner for an education of a very special kind; the book is dedicated to him.

1

THE ORDER OF MIMESIS: POISON, NAUSEA, HEALTH

It would appear, from various accounts, that we have had 'modernity', and are now, if not fully installed, in the process of entering into our 'postmodern' condition. What that condition looks like has already attracted many, and often deeply uninteresting, descriptions (the most deeply boring are those which suggest that we should get into it as quickly as possible in order to escape from Boredom). But one very powerful description is that proposed by Jean-François Lyotard, when he compares the postmodern condition to an *agon*, a place in which discourses, or different ways of forming and combining 'sentences' (the cognitive, the prescriptive, the narrative, the declarative, the normative, the performatice, etc.), meet in a relation of fundamental antagonism.[1] This view represents a very important change in the tenor of 'radical' thinking in France today. Where, in the immediate post-1968 period, we had the language of 'permanent revolution' (in, for example, the Maoism of *Tel Quel*, long since deserted for the pleasures of the psychoanalytical 'love story' or the revelations of the Bible), we now have the language of 'civil war', in which it is precisely language itself, or rather sentences, that are both subject and object of that war. What is implied by Lyotard's phrasal agonistics (and its particular bearing on the question of narrative) is a matter to which I shall want to return in a later chapter. But in terms of the general field of literary studies – although the issues involved far exceed what we ordinarily understand by the purely 'literary' – one of the casualties of this war has been the notion of *mimesis*.

Before the war (and the revolution) there was, of course, considerable and often acrimonious dispute about mimesis, but this rarely entailed attempts at its systematic liquidation. The 'mimetic' function of literature might, in certain eyes, be less interesting than other functions, but it occurred to few that it should be removed from the map altogether (although quite what was meant by the 'mimetic' was by no means a matter of universal agreement). Thus,

1

in 1953 M. H. Abrams (in *The Mirror and the Lamp*) could argue that the 'situation' of the literary text was to be understood, indeed had always been understood, in terms of four basic 'co-ordinates' or 'relations': the 'expressive' (the relation of text to author); the 'pragmatic' (the relation of text to audience); the 'mimetic' (the relation of text to world); the 'objective' (the relation of the text to itself, as a purely 'autonomous' object).[2] The kind of attention given to any one or more of these relations would vary according to individual tastes or, more importantly, historical conventions (in the Romantic period, for example, there is a characteristic foregrounding of the 'expressive'). But, as a matter of general principle, there was no necessary reason for these relations to be organised hierarchically; still less were there sensible grounds for suggesting that any one should be consigned to a merited oblivion.

Since the advent of structuralism and semiology, and then (in what Barthes called 'the runaway history of semiology')[3] their critical transformation into 'post-structuralism' and 'deconstruction', all this has changed. Both the 'expressive' and the 'mimetic' functions have been subjected to ceaseless bombardment by a series of 'sentences', at once prescriptive and proscriptive. 'Authors' have been declared 'dead', and the expressive function merely a residue of romantic individualism mixed up with a proprietorial ideology of meaning. Mimetic or representational notions have been exposed as an 'illusion', in the sense of a rhetorical trick designed to mask the arbitrary character of the literary sign, and similarly contaminated by an ideology whose effort is to convince us of an enduring (human) Nature beyond the changing and heterogeneous forms of culture and history. In short, the rout of the expressive and the mimetic has been part of that process of clearing away the débris of the ruined categories of an anthropocentric metaphysics: self, nature, presence, and ultimately Man. Conversely, Abrams's two other functions, the 'pragmatic' and the 'objective', have gained pride of place. The terms have, of course, changed. Thus, in so far as the emphasis on the pragmatic function rested on notions of literature as 'communication', it has been revised or discarded as smacking too much of intentionalist theories of meaning. On the other hand, as Genette has pointed out,[4] a major preoccupation of structuralist research, especially in its proposals for new ways of studying rhetoric, has been with the social and ideological context of the relation of text and reader, as an inquiry into the cultural circuits or 'codes' through which the text is 'realised' in the act of reading. Substantial reservations have also been expressed with regard to the notion of the 'autonomy' of the literary text (especially its formulation in the terms of Anglo-American 'New Criticism'). But the impact of Jakobson's pioneering essay on the 'poetic function' of language brought the notion back in a new, and more sophisticated, form: the poetic function brings about a suspension of the 'referential' function; it accentuates attention to the 'message pour son propre compte', to the materiality of the literary sign ('le côté palpable des signes').[5] This version of autonomy insists on the irreducible nature of *textuality* (and, from there, of 'intertextuality'); what literature talks about is not the world or the self but literature, engaged in self-reflective scrutiny of its own fabricated reality, its specific processes of construction and, under certain conditions, 'deconstruction'.

This eclipse of the 'mimetic', and what its consequences are for how we read certain texts of the past ('classics') is one of the themes of this book. In that regard, its primary aim is to outline a number of modern theoretical approaches to the idea of mimesis, and, in a more analytical vein, to relate these to a number of narrative texts produced in the period which literary history familiarly designates as the 'age of realism'. For the most part, my material and frames of reference are of French origin, although I shall also add to, and complicate, these frames by drawing upon alternative intellectual traditions. The texts I shall be chiefly examining (for reasons explained in due course) are Balzac's *Illusions perdues* and *Splendeurs et misères des courtisanes*, Stendhal's *Le Rouge et le Noir*, Nerval's *Sylvie* and Flaubert's *L'Éducation sentimentale*; while the theoretical perspectives derive in large measure from what, roughly, we can call the critical semiology developed in and around the work of Barthes, Kristeva, Genette and Derrida (although such are the self-displacing moves of modern French 'theory' it is doubtful, especially in connection with Derrida, whether the semiological project any longer holds as an adequate description). While some knowledge of the writings of these latter figures is assumed, one of the aims of the book – in accordance with the general objectives of the series in which it is published – is to give a résumé of how, and why, the idea of mimesis has been critically encountered within the wider contemporary French critique of the idea of 'representation'. Accordingly, the subsequent chapter, devoted largely to theoretical matters, sketches the elements of an 'economy' of mimesis (the term is Derrida's)[6] on the basis, or from the starting point, of some of the central propositions of this body of work. With the exception of the chapter on Flaubert (which introduces a major shift in direction), the more analytical chapters on the narrative texts are themselves broadly organised along similar lines, each chapter in turn taking up the main issues, raised successively in each of the various sections of the theoretical chapter.

On the other hand, my aims are not exclusively of an expository sort. I also attempt a more general argument about mimesis, in which the semiological and deconstructionist perspectives, while playing a vital role, are also subjected to critical examination, and partly displaced by other ways of looking at the question. For if, following Lyotard, the *agon* is now the only place in which we can 'honourably'[7] conduct ourselves (where we can escape the seductive mystifications of consensus and legitimation), it is also true that, in a universe of adversarial exchange where each competing party seeks to gain maximal advantage over the others, argument is all too often usurped by polemic. Naturally, on the battlefields of the 'civil war', local tactical considerations often rule out the protocols and niceties of more deliberative exchange, and it would certainly be disingenuous for any party to current debates about mimesis to claim exemption from polemical manoeuvres. It is indeed an index of the sensitivity of the issue of mimesis that it so regularly attracts such manoeuvres. Nevertheless, they often exact a high price. For when, in the cut and thrust of polemic, 'mimetic' automatically trips off the tongue as a taken-for-granted term of abuse (or conversely, as a taken-for-granted term of praise), this is a sign that the channels of more serious argumentation have become blocked. One of the aims of this book is to unblock those channels, to engage critically (and sometimes polemically) with what appears to have been simplified or effaced by polemic. Mimesis, I shall argue, cannot be reduced to being merely a bogus target in the contemporary version of the quarrel of the Ancients and the Moderns; it is only at the cost of a serious distortion of its complex logic that it can be pressed into the service of a particular *parti pris*.

This more general argument is difficult to summarise in advance of its detailed presentation. The difficulty is partly a matter of historical perspective. Although in many of its versions the idea of mimesis is intimately associated with a notion of stability (in the assumption of both a stable 'reality' and a correspondingly stable system of 'representation'), the actual history of the idea itself shows a quite remarkable instability. Reconstituting that history, even in barest outline, is not one of the ambitions of the present undertaking (that would require a capacity on the part of its author and a capaciousness on the part of the book that are quite unavailable). But that history is evidence that, in the case of mimesis, there is no original or core doctrine to be unproblematically recovered, and in relation to which all other accounts can then be classified as so many variants or derivatives. Although mimesis is haunted by its own 'origins' (in the perennial exegetical return to the first moments of its articulation in Western thought, Plato and Aristotle), the abundance of widely divergent commentaries subsequently produced on those canonic texts itself bears witness to a history of the continuous transformation of those origins. We cannot read the idea of mimesis independently of the multiple commentaries to which it has given rise, and in which it is now, for us, diversely embodied. Thus, while the actual history of literary mimesis is not my concern here, a recognition of its historical character, of the historical conditions determining both the theory and practice of mimesis, is an indispensable feature of the more formal approach I shall be adopting.

The problem of gaining synoptic purchase on the idea of mimesis is not, however, just a question of its multifarious historical guises. A deeper source of difficulty – but at the same time it is the very crux of the argument I wish to pursue – arises from the inherent conceptual ambiguity of mimesis itself. This ambiguity can perhaps be initially marked by the double sense of the term 'order'. Mimesis is an order, in the dual sense of a set of arrangements and a set of commands. On one interpretation, the mimetic 'command' consists, through a stress on the values of imitation and repetition, in an imperative to submit to the set of symbolic arrangements (the mimetic 'plot'), as if the latter corresponded to the natural order of things. The key question concerns the origins and status of this command. On Lyotard's model of phrasal 'enchaînement', we could say that the logical matrix of mimesis is formed from the combination, and confusion, of three (heterogeneous) kinds of sentences: a descriptive, a prescriptive and a normative. The descriptive says 'this is how things are'; the prescriptive says 'you must accept that this is how things are'; the normative says 'there is an authority validating the two previous sentences'. Just who are the addressors and addressees of these sentences, and in particular how we name the 'authority' governing the normative, is a question the answer to which is far from self-evident. Radical theory has, of course, come up with various candidates, but as Lyotard remarks, searching for the source of a normative is an intellectually hazardous business:

L'autorité ne se déduit pas. Les essais de légitimation de l'autorité conduisent au cercle vicieux (j'ai autorité sur toi parce que tu m'autorises à l'avoir), à la pétition de principe (l'autorisation autorise l'autorité), à la régression à l'infini (*x* est autorisé par *y*, qui est autorisé par *z*), au paradoxe de l'idiolecte (Dieu, la Vie, etc. me désigne pour exercer l'autorité, moi seul suis le témoin de cette révélation).[8]

In different forms and contexts, we shall find these circles, paradoxes and regressions everywhere in the contemporary argument about mimesis. Yet, if it is difficult, perhaps impossible, to identify the authority behind the authorised versions of reality consecrated by mimesis, there is, in modern French critical thought, general agreement that such versions are unequivocally authoritarian. The 'order' of mimesis is repressive and claustrating. It is part of the fabric of mystification and bad faith from which the dominant forms of our culture are woven, a 'command' belonging to the repertoire of what Althusser, in his account of the ideological foundations of representation, has termed the process of 'interpellation', whereby we are imperiously called upon to occupy fixed positions within existing historical structures, themselves posited as if made for all eternity.[9] The authoritarian gesture of mimesis is to imprison us in a world which, by virtue of its familiarity, is closed to analysis and criticism, in which the 'prescriptive' and the 'normative' (themselves tacit) ensure that the 'descriptive' remains at the level of the undiscussed, in the taken-for-grantedness of the familiar. Mimesis deals in familiarities ('recognitions'), but the recognitions it supplies are often misrecognitions ('méconnaissances'); and what is characteristically misrecognised, in the interests of conferring legitimacy on the familiar, is the arbitrariness of the symbolic forms we make and which make us.

Clearly, it would require a considerable amount of naivety or bad faith (neither currently in short supply) to reject outright the proposition that an art concerned with the reproduction of the familiar (with 'recognitions') can entail psychic repression, historical inertia and ideological hypostasis of the given. Whence the tendency in 'modernist' aesthetics to construe what is most vital in literary texts in terms of an impulse to question and rebel against the order of mimesis (broadly, what we know as the aesthetics of *defamiliarisation*). The prestige of the latter, in its varying forms, is now such as to have made it virtually unassailable. On the other hand, it is minimally arguable that ceaseless defamiliarisation (like 'permanent revolution') is a notion that is difficult to hold steadily in focus for very long without falling prey to certain optical illusions, or other kinds of misrecognition. One such possible misrecognition concerns the question of 'limits'. Are there limits to the programme of defamiliarisation beyond which we fall into a world that is totally 'unrecognisable', and what (if anything) could it possibly mean to inhabit such a world? What are the conditions and constraints in the passage from programme to *practice*? 'Practice', of course (and related expressions, 'practical knowledge', 'practical consciousness') means different things to different people. Indeed such have been its appropriations by all sides of the modern war of meanings, that late twentieth-century usage of the term will doubtless create fairly severe headaches for future lexicographers. But its conservative connotations are still powerful: any statement prefaced by the phrase 'in practice' is very likely to lead back into that mystified triangle of the descriptive, the prescriptive and the normative where we hear (though cannot name) the voice of 'authority'.

But these connotations by no means monopolise or exhaust the semantic field. One of the senses of 'practice' I want to foreground here is Bourdieu's, and in particular his insistence that the meaning of the term be rescued from the theoretical 'legalism which sees practices solely as the product of *obedience*'.[10] This also gives another context for thinking about mimesis. 'Mimesis', says Bourdieu (citing the well-known phrase of Durkheim's), is linked to 'practice without theory',[11] to practice that is non-reflexive but not, for that reason, blindly submissive to authoritarian dictat, in the way a great deal of mainstream grand theory would have us believe. Practice, in this account, draws upon resources of active initiative and informal negotiation that are quite capable of bypassing the official ('authoritarian') forms of knowledge. This would then suggest a quite different level at which to situate and interpret the order of mimesis, where the principle of negotiating and naming the world in terms of familiar, shared images and representations is fundamentally bound to all organised forms of human practice. These images and representations may, under the pressure of a certain type of analysis, be shown as embodying a large portion of illusion ('misrecognition'); in the perspectives opened up by the holy trinity, Nietzsche, Freud and Marx, they may be 'fictions' serving particular desires, interests and ideologies. But, in other ways, they are also arguably indispensable to any conceivable social reality or what Wittgenstein calls a 'form of life' (the Wittgensteinian notion of 'form of life', along with the related notion of 'language game', will become a central reference in later chapters);[12] and perhaps the supreme illusion would be in the assumption that we could live entirely without them, in a euphoric movement of 'unbound' desire and 'infinite' semiosis.

Here, then, is the area of the profound ambiguity of the mimetic 'order'. In one of its aspects, it is, as we shall have ample occasion to see in the following chapters, part of the equipment of the Censor, whose repressive work inevitably generates a rebellious move, as that which psychoanalysis calls the 'return of the repressed', or, as Barthes puts it, as a series of 'decoys' ('leurre', 'esquive') in which the terms of the given are outplayed and transgressed.[13] In another of its aspects, however, it is that to which we assent, not so much because of its tyrannical exhortations or hegemonic authority, but simply because no coherent set of human practices can escape its aegis. In short, the ambiguity of mimesis turns on the paradox of the 'limit': the famous limit of which Bataille speaks (the limit of representation) is that which, as limit, invites a crossing (no 'norms' which do not breed an impulse to 'transgression'), but which also, precisely as limit, renders such a crossing in any definitive sense impossible.

The complex, shifting relation of mimesis to the experience of the 'limit', and the strange paradoxes and anxieties engendered by that relation, constitute the essential framework of the present undertaking. Its argument accordingly requires a certain style of presentation, adapted to the paradoxical character of its object. It will perhaps already be evident that the whole of the argument rests on a consciously exploited attitude of equivocation. I argue neither for nor against mimesis, or rather I argue simultaneously both for and against, on the grounds of an ambiguity in the concept that, it seems to me, cannot be adequately handled in any other way. It is thus less a matter of adopting *a* position than of bringing different positions into play, the essence of the case lying in the relations of complementarity and contradiction between these positions. This approach implies a double movement of assertion and negation, of putting forward a certain point of view and then back-tracking on that step and replacing the point of view with another. It is a movement mirrored in the lay-out of the book where, in the section on Aristotle, the section on 'reference', the chapter on Flaubert and the conclusion, I turn back on many of the premises of previous sections and chapters. But, simply as a schematic prolegomena, a pointer in the direction of the kinds of ambiguities and complexities to be confronted, it might be instructive to begin by briefly juxtaposing three quite different approaches to mimesis, three major paradigms, which we can respectively resume under the metaphorical headings: poison, nausea, health.

Poison

Plato (or Socrates? – the question already complicates the argument in major ways) banishes the mimetic artist because to grant him *droit de cité* would be equivalent to granting a licence for mayhem. It would be akin to releasing a noxious substance into the body politic, a 'poison' for which, once released, there is no remedy in the Platonic 'pharmacy', and which therefore can be handled only prophylactically, by means of rigid exclusion. Yet despite all the apparent evidence to the contrary (and the weight of the dominant exegetical tradition issuing from it), it is arguable that Plato promulgates this decree not primarily because the mimetic artist tells 'lies'. There are quite sophisticated (sophistical?) reasons for advancing this view, which have to do with suggesting Plato's own complicity in the very 'sophistry' he himself denounces (sophistry being to philosophy, roughly, what mimesis is to art). I shall return shortly to these reasons. There are, however, grounds of a much more straightforward nature for asserting that it is not primarily the question of the 'lie' as such which worries Plato. In the first place – the text of the *Republic* is quite explicit on the point (389c) – Plato does not shrink from claiming that, *in the right hands*, the lie can be of strategic usefulness to the State (what, for example, is the ingenious kinship system devised to accommodate the requirements of the incest taboo other than an elaborate fiction, a lie determining with whom you may lie?). Secondly, and in a somewhat different perspective, there is a very important sense in which, within the terms of Plato's own account of mimesis, an 'imitation' cannot possibly be a lie, or at least is such that no-one can possibly be taken in or 'deceived' by it. For, as Socrates remarks in the *Cratylus* (432bff), an imitation can be deemed to exist only where there is a perceived difference from, as well as similarity to, the object being imitated; without that difference, however minimal, there is no longer an imitation, but rather a replica (although such are the skills of the more artful mimeticians – Zeuxis's grapes – that we may be led to take an imitation for a replica).

The banishing of mimesis arises, therefore, not, as in the familiar arguments inspired for the most part by the cave-parable of Book 10 of the *Republic*, because it contaminates by means of its clever deceptions our metaphysical apprehension of the world of Ideal Forms; not because they obscure that movement (that opening of the 'eye of the soul') towards the transparent revelation of the Truth represented in the notion of *aletheia*. The real worry is initially (certainly the initial worry in the chronology of the *Republic*) less metaphysical than political; less an anxiety about duplicity than about duplication, or less a question of truth than of taxonomy. For what is at risk in the potentially uncontrollable proliferation of 'images', the endless play of representations made possible by mimesis, is a proper sense of 'division' and classification. Through his doublings and multiplications, the mimetic artist introduces 'improprieties' (a 'poison') into a social system ordered according to the rule that everything and everyone should be in its/his/her 'proper' place. He disturbs both the law of identity and the law of differentiation, confuses the hierarchical system of category-distinctions that is fundamental to the organisation of the City: if any one person can 'imitate' being a carpenter, a soldier, a doctor, a prince, then the boundary lines of recognition and separation which alone ensure the stability of the City dissolve into a promiscuous, undifferentiated mess. In brief, mimesis is excommunicated not because it is a threat to truth, but because it is a threat to order.

Plato's critique of mimesis in these terms is, as J.-P. Vernant argues,[14] linked to the specific historical and cultural conditions of his age (and in particular to the attack on the influence of the 'illusionist' repertoire of the magician). As a general argument, however, it has echoes in many other contexts. In particular, in terms of the period and the narrative forms I shall be concerned with, the idea of doublings as damaging, simulations as subversive of the fabric of society, we will refind in that other arch-ideologue of 'order', Balzac, where (especially in *Splendeurs*) the use of disguise, the creation of copies, the circulation of the fake, are perceived as secreting, precisely, a kind of 'poison' whose effects on the social organism are devastating. Yet, in the Balzacian context, one of the problems we shall encounter in this preoccupation with the dangers of doublings concerns its implications for the place of the Narrator: to what extent is he caught up in, or alternatively exempt from, the subversive kinds of fiction-making his own fiction denounces, and what kind of ambiguities and tremors within the system of narrative itself does this difficulty produce? A similar difficulty arises with the status of the 'narrator' of the *Republic*. One of the more curious features of his resourcefully cunning argument is that the medicine he prescribes for others, he conspicuously fails to administer to himself; and the text which lays the foundations for the ideal State is itself everywhere invaded by the very mimetic poison whose elimination is an essential prerequisite of the political programme it advocates.

For the really striking paradox of the *Republic*, as of the *Dialogues* as a whole, is that Plato too plays the mimetic game. What Plato's argument attacks (the 'image', 'narrative') is exactly what he often uses to advance his argument (notably in the story of the 'cave' and the image of the 'mirror').[15] Furthermore, in the act of displacing or 'doubling' himself in the figure of Socrates, Plato deserts what, in the *Republic*, are commended as the virtues of simple *diegesis* (speaking in one's own name) for the dissimulations of *mimesis* (speaking in the name of another). One way of dealing with these paradoxes – the sophisticated/sophistical approach intimated above – is the way developed in the radical reading of Plato proposed by Derrida.[16] What the scholarly credentials of this reading are I am not competent to judge. I allude to it here because the paradoxical logic it seeks to unfold within the Platonic account of mimesis announces a theme that, in equally paradoxical ways, will be central to this book (and which indeed will eventually and inevitably implicate Derrida's own position). According to this reading, Plato/Socrates is the Sophist par excellence; were he to appear as a stranger in a foreign city, he would instantly be branded magician, sorceror, charlatan, precisely the sort of figure to be rigorously excluded from the Republic. The premiss (unquestionably questionable) of this argument is that, in the final analysis, all discursive representations of the world are 'fictions', and that Plato *knows* this. Above all, this is the case with representations that lay claim to revealing the truth (the movement and moment of *aletheia*); but it is exactly the myth of Truth that has to be 'guarded' in the interests of the proper education of the Guardians (as Heidegger notes in his commentary on Plato, playing on the relation between *bewahren* and *Wahrheit*).[17] For Derrida and his followers, *aletheia* signifies not just the process of 'revelation' but also, and simultaneously, a process of 'masking' (in the French double-entendre, *aletheia* is that which 'se dér-obe').[18] In offering itself as truth, it has, in the same moment, to disguise its discursive, man-made and therefore fictive origins, since without that activity of masking the very foundations on which the security of the State is to be built are necessarily threatened. In other words, the criteria for distinguishing between representations are in reality purely pragmatic. There are those which maintain order, which conduce to the health of the State (including pre-eminently the fiction of truth). There are those which are injurious ('poisonous'), such as mimetic representations, for these not only disturb the ideal hierarchy of things, but also, in so far as they are recognisable as 'imitations', they draw attention to the capacity of the human mind for making, inventing, *fabricating* (in the dual sense of a making and a forging) the systems under which men live. But the final irony, on this reading, is that Plato, in seeing the hopeless impasse to which this leads him, both signals the impasse and mischievously disclaims responsibility for it, by disguising himself through the 'miming' of the voice of another, the voice of 'Socrates'. Plato 'lies' about himself in order to deal with both the lie of truth and the truth of lying.

Nausea

The modern way with mimesis (understanding by 'modern' roughly the attitude issuing from Nietzsche's critique of the representational arts in *The Birth of Tragedy*) is similarly articulated on a diagnostic model of 'sickness'. In its most influential contemporary incarnation (*S/Z*), Plato's 'poison' has become Barthes's 'nausea' (not to be confused with its Sartrian version, which is both the occasion and the pretext for promoting a new, more 'authentic' kind of mimesis). In these metaphorical guises, with their common implication of organic affliction, the respective approaches they embody might appear to be very close. In fact they stand at opposite poles to each other. For Barthes, the mimetic text is 'sickening', exhibits 'une sorte de vertu vomitive',[19] not because it troubles an order in which everything is in its proper place, but, on the contrary, because it *confirms* that order. Unlike the disruptive and subversive force assigned to mimesis by Plato, in Barthes's account mimesis is construed as an essentially conservative and conserving force; it participates in the production of a stable economy of signs and meanings through its perpetual re-cycling of the 'ready-made' (the 'déjà-vu, déjà-lu, déjà-fait').[20] As in the *Republic*, mimesis for Barthes is indeed a 'copy of a copy'.[21] It is not so, however, in the Platonic sense of a series of progressively distorting moves away from the original source of truth, but rather as the uncritical repetition of a discourse itself socially taken for granted as the repository of truth: that is, the discourse which Barthes will name as the *doxa*, precisely the term which, in Plato's system, stands in opposition to truth. In this reading, the strategies of mimesis are primarily subject to the law of Repetition, and produce (in Barthes's ideal reader) the feeling of nausea by virtue of 'l'ennui, le conformisme, le dégoût de la répétition'.[22] Arresting the infinite play of difference in the interests of reproducing the static order of the same, mimesis repeats and sanctions the Given as if it were the natural order of things. Mimesis, in other words, is a function of 'ideology' and, in its modern form, of *bourgeois* ideology, proceeding from that 'tourniquet propre à l'idéologie bourgeoise qui inverse la culture en nature'.[23]

The nauseously bland securities that Barthes's version accords to the system of mimesis could not be further removed from the menacingly poisonous proliferations that figure in Plato's account. To juxtapose them is thus to encounter a transformation in which, elliptically, we can read a great deal of the curious history of mimesis. As I have already indicated, that long and complex history does not fall within the terms of this study. The purpose of the juxta-position is rather to confront two intellectual paradigms, in order to illustrate from the outset precisely that ambiguity and instability in the concept of mimesis which enables it to produce diametrically opposed interpretations, to gather into itself notions of both norm and transgression, conservation and subversion. If therefore I begin (in the following chapter) by foregrounding the terms of the theoretical approach associated with Barthes and others, it is not because of an intention to give intellectual priority to that approach above all others. The strengths of the approach are now well known, and what contemporary understanding in general, and this book in particular, owe to it is very considerable. Broadly, these strengths are three-fold. First, in so far as mimesis can be identified as a sys-tem striving for maximal semantic unity and stability, it is necess-arily caught in a process whereby it seeks to mask the initial (and therefore potentially arbitrary) choices on which it is based. One of the great merits of semiological literary analysis lies in its power to uncover not only the hidden presuppositions of the system, but also the mechanisms whereby they remain hidden (what the semiologists call the logic of 'naturalisation'). Secondly, and inter-relatedly, semiological criticism of mimesis refuses to side-step, indeed actively pursues, a question of capital importance: if *grosso modo*, the idea of mimesis encapsulates a major intellectual error (false assumptions about language and its relation to the world), then why the sheer tenacity of the mimetic prejudice; why is it that texts have so frequently proffered themselves or have been so per-sistently read in mimetic terms? This is simply a brute fact of the his-tory of writing and reading which any serious account of mimesis, whatever its particular *parti pris*, must take into consideration.

Although, as I shall argue, the terms in which semiological criticism has answered this question are not fully adequate, it is nevertheless the case that it has exceptionally interesting things to say about the conditions of efficacy of the mimetic idea in Western culture. Thirdly – and perhaps the feature of Barthes's argument that is at once its most prominent and controversial feature – it has been quite remarkably adept in describing the kinds of rhetorical force and signifying 'play' through which, in certain texts, these conditions, and the sets of expectations which accompany them, are challenged and overturned.

In this respect, my own account of how nineteenth-century narrative practice relates to the protocols of mimesis follows that of Barthes's *S/Z*, in particular that point where Barthes describes *Sarrasine* as introducing a 'trouble de la représentation',[24] a moment of breakdown in the otherwise self-assured functioning of the economy of mimesis. The tracing of such moments will be one of my central concerns, although it will also be one of my contentions that the area and incidence of these disruptive moments are far greater than is apparently implied by *S/Z*. More importantly, however, I intend the term 'anxiety' as a generalised description of an unease whose ramifications are much wider than I take those of Barthes's 'trouble' to be. By 'anxiety' I do not just mean that which precedes and precipitates an experience of breakdown in the representational system, but a worry which turns on the uncertain status of representation as such. It is the anxiety linked to the permanently unsettled condition we inhabit in relation to the mimetic 'order', as that which, on the one hand and for the reasons persuasively stated by Barthes, we wish to disobey and exceed, but which, on the other hand and for equally persuasive reasons, we acknowledge and accept. Barthes's wholesale attack on the idea of representation, as an instrument of subjugation within the symbolic order, loses sight of that ambiguity (with a corresponding swerve, in the emphasis on 'liberating' the signifier, towards a potentially regressive movement back into the seductions of the 'imaginary').[25]

Reinstating and exploring the ambiguity excised from Barthes's account is therefore an essential part of the present enterprise. An obvious starting point would be with some of the problems connected with the typology of texts which in *S/Z* Barthes sketches in relation to the idea of mimesis: the typology constructed around the terms *lisible/classique*, *scriptible/moderne* and *texte-limite*. Texts coded according to the project of mimesis are basically inert and reactionary (*lisible*), by virtue of their complicity in the ideological discourses of their age. Such texts only become interesting and alive when (as in the case of *Sarrasine*) they come up against and break through the 'limit' of mimesis, subverting the ready-made systems within which the mimetic disposition is organised. The 'modern' (*scriptible*) text transgresses this limit systematically. The 'classic' does so rarely; the classic is basically conformist, and hence within the corpus the number of classic texts which merit the accolade of being 'limit-texts' is decidedly small. In developing these classificatory categories, Barthes himself explicitly warned against using them as a blue-print for analysis and interpretation. In many quarters, it was a warning that went largely unheeded, with the result that what started life as a brilliantly suggestive and experimental account of the forces (the 'codes') determining how we read narrative quickly degenerated into a set of reified procedures; all one had to do was to plug in the codes, and all the lights would go on. The paradox of its sensational success (after the predictable resistances) was that *S/Z* rapidly produced its own *doxa*, masquerading as our liberation from the embrace of the stereotype which for so long had held and blinded so many others. In that reified form, the objections that can be raised to this typological schema are manifold. First, it seems to imply (although elsewhere Barthes vigorously denied this)[26] an exceedingly schematic literary history, according to which the texts of the past (the 'classics') so rarely encounter the 'limit' that they are effectively reduced to being but the poor relations of the modern. The alternative view would argue that historical divisions of this sort are quite deeply misleading, and that all narrative productions which seriously engage our attention in some way equivocate received systems of representation.[27] This latter view is particularly pertinent to nineteenth-century narrative, for the obvious reason that this is the period in which, under the guise of the notion of 'realism', the idea of mimesis makes one of its more spectacular historical reappearances. In the analyses of Balzac's *Illusions perdues* and *Splendeurs et misères des courtisanes*, Stendhal's *Le Rouge et le Noir* (both typically considered as archetypes of the 'realist' mode) and Nerval's *Sylvie* (more of a special case), I try to show how in fact nineteenth-century narrative continually encounters, in all kinds of problematical ways, just this experience of the 'limit'. Secondly – what is basically the other side of the same coin – one can legitimately take issue with the view of the 'modern' as resolutely anti-mimetic. In the chapter on Flaubert (often adduced in contemporary critical circles as a first instance of the 'modern'), I argue that the logic of the Flaubert text is such that the very condition of an anti-mimetic reading is the equally valid possibility of a strictly mimetic reading; each ironically shadows the other, and the text is not finally reducible to either. There are, of course, hints of this ambiguity in some of Barthes's own remarks on Flaubert, but if we draw out their full implications we find that they are of a kind which seriously compromise the categorical divisions proposed in *S/Z*. Thirdly, and most crucially of all, it must be remembered that Barthes's typological categories are not just descriptive terms, but also explicitly criteria of *evaluation*. Mimetic conventions do not produce a very high yield of 'pleasure'; on the contrary, they actually make one 'sick'. In the later *Plaisir du texte* Barthes will introduce modifications to this somewhat rigid view of the matter. But in *S/Z* the position is relatively straightforward: as product of ideology and instrument of closure, mimesis is a very inferior specimen indeed, when set along side the liberating free play of the 'moderne-scriptible' text. My own argument will be that mimesis embodies more complex tensions and requirements, of a sort which include the ideological dispositions Barthes discusses, but which are by no means exhausted by them. That mimetic arrangements halt or foreclose the field of signification I do not deny, but dispute the view that this is something which, in all cases, we should automatically deplore, or indeed that we can deplore without falling into another form of bad faith.

This is perhaps the point at which we can return to that brute fact of the obstinacy with which readers have read, and continue to read, mimetically. Barthes's explanation of this fact in terms of cultural and ideological pressures to impose a form of closure on the potentially endless, multidimensional space of signification is unquestionably a powerful one. But our tacit knowledge of the practical conditions of everyday life tells us that such operations of closure, and the communicative exchanges they make possible, are also necessary conditions of anything we might plausibly recognise as a 'form of life'. Mimetic ways of reading, and more broadly, the sorts of human transaction that depend on shared, familiar representations, survive tenaciously not just because of collective gullibility in the face of a massive ideological confidence-trick. They survive quite simply because they are ways of reading that have *droit de cité*, and to which all narrative texts, however sophisticated and equivocal, at some level of their reality lend themselves.

In this context, we can perhaps begin to recast the notion of the 'limit' in more complex terms; to speak not only of the limits *of* representation but also of representation as *limit*, of a binding and

16

ineluctable kind. It is this double sense that haunts the work of Bataille (ostensibly the intellectual inspiration of *S/Z*). Bataille's major commitments are of course resolutely anti-mimetic, notably in the running debate he maintains with Sartre's view of the representational function of (prose) literature in *Qu'est-ce que la littérature?*.[28] Where Sartre sees writing on the instrumental analogy of the transparent 'pane of glass', Bataille sees it as opaque, as resistance to the effort by consciousness to bring primary 'experience' to expression. The meaning of 'literature' lies in its strictly *impossible* situation of endeavouring to overcome that resistance, to close the gap separating experience and consciousness, while always having to acknowledge its own failure. The 'limit' (either as social rule or linguistic custom) is that which literature, in the name of experience, seeks to transgress and exceed in order to take us into the realm beyond that limit: that realm designated by Bataille's contemporary, Blanchot, as the realm of 'fire' which burns and consumes all that touches it.[29] This is the desired or imaginary movement of the text beyond the confines of all known forms of representation, into the sphere where the text ends by devouring itself, reduced to ashes in the flames of the 'unrepresentable'. On the other hand, that limit always reappears intact on the other side of that desired crossing, not only as that which ultimately cannot be transgressed, but also, and paradoxically, as that without which the idea of transgression is itself unthinkable. For, from the moment that the notions of 'transgression', the 'beyond', the 'unrepresentable' are *articulated* in or as language, they are perforce inscribed in, and hence negated by, the very logic of representation they seek to exceed (as Blanchot himself was only too well aware, the very act of *naming* the 'beyond' in the metaphor of 'fire' is already a negation of it). As long as we are in language (and we are always in it), we necessarily remain this side of the limit, inside the famous 'limits of language', understanding this, however, not so much in the sense in which the Wittgenstein of the *Tractatus* uses the phrase, but as designating the social space of communication and exchange in which the text, if it is to be understood at all, makes itself available to a given community of knowledge and practice.

The placing of the idea of the 'limit', and the space of representation it demarcates, in terms of the question of language generally is, of course, to raise issues which go far beyond the problems specific to literary mimesis. It is however a crucial reference, in so far as the extreme point of the semiological critique of mimesis is co-extensive with a questioning of the primary categories and operations of language itself: syntax, predication, naming[30] (its extreme form will be the reduction by Barthes of language to the description 'fascist').[31] To observe that this questioning process has, on the whole, been presented in 'well-formed' sentences is not just (though could easily be) a frivolous and possibly quite futile remark. One can respect the obvious dilemma it involves in the work of those who have denounced the 'tyranny' or 'imperialism' of predicative syntax, but at the same time pose it as a severely disabling difficulty in the deconstructionist undertaking. I shall try to argue this at some length in the chapter on Flaubert and in the conclusion, and, since the argument bears centrally on the question of 'originality' and the impossibility of 'transcendence', I deliberately present the paradox in one of its most ancient forms: Epimenides's Cretan Liar paradox. It is a dangerous paradox with which to play, since it can easily blow up in the face of its user. Its importance for my present purpose lies in the way it places logical constraints upon the attack on mimesis and representational discourse generally, in that any such attack is obliged, as a condition of its intelligibility, to adopt the very categories of the object it attacks. It is, of course, a paradox identical to that with which Derrida trips up Plato. Derrida catches Plato *in flagrante delicto* playing the very mimetic game he rejects. But Derrida's own deconstruction of the set of terms which support the mimetic project (truth, reference, etc.) is – self-confessedly – impossible without recourse to these terms. The paradox, as Derrida acknowledges (but, then, what is the *point* of this acknowledgement?), is that one is inside them as inside a circle.[32] The circle (the limit) is not entirely unbreachable; there are gaps through which one can 'slip'. But the influential notion of 'slippage' – developed from the psychoanalytical model of the work of the unconscious – is, yet again, deeply ambiguous: 'slippages' provide escape routes through the limit, but precisely because they are *merely* slippages (and not full-scale collapses), their existence does as much to confirm as to break the strength of that limit.

Health

The dilemmas and paradoxes (not least the paradox that in tarring mimesis one risks getting tarred oneself with the same brush) which arise from the rejection of mimesis, in the respective descriptions of Plato and Barthes, can be countered by another tradition, which views the matter in far more eirenic mood. For there is a third way with mimesis that is neither Plato's poison nor Barthes's nausea, but which, on the contrary, promotes mimesis as a model of epistemological and psychological health, as a necessary condition of human growth and maturation. In its most illustrious form, this is the way of Aristotle, according to whom mimesis is an activity and embodies an order of knowledge that are 'natural' and distinctive to man. Mimesis is a capacity, or a potentiality, rooted in nature (*physis*) and realised by human nature (*physikai*). The central argument of the *Poetics* is just this posing of mimesis, not only as the origin of art, but more generally as a congenital property of man's natural mode of constructing and inhabiting the world:

It is clear that the general origin of poetry was due to two causes, each of them part of human nature. Imitation is natural to man from childhood, one of his advantages over the lower animals being this, that he is the most imitative creature in the world, and learns at first by imitation. And it is also natural for all to delight in works of imitation.　　　　　(I448b 5–9)[33]

In this version, the ruling idea concerns a relation between mimesis and knowledge, first in the stress on the role played by mimesis in the process of 'learning' (and in particular the place of imitation in the child's developing mastery of its environment); secondly, in the stress on the 'pleasure' we experience before imitations, the pleasure of 'recognition', itself linked elsewhere in the *Poetics* to the principle of acquiring knowledge of reality. Both these emphases can, of course, be translated critically into the terms of the 'modern' way with mimesis. Aristotle's pleasure could be re-routed towards that negative aspect of pleasure which in *Le Plaisir du texte* Barthes describes, in opposition to the raptures of *jouissance*, as the feeling of banal comfort the subject experiences in refinding the familiar forms of his culture.[34] Equally, the idea of 'learning' through imitation can easily be read in terms of the psychoanalytical critique of socialisation: what the child learns in his imitative activities is simply the internalisation of the norms of the given reality-principle, a phase in entering and submitting to the symbolic order commanded by the 'Name-of-the-Father'. Yet the psychoanalytical gloss on Aristotle can work both ways. In precisely a discussion of children's imitative games (and with an explicit reference to Aristotle), Freud talks of the 'pleasure' we take in the 'rediscovery of the familiar', as a disposition of the mind, an element in the psychic economy, in terms which imply that it has functions other than those of mere passive obedience to the authority of the censor.[35] The association of Aristotle's account of mimesis, and in particular the emphasis on the importance of 'recognition', with the repressive work of the censor is a recurring theme of modern critical theory, and has produced a whole string of related associations: with the law, the father, the state, the police. We shall see how some of these analogies work in later chapters, and what some of their limitations are. For the moment it suffices to say that this reduction of Aristotle's categories to the terms of a kind of policing operation itself requires a degree of correction. It of course remains true that to rest a case on an assumption of what is 'natural' to man is minimally a delicate and problematical affair. In unproblematical form, it is legitimately open to all the attacks with which the modern critical temper has assailed it. The argument from nature is very often an argument from the natural attitude, implying that mimesis takes place in a cultural and historical void, as an unmediated encounter between world and text. Any account of mimesis which overlooks its mediated character takes us, intellectually, down a blind alley and, morally, into that space of bad faith which Barthes identifies as the legacy of the mimetic idea: the space in which the rhetoric of the natural attitude passes itself off as nature *tout court*. For Barthes, Aristotle's theory of mimesis is inseparable from his reflections on rhetoric; mimesis is essentially dependent upon rhetorical forms of persuasion. But rhetoric, in Barthes's view, is a kind of 'degradation', a fall into the stratagems of a 'public' discourse rooted in *doxa*, in norms of 'common sense' and 'current opinion', which are themselves but the reflection of an administering and manipulative ideology.[36]

The consequences of this view will be a central concern of the next chapter, especially in connection with the terms of Aristotle's notion of 'verisimilitude'. However, in its total assimilation of mimesis to *doxa* (within the negative definition of the latter), it does promote a version of the Aristotelian account which others have been anxious to resist. Perhaps the boldest and most powerful rehabilitation of the more positive claims of the Aristotelian doctrine of mimesis is that of Paul Ricœur.[37] Ricœur's reading of Aristotle, and the more general argument about mimesis and narrative which that reading serves, are complex matters, and I shall return in more detail at a later point to various features of that argument (in particular to the notion of human 'understanding' as directly linked to the notion of mimetic 'emplotment'). In broad terms, Ricœur attempts to restore to Aristotle's thinking about mimesis precisely the set of emphases which Barthes's version either removes or devalues. Ricœur also stresses the 'public' or social character of mimesis (as one of the modes of our 'being-with-others'); but he puts a quite different emphasis on it, by connecting mimesis to a principle of human cognitive projects modelled on the Kantian category of the 'productive imagination'.[38] Aristotle observes that imitation is one of man's natural means for learning about the natural world. But learning here is not just a form of passive aping. In Ricœur's gloss on Aristotle, cognitive pursuits are essentially dynamic; both the subject and object of cognition are inextricably bound to the categories of process, activity and becoming. Nature (*physis*) is not given to the mind as fixed form; the intelligibility of Nature, in the argument of the *Metaphysics*,[39] is properly apprehended as *entelechia*, as ceaseless process of becoming, or movement of the potential into the actual. To 'know' the world is, therefore, not only to register the actual, but also to bring out or make manifest what is potential in nature.

It is in relation to that project that Ricœur sees the true significance of mimesis. The invented plot of the mimetic work of art is not simply a copy of the given; its invented character makes of it a 'heuristic fiction',[40] whose completed form embodies a dynamic cognitive shaping, a realisation of what is incomplete in natural process, an extension or development of what is already potentially inscribed in *physis*. In this respect, mimesis performs the same cognitive function as metaphor; they are both modes of active disclosure. The 'best' metaphors, says Aristotle in the *Rhetoric*, are those which 'show things in a state of activity' (1411b 25). The foundation of mimesis, Aristotle says in the *Poetics*, is 'action' or movement, that is, the very basis of 'life' itself: 'an imitation, not of men, but of an action and of life, and life consists in action and its end is a mode of action' (1450a 16–17). Both mimesis and metaphor are thus discovery procedures, heuristic mechanisms for representing the movements of Nature, the poetic materialisation of the 'entelechic' properties of material life itself. In Ricœur's key term, they are the privileged means for a dynamic *re-description* of the world,[41] whereby new configurations in Nature are released, new forms of knowledge and understanding are constituted, a new relation of 'reference' to the world is installed. The inventions of mimesis, like those of metaphor (at least of 'la métaphore *vive*'), are not just the fanciful constructs of the mind arbitrarily put into the world; they are a distinctively human form of knowing what is *in* the world.

Clearly this is to raise the Aristotelian view of the 'naturalness' of mimesis to a very high philosophical order indeed. It also has visible attractions at the level of aesthetic theory, in that it extends the idea of mimesis from simple confirmation of the familiar into engagement with the unfamiliar and the unknown (indeed, on Ricœur's interpretation, mimesis is entirely compatible with the *avantgardiste* aesthetics of 'defamiliarisation'). But, equally clearly, questions start to pour in from all sides. One obvious difficulty, arising from the emphasis on mimesis as dynamic cognition, is that mimesis can easily become a catch-all term for all forms of significant art; if mimesis embraces both the familiar and unfamiliar, then either everything is mimesis or, alternatively, there is no clear criterion for distinguishing mimesis from other kinds of art to which we might wish to attribute dynamic cognitive value, but which we would hesitate to describe as 'mimetic' (e.g. the surrealist novel). More centrally perhaps, there are the numerous problems associated with the avowedly Kantian perspective within which Ricœur's reading of Aristotle is proposed (we will re-encounter similar problems in the context of Hegelian notions of narrative representation). In tying mimesis to cognition, Ricœur elevates the former to a position of considerable intellectual dignity (far removed from the nauseous pit to which Barthes would consign it). But, by the same token, his argument raises all the difficulties that attend subject-orientated theories; what guarantees the security and the authority of the cognitive 'categories' of the knowing subject; how, from these premisses, can we distinguish true cognition from mis-cognition, or the genuinely intelligible from the merely gratuitous?

Ricœur himself wrestles strenuously with this question, although largely in terms of an attempted grounding of the Kantian subject in the outer reaches of a Heideggerian ontology of being and language, where it is (at least for the present author) often rather difficult to follow him. An alternative, and more accessible, task adopted by Ricœur, however, is through phenomenology, a locating of the knowing subject in the realm of the intersubjective relations of the social world (this, moreover, is the context for his remark about the 'public' basis of mimesis, as a mode of our 'being-with-others'). Cognition, and hence mimesis, have their roots in what is humanly and socially shared (there is no 'symbolic creation which is not in the final analysis rooted in the common symbolical ground of humanity'). The appeal to Aristotle is then finally an appeal to the notion of a world intersubjectively known and held in common, with even a possible implication of a categorial universalism (the 'common symbolical ground of humanity').[42] But that approach, in turn, generates further questions; and, while I shall later try to argue the merits of the case from intersubjectivity (and specifically against the adequacy of the repeated reduction, in some of the more influential areas of modern French theory, of the 'intersubjective' to 'ideology'), a position based on a universalist presupposition is notoriously difficult to hold in place for very long, without encountering the various critiques that, in large measure, will be the concern of the next chapter.

2

THE ECONOMY OF MIMESIS

The subject of mimesis

Totalities

In describing the constituent elements of an 'economy' of mimesis, we are from the beginning faced with the theoretical difficulty of Beginnings. For Aristotle appropriate beginnings (along with middles and ends) are, of course, basic items in the structural equipment of the mimetic work of art, actualising a coherence given in Nature, although not fully realised until articulated by the work of art. Yet, even in the terms of Aristotle's own account of mimesis, there is also a problem of beginnings. Mimesis, the essence of 'art' (*poiesis*), also precedes poetry; it is the 'origin' of art, that which founds and makes art possible. The principles of knowledge, mastery and pleasure that Aristotle associates with mimesis are not just the terms of a literary practice, but also of a general strategy for living in and negotiating the world; they underlie a great many of the routine activities of daily life. On the other hand, if a generalised human mimetic activity founds artistic mimesis, it is also the case, as Sartre[1] and Sollers[2] have argued, that the forms of literary practice themselves actively furnish or influence, though in complex and diffuse ways, some of the models for the imitative practices of everyday life. Thus, within the recursive dialectic of the literary text and the 'text' of life, of books imitating life and life imitating books, the whole question of the 'origin' is rendered singularly intractable, or – as modern theory would have it – is displaced into the disoriginated and disoriginating notion of 'intertextuality'. I shall have more to say at a later stage concerning the impact of this notion on the theory of mimesis. I allude to it here for what may appear a somewhat paradoxical reason: in the very act of drawing attention to the problem of origins which besets mimesis, it can also provide a beginning, an entry-point for discussion. For if, roughly, we see the notion of the 'intertextual' as in some ways a version of the endless and unanchorable process of *intersubjective* transactions and exchanges from which a world, and its representations, are constituted,[3] we can begin to address the question of the 'subject' of mimesis by way of, precisely, the Subject, the subject-ivity of mimesis.

Such a way of going about matters is both commonplace and provocative. It is commonplace in so far as, in the wake of Ian Watt's remarkable book, we now see the rise of the novel (the modern literary form most intimately associated with the idea of mimesis) as closely tied to the development of certain rationalist epistemologies, in particular the sets of assumptions bound up with classical subject-object theories of knowledge.[4] It may be deemed provocative, however, in so far as, in many familiar ways of thinking about mimetic or realist art, the 'subject' of the subject-object relation is often elided, with a corresponding stress on the importance of the 'object' alone in the process of representation (in some versions 'subjectivity' is said to belong to an entirely different order of literary representation altogether). One of the important features of modern French theory has been the attempt not only to check that elision, but also to show what is entailed by it if it is left unchecked. It may therefore be instructive to consider briefly how that elision has manifested itself in other bodies of thought, and in particular in two books which, until recently, have probably done more than any others to shape modern understanding of mimesis: Auerbach's *Mimesis: The Representation of Reality in Western Literature* and Lukács's *Studies in European Realism* (the latter to be supplemented with the theoretical programme outlined in *History and Class Consciousness*).[5]

What, despite numerous divergences, Auerbach and Lukács have in common is an intellectual commitment to the notion of 'totality'. In Auerbach's account of the fortunes of mimesis it is largely implicit. In Lukács's account of the conceptual grounds of literary realism it is explicit, and is succinctly formulated in *History and Class Consciousness*: 'Only in this context which sees the isolated facts of social life as aspects of the historical process and integrates them as a *totality*, can knowledge of the facts become knowledge of reality . . . The intelligibility of objects develops in proportion as we grasp their function in the *totality* to which they belong.'[6] In this emphasis, there are unmistakeable echoes of Hegel (although, in the case of later Lukács, a Hegel transformed in terms of a Marxist reading of history). The exact details of the differing relations of Auerbach's and Lukács's work to Hegel's thought we may here leave on one side. What they have in common is the importance both attach to the ideal of 'totality', as supplying the basis and the validation of the representational literary arts. The aspiration of a literary mimesis is to attain, or strive for, a representation which reflects, in Hegel's phrase, the 'objective totality' of a world at a given moment of its historical realisation.[7] The term 'totality', in this context, is not to be confused with a purely empirical or quantitative notion; it does not designate the ambition of an exhaustive transcription of contingent particulars. On the contrary – this becomes a key stress in Lukács's *Studies in European Realism* – it aims at a maximum differentiation of the contingent and the essential. In Hegel's terms, the 'total' world of the text (its 'self-enclosed, self-contained world') is that which reflects the 'hidden inner necessity' of things, the 'fundamental idea', the 'innermost core and sense of an event'.[8] The authentic mimetic work thus selects and arranges the essential or representative patterns of experience, and, in so doing, grasps the underlying laws of reality and history, reveals the world in its inner principle of intelligibility. In short, the text is to world what microcosm is to macrocosm, a system of interrelated parts whose internal relations yield a model of the set of relations organising the wider totality of the world beyond.

The difficulty with this influential view lies with what the argument from the notion of totality takes for granted: the principle which allows for the unproblematic passage from microcosm to macrocosm, the criteria by which the writer decides, and which enable the reader to accept, that one set of selections and combinations is representative, where another is merely random or arbitrary. In these terms, the success of the mimetic project depends absolutely on the validity of a set of unquestioned prior choices determining the relative value of both its inclusions and exclusions. More abstractly, the argument based on the notion of totality implies both the possibility of a transcendent order of knowledge and the primacy of a transcendent knowing Subject, a privileged form of the Hegelian *Geist* ensuring and authorising the relation of microcosm to macrocosm. (The extreme version of this is to be found in Hegel's *Aesthetics* itself, in the grandiose and impossible fantasy of an epic work of art that would capture the totality of the whole world-historical process.)[9] Formulated in this way, the approach I am describing contains many echoes of the earlier epistemologies which Watt relates to the idea of 'realism'; and to that extent one would, of course, hasten to enter various caveats and qualifications: in particular, the attempt by Hegel to dissolve the static categories of previous subject-object theories of knowledge into the dynamic processes of history and the terms of dialectical logic; the historicising perspective that informs virtually every page of Auerbach's *Mimesis*; the recasting by Lukács of totality in terms of the relations between history, praxis and class consciousness. Yet, once the necessary qualifications have been made, in one form or another the basic assumption remains intact; the logical priority of an act of reflective consciousness 'in' or 'behind' the text guaranteeing the artistic choices and decisions (otherwise at risk of appearing quite arbitrary) which furnish the corner-stone of the 'totalising' endeavour. From that assumption, we could then certainly agree with J. P. Stern's view of mimetic or realist fiction as 'erected on firm grounds which reveal no epistemological cracks', or indeed as 'epistemologically naive',[10] although we might wish to reject the self-congratulatory aura which Stern sees as the natural accompaniment of this professed naivety. As with all epistemologically naive positions, naivety is purchased at a price, which is precisely what, in order to proffer itself as 'naive', it is compelled to mask; it rests on making tacit what, if brought out into the open and critically examined, might cause the whole theoretical edifice to collapse.

The triangle of representation

One of the major virtues of modern French theory has been to make visible and explicit what elsewhere has generally lain hidden, as the founding presupposition both of the theory of representation in general and, *a fortiori*, of artistic mimesis in particular. Perhaps the outstanding example of this endeavour is to be found in the brilliant virtuosity of Foucault's analysis of Velasquez's *Las Meninas*, where the whole dialectic of representation, reflexively mirrored in the structure of the painting itself, is made to turn on an element in the picture at once absent and present: 'l'invisibilité de celui qui voit'.[11] This invisible person is the painter himself (doubled in the picture), the figure whose commanding gaze circumscribes and closes an otherwise potentially endless play of reflections: he is the sovereign Subject who, positioned at the apex of the system of representation, orders its elements into a stable 'geometric' configuration ('le regard souverain commande un triangle virtuel').[12] The details of the representational paradigm extracted by Foucault from Velasquez's painting cannot, of course, be extended wholesale to

27

the other arts; as Foucault rightly stresses,[13] the specific terms of painting and literature are not strictly commensurate; to move from one to the other is to move from one order of representation to another, requiring different kinds of analysis. What can, however, be generalised from Foucault's model of the 'triangle' is the notion of the masterful Subject – the argument that the representational system works primarily by virtue of the assumed place of mastery occupied by the representing subject in respect of the universe of knowledge and understanding within which the representation is organised. This image of the 'triangle' we will find elsewhere, notably in Barthes's important essay, 'Diderot, Brecht, Eisenstein', in which he sketches the terms of what he calls a veritable 'Organon of Representation':

La représentation ne se définit pas directement par l'imitation; se débarrasserait-on des notions de 'réel', de 'vraisemblable', de 'copie', il restera toujours de la 'représentation', tant qu'un sujet (auteur, lecteur, spectateur ou voyeur) portera son *regard* vers un horizon et y découpera la base d'un triangle dont son œil (ou son esprit) sera le sommet. L'Organon de la Représentation (qu'il devient possible aujourd'hui d'écrire, parce que *autre chose* se devine), cet Organon aura pour double fondement la souveraineté du découpage et l'unité du sujet qui découpe. Peu importera donc la substance des arts; certes, théâtre et cinéma sont des expressions directes de la géométrie . . . mais le discours littéraire classique (lisible), lui aussi, . . . est un discours représentatif, géométrique, en tant qu'il découpe des morceaux pour les peindre: discourir (auraient dit les classiques) n'est que 'peindre le tableau qu'on a dans l'esprit'.[14]

Despite the difficulties that surround the term 'classic' as a term of historical description, this passage is perhaps the clearest and most wide-ranging statement of the 'perspectival' model deemed to underlie the representational arts. Three points in particular need to be retained from this account. First, there is Barthes's assimilation of the idea of literary representation to the metaphor of 'space' and, more precisely, to the geometrical image of the 'triangle'. The obvious objection that this overlooks the temporal aspect of narrative might be met, if only provisionally, by saying that the teleological structure of narrative (with its apparatus of predetermined beginnings and necessary closures) can be readily assimilated to the more static conception embodied in the spatial metaphor. Secondly, there is the emphasis on the relation of 'seeing' (the *gaze*), the posing of the space of representation as a field of vision. This has important consequences on a number of fronts. It marks what Lacanian psychoanalysis has described as the fetishising of vision as a source of knowledge, the supposedly privileged relation between 'voir' and 'sa-voir'. This in turn carries major implications for our understanding of many variants of traditional versions of literary mimesis, namely the eclipse or effacement of its specifically linguistic nature, in the reduction of representation to a relation of specularity between subject and object (precisely that subordination of the linguistic to the visual against which Foucault warns, but which has dominated Western thinking about mimesis since Plato). Thirdly, and most crucially, there is the reference to the overarching position of the hypostasised subject, the unified and homogenising agent who provides the essential guarantee of the security of the representational space he commands.

In the terms of Barthes's 'Organon', a critical theory of literary mimesis is thus intimately linked to a critical theory of the 'subject'; decomposing the former is part of the wider project of deconstructing the hypostases which enter into the construction of the latter. The initial move of semiological inquiry is to examine the real conditions and characteristics of this 'subject', once it has been stripped of these hypostasising operations. One form that this move takes is to equate the 'subject' in question with the *narrating* subject, on the basis of the narrator's unhampered access to the systems of knowledge which inform and control the text. Echoing the geometric figures of Foucault and Barthes, this approach suggests that we grasp the structure of the mimetic text as a stratified or 'hierarchical' distribution of discourses: at the apex there is the speech of the narrator; below this point there is the speech of the characters, whose varying relation to the 'truth' is measured by their degree of approximation to, or divergence from, the discourse of the narrator.[15] An example (which I choose for the remarkable purity with which it conforms to the model) is Balzac's short narrative, *Madame Firmiani*. This story is composed almost entirely of a series of conversations between different characters concerning the nature of the mysterious Madame Firmiani. All of them (on their own premisses) are plausible; none of them is true. The triumphal pleasure of revealing the 'truth' is reserved for the demiurgic narrator, a truth suspended until, in a highly characteristic gesture, the final moment of hermeneutic 'dévoilement' at which all other versions are confounded and routed.

This approach has a great deal to recommend it, especially when we recall the close link in modern fiction between the assault on mimetic expectations and the loss, or blurring, of an authoritative narrative voice (in Barthes's formulation, the impossibility of deciding the question 'Qui parle?').[16] And indeed the issue of the 'narrator', its complexities, hesitations and equivocations, will be one of my major preoccupations throughout the chapters on Balzac, Stendhal, Nerval and Flaubert (although the presence of such uncertainties in these nineteenth-century texts immediately places a question-mark over the attribution of discursive stability to the so-called 'classic'). The point which is germane to the present theoretical argument, however, is that, although fruitful in some respects, the model of the authoritative narrator standing at the apex of the triangle of representation does not adequately explain, or indeed 'explain' at all, the success of the mimetic endeavour. The limitation of the model is that it is internally self-confirming; the authority of the narrator ensures mimesis because the narrator is authoritative; it thus lacks genuine explanatory power in so far as it presupposes what it is designed to explain. To leave matters there would in fact be simply to displace the hypostasis which semiology seeks to undo from the subject to the narrator. A further question is required, which bears upon the sources and conditions of the narrator's authority itself. For the narrator of mimetic narratives is not an unconditionally 'free' subject. He does, of course, enjoy a certain latitude in positing premises and offering explanations (the range of possibilities available to the narrator of *Madame Firmiani* is very wide). At the same time the narrator is severely constrained: first, by the generic conventions of his medium; secondly (and interrelatedly) by the everyday belief systems of his readers. Balzac's narrator could not have told us, unless he were justified by a prior generic convention of a specific kind (as, for example, in the fairy tale), that Madame Firmiani was in fact a witch who flew every night to the moon. For the text to be accredited with mimetic values, the narrator's assertions must command the assent of the reader. There must be a certain 'concord' between narrator and reader, a necessary condition of which is the existence of a socially shared universe of meaning. In brief, the 'subject' of mimesis is an intersubjective entity, a socially constructed subject issuing from the 'cultural codes' which, in the wider sense Barthes gives to that term in *S/Z*, are held to underlie the whole of the organisation of the mimetic text. Following Lucien Goldmann, we might then be tempted to refer here to a 'collective subject', were it not that the term readily attracts connotations of the very transcendentalism that the argument seeks to circumvent (as, for example, in the various derivatives of Durkheim's sociology where the hypostasised subject is relocated from the level of the individual *cogito* to that of the impersonal *conscience collective*). In order to retain the necessary notion of social *process* (the production and reproduction of the social world), it would perhaps be preferable to think of the scene of mimesis as unfolding within what one sociologist has called the interactive systems of 'mutual knowledge'.[17] The social context of mimesis will then appear not as some abstract realm 'beyond' both writer and reader, but as a network of interpenetrating interpretative schemas within which writer and reader participate, both actively and passively, in a series of collaborative exchanges.

But, whatever the refinements one introduces, the leading idea here revolves around the reinsertion of the transcendental Subject into the terms of history and society. The 'subject' (if I may employ the term in its dual sense) of mimesis is irreducibly social: first, as a social product, mimesis, in its detailed articulations, is a 'subject' properly speaking for the sociology of literature; secondly, it is a product whose production is governed by a 'subject' that is itself socially constructed. 'Subjectivity' and 'objectivity' which, as we have already seen, have so often been the epistemologically taken-for-granted terms of other versions of mimesis, are decisively recast in the ideological forms of social knowledge, to which Barthes will variously give the names of the stereotype and the *doxa*:

Objectivité et *subjectivité* sont certes des forces qui peuvent s'emparer du texte, mais ce sont des forces qui n'ont pas d'affinité avec lui. La subjectivité est une image pleine, dont on suppose que j'encombre le texte, mais dont la plénitude, truquée, n'est que le sillage de tous les codes qui me font, en sorte que ma subjectivité a finalement la généralité même des stéréotypes. L'objectivité est un remplissage du même ordre; c'est un système imaginaire comme les autres . . . une image qui sert à me faire nommer avantageusement, à me faire connaître, à me méconnaître.[18]

Subjectivity and objectivity are pure fictions; uncritically accepted, they partake of the domain of the 'imaginary', as the unexamined illusions of presence and plenitude through which the categories of 'self' and 'world' are filled ('remplissage') with a mythical unity and stability; critically inspected, however, they are exposed as ideological mechanisms designed to ensure recognitions, but in fact producing the 'misrecognitions' which flow from all orders of representation – including supremely that of mimesis (the art of 'recognitions' par excellence) – when their arbitrary foundation is hidden in the congealed thickness of the stereotype.

Types and ostension

For Barthes the notion of the 'stereotype' is central to his account of mimesis, and it opens onto a theme that will play a large part in subsequent stages of my argument. The stereotype is a reduced form, or another way of describing, what we often understand as the 'type'. That typifications are basic to the ways we construct and apprehend the social world is a commonplace of the sociology of knowledge ('the social world is apprehended in a continuum of typifications').[19] That they are also basic to the constitution of mimetic or realistic fiction has been an equally commonplace proposition. The centrality, indeed the prestige, which the notion of the type has acquired in modern critical thinking about literary realism can scarcely be over-emphasised, and is in the main due to the hugely influential work of Lukács (notably in *Studies in European Realism*). Lukács 'type', it will be recalled, it always a matter of the concrete and the particular. Although it involves a certain process of abstraction away from the mere accumulation of empirical details, in terms of its actualisation in literary texts it is neither an abstract nor a static concept. It does not partake of the allegorical dimension of earlier, and more schematic, typologies. Nor is it to be confused with a notion of the 'average'; it has nothing to do with what has been called, as a fundamental criterion of realist writing, the 'middle distance',[20] a sort of fixed point midway between generality and individuality. Typification is inherently mobile: the degree of generalisation and, conversely, of individuation it embodies in any given case will depend on the position occupied by the observer along the available continuum of typifications. But, above all, Lukács's version of the type is resolutely particularistic. In a slightly more technical language, Lukács's theory is a variant of the 'type-token' relation, in that the literary strategy in question evokes and names a general class (of objects, persons, events, processes) by means of identifying individual members of that class. Literary typification is a form of imaginative *naming*, whereby the characteristic or 'essential' features of the social process are picked out and gathered into a single expressive moment of a peculiarly intense and concentrated kind ('the specific figure which concentrates and intensifies a much more general reality').[21] The articulations of the 'great tradition' of realist literature are delineated by Lukács in terms of the production and combination, at various levels of the text, of these typical moments, their global interrelations thus giving a paradigm of the underlying configurations or 'laws' of reality in one of its significant historical forms. Thus Balzac's Crevel in *La Cousine Bette* (Balzac being for Lukács the supreme practitioner of the arts of typicality) is a concretely realised figure whose individual traits, habits, mannerisms of speech are systematically invested with representative values (referring to the type of the 'bourgeoisie parvenue' in the France of the 1840s); and it is from our recognition of these representative values (in conjunction with others in the text) that the novel can be perceived as a fully adequate representation of a social reality at a given historical juncture.

What the Lukácsian notion of the type looks like when passed through the filter of semiological analysis (and in particular the categories of *S/Z*), I have examined at some length elsewhere.[22] Moreover one of the chief difficulties of the theory – what or who supplies the criteria of the type-token ratio, what ensures that the typifications will be recognised as such – rejoins the problem we have already seen to be at the heart of the related notion of 'totality'. What I want to do here is to complement that critical perspective by way of a brief detour through a rather different theoretical context: Wittgenstein's critique of the principle of 'ostensive definition'. At first sight that might seem a singularly inept way of promoting the sadly resisted cause of cross-Channel dialogue. But in any case – for reasons that will be immediately apparent – I intend the relation in question to be taken only in the spirit of an extremely loose analogy. The common ground I posit between the two lies in the significance each attaches to the principle of the 'representative example' (or what, in the *Rhetoric*, Aristotle calls the *paradeigma*). Ostensive definition is the act whereby the meaning of a name is explicated by physically pointing to or showing (sometimes accompanied by the verbal demonstrative 'this' or 'that') a particular example of the general class of objects which the name denotes. It will, of course, be immediately clear that, on strictly logical grounds, there can be no case whatsoever for extending this to the way literary language works, or indeed any kind of language (other than pure deictic utterance). While, following a suggestion of Wittgenstein,[23] it may be plausible – although problematical in the light of the famous duck/rabbit example – to ascribe ostensive potential to iconic representations (such as a drawing), this cannot be true of verbal representations (unless we are prepared to endorse that subordination of the linguistic to the visual which has so bedevilled the history of Western thinking about mimesis). Literature is language, and in any literal sense language cannot be said to 'point' to anything, except perhaps itself. On the contrary, it is language which provides the names which, under the premises of ostensive definition, it is the task of the physical gesture of pointing to elucidate; to return to an earlier emphasis, literary typification is a process of *naming* and, accordingly, must not be confused with the very different operation of *pointing*.

As such we might therefore be tempted to jettison the analogy between typification and ostension without further ado. There is nevertheless an important, if loosely metaphorical, sense in which we can describe Lukács's theory of the type as entailing a kind of 'pointing', in ways which moreover have exercised considerable influence on how we understand the workings of the mimetic text. In the account of typification developed by Lukács, as a movement from the particular to the general mediated by the 'representative example', the latter could be seen figuratively as a literary equivalent of the pointing finger of ostensive definition: the purpose of its particularity is to indicate, or *show*, the more general class of which it is both member and illustration. This notion has a lineage that goes back to the nineteenth century. It echoes, for example, the prescriptive emphasis given to the idea of 'showing' in the Jamesian aesthetic of narrative, and the link with the larger representational functions James elsewhere assigns to the novel precisely in terms of the notion of the 'typical' ('Art is selection, but it is a selection whose main care is to be typical').[24] This has a close parallel with the thinking of Lukács. In particular, James's 'showing/telling' opposition is very similar to the distinction drawn by Lukács between *erzählen* and *beschreiben*.[25] *Beschreiben* is a mode of writing which, like James's 'telling', informs us about the world in a merely superficial and inert way, which approaches the world from the outside. *Erzählen*, on the other hand (literally translated as 'telling', but in fact close to the spirit of James's 'showing'), designates a mode which seizes the world from within, in the lived immediacy of particular situations and processes, which, by virtue of their concrete illustrative value, are indicative of the immanent structure of a more general reality. In brief, it is a mode which entails a form of *exhibiting*: the general is made available by the exhibiting of a concrete instance which gathers into itself the characteristic properties of the social world.

The analogy thus yields a rough and ready equation whereby, in the art of typification, particular is to general what, in ostensive definition, example is to class, and it is in these analogical terms that we could therefore tentatively describe the mimetic project as based on a form of ostensive drive.[26] Consequently the difficulties in

Lukács's theory (together with the means of correcting them) might be usefully clarified by way of those associated with the operations of ostensive definition. The difficulty with ostensive definition, as Wittgenstein argues, is twofold: either it in fact tells us nothing at all ('defines' nothing), or it requires presuppositions of a sort which render its logic entirely circular. In its first aspect, what is supposed to be the most precise form of definition possible – pointing to an actual instance – recedes into an indefinite indeterminacy ('an ostensive definition can be variously interpreted in every case');[27] as in Jakobson's famous example of the packet of Chesterfield cigarettes (the white man who replies to the Red Indian's question 'what is "Chesterfield"?' by pointing to a packet lying on the ground),[28] not only is the range of interpretative possibilities which confronts the Red Indian indefinite, but, without other information, he has no way of deciding which interpretation is the correct one (cigarettes in general, tobacco, cigarette paper, paper, packets, all objects of this shape and colour, and so forth). In its second aspect, it collapses into pure tautology. For the other information that would enable him to determine the correct relation between the name 'Chesterfield' and what his interlocutor is pointing to presupposes precisely what our Red Indian has all along been trying to find out: he will only know that the pointing finger indicates a *brand* of cigarettes if, in some form or other, he already knows that 'Chesterfield' 'means' a brand name. In other words, he cannot control the interpretative field without what Eco calls 'a prior stipulation of pertinence',[29] which, however, already contains within itself the meaning which the ostensive gesture is supposed to define; as Wittgenstein says, 'One has already to know (or to be able to do) something in order to be capable of asking a thing's name.'[30]

Thus, without a prior grasp of the pertinent level or system of classification involved, the gesture will remain either unintelligible or open to endless interpretation. There is nothing inherent in the activity of pointing itself to explain the precise nature of the intended relation of 'token' to 'type'. Since the ways in which the world can be classified are theoretically endless and, in an important sense, arbitrary (an emphasis beautifully captured in Borges's imaginary Chinese system of classification), any ostensive act will make sense only from within a socially shared context of knowledge and reference; in Wittgenstein's terms, to play the 'language-game' you need to be part of, or to understand, the relevant 'form of life'. This constraint has important implications for any theory of mimesis which takes the principle of the 'type' as one of its primary supports.

The socially bounded character of the logic of typification and classification – a constant epistemological theme in social theory since the pioneering work of Durkheim and Mauss on primitive classification[31] – applies *a fortiori* to the mimetic types of narrative. The gestures and mannerisms that make Crevel the particular representative of the general type of the 'bourgeois parvenu' could, in another culture or 'possible world', be, let us say randomly, signs of moral distinction or symptoms of insanity. To recognise these as tokens 'pointing to' a general type or class requires a culturally embedded system of agreed conventions comparable to that required by ostensive definition, a socially acknowledged 'stock of knowledge' which – often unconsciously or tacitly – directs and instructs both reader and writer. Or, to return to the Aristotelian reference, the *paradeigma* can function as both mark and demonstration of a general state of affairs by virtue of its place within a *rhetoric*, as a tactic in a set of discursive practices (those, for example, of the law courts) for persuading and confirming that such and such is the case.

Contract

These largely informal 'stocks of knowledge', and the underlying agreements that sustain them, can be formalised in terms of another model which, both in the semiological literature and elsewhere, has played a large part in the analysis of fiction: the model of *contract*.[32] 'Contract', in this context, designates what Barthes has called 'l'échange réglé sur quoi reposent la marche sémantique et la vie collective',[33] and within which, among other things, the practice of narrative mimesis is inscribed. In respect of the latter, we are in fact dealing here with a kind of double contract, the one both presupposing and doubling the other. First, there is the set of agreements between the reader and writer as to what forms a faithful 'representation'; but that understanding, in turn, is possible only by virtue of a prior and wider set of agreements as to what constitutes 'reality' itself. As Sollers puts it, in his characteristically polemical way (since for him such 'contracts' are always sources of mystification, they must be denounced): 'le réalisme . . . ce préjugé qui consiste à croire qu'une écriture doit exprimer quelque chose qui ne serait pas donné dans cette écriture, quelque chose sur quoi l'unanimité pourrait être réalisée immédiatement. Mais il faut bien voir que cet accord ne peut porter que sur des conventions préalables, la notion de *réalité* étant elle-même une convention et un conformisme, une

36

sorte de *contrat tacite* (my italics) passe entre l'individu et son groupe social.'[34] The mimetic text thus comes into being, through a process of exchange, through its insertion into what Julia Kristeva describes as a four-term 'circuit d'échange (réel-auteur-œuvre-public)'.[35] The specific mediations uniting these terms are, of course, extremely complex, but the general point turns on a circular principle of reciprocity at the level of the symbolic, whereby the text acts as the locus in and through which signs and meanings are exchanged; the reader gives credence to the mimetic claims of the text in return for confirmation by the writer of the reader's expectations.

I shall consider the analytic opportunities offered by this model in the chapters on Balzac and Stendhal (where in particular I shall be concerned with tracing what happens when the contract between writer and reader breaks down). But, as a general theoretical model, its potential usefulness should not be allowed to obscure its very real limitations. These limitations are of a twofold sort. The first is that, as a formal concept deriving essentially from legal and political discourse, contract carries the presumption of a 'sovereign subject' entering freely into an agreement with another party. That presumption cannot, however, be easily transferred to the more informal version of contract we are concerned with here. The difficulty in question is well represented by the problems we find in Saussure's use of the idea of contract to describe language as a social institution. In order to make sense of the notion of the 'arbitrariness' of the sign, Saussure has to posit *langue* as a system of contractual values (words signify in the way they do by virtue of agreed conventions). But – in an echo of the difficulty encountered, in the *Cratylus*, by the voluntarist argument of Hermogenes with the notoriously provocative example of the name given by the Master to the Slave – the contract of language is not one that is freely entered into by autonomous and sovereign speakers. The 'agreements' in question are always transmitted to the individual, unconsciously or taken-for-grantedly, from society and tradition which impose them, if not coercively, then by the inescapable 'poids de la collectivité'.[36] Moreover, no speaker has the right to secede from the contract (although he may play around at its margins), except at the price of ceasing to be a speaker at all (there can be no 'private language'). The individual is thus 'pre-installed' in the collective reality of language before his arrival on the scene as a speaking subject; in the now famous emphasis, he is as much 'spoken' as 'speaking'. If, therefore, it is still plausible to speak of language as contract, it is a contract which, from the point of view of the individual, is drawn up, signed and sealed long before he himself is engaged in its clauses. (These difficulties will, in different forms, be central to the nineteenth-century novel, where an obsession with values such as freedom, spontaneity, originality, will be constantly met and threatened by the massive weight of inherited and reproduced discourses, in a complex of tensions that will implicate the discourse of the novel itself as a medium of social representation.)

The second objection to the contract model is of the type that can be levelled at all 'holistic' or 'consensus' theories of society and its symbolic apparatus, which, with their characteristic emphasis on social reality as essentially integrated, closed systems, perforce overlook specific forces and pressures which it has been the business of an alternative social theory to bring to the fore. Briefly, these would include: first, relations of power and 'interests', in terms of which the consensual model can be reformulated in the more radical notions of hegemony and domination; secondly, relations of contradiction and conflict, as the area in which the consensual fabric comes under strain, or even comes apart at the seams. And indeed most of the critics and theoreticians of mimesis who have had recourse to the model of contract have been quick to register the appropriate qualifications: thus, Sollers' reference to the 'contrat tacite' is followed by a remark which leaves us in no doubt as to the system of power relations not only to which the 'contract' belongs, but of which it is also the servant ('est déclaré réel, dans des circonstances historiques données, ce que le plus grand nombre *à travers le nombre au pouvoir, et pour des raisons économiques précises*, est obligé de tenir pour réel').[37]

For these reasons it is therefore essential to correct the model of contract in respect of its potentially misleading implications; and in its particular bearing upon the logic of mimesis, we might usefully return here to Barthes's essay 'Diderot, Brecht, Eisenstein', in connection with one of the key figures in his description of the economy of representation: the Law. The appeal to the Law occurs in the context of Barthes's discussion of a central component of representational art: what (citing Lessing) he calls the 'instant prégnant' and of which he gives as chief examples Diderot's 'tableau', Brecht's 'Gestus' and Eisenstein's 'shot'. The 'pregnant moment' is that artistic construct which enables us to read 'd'un seul regard . . . le présent, le passé et l'avenir, c'est-à-dire le sens historique du geste représenté'. In some respects, the notion of the pregnant moment is not unlike Lukács's 'typical' moment of realist literature. (In other respects, it is, as Barthes strongly underlines, radically different, notably in the self-conscious abstraction from linearity character-istic of the Eisenstein shot and in the insistence of the Brechtian gestus on laying bare the conditions of its production.) What the two have in common, however, turns on the extent to which both strategies construct an image from which a 'total meaning' can be read (albeit that in the Brecht example the image is offered to its audience for critical appraisal). In both cases, therefore, an actual or potential hypostasis is involved, or, as Barthes puts it, a *fetishism*. For what authorises the representative or total semantic value of the 'moment' if not the 'fetishist subject' which, as we have already seen, Barthes poses as the subject who controls the 'geometrical' space of representation? And the origins of this subject, once deconstructed, are revealed as nothing other than the hegemonic authority of the Law ('Ce lieu d'origine est toujours la Loi . . . cette Loi qui regarde, cadre, centre, énonce.')[38] It is the Law which regu-lates the economy of mimesis. It determines the area of the rep-resentative and the significant, in the same way that it legislates what is constitutive of 'reality' itself, and, correspondingly, consigns to silence and oblivion, refuses (as unrepresentative or insignifi-cant) that which does not conform to the models of intelligibility it proposes. As such, it is closely aligned with forces of repression and censorship. The Law, in this sense, is an instrument of power, and is directly bound to a function of 'policing'. This replacement of the blander emphases of a contractual theory of the relations between language, meaning and narrative by the notion of a form of cultural 'policing' is a recurring theme of modern French theory; the most trenchant statement of this view is Derrida's claim that narrative 'responds to a certain "police", a form of order or law . . . In this sense all organised narration is a "matter for the police" ', held within what, in the same essay, Derrida poses as 'the whole prob-lematic of juridical framing and of the jurisdiction of framing'.[39]

The catchment area which Barthes gives to the notion of the Law is, of course, very wide, perhaps unmanageably so; it includes all those entries on that long list of despots of 'Western symbolicity'[40] which are candidates for rigorous semio-critical treatment. We might also feel, if only in a generally intuitive way, that Derrida's approach represents a somewhat restrictively penitential view of the matter of narrative. Yet, although I shall argue against the adequacy of this view, as failing to give fully satisfactory terms for an understanding of mimesis, it does direct attention to an aspect of the

question that is of major importance. In a more immediately practical way, we could test its importance by briefly considering some
of the instances of direct intervention in literary affairs of this sort
by those institutional custodians of the Law, the organs and officials
of the State (academies, courts, police, magistrates, censors, etc.).
The history of such interventions, in the context of the general
theory of representation, remains to be written; properly done, it
would make a vital contribution to the sociology of literature. Here
I shall mention just three, historically widely separated, cases (the
first of which I shall discuss more extensively in the next section). In
the seventeenth century, there is the case of the formal strictures
brought to bear by that political invention of Richelieu, the French
Academy, on Corneille's *Le Cid*: the argument that the marriage of
Chimène to Rodrigue, although historically true, was not the sort of
thing a young woman *of her type* would normally do, and which,
therefore, should have no place in a literary text aspiring to represent more than mere historical contingency. Secondly, there is the
example, in the nineteenth century, of the argument put forward by
the prosecutor at the trial of *Madame Bovary* (motivated, as is well
known, by directly political considerations): that the 'proof' of
Flaubert's obscene and blasphemous intention lay in the fact that, in
the convent episode, Emma's commingling of religious and erotic
feelings in her devotion to Christ could not conceivably be deemed
an accurate representation of the psychological condition of young
girls educated in the French convents.[41] Thirdly, in the twentieth
century, there is the droll account by Brecht of his meeting with the
official Censor to discuss the suicide incident in the film *Kühle
Wampe* (the suicide of the young worker precipitated by the housing
crisis). To Brecht's claim that the episode was based on a
documented case, the Censor replied that he had no objection whatsoever to its inclusion in the film as an isolated incident; what was
not acceptable was the film's implication that the despair the suicide
evokes might correspond to a 'typical' state of affairs; as Brecht
sardonically concluded: 'He had read us a little lecture on realism.
From the standpoint of the police.'[42]

All these cases are so many occasions of the authoritarian
incursion of the 'Law' in an attempt to condemn, mutilate or mould
the shape of an artistic representation from declared assumptions as
to what should constitute the criteria of a 'true' representation. Of
course, for Barthes the controlling and coercive presence of the Law
is far wider and more insidious than is indicated by these explicit
institutional judgements and directives; in the final analysis, it

saturates language itself as the medium of our day to day exchanges with others, and invades almost every recess of our psyche. This is arguably to make of the notion of the Law something so ubiquitous that what is lost is any sense of what distinguishes it from other forms of determination; it is moreover an emphasis which reduces our relation to representations entirely to the terms of a passive obedience to what is dictated from an 'elsewhere'. However, the claim that the model of contract often disguises other kinds of relation (such as those of power) is deeply pertinent to any argument about the social and ideological context of mimesis. What is, or can be, masked by the model (forces of repression, censorship, prohibition) I shall try to bring into greater prominence in the following section. It also gives an important focus for understanding those moments of resistance to socially ordained systems of meaning in the narrative texts I shall be examining in subsequent chapters. On the other hand, I would not wish the central implication of the argument from contract to be lost from sight. To stress the *negotiated* character of the social knowledge informing the agreements on which the mimetic text is mapped out does not entail returning uncritically to the assumption of the unconstrained 'free' subject; nor (by definition) does it rule out the possibility that, as negotiated knowledge, it is, under different circumstances and requirements, re-negotiable. It does however imply that there is more to these 'agreements' than a reduction to the terms of repression and control will allow, and it is from that position that I shall later argue that there is more to the social contract of mimesis than a construction of reality built to the specifications of the 'police'.

On verisimilitude

Aristotle and the detective novel

'In general, art either imitates the works of nature or completes that which nature is unable to bring to completion . . . The relation of that which comes after to that which goes before is the same in both.' This claim in the *Physics* (199a 15–20) restates the general relation between art and nature we have already encountered in Aristotle's discussion of mimesis in the *Poetics* (art as imitation of what is both actual and potential in nature). But it also supplies further criteria for defining the character of that relation: things happen in art as they do in nature, or, more exactly, the *order* in which they happen is the same ('the relation of that which comes after to that which goes before is the same in both'). The axis of similarity or identity is therefore that of an order of temporal relations, whose unity is assured by an assumed principle of teleological coherence. The 'motivation' of the work of art (of its dispositions as an integrated system of beginning, middle and end) doubles, or completes, causal sequences whose unfolding can be apprehended both retrospectively and projectively. At any given point in the system of nature and the system of mimesis, we should, under the appropriate cognitive conditions, be able in principle to infer correctly what precedes as a determining instance (what 'goes before') and what succeeds as a consequential outcome (what 'comes after'). Mimesis is thus linked cognitively to the capacity of the human mind to draw reliable inferences in terms of both antecedents and consequences. The formalised representation of this capacity includes the deductive inferences of logic and the inductive inferences of science; and to the extent that mimesis is shaped by these modes of reasoning, it would appear to rest on exceptionally secure intellectual foundations.

Recent research and interpretation have suggested, however, that the basis of Aristotle's theory of inference is not as firm as it might appear.[43] It has been argued that the purity of Aristotle's logical and scientific models is often adulterated by the tacit presence of what are in fact semiotic conventions of inference; that the integrity of logic and science can be threatened by incursions from rhetoric and 'dialectics', notably by the impure or probable syllogism, the *enthymeme*. The *enthymeme* is the argument whose major premiss derives from common opinion (the *doxa*), and it is a form not only central to Aristotle's analysis of rhetoric, but which also bears directly on his account of mimesis. A great deal of the interest of these points of uncertainty in Aristotle's thought is that they give a framework for discussing that fundamental yet highly problematical feature of the theory of mimesis, the doctrine of verisimilitude or, in the term I prefer to use, of *vraisemblance*. Many of the central portions of the *Poetics* are taken up with reflections on the *vraisemblance* of literary plots. But, to a large extent, they turn on a set of distinctions which, around the question of 'inference', mark exactly the troubling intersection of logic and rhetoric; and that intersection complicates the issue in ways which the metaphysical assurance of the passage from the *Physics* does not acknowledge. I shall return shortly to Aristotle's interpretation of *vraisemblance*, and, more specifically, to the important reading of Aristotle that has taken place in the work of the semiologists.[44]

First, however, in what might seem like a leap from the sublime to the grotesque, I should like to broach the question of *vraisemblance* by way of the example of the detective story.[45] The form of the detective novel is of value to the theory of *vraisemblance* in at least two respects. First, it is a form whose conventions lend support to the view that the *vraisemblance* of fiction is primarily a matter of *genre*: the 'internalised probability-system' which readers bring to novels is, as Kermode argues, generically determined;[46] it refers to sets of convention and expectation in terms of which items in the text will be deemed plausible not because they typically occur in real life, but because they typically occur in texts of this sort; because they conform to what we characteristically encounter in the literary genre in question. These are not necessarily identical with the expectation-systems of everyday life, indeed they may be radically discontinuous with them. The detective novel provides a good illustration of this argument (but, at the same time, also of some of its limitations). The central requirement of the detective novel is that the actual culprit should be the individual who, on the reader's interpretative assumptions, is the least likely candidate (although, in the game of double-bluff that this can generate, sophisticated modern writers of thrillers have played around with this requirement). In its classic form, however, the detective novel is constructed from two apparently conflicting systems of *vraisemblance*: the *vraisemblable* of the reader through which he misreads the signs; the *vraisemblable* of the detective (or rather the supervening *vraisemblable* of the text) through which the signs are read correctly. In other words, a generic *vraisemblable* (the Wisdom of the detective) reverses or overrides the *vraisemblance* of everyday life on the basis of which the reader has classified the characters into plausible and implausible suspects. Two sets of assumptions and inferences at work around a body of 'clues' compete, and, in that competition, may be said to disturb the collaboration of those two codes whose interlacing Barthes specifies as part of the organisation of the mimetic text: the 'cultural code' and the 'hermeneutic code'. The reader's interpretations derive from the cultural code; the detective's belong to the hermeneutic, whose final revelation of Truth displaces the Error produced from within the former.

There is, however, a fallacy in this analysis. For the *vraisemblable* of the detective is not in fact fundamentally different from that operated by the reader; it does not deploy a different logic. The rules of inference remain the same, but are simply applied more efficiently. The sense we have of discontinuous systems is but a ruse designed to protect the surprise effect of the final revelation; it is an illusion that, once it has served its purely local purpose, is dispelled in that happy drawing-room reunion where, as detective explains and exonerated suspects nod in agreement, the 'hermeneutic' and the 'cultural' rejoin hands as the mutual agents of the 'police-force' of intelligibility. The case of detective fiction is, of course, a somewhat specialised one. But its clarity is such that it might lead towards a similar recuperation of the 'generic' into the 'social' in the case of more complex literary forms. For instance, it is often argued that, given its extremely stylised nature, tragedy evinces a *vraisemblable* that is entirely generic in character. It would not be difficult to give criteria for that assumed autonomy: in seventeenth-century tragedy, for example, the requirements concerning the 'unities' (what the romantics will later try to take apart in the name of a greater 'realism'); or the fact that the transposition of the speech styles of tragedy and daily life from one to the other would, in both cases, be experienced as quite peculiarly implausible. On the other hand, the reasons why in a 'high' literary form such as tragedy certain personages have to speak in certain prescribed ways (the *style noble* for noble characters) derive, in part at least, from assumptions of a social, as distinct from exclusively literary, character concerning the appropriate conduct of such personages in real life; Hugo's famous 'Hein!' inserted into the discourse of the queen in *Ruy Blas* 'transgresses' (in its own limited way) a *vraisemblable* of tragedy, not just as a challenge to a set of inherited generic norms but also as an intended provocation of entrenched social values (noble persons never speak in 'vulgar' ways).

One could enumerate other examples of this kind of relation between the generic and the social. They might also help to connect Auerbach's presentation of the internal history of mimesis as the changing fortunes of a hierarchical system of 'levels of style' to the conditions of a wider cultural history (although that would entail an historical sociology of knowledge on a scale so vast as to be almost unimaginable). The main point at issue here, however, is the way these examples draw attention to a difficulty of a general order in any 'generic' theory of *vraisemblance* (one of the structuralist claims – that it is simply a matter of separating out different 'levels' of *vraisemblance*, which in some texts interweave and in others do not – does not meet this difficulty): namely, the problem of the *origin* of literary genres. This is not an easy question to handle. One of the most sophisticated attempts to answer it (Todorov's) comes up with the perhaps somewhat unenlightening conclusion that the origin of genres is genres.[47] There is indeed a chicken-and-egg dimension to the problem. What, for instance, are the respective founding roles of 'convention' and 'expectation' in the constitution of a genre; which has logical and temporal priority over the other, and, if we could successfully negotiate that question, what then would be the origin of the prioritised item? What, in these terms, would we do with the conflicting models of *vraisemblance* at work in *Don Quixote*? The Don's own models appear to be unambiguously 'generic', derived from the literary romances, while Sancho Panza's seem to come from the practical sphere of ordinary life. Yet the bookish sources of Quixote's notions of the world express codes of conduct that were once embedded, if only intermittently and incompletely, in a real social context (the codes of knightly conduct); while Sancho's *vraisemblable* will, through various processes of diffusion, itself become a 'bookish' source for a model of common sense not only in everyday life, but also for many of the texts of literary 'realism'. The imbrication of the forms of social practice and literary practice, each shaping the other while being itself shaped by them, radically disoriginates both. This must apply with even greater force to texts which make systematic mimetic claims for themselves, with the consequence that a genre-specific theory of *vraisemblance*, while having useful things to contribute, would also be quite seriously deficient.

Inference and index

The second point of interest arising from the example of the detective story involves the phenomenon of the 'clue'. The clue is very close to what the semiologist knows as the 'index' (in French both senses are contained in the term 'indice', and unquestionably part of Robbe-Grillet's fascination with the form stems from the opportunity it provides for playing ambiguously between the two senses). As far as I know, a semiological account of literary *vraisemblance* from the point of view of the theory of the index has not been attempted, although the relation is, I think, fundamental.[48] Given the proliferation of usages that in recent times has developed around the term, I should make clear what the context here applies. Although I am, of course, concerned with the representation of the index in language (in literary texts), I am not using the

term in the restricted sense in which linguistics uses it to denote the
verbal indices (the anaphoric and deictic 'shifters'). Secondly, I
shall not touch upon the looser adaptation of the term by Barthes (in
'Introduction à l'analyse structurale des récits') to describe a literary
code from which 'characters' are constructed (in *S/Z* 'index' is
replaced by the far more satisfactory 'seme'). Rather, I follow the
classic definition given by Peirce, within his general taxonomy of
signs, as that which stands in a *causal* relation to what it represents
(in an earlier terminology, it would be called a 'natural sign'). The
index is a sign which enables us to draw a whole range of inferences
whose accuracy, by virtue of the purported causal relation of the
index to its object, can rarely be in doubt; although in many cases
the precise nature of the relation may be unclear (a blush on a person's face, for instance), the index *can never lie*. The interpretation
of the index is thus of an inferential order that can proceed confidently in any temporal direction: the present (smoke → fire); the
past (track → animal); the future (thunder → rain). Although, even
on a purist definition, we can make interpretative mistakes with an
index, a universe in which all signs were indexical would be a
semiotically very safe place indeed. Similarly, a literary text organised according to the same principles could rest assured of its complete mastery of the intelligible world. And is not this precisely one
of the possible senses of Aristotle's equation of mimesis and nature
in terms of the assertion that 'the relation of that which comes after
to that which goes before is the same in both'? Do we not also refind
it in Balzac's eager endorsement of the proposition that 'De part et
d'autre, tout se déduit, tout s'enchaîne. La cause fait deviner un
effet, comme chaque effet permet de remonter à une cause' (ix,
475), and in his corresponding effort to construct a narrative
architecture whose scaffolding would be but a structure or chain of
'indexically' interrelated items (so that, as Balzac himself affirms,
from any point in the system we could always read backwards or forwards to infer infallibly what 'goes before' and what 'comes after')?

The trouble with this impressive aspiration is not just that,
semiologically speaking, it often confuses manifestly non-indexical
signs with indexical ones; it also reflects a trouble within the notion
of the index itself. The difficulty with the concept of the index lies at
the very heart of what is presupposed in its definition: its assumed
causal status. So problematic is this assumption that one recent
taxonomy has proposed that we separate out the temporal and the
causal attributes of the index, reserving the latter strictly for the
'signal' or 'symptom'[49] (a brilliant practical account of this difficulty

is to be found in Foucault's history of the confusion between medical 'signs' and 'symptoms' in *Naissance de la clinique*).[50] For a great many items that a taxonomist might be tempted to put into the class of the index express relations instituted not by nature but by culture, which, however, are made to appear as if they were relations of nature. A radical version of this critique, inspired by the Humean problematic of 'causality', might argue that all 'indexical' inferences are of this sort; that even the process of scientific inference is ultimately grounded in 'rhetorical' conventions. A more modest version would certainly claim that many of the signs which everyday life routinely imbues with causal meaning (including the 'lay' reception of science) in fact embody associations based on custom and habit. The inferences we draw from them are – legitimately – authorised by custom (what we can normally expect to occur given *this* particular ordering of the world), but would not be possible without the intermediary of a socially conventionalised activity of interpretation. In such cases, we would therefore have to modify Peirce's definition of the index (a modification Peirce himself hinted at in his suggestion that all inferences are 'semiosic' acts):[51] what the semiologist classifies as an index, or rather what a given society treats as an index, will depend critically on what that society *assumes*, by dint of repetition and familiarity, to be causally related. This, of course, would render the concept of the index exceedingly 'fuzzy'. But that fuzziness might itself be construed as having a very precise function, as a constituent of the cultural glue which enables a society to perceive itself as a stable and knowable reality.

Many of the 'stocks of knowledge' of everyday life function in this way, sheltered beneath a symbolic canopy woven from a tissue of tacit maxims and enthymemes that have been ideologically translated into natural truths (the occulting of the enthymeme, remarks Eco, is one of the key points for the semiological analysis of 'ideology').[52] They legitimate arguments based on received opinion as watertight causal explanations; or, in other words, furnish the context in which the clue, the sign, is invested with the authority of the index. A particularly clear example of this process is given by the discursive practices of the law courts (doubly instructive when we recall that legal disputation is one of the main sources for Aristotle's codification of rhetoric). The theory of jurisprudence shows us, of course, that the structure of forensic reasoning is immensely complex (except in societies where trials are transparently rigged). But one area in which legal debate is regularly contaminated by enthymemic reasoning, or rather by its ideological transformation,

47

is in its deliberations upon the question of 'motive'. As Barthes illustrates, in his remarkable essays on two modern trials (in *Mythologies*),[53] legal arguments about motive, or its absence, frequently have recourse to what are culturally sanctioned typifications of human conduct, but which, in the play of the argument, are explicitly adduced as causal laws of 'human nature'. The example of legal argument is also instructive in another respect. The inferences and judgements of this type that it makes are not just appeals to pre-given stocks of knowledge; they are also practical interventions: in the form of publicly declared and recognised 'cases' and 'precedents', they become themselves interpretative paradigms which feed back into, reinforce (and sometimes modify) these stocks, thus providing a perfect image of the recursiveness of the social world.

A similarly recursive dialectic informs many levels of mimetic narrative. The techniques of 'motivation' it uses for the construction of plots and characters often produce versions of events and behaviour whose assumptions closely resemble those of the argumentative forms deployed in the law courts around the issue of 'motive'. Furthermore, not only does mimetic fiction draw parasitically on the tacit assimilation of convention-bound readings of reality to the model of a causal ('indexical') interpretation of reality; in putting these versions of 'human nature' into cultural circulation, it can be seen as actively taking the ideological initiative with that model: like legal 'precedent', it returns to society the terms in which the latter's self-image can be confirmed and strengthened. This may explain in part why, from Kafka to Camus, the phenomenon of the 'trial' has been such an important image in the attack mounted by the modern novel on traditional narrative psychology. In respect of Camus's *L'Étranger*, for example, in which the court desperately searches for, and the hero resolutely refuses to supply, a motive for his actions, it is arguable that the central figure of the trial (on both sides of the dock) is the Novel itself: the prosecutor seeks to interpret Meursault's crime in the terms consecrated by the Novel: Meursault's stubborn resistance to those interpretative moves is a resistance to the forms of explanation endorsed by the traditions of the genre. Similarly, what makes Robbe-Grillet's play with the 'clues' of the detective story more than just a frivolous game is that its structure gives a pretext for a more extensive questioning of the role played by the novel in manufacturing the ideological cement with which a society holds its world together. In ironically focussing the surreptitious sliding between the conventional and the causal, in showing the insecurity of the inferences whose stability is otherwise taken for granted, Robbe-Grillet takes apart the 'indexical' fabric of a whole cultural formation. The parody of the detective in *Les Gommes* and the satire of the court in *L'Étranger* are part of that general modern enterprise of challenging the 'law' of narrative, the authority of its *vraisemblable*. But then perhaps the 'modern' has simply picked up, in its self-consciously programmatic way, on a theme that has been implicitly available since the beginnings of the theory of literary verisimilitude. This is the moment to return to Aristotle.

Eikos *and* doxa

For, although he does not pursue the implications of what he suggests (had he done so, scholarship might have been spared a great deal of interpretative labour), Aristotle brings the whole issue out into the open, or alternatively gives the game away – in the distinction frequently drawn in the *Poetics* between the 'necessary' (*anagkaion*) and the 'probable' (*eikos*).[54] Although almost casually presented as the terms of a simple alternative confronting the artist ('the probable or necessary sequence of events', 1452a 23–4), the distinction is crucial. The 'necessary' designates the area of natural truths (the truths of Nature), as articulated by logic and science. The 'probable', on the other hand, is more a rhetorical category, an element in the social arts of 'persuasion' (the *pithanon*); its link with rhetoric (the 'persuasive' story being to the *Poetics* what the 'persuasive' argument is to the *Rhetoric*) is brought out in the famous stipulation (1460a 27) that 'for the purposes of poetry a likely impossibility (*pithanon adunaton*; is always preferable to an unconvincing possibility (*apithanon dunaton*)'. Aristotle himself does not have much to say about the place of the 'necessary' in the structure of the mimetic work; he does have more to say (although, for our purposes, unfortunately not enough) about the place of the 'probable'. Whether this disjunction betrays a moment of unease in Aristotle's thought (since the intrusion of rhetoric inevitably weakens the integrity of the systems he elsewhere affirms), or simply a moment of shrewdness, we shall never know. It does however re-orientate the argument about the form of mimesis in a fundamentally different direction; it pushes the argument away from the certitudes of a teleological metaphysics towards an emphasis on the more contingent constraints of a social context, within which the artist has to 'persuade' an audience in large measure by the cultural frames of meaning to hand. Presumably, in an ideal Aristotelian world, mimetic plots would unfold according to pure laws of teleological 'necessity'; such an eventuality would indeed be the supreme guarantee of the relation between art and nature stipulated in the *Physics* (i.e. the guarantee that 'the relation of that which comes after to that which goes before is the same in both'). In the practical world, however, Aristotle recognises that the coherence and credibility of narrative have more frequently to depend on the rhetorical poor relation of the logically 'necessary', the merely 'probable', the network of enthymemes and maxims that enables us to infer what, under generally familiar conditions and by general consent, is *likely* to be the case. For the 'probable' is epistemologically far more precarious than the 'necessary'. It may, from time to time, have usurping designs on its definitionally superior brother, as a creature of custom that would like to be perceived as consecrated by the laws of nature. But its actual authority, as Aristotle is aware, is not the voice of metaphysical necessity but the philosophically far less reliable voice of the *doxa* ('common opinion', or that system of socially shared meaning and belief determining what members of the community generally take to be the case).

This apparent dilution, within the terms of Aristotle's thinking, of the conceptual foundations of mimetic art has formed the basis of a substantial body of recent work, in particular the attempt by the semiologists to reactivate the Aristotelian text in support of their own critical interpretation of the notion of *vraisemblance*. The main emphasis of that interpretation lies in the proposal to arrange a marriage between the theory of mimesis and the theory of rhetoric, through the suggestion that the literary *eikos* of the *Poetics* should be subsumed under the larger category of the *doxa*.[55] In these terms, what, in a given historical context, is admitted as *vraisemblable* in a fictional text arises from the diffuse 'doxal' text through which a society achieves a consensus on such general categories as the 'rational', the 'normal', the 'plausible', etc. In Genette's summary of this account, the *vraisemblable* articulates the relation of a literary text to a set of social and institutional 'norms': 'ce qui définit le vraisemblable, c'est le respect formel du principe de la norme, c'est-à-dire l'existence d'un rapport d'implication entre la conduite particulière attribuée à tel personnage, et telle maxime générale implicite et reçue.'[56] The *vraisemblable* thus derives from a code according to which the intelligibility of a particular action or sequence of actions in the literary text is vouchsafed by a set of norms silently posited in the text, and which correspond to the norms through which a society constructs a general representation of its own reality.

As a piece of Aristotelian exegesis, this reading has in fact somewhat problematical credentials, and the guardians of scholarly rectitude might well be tempted to see in it merely another instance of 'Gallic' irresponsibility with the canonic texts of the past (less a respectable marriage between the *Poetics* and the *Rhetoric* than a promiscuous mish-mash).[57] Minimally, it is a reading that does require a considerable amount of inferential juggling and cross-referencing between the two texts, and it is certainly the case that practitioners of the art have not been conspicuously ready to cite detailed sources. But, apart from the question of exegetical accuracy, the interest of this approach lies in the effort to confer on the notion of *vraisemblance* a specifically sociological or anthropological dimension; to establish a relation between the expectations readers bring to bear on the performance of the mimetic text and what, in sociological theory, are sometimes called the 'background expectancies' we use in the interpretation of the social world. For the postulated link between the *eikos* and the *doxa* implies that the former is to be seen as belonging to the network of interlocking discursive forms shaping the 'natural attitude' of society, that space of 'common sense understanding' within which is constituted, in Alfred Schütz's phrase, 'the world known in common and taken for granted'.[58] *Vraisemblance* is a system of conventions and expectations which rests on, and in turn reinforces, that more general system of 'mutual knowledge' produced within a community for the realisation and maintenance of a whole social world. This knowledge is not primarily theoretical; rather it is what the sociology of knowledge refers to as 'pragmatic' knowledge – essentially, a set of socially constructed typifications in respect of which the world is expected to behave in certain more or less regular and predictable ways. As a form of knowledge sustained largely by means of collective agreements, it can be represented by that model, or metaphor, whose role in modern thinking about mimesis I have previously discussed: the model of contract. As Olivier Burgelin has suggested,[59] we may grasp *vraisemblance* in terms of a 'contractual' model of communication and exchange, whereby reader and writer participate collaboratively in the creation of a stable economy of meaning. Or, as Leslie Hill argues,[60] the *vraisemblance* of the fictional text is assured by virtue of reader and writer engaging in a 'contract of mutual recognition', a contract of meaning which meshes into that general network of agreements from which a society demarcates its boundaries between sense and nonsense, the typical and the anomalous, the normal and the abnormal.

Vraisemblance *and censorship*

This relation of mutual confirmation uniting the *eikos* and the *doxa* suggests therefore that, at one level, the *vraisemblable* has specific ideological properties; that it is an ideological 'opérateur' whose prime task is to contribute to stabilising and legitimating the given order of things. In Burgelin's economic metaphor, its function is to exert maximum 'deflationary' pressure on the society's economy of signs and symbols, to maintain a cultural situation in which meanings are simply repeated and redistributed rather than changed. Moreover, since (as we have seen) the model of contract often masks relations of force and repression, the *vraisemblable* can be said to fulfil the dual role of guardian and censor ('le vraisemblable est l'expression de la censure').[61] As part of a system of knowledge whose functions and conditions of existence are intimately related to prevailing relations of power, it acts both to protect the values of the official culture and to exclude (as *invraisemblables*) those representations which threaten the hegemony of the universe of established meanings – a role from time to time publicly institutionalised, as with the foundation of the Académie whose pontifical enunciations on *vraisemblance* embodied not only specifically aesthetic judgements on the 'proper' conventions of literary forms, but also judgements that extended across the whole field of the normative culture of the time.

Perhaps nowhere is this rationalising and repressive function more apparent than in connection with the *moral* systems of society, the specifically moral injunctions embedded in the social contract of meaning. Durkheim argued that social reality is primarily moral reality. The *conscience collective* (or *consensus universel*) consists essentially of a set of consensual moral norms, whose internalisation by social actors is a constitutive condition of the very existence of society. I have already suggested that any inquiry into the social context of mimesis should treat Durkheimian models of interpretation with some circumspection. They do, however, raise an issue that is directly related to the functions of *vraisemblance*: the importance of the *tacit* nature of moral belief. For the social efficacy of such norms lies to a large extent in their implicit, or taken-for-granted character. 'The implicit is the necessary foundation of social intercourse', writes Mary Douglas,[62] and it is precisely by virtue of a body of tacit collusions and unexamined assumptions that the binding authority of a 'morality-sustaining' universe can be accepted. But, since the assumption of free choice (and therefore the making explicit of the criteria of moral action) is part of the definition of the moral, there necessarily arises serious difficulty over the idea of the unconditionally binding authority which the implicit nature of moral belief both presupposes and enforces. Societies evolve various ways of dealing with this difficulty, from religious to legal sanction, but the most effective (because generally unnoticed) lies in the ingenious solution of presenting moral ideas as if they were in fact something else, or as if they originated in a source other than moral choice.

For the profoundest operation of the tacit ideology of a society lies not in instituting a set of moral values as such, but in masking the origins of prescriptive sanctions, by re-routing the terms of the moral order into the circuit of another order of discourse: that of causal statements and logical predictions. As Mary Douglas again puts it, 'although the moral order and the knowledge which sustains it are created by social convention, if their man-made origins were not *hidden* they would be stripped of some of their authority'.[63] The major ideological move in achieving this result is to identify the moral order with that of 'common sense', itself idenfied as corresponding to the 'natural' order of things; the moral 'contract' may be written by men, but it is presented and experienced as a charter handed down by Nature. It is the process whereby an 'ought' is transformed into an 'is', whereby moral imperatives (what people are required to do) are disguised in the form of descriptive and predictive statements (what everybody does, or is likely to do, as a matter of course). It is from this reduction of ethical norms to naturalistic laws, specifying the area of what is plausible, normal, natural, that moral action can be presented as natural action, and infractions of moral norms as nothing other than a departure from the order of 'reality' itself (as implausible, abnormal, unnatural and, in its extreme form, as 'mad').

Many of the ambiguities in the concept of *vraisemblance* revolve around this confusion of prescriptive norms with predictive models of behaviour. We already have a glimmering of this confusion in that moment of terminological instability in the *Poetics*, where Aristotle outlines his theory of mimetic 'character' (chapter XV): apparently distinct notions ('proper', 'appropriate', 'decorous', 'true to life') combine in the presentation of the argument in ways that tend to blur the lines of semantic division between them (this is especially the case with the terms 'indecorous' and 'inappropriate'). But for a more systematically developed example, we might turn to that emphasis in seventeenth-century poetics which sought to establish a relation between *vraisemblance* and *bienséance*. Despite considerable scholarly effort, the logic of this connection has remained quite irritatingly opaque. It may well be, however, that the main reason why we have experienced such difficulty in clarifying the concepts in question is because their interrelations and distinctions were by no means clear within seventeenth-century discourse itself. As René Bray's impressive reconstruction shows,[63] entering the terminological universe of seventeenth-century literary debate is like trying to cut one's way through a semantic jungle or, better, trying to find one's way out of a semantic circle. The major terms of the discussion (*vraisemblance*, *raison*, *nature*, *bon sens*, *bon goût*, *bienséance*) not only mutually imply each other, but in many respects furnish the materials for the definition of each other, in a movement that is entirely circular. If we were to apply to this vocabulary the technique of 'path-analysis' developed by modern semantics, we would come up with an exceptionally complicated 'compositional tree', in which it would be by no means clear which was trunk, branch or foliage.

It may be, however, following the later Wittgenstein's recommendations, that the headaches created by trying to negotiate this circle derive not so much from the inherent logical intractability of the concepts, as from adopting a wrong way of looking at them: change the angle of vision and the headache might go away. For many of the difficulties do disappear if, following Wittgenstein's example, we concentrate less on the logical requirements of abstract definition and more on the practical 'uses' of these concepts in their particular cultural context. It is eminently possible that the areas of confusion arise not from our own inability to understand, still less from technical deficiencies in seventeenth-century discourse, but from specific ideological demands placed on that discourse in the seventeenth-century world. Accordingly, instead of trying to convert confusion into clarity, we should see the 'confusion' itself as forming an active part of the cultural meaning and ideological function of the concepts in question. As the philosophers of the social sciences remind us, always to look for rigour and precision in the conceptual systems of a given culture or period is often to miss half the point, since the purpose of many such systems lies less in conforming to an ideal model of 'rationality' than in protecting and legitimating the pursuit of non-rational pragmatic goals; the uncertainties, overlaps and ambiguities of key terms within the given conceptual field may well correspond to certain 'strategic ambiguities'[65] which it is in the interests of a society, or a particular social group, to maintain.

The overlapping relation between *vraisemblance* and *bienséance* in seventeenth-century thought is an exemplary instance of this type of ambiguity maintenance, of the 'logically illicit transformation'[66] of one concept into another, in the service of the pragmatic requirements of the seventeenth-century aristocratic *doxa*. Strictly speaking, *vraisemblance* and *bienséance* form two quite separate codes, based on two distinct orders of knowledge: one is logical, centred on the probabilities and predictabilities of actions and events; the other is ethical, concerned with norms of 'correct' or 'proper' behaviour. Thus, as in the famous *Querelle du Cid*, to which I have previously alluded, the judgement that Chimène's projected marriage to Rodrigue represents a major artistic error on Corneille's part, because typically a young woman of honour *would* not do this sort of thing, is a judgement according to the code of *vraisemblance*; whereas the judgement that it is an error because a young woman of honour *should* not do, or should not be represented as doing, this sort of thing, is a judgement according to the code of *bienséance*. As Genette has elegantly demonstrated,[67] through his play on the ambiguity of the verb 'devoir' (connoting both *obligation* and *probabilité*), the two judgements in practice overlap and interpenetrate to the point where they are virtually indistinguishable.

Yet, in pointing to this imbrication of codes, Genette does not fully bring into focus the essential process, precisely because he does not comment on the functional significance of this relationship of overlap. Genette is quite right to stress how, in seventeenth-century thinking, the code of *vraisemblance* can gather into itself judgements drawn from the code of *bienséance*, but wrong to infer that it is consequently a matter of 'indifference' as to which code the critic will deploy in delivering his assessment of the 'plausibility' of the literary representation ('On peut donc *indifféremment* énoncer le jugement d'invraisemblance sous une forme éthique . . . ou sous une forme logique').[68] For the language of *vraisemblance* and the language of *bienséance* are not conceptually equivalent, and thus capable of being exchanged at will to mean exactly the same thing (if this were the case, then the severe difficulties scholars have always encountered in this area would simply evaporate). Rather the relationship is less one of logical equivalence than of logically 'illicit' substitution, the covert rationalisation of the one by means of the other. The two terms constitute a space of ambiguous meanings and shifting identities, whose purpose is the elision of one code into the terms of the other, so as to confer on the ethical injunction the alibi of the rational and the natural; what is held to be ethically proper can thus be proffered in the guise of what is held to be rationally normal or natural. It is almost certain that the main reason why seventeenth-century susceptibilities were so outraged by Chimène's marriage was because it infringed a moral code centred on familial relationships (father before lover, obedience before desire). Yet since that code, like all moral codes, is questionable, the case against Corneille is immeasurably strengthened if Chimène's 'immoral' behaviour is recast as 'unnatural' behaviour, as *invraisemblable*, situated beyond the bounds of the prevailing norms of 'reason' or 'common sense'; in brief, not just the infringement of a moral taboo, but a violation of intelligibility itself. In this way, the offence against the standards of *bienséance* is naturalised as an offence against *vraisemblance*; or, to put it the other way round, the appeal to the authority of *vraisemblance* is a way of simultaneously masking and yet legitimating a prior appeal to that area of the *doxa* occupied by the prescriptions of *bienséance*.

The seventeenth-century quarrel over *Le Cid* suggests, therefore, the existence of an intimate link between the forms of *vraisemblance* and the operation of a strategy of moral censorship and control. It is moreover significant that, in this particular area, the object of that censorship should be desire, and more specifically *feminine* desire. It is a pattern that we will re-encounter in connection with contemporary responses to nineteenth-century narrative. I have already cited the Prosecutor's attempted demonstration of the 'obscene' intention of *Madame Bovary* on the grounds of the 'implausibility' of Emma's mingling of erotic and religious fantasies. Similarly – in the example I want to explore more extensively in a subsequent chapter – it is a recurring theme in nineteenth-century criticism of Mathilde de la Mole's affair with Julien Sorel: so disturbed is the conservative critical mind by the transgression of 'proper' codes of conduct entailed by Mathilde's desire for the plebeian Julien that, through a piece of deftly self-protective sleight of hand, it can cope only by denouncing the episode on the grounds that Stendhal must have written it with scandalous disregard for the elementary requirements of literary probability. One of the most complex and intense moments of Stendhal's novel is thus banished from the territory of 'proper' representation, condemned by the critical magistracy as being but the delinquent product of an aberrant imagination.

Accordingly, we might construe one of the ideological functions of *vraisemblance* in terms of what Deleuze has called the 'territorialisation' of desire and Foucault the 'discursive policing' of sexuality.[69] *Vraisemblance* is part of the cultural apparatus for coding and demarcating the field of desire within the terms of what the society proposes as the self-evident or the natural; or, in Foucault's account, it serves that tendency to naturalise the rules governing the discursive and institutional organisation of sexuality, so that transgression of the rules becomes an offence against nature itself: the 'contre-la-loi' becomes equated with the 'contre-nature'.[70] I have already suggested that the metaphor of 'policing' by no means exhausts the order of mimesis, and I shall later also raise certain queries with regard to Deleuze's notion of 'territorialisation' (it is explicitly linked to the question of mimesis in *Mille Plateaux*). Nevertheless, there remains considerable historical evidence in support of the view that the logic of *vraisemblance* is in many ways tied into the logic of censorship, that logic so brilliantly mapped by Foucault, with whom, therefore, we might, for the moment, leave the last word:

La logique de la censure: Cette interdiction est supposée prendre trois formes; affirmer que ça n'est pas permis, empêcher que ça soit dit, nier que ça existe. Formes apparemment difficiles à concilier. Mais c'est là qu'on imagine une sorte de logique en chaîne qui serait caractéristique des mécanismes de censure: elle lie l'inexistant, l'illicite et l'informulable de façon que chacun soit à la fois principe et effet de l'autre: de ce qui est interdit, on ne doit pas parler jusqu'à ce qu'il soit annulé dans le réel; ce qui est inexistant n'a droit à aucune manifestation, même dans l'ordre de la parole qui énonce son inexistence; et ce qu'on doit taire se trouve banni du réel comme ce qui est interdit par excellence. La logique du pouvoir sur le sexe serait la logique paradoxale d'une loi qui pourrait s'énoncer comme injonction d'inexistence, de non-manifestation et de mutisme.[71]

The language of mimesis

Mirrors and windows

Any theory of literary mimesis which takes the term mimesis in the literal sense of 'imitation' is likely to be stopped dead in its tracks before a problem of an elementary sort. For, strictly interpreted, the idea of a *literary* mimesis calls attention to a difficulty so obvious as to appear pedantically trivial, were it not that a great deal of the history of the idea has been taken up by a confrontation with, or avoidance of, this very difficulty. The problem is this: if, following Plato, we pose the order of mimesis as a relation between an 'original' and a 'copy', then, apart from the marginal (but still problematical) cases of onomatopoeia and the ideogram, in what sense can we say that language 'copies' anything; in respect of what can its properties be held to produce an 'imitation' or a 'likeness'? The only moderately obvious (but also deceptive) answer to this question is that what language imitates, and all that it can imitate, is language itself. In its classical form, this notion turns on the distinction between *mimesis* and *diegesis*. In Book III of the *Republic*, Plato divides narrative poetry into two modes: narration proper in which the poet relates events in his own voice ('diegesis'); dialogue (and reported monologue) in which the poet 'imitates' the voice of others. Language can thus be said to behave mimetically only in the restricted case of speech (which is one reason why Aristotle gears his discussion of mimesis to the specific case of drama). But, if this distinction has the virtue of giving what seems to be a clearly defined answer to our question, it also suffers from serious drawbacks. In the first place, the division of the text into 'diegetic' and 'mimetic' necessarily entails that the concept of mimesis can never be used, with the possible exception of drama, to describe the character of a literary text as a whole; there can be no such thing as a mimetic narrative *tout court* (apart perhaps from a narrative entirely in reported speech). More specifically, the notion of 'diegesis' writes out of the scenario of mimesis precisely that feature which, from another point of view, we have elsewhere identified as a key constituent of the mimetic text: namely, the commanding position occupied by the narrating subject in the economy of mimesis. Secondly, the argument that, through the reproduction of speech patterns, language *imitates* language is in an important sense logically flawed. As Genette points out,[72] in his account of the thinking of Plato and Aristotle on narrative and drama, the true logical status of the claim that language imitates language is in fact that of pure tautology. In the case of narrative or dramatic speech, what we have in principle is not so much a relation of imitation as of duplication, the giving of a further instance of the same; the argument thus eliminates that element of difference between 'original' and 'copy' which enables us to recognise that a mimesis is taking place.

Beyond this restricted context, however, the difficulties with the question proliferate almost uncontrollably. Depending on one's point of view, this prospect is likely to lead us to see the question either as plunging us into deep and treacherous philosophical waters, or as having occupied a quite disproportionate amount of time and space. In addressing this question myself, I propose to take the latter view. One consequence of this is to make a move which, given the nature of my topic, will doubtless appear somewhat extravagant, if not entirely illicit: to bypass, as something of a red herring, the long and complex history of the grounding *ocular* metaphor on which so many answers to the question have been traditionally based (the notion of language either as 'mirror' or as 'window', as that which 'reflects' or that which is 'transparent'). My reason for doing so is not to write off as incoherent the intellectual ambitions of this tradition, from the presumed superiority of our post-Saussurean vantage point; that would be rather like adopting the position of someone ticking off Plato for having led us for over two thousand years up the philosophical garden path. From the post-Saussurean perspective, that tradition will, of course, seem incoherent. But, if we reject it categorically in this way, we are then faced with the prospect of spiriting away a very substantial portion of our own intellectual history. Richard Rorty has argued that we do indeed need to free ourselves from the ocular metaphor, as placing impossible demands on both the definition and the enterprise of 'philosophy'. But he also points out that the history is after all *there*, and that we cannot deal with it simply by treating it as some grotesquely prolonged aberration: 'There was, we moderns may say with the ingratitude of hindsight, no particular reason why this ocular metaphor seized the imagination of the founders of Western thought. But it did, and contemporary philosophers are still working out its consequences, analysing the problems it created, and asking whether there may not be something to it after all.'[73]

Reviewing that history is mercifully not part of the brief of this book (still less inquiring as to whether 'there may be something to it after all'). But the tradition yields an extraordinarily rich and fascinating story. If the context is that of the history of epistemology, it will include such diverse chapters as the place of language in the apprehension by the 'eye of the soul' of the sphere of Ideal Forms (Plato); the terms in which language assists the passage from 'innate' ideas to knowledge of the external world (Descartes); how the structure of propositions gives a 'picture' of the logical structure of reality (early Wittgenstein). Where it concerns speculations on the 'origins' of language, we will be returning to the various theologies of prelapsarian origins: the story of the pre-Babel condition where Adam gives names to things in a fixed relation of designation that is divinely ordained; or the argument of the *Cratylus* about the mimetic sources of 'primary' words (the argument about the 'natural' or 'conventional' basis of language that will resurface in very many different areas, notably in some of the great linguistic and aesthetic debates of the eighteenth century). In the context of the history of rhetoric, it is the debate contrasting the notion of a 'natural' language of representation, in the sense of the plain and the unadorned, with the seductive and deceptive 'cosmetics' of rhetorical embellishment. In the context of the impact of the natural sciences on literary thought (as in the nineteenth century), it is the reactivation of the metaphors of ocularity and specularity in the effort to define for literature the grounds of a neutral, value-free vocabulary of description. Or, quite simply, it is a metaphor mobilised to defend literature from the pressures of official or unofficial censorship; when Stendhal famously compares the novel to a 'mirror' travelling along a highway, it is in order to resist the imposition of taboos on the subject matter of fiction: the novel must show the mud on the road as well as the more fetching and elevating view of the blue sky.

My ostensibly cavalier attitude to this weighty tradition is, however, rooted in more modest and parochial considerations; it has to do with how residues of this prestigious metaphor have informed some of the more taken-for-granted habits of thought from which literary theory today has often 'theorised' the assumptions about language that are built into the project of literary mimesis. My claim is that these residual echoes have generated in modern critical discourse a kind of ritual sparring over a falsely posed issue (or indeed over several issues); and that, accordingly, in order to examine in more coherent ways the assumptions about language on which the practice of mimesis depends, we need to move the discussion to quite different conceptual ground. In particular we need to ask ourselves if any useful purpose is served by what, from the various metaphors inherited from the tradition, has tended to be (at least in France) the particular catch-word of this modern ritual: the term 'transparency'. This may be thought an arbitrary restriction, given the role played by the other variants of the ocular metaphor, notably of course, the idea of 'reflection'. But, while the term 'reflection' continues to be active in the vocabulary of literary discussion, it is, I think, fair to say that it no longer functions as the dominant term of this particular theoretical debate (especially since the decisive shift, within Marxist accounts of cultural formations, from the idea of 'reflection' to that of 'mediation').

'Transparency', on the other hand, has continued to have a field-day. In *Qu'est-ce que la littérature?* Sartre compared language (specifically prose) to a *vitre*, a pane of glass through the transparency of which the gaze of the reader passes to an immediate apprehension of the world; the transparency of the linguistic sign is what guarantees its efficacy as a means of 'unveiling' the truth of things.[74] For those on the other side of the argument, the assumption of the transparency of language is the very core of the ideological mischief which the idea of a mimetic or representational literature seeks to perpetrate. But this, basically, is a reduction of the tradition to intellectual melodrama, sparring with a straw man. Perhaps, as analogy, the notion of 'transparency' has satisfied some limited needs of twentieth-century polemic. But its subsequent fate has far outrun those local and limited uses. The more it has settled into being a fixed and taken-for-granted item in the currency of critical exchange, the more it has moved the real argument down a blind alley. In so far as escaping from ritual postures is a necessary condition of engaging with the real argument, then of all our ritual terms, 'transparency' is pre-eminently the one that should be consigned without delay to the critical waste paper basket.

Madame Aubain's barometer, or the referential illusion

I

If recourse to the optical metaphors which have traditionally governed accounts of the relation between language and mimesis only succeed now in generating categories of straw, what then is the area in which this relation can be more usefully discussed? One major alternative line of enquiry is by way of the claim that what marks the language of literary mimesis is its *referential* character. The language of the mimetic text does not 'mirror' reality, is not 'transparent' to reality; it 'hooks' on to reality by virtue of a relation that holds between linguistic expressions and what they stand for in the world (objects, places, persons, states of affairs, etc.). By exploiting the referring properties of language, the mimetic text knits the order of 'fiction' into the order of 'fact', and thus ensures that process of recognition whereby the reader connects the world produced by the text with the world of which he himself has direct or indirect knowledge.

This is certainly a claim of a logically quite different sort from that which underlies the metaphors of 'mirroring' and 'transparency' – it is important to stress this difference since in much contemporary debate the two are frequently used as if they were synonymous. It is nevertheless the case that the terms in which the claim is ordinarily advanced (or disputed) in literary criticism are often extremely vague. Intuitively it seems appropriate to talk of certain features of Balzac's descriptions of Paris in the *Comédie humaine* as 'referring' to the characteristics of a real city, or of Stendhal's account, at the beginning of *La Chartreuse de Parme*, of the entry of the Napoleonic army into Italy as referring to an actual state of historical affairs (this does not of course preclude these items from performing other functions at other levels of the organisation of the text). But intuitive talk is often loose talk, and may require considerable tightening up. A hard-nosed linguist or philosopher of language, reviewing the way in which the terms 'refer', 'referential', 'referent' frequently behave in literary argument, might well arrive at some dismaying conclusions. In more aggressive mood, he might feel inclined to put to the parties engaged in this literary debate a number of unsettling questions. It does not necessarily follow that such an interrogation, though doubtless bracing, would bring the debate to a successful conclusion. It might shake us out of habits of intellectual laziness, but not perforce provide any sure guide as to the direction in which one might profitably take the literary argument. The linguistic and philosophical literature on the theory of reference is inordinately extensive and complex, and it is easy, within this form of inquiry, to become paralysed by interminable technical niceties. Furthermore, for both linguists and philosophers the topic is still deeply controversial; within the corpus there are various and diverging theories of reference.

Nevertheless if we are to entertain seriously the claim that the language of literary mimesis 'refers' to reality, there is some virtue, if only in the interest of preliminary clarification of terms, in attending to some of the things that linguists and philosophers have to say on the subject. Most theories of reference specify a function, a set of conditions and a presupposition. Functionally, a reference is distinguished from other linguistic categories on the grounds that its specific purpose is to pick out or identify a particular, an individual member of a class of entities. Secondly, it is often held that the conditions of a reference include a set of grammatical and contextual constraints on the capacity of an expression to perform this function (such as the presence of possessive adjectives, demonstrative pronouns, deictic adverbs, and other 'indexical' devices). Thirdly, reference normally involves an existential presupposition: one can only refer to something that is held to exist in the world (or, in

Frege's terms, something in the world about which statements possessing truth-values can be made).

All of these assertions are open to dispute and modification, and not all are necessarily co-present in a given theory of reference. They do, however, provide a rudimentary analytical framework within which one can begin to correct the laxity of usage that often accompanies literary discussion of the question of reference. In particular, they prompt two considerations. First, on the above criteria, the number of expressions that can be properly described as 'referring' is limited; it will therefore not do to describe whole stretches of connected discourse, let alone whole texts, as uniformly referential; one has to discriminate, break down the discourse into its functionally distinct constituents. This constraint may be thought overrestrictive, especially in the light of the powerful version of reference developed by Frege, which necessarily allows for connected discourse to be referential, in so far as the question of reference is directly related to the 'truth-values' of sentences, propositions and descriptions. Frege's insistence on reference as linked to truthvalues, however, raises, in acute form, the second consideration: whether, under any circumstances, the language of a *fictional* text can ever be held to possess referring properties. The example of a non-referring sentence Frege gives is Homer's 'Odysseus was set ashore at Ithaca while sound asleep' (adding, in a footnote, that we perhaps need a special term for the class of signs that have only sense and no reference).[75] Similarly, Searle's 'speech-act' theory of narrative argues that, apart from the inclusion of certain kinds of proper names, fictional discourse is definitionally non-referential; on the existential presupposition, there can be no referents in an imaginary world (other than subsequent mentions of fictive entities already established in that world).[76]

This is indeed a pertinent (though, some would say, pedantically obvious) consideration. For how, if we felt so inclined, might we go about identifying the 'referents' of a fictional text? A certain class of proper names would presumably present little difficulty; in the examples from Balzac and Stendhal grasping the referents of the proper names 'Paris', 'Napoleon', 'Italy', requires no further specification (although some theories would require supporting contextual information – the 'principle of identifying descriptions' – to avoid potential ambiguity or misidentification). Similarly, the mention of the 'rue Neuve-Sainte-Geneviève' in the Paris of *Le Père Goriot* is unproblematically referential (at least to a nineteenth-century reader; is its referential status altered by the fact that the street was subsequently renamed the 'rue Tournefort'?).[77] But what of the 'pension bourgeoise' that is situated within it? What is the referent of the 'Pension Vauquer'? What are the referents of its inhabitants and its furnishings? What is the referent, to pick out but one detail of that famous description, of 'un baromètre à capucin qui sort quand il pleut'?[78] Or what, to take a virtually identical example from another text, is the referent of Madame Aubain's 'barometer'?

Madame Aubain's barometer appears as an item in a description of that lady's drawing room in Flaubert's *Un Cœur simple*: 'un vieux piano supportait, sous un baromètre, un tas pyramidal de boîtes et de cartons.'[79] It probably led a rather humble, possibly entirely unnoticed, literary life, until it was elevated by Barthes to a position of some prominence in his important paper, 'L'effet de réel'.[80] We do not know if Madame Aubain ever consulted her barometer (in the same way that we do not know, or care, how many children Lady Macbeth had). Barthes, however, consults or 'reads' it as a register of considerable perturbation in the literary atmospherics of the Flaubert text, and, by extension, in the text of 'realist' writing in general. For Barthes, Madame Aubain's barometer is 'worrying', even 'scandalous'. Sandwiched anodinely between two other, semantically richer substantives, it is precisely its anodine, almost self-effacing character, that is the source of Barthes's worry. What is it doing there, what is its 'function'? From the point of view of a structural description of the text, it seems quite useless ('un détail inutile'); it is resistant to meaning, or rather, it resists the coding operations whereby meaning is produced. Unlike its immediate neighbours, which appear to be governed by a connotative code ('vieux piano' connotes bourgeois standing; 'un tas pyramidal' connotes disorder, and together the two connotations join along one of the main thematic axes of the text), 'baromètre' is relatively uncoded, conveying no semantic information beyond its literal denotation. It is not a sign on which one can gain any interpretative purchase; it is void of connotative force. One could, of course, argue that, semiologically speaking, Barthes is being here a shade pessimistic; giving up, as it were, the semiological ghost in the face of the apparently intractable. Since weather, in Flaubert's Normandy, is predictably boring, the barometer could be connotatively construed as signifying the Futile (it is exactly the sort of thing we might expect to find Emma Bovary consulting on a grey day at Yonville, in the forlorn hope that signs of a change in the weather herald signs of a change in her life).[81] That Barthes does not countenance these interpretative possibilities is, however, relatively unimportant. On his assumptions, the intriguing and paradoxical point is that here we have a sign that does not signify (beyond its literal sense). Yet, such are the paradoxes of semiotics, a sign that does not signify must, by virtue of that very fact, be significant. Barthes's paradoxical question, therefore, is: what is the significance of this 'insignificance'? His reply to that question is ingenious:

Sémiotiquement, le 'détail concret' est constitué par la collusion *directe* d'un référent et d'un signifiant; le signifié est expulsé du signe, et avec lui, bien entendu, la possibilité de développer une forme du signifié . . . C'est là ce que l'on pourrait appeler l'*illusion référentielle*. La vérité de cette illusion est celle-ci: supprimé de l'énonciation réaliste à titre de signifié de dénotation, le 'réel' y revient à titre de signifié de connotation; car dans le moment même où ces détails sont réputés dénoter directement le réel, ils ne font rien d'autre, sans le dire, que le signifier: le baromètre de Flaubert, la petite porte de Michelet ne disent finalement rien d'autre que ceci: *nous sommes le réel*; c'est la catégorie du 'réel' (et non ses contenus contingents) qui est alors signifiée: autrement dit, la carence du signifié au profit du seul référent devient le signifiant même du réalisme: il se produit un *effet de réel* . . . [82]

This is perhaps taking a semiological sledgehammer to crack what may be a relatively small nut. It is also the case that the interests of clarity are not greatly served by the somewhat arcane character of the formulation. But the general import of Barthes's argument should be clear. Since Madame Aubain's barometer does not exist (other than in the fictional world of *Un Cœur simple*), the word 'baromètre' cannot properly speaking be deemed referential; it cannot refer because it does not satisfy the existential presupposition that is one of the conditions of a theory of reference. Rather what the term does is to *appear* to refer; as the speech-act version of fictional discourse would argue, it 'pretends to refer'.[83] It mimes the referring properties of ordinary language, creates an 'illusion' of reference. Or, in Barthes's complex adaptation of Hjelmslev's terms, it is not so much a denotation, as a connotation of a denotation. And to this connotative masquerade corresponds a precise semiotic function: the purpose of the 'détail concret' is to signify the Real *tout court*; the mirage of reference is a trick performed by the language of the realist text to convince us of the text's mimetic credentials. The discourse is not in fact in the slightest degree interested in barometers and the like. It is, however, greatly interested in manipulating certain verbal signs at once to mark the convention of Realism and to mask its conventional basis. In brief, the illusion of reference in fictional discourse is yet another instance of the naturalisation of the sign.

The semiological way with reference in fictional narrative is thus to re-define it in terms of the workings of a *code* of representation and signification; as Barthes puts it in *S/Z*: 'le référent n'a pas de "réalité" . . . ce qu'on appelle "réel" (dans la théorie du texte réaliste) n'est jamais qu'un code de représentation (de signification)'.[84] One might of course object that this is all so much huffing and puffing to tell us what, in simpler terms, we knew already; no reader (unless he were like the proverbial *ingénu* who objected to the conventions of opera on the grounds that people do not communicate like that in real life) would pause for a second to inquire as to the 'real' existence of Madame Aubain's barometer; as a 'competent' reader of fiction, he knows he is in a fictional universe of discourse. There is, however, more to the semiological way with reference than the account I have given of Barthes's case might imply. Indeed that account is in some respects deeply misleading, and what I have left out not only concerns the nature of Barthes's argument in particular, but also raises problems in semiological theories of reference in general. For Barthes is not just arguing, in the manner of speech-act theory of fiction, that fictional discourse 'pretends' to do what non-fictional discourse actually does. He is arguing, more radically, against the notion of reference altogether. For in the examples he gives, Barthes does not confine himself to fictional texts: alongside Flaubert's barometer there is also an example taken from an *historical* text (the 'porte' of Charlotte Corday's cell in Michelet's *Histoire de France*). It is true that in a great deal of recent theory of historiography, the distinction between historical narrative and fictional narrative has become increasingly blurred.[85] Nevertheless, if the notion of the 'referential illusion' is extended in this way, a much larger, and epistemologically more problematic, claim is being made. It is that we should reject (as 'illusory') any assumption of a referring relation obtaining between language and the world in any discursive context whatsoever.

This is the point at which Barthes's position echoes that wider semiological endeavour to 'expel' all referential considerations from its theory of language and signification; to exclude from the scenario of language any assumption of what Derrida calls 'le dehors référable du langage'.[86] The origins of this position are to be found for the most part in the work of the founding fathers of semiotics, Saussure and Peirce. Saussure's emphasis on the arbitrary nature of the sign required, or at least appeared to require (until Benveniste showed that Saussure's theory actually presupposes what it seeks to suppress),[87] a systematic exclusion of the 'referent' from any proper description of how language functions. Language, on this view, is an autonomous, internally regulated system; the sense of signs is determined differentially within the system by means of their relations with other signs, and not referentially in terms of an assumed relation with an external reality. Peirce's version of a very similar approach revolves around his theory of 'interpretants'. Signs acquire their meaning as the result of a process of semiotic interpretation, in which other signs act as interpretants to previous signs. The meaning of a sign is always, and can only be, explained by way of other signs. Thus, there is theoretically–though not in practical daily life – no end to the process of interpretation; signs can always be substituted for other signs, in an endless stream of interpretation or 'unlimited semiosis', whereby all possibility of a final or settled relationship between language and the world is, as Derrida will put it, permanently 'deferred'. Within this theoretical perspective, what we normally call the 'referent' simply disappears, or rather it reappears, but as the *product* of signification. The referent does not exist outside the linguistic system, it is articulated within and by that system. As Peirce says, the object is always 'the object as the sign itself represents it, and whose Being is thus dependent upon the Representation of it in the Sign'; or again, 'the object of the representation can be nothing but a representation of which the first representation is the interpretant'.[88] 'Object', 'being', 'representation', 'sign' are all indissociable, gathered up in a continuous flow of 'interpretation', irreducible to any fixed point outside that flow. It has been from positions of this kind that later semioticians, such as Eco, have proposed that the question of reference be subsumed under semiology as a branch of cultural semantics. Referents, in Eco's terms, are 'cultural units', the products of a cultural *découpage* operated upon the otherwise undifferentiated continuum of the world ('A cultural unit can be defined semiotically as a semantic unit inserted into a system');[89] the 'objects' we perceive and name as objects are the creation of the semantic systems, or what Eco sometimes calls the 'encyclopaedic systems',[90] we deploy to shape and classify the world, and there are as many ways of 'cutting up' the world as there are systems to hand for that purpose.

To recast the notion of the referent as something semiotically produced rather than pre-semiotically given, as intelligible in terms of the concept of 'interpretation' rather than that of 'fact', is to make a philosophically radical gesture. Its implications for our understanding of the language of narrative mimesis are considerable. Fredric Jameson has remarked that the so-called 'raw material' of narrative (the human social world) is always 'already meaningful' prior to its interpretation by narrative.[91] In the terms of the semiologist, this would then mean that the primary relation involved in mimetic literary practice is not the relation 'word/thing', 'text/world', but a relation of *representations*. The order of mimesis and the order of 'reality' confront each other as homologous systems of signification. The language of mimesis re-presents not the world but the world as already organised in discourse. Whence the need to attend to the literal sense of the cornerstone of the economy of mimesis, the *vraisemblable*. Literally, as Julia Kristeva reminds us, it means 'resembling the true' (and not, as is sometimes thought, 'resembling the real').[92] The 'true' is a property not of the world but of propositions about the world. It is a discursive not a 'natural' category, and thus the relationship which any text maintains with it is strictly inter-discursive, or, in the now influential term, 'intertextual'; the aspiration of mimesis, as Moshe Ron suggests, is to produce not a semblance of the real world, but a 'semblance of true discourse' about the world.[93]

This 'true discourse' is not, of course, the discourse of the philosopher or the scientist (although these can be relevant to the extent that their terms enter into lay discourse); its 'truth conditions' are furnished by the belief-systems of a given culture; they are governed, as we have already seen, by what, within the prevailing forms of the *doxa*, is generally held to be the case. In other words, mimesis is a re-presentation (in the terms of the generic requirements of the given literary form) of a representation that is itself socially and historically produced, thus opening that dizzying perspective – most dizzyingly explored by Derrida – of an endless chain of representations for which there is no founding or 'original' moment outside the movement of the representational process itself. For Derrida a condition of the discursive world of the 'intertextual' is its irreducibly disoriginated character. Efforts to harness representation to an original and anchoring represented would be to fall back onto the myth of referentiality which naive theories of mimesis ostensibly seek to promote. In the perspective of intertextuality, the notion of the 'referent', as solid guarantee of the text's relation to the real, is dissolved into what Barthes, in a specialised sense, calls *Référence*, understood as that 'subtile immensité d'écritures' in which representations are held, repeated, re-written, transformed, without any possible reduction to an original referent.[94] This evaporation of the stable referent is, of course, exactly what Barthes sees the convention of the 'reality-effect' in realist writing as attempting to mask. To unmask it therefore is to encounter that 'trouble de la représentation' which Barthes identifies as the critical moment of *Sarrasine* (and, more generally, of the 'texte-limite'): the feverish circulation of signs around an absence that we may describe, at one level, as the dilemma of the lost Referent. This dilemma manifests itself in a number of ways in nineteenth-century narrative. But, as I shall argue in a subsequent chapter, it is in Nerval's *Sylvie* that the problem of the relations between representation, origin and referent is most dramatically encountered. The 'stage' of the Nervalian text is, precisely, the place of the lost Referent, and the anxiety that loss engenders in the text, in the form of a desperate quest for what can never be found, marks one of the high points in nineteenth-century literature of that 'anxiety of representation' which arises when the security of the assumptions which underpin the mimetic project is called into question.

II

The semiological removal of any component of reference from the 'signifying play' of language attacks the possibility of literary mimesis at its very foundations. To deny that there is some form of relation between language and an object-world is to undermine the theoretical supports of mimesis in a manner that leaves them strictly beyond repair. The issue of 'reference' is thus in many respects the crux of the question of mimesis. We need therefore to ask ourselves if the semiological attack on the notion of reference is entirely satisfactory. We might, for instance, inquire whether the semiological account is intrinsically self-contradictory. Is what Barthes and Derrida have to say about reference true? If it is true, does it not then follow that their statements on the subject 'refer' to something that is the case? If, as in the semiological emphasis, reference is to be 'bracketed' in favour of the endless disseminative movement of language, then the parentheses have to be removed from the discourse doing the bracketing job; as one critic has put it, 'even to mention the identity of a code presumes some component of reference: that which designates the elements of the code as belonging together'.[95] Thus, by a stubborn, if paradoxical, logic, reference intervenes at the very moment it is being denied, as a condition of possibility of that denial. This may seem a trivial objection, mere logic-chopping. But, as I have previously suggested, semiological and post-structuralist theory is haunted by paradoxes of this sort, and the self-defeating character of arguments developed within these paradoxical positions is a matter I shall return to in a more extended form at a later point. There are, however, other grounds for suggesting that semiological theory has failed to develop an adequate account of reference; that indeed it has often bypassed a problematic that, in other philosophical traditions, has been an object of scrupulous attention. In the case of Saussurean linguistics and Derridean deconstruction, these limitations have been extensively discussed elsewhere.[96] For present purposes, I shall return to Barthes's paper, 'L'effet de réel', and focus on some of the problems in the presentation of his notion of the 'referential illusion', especially since it is above all here that the general semiological critique of reference is specifically linked to the particular question of narrative and 'realist' writing.

The nub of the matter turns on Barthes's working definition of reference itself. There are here two overlapping difficulties. The first concerns exactly what definition is being used; the second the theoretical status or value of that definition. These twin difficulties derive in large part from a stylistic property of Barthes's text: the extension of the technical terms of semiological analysis into those of figurative discourse.[97] In the passage quoted above where Barthes maps out what he understands by the 'referential illusion', his major logical and analytical claims are inseparable from a series of rhetorical manoeuvres: metaphors ('collusion', 'expulsion') for the idea of the 'referential illusion'; personification for the idea of the 'reality-effect' ('nous sommes le réel'). It might reasonably be said that these devices are just a convenient shorthand for what could be spelt out at greater length in analytical form. The problems arise when we actually try to spell it out in this way. What, for example, is entailed by the personification of Michelet's 'porte' and Flaubert's 'baromètre' as 'saying' to the reader 'nous sommes le réel'? The rhetorical move is certainly eye-catching; it presents the arresting spectacle of language being personified in order to show how language seeks to deny itself *as* language. The trouble with this, however, is that there does not appear to be any relay back into analytical discourse which will produce anything other than non-sense. The implication of 'nous sommes le réel' is that the words of the text try to perform a kind of disappearing act upon themselves; the text plays a trick whereby the reader undergoes the 'illusion' of being confronted not with language, but with reality itself; the sign effaces itself before its 'referent' in order to create an 'effect': the illusion of the presence of the object itself. The reader believes he is faced not with words, but with things, as if the referent were actually *there*, in the statement. What in fact he is faced with is, of course, not things, but a rhetorical category ('la catégorie du réel'). But Barthes's hypothetical reader *does not know this*; he is bewitched by the stratagems of realist writing into confusing category with thing (otherwise there could be no sense in positing him as the victim of an 'illusion'). To maintain such a position vis-à-vis the text, such a reader would have to be in a state approaching hallucination. The association of hallucination with mimesis is indeed a theme that goes back to Plato. Yet it is difficult to believe that Barthes is asking us to believe that this is actually what happens to ('naive') readers of *Un Cœur simple* or *Histoire de France*. Assuming that Barthes cannot in fact be asking us to believe that, the point, then, is that the rhetorical device supplants rather than serves argument. It promotes the idea of a relationship between language and reality that is rightly described as an 'illusion', but leaves us in a state of complete uncertainty as to who could ever fall victim to such an illusion in the first place.

A similar invasion of argument by rhetoric occurs at the point where Barthes gets closest to a straight definition of reference: 'la collusion directe d'un signifiant et d'un référent; le signifié est expulsé du signe'. 'Collusion' and 'expulsion' are metaphors, and moreover loaded metaphors. The former in particular suggests that we look for a guilty party. The difficulty lies in finding a culprit. It is true that one of the quirkier moments of a certain brand of modern empiricism (Russell's) held that the meaning of a name *is* the object to which it refers, and can therefore only be supplied by the presence of the object at the moment of the utterance of the name. This bizarre notion (which, among other things, entails that the meaning of names has to be contingently reinvented over and over again on each occasion of utterance) has long been discredited, notably by the philosopher who for a time came under its spell, Wittgenstein. No serious proponent of a theory of reference today would adopt the terms of Barthes's definition. However it might be that an expression can be held to refer to objects or states of the world, no-one, except under very special philosophical conditions (such as Kripke's causal theory of the 'rigid designator'), would argue that it is in the form of a 'direct' passage from 'signifier' to 'referent'. Indeed the most influential philosophical account of reference we have (Frege's) insists upon the centrality of what

Barthes's definition explicitly discounts: namely, the mediating role of 'sense' (*signifié*) in the performance of an act of reference. Whatever else we do on reading 'baromètre' in Flaubert's text, we do not hallucinate an object in place of a word. And if we succeed in attaching the word to an object, such a connection could not be made without passing through the public sense of the word. Thus, Barthes's attack on reference as 'illusion' amounts to tilting at an intellectual windmill. He resurrects, in his own way and for what seem to be polemical purposes, that elementary confusion in one version of Russell's theory of reference: confusing the *meaning* of a name with the *bearer* of the name.[98] In short, Barthes here mobilises his combined semiological artillery and rhetorical infantry to fight what appears to be an imaginary enemy in a phoney war.

This remarkable blind spot in the semiological approach to the question of reference presumably reflects that long-standing determination from Saussure onwards to sever language from any kind of relation to an object world. Evidently, that severance is easily executed if the primary definitions on which the semiological hatchet falls are made of straw. One negative consequence of this is that it seems to lead, despite vigorous assertions to the contrary, towards a new sort of metaphysics; the emphasis on language as 'pure form', as internal 'play of differences', can lead to a hypostasis of language that resembles a kind of linguistic idealism. That risk is, of course, always potentially there in the refusal of philosophically 'realist' theories of knowledge and language, on a spectrum from individual solipsism to collective 'subjectivism' (what Bernard Williams has called 'first-person-plural idealism').[99] But the risk might at least have been reduced if, in its main formative stages, semiological thought had not so conspicuously failed, or refused, to address itself seriously to certain theoretical alternatives, in which a relationship of language to world is maintained without relapse into those naive versions of reference on which semiological criticism has arguably expended so much wasted energy. (The belated 'discovery' of some of these alternatives by modern French theory is the sad philosophical story told by Jacques Bouveresse.)[100]

One such alternative – now under much literary critical scrutiny – is offered by the late Wittgenstein of *Philosophical Investigations*, in particular the perspectives opened up by the stress on the interaction of 'language games' and 'forms of life'. Although for the analytical philosophers the exact position of the *Investigations* on the issue of reference is still a matter of dispute, it is undisputed that Wittgenstein here turns against earlier 'correspondence' theories of language and reality, notably in the crucial attack on the principle of ostensive definition. The problem of reference (in the sense of uniquely experienced and identified particulars, such as 'private' identifications of redness in relation to the colour term 'red') is displaced into the field of 'meaning', in its broadly Fregean sense of publicly shared semantic categories. What is known, or knowable, through language is what is constituted as known, and knowable, by a community of speakers who are, at once and indissociably, players of a language game and participants in a form of life. This approach has features in common with certain aspects of semiological thought. It recalls to some degree the semiological recasting of the referent as a product of the semantic orders that derive from a *découpage* controlled by cultural conventions; Wittgenstein's language games look very like the semiologists' 'cutting up' of the world according to different semantic fields.

The critical difference, however, is that Wittgenstein avoids the potential idealist implications of this view by his insistence upon language as a medium of social practice: in the famous emphasis, to know a language is to participate in a form of life as a set of practical activities. This insistence has two major consequences. First, in the importance attached to the notion of practical activity, language is reinstalled as the medium of a community's relation to an object world. Language is tied to 'use', to what has to be done both in and on the world; signification, action and objects intermesh in ways that the doctrine of pure or unlimited semiosis tends to disregard. Secondly, the foregrounding of the social context of language use, the interlacing of language game and form of life, places effective limits on the process of semiosis. The 'rules' for the production of meaning are given in the relations of practice that engage a community of speakers. Such 'rules' (and the various 'interpretations' to which they give rise) are not, Wittgenstein argues, timeless essences of language; they are socially created both in and for the pursuit of practical social ends, and are maintained by means of public agreements. But they are necessary conditions and constituents of any conceivable form of life. All such worlds (and there are no others) are thus, if only provisionally, bounded worlds. In the playing of any given language game, the process of semiosis has to *stop* somewhere, if the game is to be successfully played ('Do not say: "There isn't a 'last' definition." That is just as if you chose to say: "There isn't a last house in this road; one can always build an additional one".').[101]

Indeed Peirce himself, the high priest of the theory of unlimited semiosis, realised that the infinite openness or regression to which his theory committed him was checked by the routine requirements of everyday life. The theoretically endless stream in which signs act as 'interpretants' to other signs, in practical reality, will come to rest in a 'final interpretant'. The criterion of this final interpretant is not logical, but pragmatic, and is identified by Peirce with 'habit'.[102] Habit circumscribes the universe of semiosis. Habit can, of course, be taken evaluatively in many different directions. In Peirce's argument, it is neutral, simply a fact of how semiosis actually works in any given social context. In the arguments of Peirce's successors, however, it generally receives a bad press, as an ideological instrument of closure brought to bear on the otherwise open-ended movement of signification. In *S/Z*, for example, it is directly linked to the operations of what Barthes calls the 'referential code', the referential in this context designating that body of routine truism and taken-for-granted belief wherein ideology 'sickeningly' takes command of the discourse of representation. There is clearly a strong conservative implication in the invocation of the notion of habit. Yet, although it lends itself in obvious ways to familiar strategies of legitimation and control, it does not automatically follow that it is entirely reducible to being a form and effect of ideology. Habit, as Bourdieu says, is more than just 'mechanical assembly or preformed programme'; it is an active and flexible instrument in the construction of the *habitus*.[103] Habitual knowledge embodies many of the interpretative schemes we all use, and must use, to make sense of the world we in-habit; without it, no recognisable characterisation of the world is possible (including the semiological characterisation).

This, I take it, is what the notion of habit might look like when seen from the point of view of Wittgenstein's emphasis on the social practices which compose language games and forms of life. It might, accordingly, give us a different way of looking at the frames of 'reference' deployed by the mimetic text. We could, following a suggestion of Moshe Ron, describe mimesis itself as a form of language game, based on a set of agreements between a 'mimetic author' and a 'mimetic reader'.[104] I have tried to describe some of the 'rules' of this game in the preceding sections of this chapter, on the model of an 'economy' of transactions and exchanges between writer and reader in particular social contexts. It is a game whose 'making' of meanings, to adopt Gombrich's terms, entails a degree of 'matching' to the meanings embedded in the norms of common use and understanding at work within a given form of life (although we should strenuously resist the Popperian implication of Gombrich's making and matching, as an historical process of ever-increasing approximation to a fully 'true' representation of the world). But this, finally, is perhaps what we really mean when we speak of the capacity of the mimetic text to 'refer' to a world. It is, yet again, a matter of shared recognitions, or a matter of 'contract'. This is not, of course, the only game that can be played. Another game, which modern critical theory has taught us to play with considerable ingenuity, is that of breaking the 'rules' of the mimetic contract, in the effort to liberate the text from the accumulated weight of customary expectation (the *déjà-écrit*).[105] I shall play this game myself in some of the following chapters, although my main purpose there will be to question that curious shibboleth, the notion of the 'classic readable text', with which this very body of critical thought has been so closely associated; if 'rule-breaking' is to be the order of the day, we should certainly not allow a narrow historical conception of literature (the division between the 'classic' and the 'modern') to exclude a whole class of texts of the past from that endeavour.

But an equally important consideration is that there may be limits to the activity of rule-breaking, beyond which it collapses into the fundamentally unmanageable or even into sheer unintelligibility. In playing the mimetic language game, the crucial issue is still that of distinguishing between what, on one side of a more general argument, Sollers has called submitting to the 'ideological caress'[106] and, on the other side, what Kermode has called that 'necessary element of the customary which enables (literature) to communicate at all'.[107] It is a difficulty which returns us to the remarks on the ambiguous status of the mimetic 'command' with which I began. What this command requires us to endorse we may wish to reject at those points or in those circumstances where it is felt that the command is suffocatingly ('nauseously') ideological; this is the area where an anti-mimetic, anti-representational aesthetics joins with a politics uncovering and refusing a work of 'repression' at work within dominant forms of representation. On the other hand – and this too implies a politics, the terms of which are complex to a degree – we accept that command in so far as we hold to the value of forms of interaction and communication to which certain kinds of *recognitions* are indispensable.

For 'recognition' – in its original form, the *anagnorisis* which in the *Poetics* Aristotle describes as the pivotal moment in the structure of the mimetic plot – is one of the constitutive 'rules' of the mimetic language game. The various extended senses which modern exegesis has given to Aristotle's *anagnorisis* is a topic to which I shall return in a later chapter. But one of the directions in which it could be taken is towards a major emphasis in philosophical theories of reference. In Frege's account, for example, the 'route' to the referent through language (more specifically, via the public categories of 'sense') is basically the means whereby we are enabled 'to recognise the object as the same again'.[108] Reference is thus linked to the notion of recognition, to a re-presenting of the object in ways that keep its criteria of *identity* intact. Recognition in the *Poetics* is also concerned with questions of 'identity' – in particular that of persons, as a kind of mapping of proper names and identities within the great family plots of tragedy and epic poetry. As such it could be argued that reference belongs to mimesis as part of a general process of 'reminding'; although recognition can incorporate surprise (the 'surprise' of recognition mentioned by Aristotle), its primary function is to reinstall us in a world that is familiar.

Recognising 'the object as the same again' is, of course, a notion that is nowadays deeply uncongenial to our ways of thinking about art. The effect of reading a great novel is precisely that things are never quite 'the same again'. Art breaks open the congealed, homogeneous surface of the given world and propels us into the domain of the multiple and the heterogeneous, into an adventure of invention and discovery. On this view, the cognitive power of art is therefore in inverse proportion to the recognitive strategies of everyday life, or, as the Formalists have taught us, art is at its most cognitively powerful when it *defamiliarises* the object and gives us a new perceptual access to the world. But the renewing and transforming excitements of *ostranenie* are perhaps purchased at a certain price. In the assumption of the radical discontinuity of literary language and everyday language, and the corresponding emphasis on the autonomy of the literary text, the detachment of its 'inside' from its 'outside', there is a potential drift towards a wholly a-historical and a-social conception of reading and writing. What comes to constitute the sphere of the 'aesthetic' par excellence is the aleatory play of the signifier, given over to processes of fragmentation and randomisation, to the pleasures of the moment, the irreducible particularity of the *maintenant* severed from any recognitive relation with a past. Thus, the refusal of the 'outside' (the relation of reference) by many forms of *avantgardisme* is specifically the refusal of the outside of history, of historical and social mediations.

But in the concerted effort to elude the tyranny of the stereotype and the inertia of repetition, there is always the risk of a collapse back into a sort of romantic individualism. I do not mean that, in the most sophisticated forms of this effort, this collapse necessarily occurs. A case in point is the continuing controversy that surrounds the implications of 'late' Barthes. Barthes's notions of *jouissance* and *atopia* are easily read as embodying a libertarian 'subjectivist' retreat from history and society, but this is to misread and over-simplify the complex tensions of these late texts, where in fact the 'historical' remains a constant and essential, if somewhat oblique, reference in the tactic of displacing all oppressive strategies of sys-tematisation and totalisation. It is, however, abundantly clear that, in many of the appropriations and applications of these late texts, what Barthes struggled to resist is exactly what has been effected in his name. *Jouissance* has all too readily become the banner under which certain modernist commitments have carried out what we might call a neo-romantic 'privatisation' of the aesthetic. Barthes's difficult *atopia*, in other hands, has been reconstituted as the ludic playground in which the individualist subject can traffic with the 'body', 'desire' and 'fantasy', in a manner that is by no means incom-patible with a consumerist economy of signs and meanings. What Barthes understood as 'mon corps', 'mon corps de jouissance' (and 'mon sujet historique'),[109] has become, with alarming regularity, quite simply an unacknowledged proprietorial 'my', from which it is notably any sense of historical determinations that has been excised.

The argument *for* mimesis rests to a large extent on a resistance to this potential reduction of public to private, history to individual, and this is mainly why I have made the question of reference some-thing of a turning point from which to review critically some of the positions outlined earlier in this chapter. Such an argument has of course its own risks: broadly, the risk of a return to the ideological stereotype entailed by the invocation of 'history' either as an appeal to 'tradition' or as a neo-Stalinist politics of representation. The question therefore is whether there is an alternative route, avoiding both the Scylla of conservative traditionalism and the Charybdis of coercive totalitarianism, but without falling back into the indi-vidualist aesthetic of pure 'originality'. One possibility lies with Ricœur's notion of 'productive reference'. I have already mentioned Ricœur's account of mimesis as dynamic *praxis* (and the fuller implications of that account I shall discuss in the concluding chapter). Ricœur describes artistic mimesis as a 'configuration', in the terms of fiction, of what is already a 'prefiguration' of the world of human actions; the configuring agency of the mimetic plot is a 'production' (*poiesis*) actively shaping human doings into an intelligible whole, disclosing and augmenting meanings that are already to be found, although in less articulated form, in the 'pre-narrative' shapes of human experience of the world.[110] The relation of reference is thus designated as 'productive' in the sense of deriving from a series of workings and re-workings that move from the non-narrative through pre-narrative to narrative as such. The non-narrative (inchoate happenings) is necessarily mute, without shape, beyond (or prior to) human discourse and intelligibility. Pre-narrative shape derives from what, in the vocabulary of hermeneutics. Ricœur calls a 'pre-understanding' that is irreducibly social and historical in character: 'the pre-understanding common to the poet and his or her public of what action, or rather acting, signifies'. It rests on a 'community of meaning preliminary to entering into fiction', a socially shared 'repertory' whose existence 'implies having mastered the whole network of practical categories by means of which the semantics of action is distinguished from that of physical movement and even from psycho-physiological behaviour'.[111]

The attractions of Ricœur's view of mimetic reference are manifold. The dynamic emphasis on configuration means, for example, that artistic fictions are not condemned to inert repetition of the paradigms given in the social 'repertory' of pre-understanding. The work of fiction can, indeed, contest, transgress, break up the paradigms, and, as such, is entirely compatible with formalist and deconstructionist notions of defamiliarisation and disruption. On the other hand, the relation of reference to a world known and held in common is maintained in so far as a condition of intelligibility of even the most transgressive fictions (those which yield the greatest 'play with the constraints of the paradigms') is their grounding in the 'pre-understanding' which marks the point of 'intersection of the world of the text and the world of the hearer or reader': 'it remains true that, despite the break it introduces, fiction would never be understandable if it did not configurate what is already figured in human action'.

I shall give, in my concluding chapter, a further account of various aspects and implications of Ricœur's approach to mimesis. The particular feature of that approach which needs to be stressed in connection with the notion of 'productive reference' is Ricœur's view of 'pre-understanding' as itself a form of active work upon the world, as a mode of *practice*. I wish to retain this view of 'pre-

understanding' in the form of what is sometimes called 'tacit knowledge'. The latter is close to what I have already called 'habitual
knowledge', but freer than the latter from connotations of passive
repetition of the unreflectingly given. In certain areas of contemporary social theory the concept of tacit knowledge has been
developed in exceptionally rich ways. Its importation into literary
theory has, on the whole, been a somewhat diluted and
impoverished one. There, the tendency has been to see it as essentially monolithic and manipulative, and so far, in my own argument,
I have more or less followed this tendency. But like Ricœur's
'repertory', tacit knowledge is not in fact one homogeneous thing.
There are different kinds of tacit knowledge arising from different
practical exigencies, although quite how we distinguish them, how
we map the geography of tacit knowledge, deciding what belongs in
which spaces, whether the boundary lines between the spaces are
clear or fuzzy, is a difficult undertaking. It will not do, however, to
construe it as just an effect of ideology, as a reflection of the nexus
of power relations and economic interests articulated in the familiar
notion of 'hegemony', and under which 'tacit knowledge' then
appears as merely a confidence trick perpetrated by the rulers on
the governed. The 'governed' are not a population of sleepwalkers.
And, although the 'tacit' can degenerate into the negativity of *doxa*,
we must not overlook its more active guises and possibilities, as represented, for example, in Bourdieu's account of the social world,
where the 'tacit' is linked to the notion of *practical knowledge*, to
lived experience and local encounter; where alongside acknowledgement of the forces of domination and coercion, there is also the
emphasis on negotiation, the negotiated – and therefore
re-negotiable – forms of knowledge through which we take up a
relation to an object world; finally, the importance attached by
Bourdieu to the idea that the actor or 'practical operator' possesses
equipment for the monitoring of his day to day exchanges with
others in a common *Lebenswelt* (as opposed to the notion of the
actor as a purely passive subject caught in the hypnotic trance of
ideology).

These seem to me to be considerations, of a complicating and
enriching kind, which need to be fed into our understanding of the
mimetic 'language game', the 'mimetic contract' and, in that context, the question of 'reference'; and it is largely in these terms that,
in the concluding chapter, I shall broach the possibility of a certain
retrieval of the idea of mimesis. Naturally there are numerous problems with this way of going about things. It could be objected that

Ricœur's notion of 'productive reference' is so flexible (it can be made to do virtually anything within the general constraint of 'intelligibility') as to be analytically weak; and, moreover, that 'production' and 'tradition' do not make quite such easy bedfellows as Ricœur implies. Finally, in the perspectives drawn from Wittgenstein, the model of the 'form of life' can appear rather blandly holistic and static, implying a more or less integrated society based on a happily negotiated consensus. Against that implication we should set Wittgenstein's insistence on the heterogeneity of language games, and its elaboration by Lyotard, in *La Condition postmoderne*, as an 'agonistics' of conflict and dissent. In the postmodern *agon* there is no arbitrating meta-language, only heterogeneity and dispersion ('une dissémination des jeux de langage') and, hence, irreconcilably different and competing positionings of the 'referent'. Consensus is but a utopian 'horizon', and contract merely the 'contrat temporaire' ensuring the rules (themselves provisional) under which a particular game can be played. Any move beyond this minimalist stance must be treated with considerable suspicion, as a repressive bid for authority whose ultimate goal may well be the neutralisation of, or the 'terrorist' imposition of silence on, all forms of difference.[112]

What, from these general positions, Lyotard has to say about the specific question of narrative is another matter to which I shall return in the concluding chapter. It will be clear, however, that in this radical reading of Wittgenstein's notion of the language game, we find again many of the problems I have previously discussed in connection with 'contractual' theories of society and representation. And, since in the next three chapters I shall be concerned with the ways in which certain nineteenth-century 'classics' occupy a troubled or transgressive relation to conventions of contract and consensus, it is perhaps worthwhile to conclude this section with a reminder of some of these difficulties. I should like to do so by way of a brief consideration of a relatively recent theory of reference, associated with the work of Saul Kripke, and its corollary in the work of Hilary Putnam, the 'division of linguistic labour' hypothesis.[113] The causal theory of reference is complex and, in some of its aspects, both obscure and controversial. But the broad thrust of the argument is to try to 'fix' reference (by means of what Kripke calls 'rigid designators') in a way that both overcomes the potential instabilities in Frege's semantic model (what Frege acknowledged as the unsettling 'fluctuations of sense')[114] and also resists the implicit relativism of conventionalist or 'pragmatic' accounts of reference.

Kripke's view argues that we attach words to things because others have regularly and reliably done so in the past, in virtue of some original 'baptism' of the object. Referential links fixed in the past are causally transmitted to succeeding generations in the linguistic community, unless and until successfully challenged by somebody else. This process is further assured by what Putnam calls a 'division of linguistic labour'. In order to operate language referentially, it is not necessary that in every case all members of the speech community be able to identify or recognise the objects ('referents') to which the designator is attached. All that is required is a division of linguistic labour according to which there are in the society experts authoritatively accredited with the capacity to make these identifications on behalf of the laity; in Putnam's example, while we can use the word 'gold' reliably in a whole range of verbal and practical activities connected with the object gold, we cannot all identify gold, in the sense of being able to say that *this* is 'gold' as distinct from some other thing (for example, a fake).[115] But, on Putnam's model, a sufficient condition for the referential system continuing to work effectively is that there is some person (an 'authority') who *can* make the identification in question. The 'division of linguistic labour' hypothesis thus overlays the rigidly causal basis of transmission with a social context of trust. Hence, in so far as the rigid designator remains rigid by virtue of a code of trust holding between the laity and the expert, the theory can then be plausibly glossed as a modified version of a 'contractual' theory of reference; and its specific articulation is such as to render the problems of such a theory highly visible.

These are minimally threefold. First, the historical explanation presumes as non-problematical a whole fable of 'origins', an inaugural ostensive 'baptism' of the object at the beginning of the causal chain. Secondly, the distinction between expert and lay, the initiates and the ignorant, opens on to the possibility that is always the negative side of contract, the spectre of *forgery* which haunts all contractual arrangements, and which returns us exactly to the terms of the Derridean critique (in, for example, the notorious exchange with Searle).[116] Thirdly, once the conventions of trust on which the referential system is deemed to rest are separated from the (somewhat cosy) notion of freely negotiated mutualities, and are instead linked to the principle of the division of labour, we are back in the world of a socially stratified distribution of knowledge and, therefore, of relations of power, authority and dependence – that is, precisely those hierarchical forms which the more traditional versions of contract have so often been accused of attempting to mask. In this regard, Putnam's particular example of 'gold' is a revealing choice. Gold has often been posed analogically as the emblem of a grounded system of sense and reference, and it brings us to the threshold of the novelist in whose work that analogy is particularly active. Barthes remarks in *S/Z* that for the 'economy' of the Balzacian text 'le sens est d'or'.[117] Gold is the symbol of both economic and semantic stability, a kind of guarantee of a secure relation between sign and value, representation and represented. Gold is the literal and metaphorical underpinning of a certain 'accumulation' (of wealth, of wisdom) which permits goods, money and signs to 'circulate' in an orderly way. But what actually happens within and to the channels of 'circulation' in the Balzac novels I shall now go on to consider (and its corresponding implications for the system of narrative representation), is a quite different story.

3

BALZAC:
NARRATIVE CONTRACTS

Le récit-contrat

As the complex legal plot of *Splendeurs et misères des courtisanes* moves towards its climax in the Conciergerie prison, Balzac suddenly bursts into rhapsody over a saying attributed to Royer-Collard:

L'une des gloires de Royer-Collard est d'avoir proclamé le triomphe constant des sentiments naturels sur les sentiments imposés, d'avoir soutenu la cause de l'antériorité des serments en prétendant que la loi de l'hospitalité, par exemple, devait lier au point d'annuler la vertu du serment judiciaire.[1]

In the priority assigned to the 'law of hospitality' over the 'judicial oath', an ancient moral notion is recovered. In local context, it is adduced to criticise Lucien's betrayal to the legal authorities of the true identity of Carlos Herrera, but it could well apply, by extension, to a great deal of the *Comédie humaine*. The 'judicial oath', and its counterpart, the commercial 'contract', are for Balzac the characteristic forms of human negotiation and exchange in the modern world, displacing and despoiling the more informal and natural network of bonds and mutualities (such as those invested in the 'law of hospitality') perceived as belonging to a lost pre-Revolutionary world, and more precisely, in the immediate historical juxtaposition that always returns in Balzac, to what he sees as the ease and poise of the culture of the *ancien régime*.

This is a point in Balzac's thinking at which historical imagination and reactionary fantasy begin to coalesce (although, as I shall argue, there is more to Balzac's 'reactionary' politics than a mere intellectual liability). Nostalgic fantasies of this type about life under the *ancien régime* abound in the *Comédie*.[2] One concerns the social conditions of narration. In *Autre étude de femme*, Mlle des Touches receives her evening company in two stages: the first is open to all-comers from the *beau monde* and counts for nothing ('D'abord une soirée officielle à laquelle assistent les personnes priées, un beau monde qui s'ennuie'). The second takes place after midnight, and is restricted to an élite of kindred spirits who, in the intimacy of the 'petit salon', gather together to enjoy the pleasures of true sociability: 'la véritable soirée . . . où, comme sous l'ancien régime, chacun entend ce qui se dit'. This state of happy reciprocity is described as 'une heureuse protestation de l'ancien esprit de notre pays joyeux', one of the main forms of which is the telling of stories ('la conversation devenue conteuse . . . '). Narrative exchange, in this context (two stories are told, one by de Marsay, one by Bianchon), belongs to a highly protected code of social exchange founded on a ritual of exclusion and solidarity: the vulgar have gone home, the servants have withdrawn; seated cosily around the fire, the characters converse and recite, untroubled by interference from the outside world of difference and conflict. In Mlle des Touches's 'petit salon' discourse recovers its ancient rights according to the law of hospitality (III, pp. 207–10).

That the occasion is an object of fantasy (or, just conceivably, of irony) is clear from the internal evidence of the text itself. We need only consider the composition of this felicitous recreation of *ancien régime* ambience; it includes *inter alios*: Bianchon (the arriviste doctor), de Marsay (now 'premier ministre' under the very Louis-Philippard régime which the text denounces as anti-cultural), Blondet (whose corrosive *esprit* is identified in *Illusions perdues* as one of the major symptoms of cultural decay in modern France), the banker Nucingen, his wife Delphine (née Goriot), and her lover Rastignac, along with a sprinkling of illustrious Faubourg Saint-Germain names. Perhaps it is all intended as a nineteenth-century version of a sentimental memory of the convivial gatherings of cultured aristocrat and *philosophe* in the salons of the Enlightenment. But the mis-match of fantasy and personnel is not really the point. For its very absurdity is instructive, in at least one negative aspect. It is impossible to gloss this scene of narrative exchange as an instance of what Barthes, in his analysis of *Sarrasine*, has called the *récit-contrat*, the story where 'la narration devient théorie (économique) de la narration', in which the represented exchange between narrator and interlocutor doubles back on, or mirrors, the condition of exchangeability, both material and symbolic, in which according to Barthes *all* narrative is held.[3] The contractual structure analysed in *Sarrasine* (story for sex), Barthes also generalises, in a perspective that runs from Balzac back to *The Thousand and One Nights* (story for life). But that transhistorical view disregards what so much of the history and the ethnology of story-telling show: that, in very many cultures, story-telling has nothing whatsoever to do with either the spirit or the letter of 'contract', and everything to do with the laws of hospitality and sociability.[4]

For narrative to be thought of as subject to contractual relations, it must meet at least two conditions: as an item in an economic exchange, it is given on the understanding that it will bring a profitable return (the expectation can, of course, remain unfulfilled, as in *Sarrasine*); as an item in a process of 'symbolic' exchange (in a system of communication), it must give the listener/reader a return on his investment of trust in its narrative credentials; it must supply the pleasures of narrative information and disclosure in ways that confirm the 'economy' of signs and meanings within which the listener or reader operates. In this sense, the notion of 'contract' signifies the exact opposite of 'sociability' and its supporting conventions of mutual trust and understanding. Contracts are regulative mechanisms designed to guarantee the terms of an exchange between individuals in a social context where those terms might otherwise be betrayed by either of the parties. The régime of the contract is based on the sense of mistrust which is the inevitable accompaniment of a society devoted to the pursuit of private interests; it presupposes, as that against which it seeks to protect itself, the ever present possibility of the swindle and the fraud, the possibility of systematic forgery behind the façade of public agreements.

This may be thought an unduly restrictive view of what is entailed by the notion of contract (especially since I have previously argued that it is important to keep in play what is most informal and flexible in that notion). If I emphasise here the terms of the legalistic version of contract, it is in order to focus what Barthes's universalist application of the model of contract to Narrative *tout court* appears to neglect, but what Balzac never forgets, since it defines exactly the problem of his own situation as a writer in the nineteenth century: namely, that the assimilation of narrative to the contractual, in its strictly juridico-economic sense, has a specific historical context, inseparable, as Tony Tanner has suggested in a more general argument, from the developing forms of economic individualism and bourgeois social relations.[5] For Balzac, writing in the period of the July Monarchy, the perception of narrative as an object of contractual exchange is inextricably linked to that particular historical experience, and to that final transformation in the complex itinerary of the term 'contract' through the discourses of the eighteenth and early nineteenth centuries, whereby it is visibly and inalterably aligned with the ideology and practices of 'commerce'. Whence the meaning of Mlle de Touches's salon: its mixture of intimacy and sociability represents Balzac's alternative to the purely contractual. Its condition is the willed, if temporary, suspension of private interests and individualist gain ('la familiarité la plus douce fait oublier à chacun ses intérêts . . . Là, nul ne pense à garder sa pensée pour un drame; et dans un récit, personne ne voit un livre à faire. Enfin, le hideux squelette d'une littérature aux abois ne se dresse point', pp. 208–9). Nobody here is obliged to meet the terms of an exchange transaction; what is given in the act of story-telling is 'freely' given ('la générosité dans les idées', p. 208), from conventions so relaxedly taken-for-granted as to appear entirely 'natural'; communication occurs spontaneously and uninhibitedly, signs and meanings are instantly and fully intelligible ('chacun entend ce qui se dit', p. 207); it is a culture whose agreements are so deeply rooted that they are not perceived as such; to this occasion there are no 'signatories', only unselfconscious participants.

In order to work, this idealised representation must, of course, wipe out a great deal, but its meaning should now be clear: it marks, as fantasy, the distinction, in Balzac's mind, between the *ancien régime* and the nineteenth century; or, in Léo Mazet's terms, the shift from the imaginary paradise of the *récit-don* (the 'échange idéal') to the realities of the *récit-monnaie* (the 'échange malheureux').[6] What is inscribed in Balzac's notion of the contract is the cultural equivalent of the Fall, the passage from an Adamic innocence of story-telling to its irretrievable corruption. In the large gallery of Balzac's megalomaniac identifications there is, alongside Prometheus, Napoleon and the others, also the figure of Adam. Balzac, declares Balzac, will be to narrative what Adam was to nomenclature: 'J'ai lu quelque part que Dieu mit au monde Adam le nomenclateur en lui disant: te voilà homme! ne pourrait-on pas dire qu'il a mis aussi dans le monde Balzac en lui disant: TE VOILA CONTE?'[7] The exact meaning of this extraordinary flight of fancy is far from self-evident, but it presumably connects with that dream of an uncontaminated, prelapsarian language of representation which we shall encounter elsewhere in Balzac's writings (notably in *Louis Lambert*). Perhaps it is also a more flamboyant and grandiose projection of the idea of the 'pre-contractual' state of grace that characterises the culture of Mlle de Touches's salon, and as such is linked to a cultural politics in which an idealised past is played off against an irredeemably tarnished present. In any case, in Balzac's seminal diagnosis of the latter condition (*Illusions perdues*) we will find the corresponding Biblical counter-image to that of Adam the primordial name-giver – in the comparison of the modern world of the literary and journalistic trade to the Tower of Babel, the place of the pollution of language and the adulteration of meanings. We also find another, related image – the image of the Bazaar. To enter the world of *Illusions perdues* is to pass from the gallery of hero-figures that includes Adam into another gallery, the 'bazaar ignoble' of corrupt and unregulated exchange: the Galeries-de-bois.

The bazaar of Paris: deals, signatures, forgeries

Illusions perdues and *Splendeurs et misères des courtisanes* (which I propose treating here as one continuous narrative) do not display the same self-reflexive structure that we find in many of the shorter 'frame' narratives of the *Comédie humaine* (those stories in which, within the frame, the narrator tells his tale in exchange for something else), and hence their involvement in the model of the 'transaction' is not so immediately visible. The transaction is, however, the dominant, indeed saturating mode of human relationship and activity in the social world these novels represent; and that saturation, I shall argue, turns, reflexively and anxiously, back on the terms and forms of the narrative representation itself. The society of *Illusions perdues* and *Splendeurs et misères des courtisanes* is one almost infinitely permeable to the fetishism of the commodity. Human 'commerce', in its widest sense, is here reduced to its strictly economic sense. The notion that virtually everything is for sale reaches into every aspect and every recess of public and private life. Bodies, minds, identities are treated as goods, installed in a circuit of exchange of which money is the universal measure of value. Ideas, thoughts, opinions, as well as material products, are 'worth' what they will fetch on the market place of reputations and positions; the bookseller buys the favourable review from the literary critic ('des articles lus aujourd'hui, oubliés demain, ça ne vaut à mes yeux que ce qu'on les paye', p. 422); the theatre manager purchases applause from the hired 'claqueur'. Language itself, the medium of transaction, is also its object ('nous sommes des marchands de phrases', p. 422), a fluctuating value on the stock-exchange of discourse. Even that primary linguistic marker of personal identity, the proper name, is a marketable asset. Lucien, the seller of his work (his property), *becomes* himself the commodity to be sold, as the name around which a reputation will be manufactured and marketed – the name 'de Rubempré', which itself can only be acquired by means of a deal, a royal ordinance given 'en récompense des services que vous rendrez au Château' (p. 430).

Doing deals is what keeps most of the characters going, and what keeps the plot going (it is the engine of the 'deal' between writer and reader). Structurally, both texts are framed by the deal, both are inaugurated and completed by a series of dubious exchanges (two of them figuring among the most spectacular of the *Comédie humaine*): in *Illusions perdues*, Séchard and David, Vautrin and Lucien, David and the Cointet brothers; in *Splendeurs*, Vautrin and Lucien, Esther and Nucingen, Vautrin and M. de Granville. These vary from the informal pact (the Mephistophelian pact between Vautrin and Lucien, the arrangement whereby Vautrin ends up as an agent of the secret police) to the formal contract (the purchase of David's paper-making patent and printing presses by the Cointet brothers). What most of them have in common, however, is a strong admixture of the fraudulent: Séchard cheats David of his rightful inheritance; the Cointet brothers enmesh David in a labyrinthine legal and commercial intrigue, one of the key components of which is a forged letter (an intrigue, moreover, made possible by Lucien's earlier forgery of bills of exchange in David's name); Vautrin and Lucien mount a breathtakingly audacious confidence trick to secure an entry into the world of the Faubourg Saint-Germain; Esther dupes Nucingen into parting with a million (itself acquired through illicit practices on the stock market); Vautrin and M. de Granville conspire to rig due process of law, whereby Vautrin gets a pardon, and a job, in return for the love-letters so potentially embarrassing to the Court.

Deals, pacts, contracts are thus shadowed by the spectre of forgery (a perspective resumed in the chapter heading of *Splendeurs* – entitled 'Faux abbé, faux billets, fausses dettes, faux amour', p. 180). Much of the action turns on fabricated publications, falsified documents, on the drama of the *signature*. Signatures (to articles, commercial contracts, promissory notes, bills of exchange, wills, royal ordinances, *procès-verbaux*) proliferate in the text, as perhaps the most precious, and most deceptive, 'commodity' of all. To what you give your (or somebody else's) signature, or conversely from what you withhold it, are decisions of major consequence. Part of Lucien's education as a journalist consists in learning when to sign an article and when to leave it anonymous, when to sign with 'C', with 'L', with 'Rubempré' (p. 421). The advancement of his social

fortunes depends critically on the King's initial refusal and subsequent granting of his signature to the ordinance authorising
Lucien to bear his mother's aristocratic name. Camusot, the
examining magistrate, makes the fatal error of signing the *procès-
verbal* of Lucien's interrogation before consulting with the
Procureur-Général (who wants the record suppressed). Above all,
the plots of both novels revolve in large measure around the
phenomenon of the *forged* signature: in *Illusions perdues*, Lucien's
forgery of bills of exchange precipitates the sequence of events that
leads to the ruining of David; in *Splendeurs*, Vautrin's scheme to
raise money for the purchase of the Rubempré estate involves
exploiting 'une Bourse des effets faux aux environs du Palais-Royal,
où, pour trois francs, on vous donne une signature' (p. 187): the
signature of the 'célèbre escroc', Georges d'Estournay, on the
fictitious bills of exchange made out to Esther as the 'debt'
Nucingen will have to pay off as the price for her body.

The signature, guarantee of contract, here guarantees nothing. It
founds a process of circulation and exchange in which things are not
as they appear, not what they *represent*. The forged signature not
only opens on to the familiar Balzacian theme of the 'tainted'
fortune (the fortune of dubious origins); more generally it points to
that problematical relation between origin and representation,
identity and sign, of which the whole of the Rubempré cycle is an
extended exploration. The signature poses a problem of 'legibility',
the difficulty of distinguishing between the true and the false, a
problem of *assessment*. 'Ce que vaut chaque signature' (p. 482) is
the question raised by the money broker Barbet, when requested by
Lucien and Lousteau to cash the bills made out by the near bankrupt
book-sellers, Fendant and Cavalier. The exploration of the wider
implications of that question undertaken by these two novels forms
part of Balzac's general project of depicting *l'envers de l'histoire
contemporaine*, in the negative sense of the underbelly of the
mercantilist ethic, where not only can everything be bought and
sold, but where what you buy may well be false goods, a deceptive
copy, a simulation. It, moreover, gives a precise historical context to the question towards which we ourselves must move in
respect of these very novels: the question posed in abstract terms by
Barthes around the notion of the 'exchange value' of narrative
('Que "vaut" le récit?'):[8] what is the 'value' of the narratives bearing
the signature 'de Balzac'?

The 'transformation commerciale'[9] of writing and publishing into
the speculative commodity is, as Lukács argues,[10] the great organis-

ing theme of *Illusions perdues*. Blondet calls it 'une boutique où l'on vend au public' (p. 356). The image of the 'shop' is exactly right, and – following that characteristic strategy of the *Comédie humaine* whereby the part is made to stand for the whole – it is used by Balzac in the form of an extended structural metonymy for the complete world of *Illusions perdues*. If being in that world is like being in a vast shop, what more adequate representation of it (although at the same time equivocating the very notion of the 'adequacy of representation') than that 'bazaar ignoble', the Galeries-de-bois? Along with the Opéra, the Panorama-dramatique, the Newspaper Office, the Galeries-de-bois is one of the privileged *topoi* of *Illusions perdues*. It brings together, in one thematic configuration, the process of exchange, the problem of legibility, the tenuous distinction between the genuine and the fake. Entering the Galeries-de-bois (in the attempt to sell his poetic 'flowers', *Les Marguerites*) is for Lucien a decisive stage in his initiation into the ways of Paris. It is like entering the domain of an *anti-physis*, in which Nature is negated by the squalid ruins of Culture, a realm of pure artifice whose emblem is *paper*; in which real flowers are perversely festooned and choked by the 'fleurs de rhétorique', the chaotic débris of 'maculature', by 'prospectus' and 'les débris de mode' (p. 289): rhetoric, the prospectus, fashion, three modes of persuasion, of cajoling the customer into parting with his money in exchange for the false promise and the shoddy illusion.

What (for Lucien) is fascinating and (for Balzac) alarming about the Galeries-de-bois is their capacity for seduction. The 'disreputable bazaar' is the place where you can buy virtually everything (from hats to sex), and the place to which virtually everybody comes, in a promiscuous mingling of groups, trades, professions, classes. It is at once a meeting-place and a melting-pot, where 'les personnes comme il faut, les hommes les plus marquants étaient coudoyés par des gens à figure patibulaire' (p. 295). The 'monstrueux assemblages' (p. 295) which occur there are like a résumé of the Parisian population, but they are 'monstrous', and hence disquieting, because they blur the contours of the social map, bring together what should be kept hierarchically apart. Alongside 'les commerces les plus singuliers' of the Galeries ('ventriloques, charlatans de toute espèce', p. 292), there are milliners, tailors, flower girls, booksellers, joined 'avant et après la Bourse' by bankers, merchants, politicians, publishers, intellectuals, poets, and prostitutes, all engaged in the common pursuit of peddling their wares, putting into circulation financial tips, political intrigue, books, information, news, gossip, sex:

> Ce sinistre amas de crottes, ces vitrages encrassées par la pluie et par la poussière, ces huttes plates et couvertes de haillons au dehors, la saleté des murailles commencées, cet ensemble de choses qui tenaient du camp des bohémiens, des baraques d'une foire, des constructions provisoires avec lesquelles on entoure à Paris les monuments qu'on ne bâtit pas, cette physionomie grimaçante allait admirablement aux différents commerces qui grouillaient sous ce hangar impudique, effronté, plein de gazouille-ments et d'une gaieté folle, où, depuis la Révolution de 1789 jusqu'à la Révolution de 1830, il s'est fait d'immenses affaires. Pendant vingt années, la Bourse s'est tenue en face, au rez-de-chaussée du Palais. Ainsi, l'opinion publique, les réputations se faisaient et se défaisaient là, aussi bien que les affaires politiques et financières. On se donnait rendez-vous dans ces galeries avant et après la Bourse. Le Paris des banquiers et des commerçants encombrait souvent la cour du Palais-Royal, et refluait sous ces abris par les temps de pluie . . . Il n'y avait là que des libraires, de la poésie, de la politique et de la prose, des marchandes de modes, enfin des filles de joie qui venaient seulement le soir. Là fleurissaient les nouvelles et les livres, les jeunes et vieilles gloires, les conspirations de la Tribune et les mensonges de la Librairie.
>
> (pp. 290–1)

The Galeries are dominated by the figure of the pedlar, above all by the 'pedlar of prose'. Lucien's destination, inside the Galeries, is Dauriat's bookshop, and his entry into it a veritable *rite de passage* from innocence to knowledge. The recurring term of the conversation in the bookshop is the word 'deal' ('affaire'). In the space of an hour or so, Lucien is wide-eyed witness to the making, or disclosure, of at least eight transactions: the contract for the novels of Paul de Kock; the sale by Finot of complimentary theatre tickets to Braulard; the 'fixing' of a review of Ducange's novels; Finot's discounting of Lousteau's bill of exchange; Dauriat's purchase of a weekly journal; the payment of the *Journal des débats* for Blondet's article on Nathan; Dauriat's bribery of Blondet for the same article; Finot's proposal to enter into partnership with Dauriat on the newspaper venture. It is no wonder that Lucien makes the connection metaphorically between the two activities that are literally contiguous in the Galeries, the sale of books and the sale of bodies: 'A l'aspect d'un poète éminent prostituant la muse à un journaliste, y humiliant l'Art, comme la Femme était humiliée, prostituée sous ces galeries ignobles, le grand homme de province recevait des enseignements terribles' (p. 301). Prostitution, as is commonly pointed out, provides the metaphorical matrix in *Illusions perdues* for the interlinking of the different worlds of literature, publishing, commerce and politics; it spreads metaphorically across the text in a way that corresponds to Balzac's sense, in his later work, of prostitution as a kind of 'disease' spreading throughout the whole society. But what matters here is not so much the moralised representation of the prostitute in the quasi-medical analogy. The prostitute is the representative figure of the Galeries for two interrelated reasons: first, because the exchange of sex for money is the form in which the foundations of the 'contractual' relationship are made brutally visible (the prostitute-client relation is 'the reverse mirror-image of the bourgeois ideal of the good contract, but arguably the very structure of its bad conscience');[11] but, secondly, in the emphasis on her clothes and make-up ('habillées comme des princesses', p. 294), the prostitute finds her place, alongside the 'ventriloquist' and the 'mountebank', in that series of 'singular avocations' where what is on offer is a false imitation.

The Galeries are the site of a generalised charlatanism. Its perfect expression is the Cosmorama trafficking in 'images', or the fairground booth to which the customer is lured with nothing other than the promise of a metaphysical article: '*Ici l'homme voit ce que Dieu ne saurait voir. Prix: deux sous.*' The trick is simple: 'L'aboyeur ne vous admettait jamais seul, ni jamais plus de deux. Une fois entré, vous vous trouviez nez à nez avec une grande glace. Tout à coup une voix qui aurait épouvanté Hoffmann le Berlinois, partait comme un mécanique dont le ressort est poussé: "Vous voyez là, messieurs, ce que dans toute l'éternité Dieu ne saurait voir, c'est-à-dire votre semblable. Dieu n'a pas de semblable"' (p. 292). That particular hoax sums up the whole of the Galeries, just as the Galeries, in the extraordinary energy and density with which they are portrayed, may be said to sum up the whole of *Illusions perdues*. It is often claimed that *Illusions perdues* is in part modelled on the *Inferno*, as an adaptation of Dante's hell to the life of the modern city. But the terms of the writing of the Galeries might well lead towards another reference: Plato's *Republic*. As hall of illusions, the Galeries admit to the city everything and everyone that would be rigorously banished from Plato's city; they realise Plato's nightmare of an invasion of the body politic by the charlatan and the magician, the disturbance of hierarchy by the circulation of false images and deceptive signs.[12] In short, the importance of the Galeries-de-bois episode is that it brings together a politics and an aesthetics, around the worried awareness of the dangers that are incurred by an uncontrolled and degraded *mimesis*.

In this regard, there is one other member of the shifting population of the Galeries for whom the question of appearances, the matter of 'costume', is of paramount importance, who is indeed the consummate practitioner of the culture of *maquillage*: the dandy or the fashionable young-man-about-town. Moving within the confused mix of social classes in the Galeries, the dandy is in many ways the point of maximal ambiguity in that mix. He is the focus of an uncertainty of perception, of recognition and classification that, as the century unfolds, will become a veritable 'perceptual panic',[13] in which the basic categories of social distinction go into a kind of vertiginous spin. Balzac's interest in the phenomenon of the well-dressed young man dates from his early journalistic contributions to that minor, but immensely revealing genre of the period, the *Physiologie*, the *Traité*, the *Monographie*, the *Code*.[14] What, in terms of the relation between journalism and the social history of the period, the genre shows is the attempt to negotiate a deep anxiety with regard to the mapping, the 'legibility', of the social landscape of the modern city, that highly mobile, ceaselessly 'turning' landscape (what Lucien experiences as 'la rapidité du *tournoiement* parisien', p. 171), in which the perception of ranks and occupations, origins and identities, can no longer reliably orientate itself within a fixed structure of differentiation. The argument, insistently repeated, of the *Physiologie de la toilette* and the *Traité de la vie élégante* is that material changes in the post-Revolutionary economic and social formation (the frenetic pursuit of private interests, the increasing degree of social mobility around the phenomenon of *arrivisme*, the displacement of aristocratic rule by the combined forces of 'le talent, l'argent et la puissance') engender a corresponding problem of social semiotic, an attenuation, even an obliteration, of the traditional markers of class difference:[15] 'Par quel signe extérieur', asks Balzac in the *Physiologie de la toilette*, 'distinguer le rang de chaque individu?'[16] The *Physiologie* and the *Traité* are at once a statement of this problem, and an attempt to solve it by providing a 'map', the essential form of which derives from a special alertness to sartorial codes; they propose the elements of a science of vestignomonics that will, in theory, have some of the certainties assigned to physiognomonics and pathognomonics in the forms of contemporary scientific thought derived from Lavater.

One of the professions of the Galeries-de-bois is that of the tailor, and the Tailor, Balzac tells us in the *Physiologie*, ensures nothing less than the passage of man from the state of nature to the state of 'civilisation'. Clothes provide what is vital in this view of 'civilisation', a stock of 'signes matériels' for the construction of a social taxonomy, within which everyone is perceived as occupying their 'proper' place according to the principle of the division of labour and the differentiation of classes. Under the old régime the sartorial map is entirely free of confusion, *ancien régime* manners are, so to speak, semiotically stable, even inert: 'Sous l'ancien régime, chaque classe de la société avait son costume: on reconnaissait à l'habit le seigneur, le bourgeois, l'artisan.'[17] In the more fluid forms of contemporary society, the codification is less clear cut; the division of labour is still the organising principle of society, but the ideology of 'equality' and the advance of the bourgeoisie have brought an increasing degree of sartorial uniformity: 'Enfin les Français devinrent tous égaux dans leurs droits, et aussi dans leur toilette, et la différence dans l'étoffe ou la coupe des habits ne distingua plus les conditions. Comment alors se reconnaître au milieu de cette uniformité? Par quel signe extérieur distinguer le rang de chaque individu?'[18]

The answer lies in the development of a more inventive, subtle semiotic, largely through cultivation of the sartorial 'nuance'. Nuances of dress – the main example in the *Physiologie* is the art of tying the *cravate*, and the example will be picked up in *Illusions perdues* – become in the *Traité de la vie élégante* the basis for articulating a whole set of finely shaded meanings which, at least for the initiate, will reinstall a system of discriminations and recognitions. Yet, at the very moment of solving his problem, Balzac in effect reinvents it. The *Traité* divides the population of Paris into three classes: 'l'homme qui travaille, l'homme qui pense, l'homme qui ne fait rien'.[19] Balzac's sartorial recommendations are specifically addressed to the last of these, the man of private means, whose exploitation of 'nuance' will give what, in the *Physiologie*, is called 'le critérium auquel on reconnaîtrait l'homme comme il faut et l'homme sans éducation'.[20] But 'l'homme qui ne fait rien' is, in contemporary social conditions, an ambiguous class; it includes both the man of means and the aspirant parvenu, the 'fils d'un comte' and 'l'homme de talent'.[21] In the case of the fashionable aristocrat, form signifies a substance; his elegance is a sign of identity backed by collateral (family name, inheritance, capital). The parvenu dandy, however, masters the art of the nuance in order to appear what he is not, to give out the sign of a 'value' (a social identity) which is in fact false, a sign without a grounded signified ('grounded' to be taken here as connected with the literal sense of the possession of land, the fortune based on 'real' property – whence the crucial importance, in *Splendeurs*, to Vautrin's schemes of acquiring the Rubempré estate). Balzac's recommendations for a code of differentiation thus give the recipe by which that code can be manipulated to produce a confusion, and a travesty, at the heart of the clarity for which the code is devised.

This is exactly the ambiguity depicted in *Illusions perdues*. It is true that the text returns repeatedly to the topic of clothes as a means of social interpretation and demarcation, as a shorthand way of slotting its characters into instantly recognisable categories ('ce costume . . . convenait si bien à ses vices et ses habitudes que . . . ', p. 9). But the real interest of clothes revolves more around a blurring than a clarifying of the social map; and in *Splendeurs* this will become wildly endemic, in that melodramatic proliferation of disguises which, however, are consistently posed metaphorically as a problem of 'textual' interpretation, as a sign of the developing opaqueness of the modern city. From the point of view of Lucien's ambitions, the question of costume is the one formulated by the narrator: 'La question du costume est d'ailleurs énorme chez ceux qui veulent paraître avoir ce qu'ils n'ont pas; car c'est souvent le meilleur moyen de le posséder plus tard' (pp. 176–7). Lucien's early days in Paris – his first evening at the theatre, the 'jour néfaste' (p. 279) at the Opéra – are an object lesson in the exigencies of sartorial self-presentation:[22] the discarding of the 'bel habit bleu', the nankeen trousers and the white cravate; the mistake of the initial purchase at the tailors of the Palais-Royal; the rectification of the error *chez* Staub, that stopping-off place for every aspirant dandy in the *Comédie*. Suitably attired in 'cet élégant mobilier des élégants' (p. 450), Lucien can set about his objective of passing from the 'zero' condition of a nobody ('n'être rien à Paris', p. 171) to being a somebody; in the bazaar of Paris, the clothes purchased at Staub's are an investment – the return on which is the fabrication of a spurious social 'value', the putting into circulation of an identity that is an impersonation, that is without the collateral of a secure origin.

The effort, in the mode of forgery, to compensate for that absence of collateral (obtaining the name 'de Rubempré', the Rubempré estate, the marriage into the Grandlieu family) will be the incredible story of *Splendeurs et misères des courtisanes*. At the end of *Illusions perdues*, just before Lucien meets Vautrin, he will himself employ the mathematical analogy of the 'zero' condition: 'Certains êtres sont comme des zéros, il leur faut un chiffre qui les précède, et leur néant acquiert alors une valeur décuple' (p. 698).

Vautrin will offer to be the agent of that miraculous mathematical conversion of zero into ten, beginning (in the opening chapter of *Splendeurs*) with Lucien's triumphal appearance at the masked ball at the Opéra. Or, in Vautrin's metaphor, he promises to make of Lucien a kind of 'bright coin' (p. 715), shining but counterfeit, false currency minted by the master-forger of the *Comédie humaine*, and inserted into the circuit of social exchange in such a way as to create havoc and pandemonium. With the reappearance of Vautrin, the anxiety concerning imitations, doublings, 'unlicensed' mimesis will become a veritable panic.

Brokers (I): Vautrin and Lucien

At the moment of his arrest in *Le Père Goriot* (II, p. 1016), Vautrin describes himself as one 'qui proteste contre les déceptions du contrat social' (adding that this makes him a disciple of Jean-Jacques). The Social Contract, and its latter day transformation, the Napoleonic Code, are empty fictions, the legal façade behind which the 'respectable' citizen cheats and swindles. The art of modern life, in Vautrin's great lesson to Rastignac, is in finding the gaps in the Code, 'les mailles par où l'on peut passer à travers le réseau du Code. Le secret des grandes fortunes sans cause apparente est un crime oublié, parce qu'il a été proprement fait' (p. 942). Similar notions will reappear in Vautrin's long disquisition to Lucien on the 'secret history' of modern France:

En France donc, la loi politique aussi bien que la loi morale, tous et chacun ont démenti le début au point d'arrivée, leurs opinions par la conduite, ou la conduite par les opinions . . . De là, jeune homme, un second précepte: ayez de beaux dehors! cachez l'envers de votre vie, et présentez un endroit très brillant . . . Dès lors vous ne serez plus coupable de faire tache sur les décorations de ce grand théâtre appelé le monde. Napoléon appelle ça: *laver son linge sale en famille*. Du second précepte découle ce corollaire: tout est dans la forme. (pp. 714–15)

Contracts, Codes, Laws are thus resumed and devalued in the emphasis on 'form', on forms without substance, a play (a 'theatre') of fraudulent deceptions.

Vautrin, the outlaw, simply takes the logic of this diagnosis of the laws to its extreme point, to destabilise further what is already a highly unstable economy of signs and meanings by means of systematic deceit and forgery. Apart from 'abbé', the generic term most commonly used in the text to designate Vautrin is 'faussaire' (of which 'abbé' is, of course, but one of its manifestations).

The nodal point of a complex web of transactions, Vautrin is not just an outlaw in the ordinary sense of his criminal activities, but also in the sense of manipulating and equivocating the 'law' which governs the signs of identity. Outside society, he nevertheless continues to circulate incognito within it by virtue of his formidable proteanism and his 'colossal' capacity for trickery ('ce colosse de ruse', p. 362). To the multiple disguises required for the plot (priest, diplomat, magistrate, commercial traveller), he, and Balzac, will add, in the form of metaphorical representations and self-representations, the roles of surrogate banker, father, author, poet. Ceaselessly self-metamorphosing, Vautrin makes of himself the very emblem of the undecipherable.

The elaborate intrigue mounted against Contenson and Corentin is described as 'un texte indéchiffrable' (p. 267). Vautrin's mastery of the sign extends even to its literal inscription on his own body; his transformation into the abbé Carlos Herrera includes erasing the physical marks with which society has stamped his place (as convict) in the order of things. Chameleon and imposter, Vautrin embodies the principle of an infinitely variable exchange-rate. One of the precepts he enjoins on Lucien is that a man can be what he decides to be, that this destiny is 'worth' whatever value he chooses to put on it ('Une destinée vaut tout ce que l'homme l'estime', p. 709). In this assumption, Vautrin is in fact cruelly deluded, and that delusion will provide one of the major codas of the whole novel. But around Vautrin 'values' anarchically fluctuate and multiply, are endlessly diversified and relativised – signs, identities, beliefs, currencies. Archetypal criminal of the *Comédie humaine*, Vautrin is also, in a sense, one of its great capitalists, or rather he incarnates the spirit of anonymously mobile capital, its origins opaque, its transactions murky, its 'life' that of continuous circulation. It is entirely appropriate that he is banker to the *pègre*, and can play the Stock Exchange, trebling the value of the convicts' funds in a single coup. Everywhere and everything, Vautrin is the very image of a universal convertibility, of an exchange-rate without the underpinning foundation of a 'gold standard'.

Vautrin is thus ideally placed to act the part of mentor to Lucien or, to pursue the commercial analogy, to act as a kind of 'broker'. Vautrin advises Lucien on what he is 'worth', on how to invest the bright coin he himself will mint. He is the broker of information and knowledge, transacting (or promising to transact) nothing less than total intelligibility and total mastery. Himself the 'texte indéchiffrable', he claims complete authority over the decipherment of the text of society, uncovering the 'secret history' behind the 'official history', exposing the lie of Contract, Code and Charter as the succeeding expressions of, or diluted accommodations to, the great but empty promise of the French Revolution. The 'pact' with Lucien is Vautrin's means of at once exploiting and outplaying the fraudulence of the social 'contract'. This undertaking entails primarily the creation of a double forgery (at one point in the text he is called 'le double faussaire', p. 243): Lucien the 'fake' aristocrat, through whom, in turn, Vautrin can envision a doubling of himself, the vicarious living out of a desired identity. In this fantasy, Lucien will be, precisely, a *phantasma* (in the ancient sense of a false semblance), a reflection, or indeed, in the connection made by Plato in the *Sophist*, a mimetic 'work of art':

Je veux aimer ma créature, la façonner, la pétrir à mon usage, afin de l'aimer comme un père aime son enfant. Je roulerai dans ton tilbury, mon garçon, je me réjouirai de tes succès auprès des femmes, je dirai: – Ce beau jeune homme, c'est moi! ce marquis de Rubempré, je l'ai créé et mis au monde aristocratique; sa grandeur est mon œuvre, il se tait ou parle à ma voix, il me consulte en tout.　　　　　(*Illusions perdues*, pp. 724–5)

Equipped with name, capital and estate, 'Lucien était la splendeur sociale à l'ombre de laquelle voulait vivre le faussaire – "Je suis l'auteur, tu seras le drame" . . . ' (*Splendeurs*, p. 103). This 'play' (a play within a play, within the 'theatre' of Paris) sets in motion a spiral of fictions which ultimately threatens the interests of the State itself. Lucien the sham aristocrat and Vautrin the sham author generate a confusion of signs, roles and identities that parallels the social disorder predicted by Plato if the impostures of the mimetic artist are allowed within the precincts of the City. Lucien, the false copy, circulates in society like a poison, a *phantasma* secreting a *pharmakon* which will produce violence, death, suicide, delirium, a crossing of sexual desire, financial dealings, and political machination in which the 'proprieties' of hierarchy are radically transgressed.

Moreover, the anticipated last act of that play is the one thing its author cannot in fact guarantee. Vautrin's elaborate plan comes crashing to the ground; the doublings of which he is the author release forces which run beyond his apparently omnipotent control; creator of disorder, he cannot himself fully command the field of that disorder. From the moment of Esther's suicide, the plot of *Splendeurs* runs riot, largely in the form of a series of messages and letters that cross, conflict, arrive too late or cannot be transmitted;

the communicative circuits get blocked, seize up, go wild. It is customary to describe this sequence in *Splendeurs* as the lowest point in what is already low melodrama. Indeed Maurice Bardèche argues that the real trouble with the 'impossible' plot of *Splendeurs* is the impossible premiss on which it is based:[23] the assumption by Vautrin in the first place that the scandalous origins of Lucien's fabricated fortune could have been successfully masked; thus, by virtue of a false premiss, Balzac himself is complicit in the business of counterfeiting, has seduced us with a 'fake' narrative. But that is to miss an important implication: Vautrin's error is exactly what, in more general terms, the novel is about – the emptiness of 'guarantees' and the worthlessness of 'signatures'. In signing the pact, Vautrin does not merely promise Lucien a destiny, he *guarantees* it ('je vous garantis . . . ', p. 718). But in the world of *Illusions perdues* and *Splendeurs et misères des courtisanes*, nothing can be guaranteed, the pledge of pact or contract underwrites nothing. Vautrin's attribution to himself of demiurgic powers rests on the false dream of total individual control. His claim that an individual's destiny is worth whatever price he puts on it is the one thing that the ever-shifting, mobile landscape of modern society renders impossible. To the question, what then is Vautrin 'worth'?, we may be tempted to reply 'nothing', a reply indeed perhaps written into his very name ('Vautrin – vaurien – vaut-rien'). When 'l'échéance du diable' (p. 99) arrives, we find that it has no cash value.

Furthermore, this collapse of 'economies' has implications for the position of Balzac vis-à-vis his own text, his reader, and, more broadly, for the problematic and anxious relation he maintains in respect of the project of a narrative mimesis. I shall turn to this question in more detail in the next two sections. But some of the terms of that discussion can be adumbrated here by commenting on the implications for Balzac's narrative of Vautrin's 'creation', Lucien de Rubempré. Lucien's instability is often noted, and is usually explained in the terms of psychological characterisation (his weak and volatile nature). But that psychology also possesses wider thematic and structural meanings. Lucien encapsulates the theme of pure 'exchange-value'; he is all things to all men, he 'is' whatever he offers for exchange in any given situation (friendship, love, treachery, Liberal politics, Royalist politics, honest writing, mendacious writing). Behind these various incarnations, Lucien is a mere cypher (a 'zero'); without a centre, he is only as he appears to be, and appearances fluctuate according to circumstances. He is a space of 'values' that vary according to the laws of circulation. Yet that 'circulation' is exactly what generates the shape and development of Balzac's narrative; as structural 'device', it is Lucien's mobility which makes possible the system of connections binding together the different social milieux explored in *Illusions perdues* and *Splendeurs et misères des courtisanes*.

Moreover, as Vautrin's 'creation', he is not only what ensures Vautrin's return to Paris; Lucien ensures, for Balzac, the return of Vautrin to the *Comédie humaine*; he is the condition for the continuation of the narrative. In the closing pages of *Illusions perdues*, Petit-Claud remarks of Lucien (on the discovery that he has not in fact committed suicide): 'Ce n'est pas un poète, ce garçon-là, c'est un roman continuel' (p. 735).[24] The story of Lucien is a story 'to be continued'; there is much narrative mileage to be gained from keeping him alive. *Suite à venir* is the implicit promise of the ending of *Illusions perdues*, and in particular a promise of the special kinds of narrative excitement that the return of Vautrin will bring. It is also the standard ending of the instalment form in which *Splendeurs* was published. The phrase 'suite à venir' at the bottom of the *feuilleton* expresses one of the most basic relations of the narrative contract, that between the desire of the reader to know more and the promise of the narrator to give gratification. What is literally bought by the subscriber to the newspaper is a guarantee of the satisfactions anticipated by suspense; the subscription is an advance purchase of narrative completion. This has to be taken in its properly economic sense: subscriptions were payable in advance, and although newspapers were, of course, bought for other reasons, it is known that the inclusion of the *roman-feuilleton* from 1836 onwards was a major cause of vastly increased circulation figures (witness, for example, the letters of outrage to the *Journal des débats* at the interruptions to the regular supply of the instalments of Sue's *Les Mystères de Paris*). It is significant that *Splendeurs* (especially its last section, 'La dernière incarnation de Vautrin') was one of Balzac's commercially most successful novels, perhaps the closest he came to writing in the idiom of the contemporary popular novel ('Je fais du Sue tout pur').[25] In that respect, we may say that *Splendeurs* provided the pleasures its 'public' paid for.

But at another level of the transaction (the 'contract') – the level of social and ideological confirmations – it is by no means certain that it delivers the required goods. *Splendeurs* is a major example of the narrative prototype for what will later become the detective story. As Walter Benjamin argued, these literary developments have to be seen in the context of a wider social and cultural history.

The detective novel, like its precursors, tells of the 'hunting' of the criminal transgressor, and of the difficulties of conducting that operation in a mass urban population ('the original social content of the detective story', observes Benjamin, 'was the obliteration of the individual's traces in the big-city crowd').[26] In the popular fiction of the period these difficulties are invariably overcome: the 'traces' are recovered, and the malefactor successfully identified and punished. But, in relation to the wider history, it is possible to read these fictional resolutions as compensatory fantasy for what, in the society, is a wide-spread source of disquiet on the part of the authorities: how to 'track' identity and control behaviour in an increasingly dense and opaque urban society (the connection between the model of 'hunting', the detective novel and forms of social control in the nineteenth century we shall encounter again, in terms of Carlo Ginzburg's notion of the *paradigme cynégétique*).[27] *Splendeurs* belongs centrally to these developments: its plot is about the detection of 'traces', the unmasking of an imposter and a final restoration of 'order'. But, in its closing stages, the more it seeks to clarify and resolve, the more confusion it produces, to the point where the 'authority' of the discourse which takes the narrative in charge is itself jeopardised.

Brokers (II): narrator and reader

In the 'cours public et gratuit' on the legal fate of the unpaid bill of exchange which Balzac generously offers the reader of *Illusions perdues* ('il n'y a rien de moins connu que ce que tout le monde doit savoir: LA LOI!), he makes, though partly withholds, a pun: 'Ainsi, *en Banque* . . . dès qu'un effet transmis de la place de Paris à la place d'Angoulême est impayé, les banquiers se doivent à eux-mêmes de s'adresser ce que la loi nomme un *Compte de retour*. Calembour à part, jamais les romanciers n'ont inventé de conte plus invraisemblable que celui-là . . . ' (pp. 587–8). Given the worry about the pun, and the language of *esprit* generally, expressed in *Illusions perdues*, we may note the hesitant way in which the pun is introduced ('Calembour à part'). Putting the pun on one side is a precaution we might render as implying the notion of taking a 'risk' ('if we may risk a pun'). What, then, is being risked? Perhaps, as is often suggested with regard to the 'promiscuous couplings' of word play, a possible offence to a code of social and linguistic propriety, analogous to the transgression of narrative *vraisemblance* which, so Balzac tells us, this 'conte' about a 'compte' entails. But what, then, is the return on the risk? Presumably it is, despite (or because of) the emphasis on *invraisemblance*, a gain in understanding. Novels and bills of exchange have metaphorically something in common: they are a form of contractual note, promises to pay the bearer; they assume a system of *credit*. But, whereas the bill of exchange that is the subject of this story is a dishonoured one (Lucien's forgery), the assumption Balzac appears to make about the creditworthiness of his own discourse is that it can command complete public confidence: the accuracy of the 'account' of the legal documents surrounding the forged bills of exchange 'est garantie, elle a été copiée' (p. 596).

Balzac's 'copies' are thus quite distinct from the false copies that circulate in the story. Balzac's 'accountancy' is impeccable, everything entered in its proper place within the fully responsible balance sheet of Truth. Like the police file described in *Splendeurs* as a kind of ledger ('ce calepin universel, bilan des consciences, est aussi bien tenu que l'est celui de la Banque de France sur les fortunes'), and which contains 'la vérité condamnée à rester dans son puits, comme partout et toujours' (p. 392), Balzac's novels open and complete the file on modern life, they uncover and record what in the *Avant-propos* is called the 'sens caché' of reality. The narrative structure of *Splendeurs* proceeds as a progressive hermeneutic *dévoilement*; that of the *Illusions perdues* as a kind of ceaseless 'stock-taking'; initial information is followed by sequences of action that are subjected to retrospective review and assessment: Lucien's life at Angoulême is entirely reinterpreted on his arrival in Paris; his first few weeks in Paris are, with the help of Lousteau and D'Arthez, made an object lesson in the necessity of discarding false assumptions; while, at the end of the novel, the total story of his 'illusions' is systematically *revu et corrigé* by Vautrin. But standing beyond all these perspectives is that of the narrator himself. Indeed, in vital respects, the Balzacian narrator appears as the reverse of Vautrin, in all the latter's various guises. Whereas Vautrin, in his role as 'banker', will speculate and defraud, the narrator will control the circuits of semantic exchange from a position of securely 'accumulated' knowledge and wisdom ('knowledge' here being strictly cognate with the primitive accumulation of capital); whereas Vautrin the phoney 'father' will produce a fake offspring, Balzac's 'child'[28] will be entirely legitimate, carrying the traces of the patrimony of truth; whereas Vautrin the author ('Je suis l'auteur, tu seras le drame') will produce a false mimesis, Balzac will give us the genuine article. Balzac's narrator is someone in whom we can place our trust, a 'broker' who will supply the reader with the requisite language and interpretative strategies for understanding the modern world.

To play in this way with pun and metaphor, as modes of a certain *mise en abyme* of Balzac's narrative discourse, should not be taken in any way as an attempt to assimilate the text of Balzac to the modernist (or 'postmodern') aesthetic of the polysemic and self-reflexive moves of the signifier. The analogies in question are not to be read as an anachronistic imposition from a later twentieth-century perspective. On the contrary, they belong to the historical context of Balzac's writing and, as we shall see, the reflexivity they install at the heart of the writing bears, precisely in virtue of that historical situation, a very different meaning from that of the jubilatory manoeuvres of the 'modernist' text. The reflexivity in question is not jubilatory, but anxiety-laden, and the metaphors which enact it derive from an essentially conservative desire to maintain a stable unit in the currencies of exchange; to warn against the dangers of 'polysemy' in a society seen as taking up, through the alibi of a 'free' circulation of meanings, a deeply irresponsible attitude to language.

The narrator's discourse is implicitly, and often explicitly, posed as the antithesis to this dangerous irresponsibility with regard to the use of signs. The problems of decipherment and legibility dramatised in the plot of masks and disguises will, in the hands of the narrator-pedagogue, simply disappear. Thus, Contenson's thoroughly effective disguise is nevertheless thoroughly transparent 'pour ceux qui savent déchiffrer un costume' (p. 127); Corentin may be for Nucingen 'ce qu'est, pour un archéologue, une inscription à laquelle manque au moins les trois quarts des lettres' (p. 164), but the narrator will provide (has already provided) for the reader what is deficient in Nucingen's perception. The teeming mass at the masked ball at the Opéra may appear the very paradigm of perceptual disorientation and interpretative blockage, but, under the lucid gaze of the narrator, all its secrets of origin and identity are rendered entirely readable: 'Qui n'a pas remarqué que là, comme dans toutes les zones de Paris, il est une façon d'être qui révèle ce que vous êtes, ce que vous faites, d'où vous venez et ce que vous voulez' (p. 6).

What, therefore, is promised by the narrator is a transformation of the opaque landscape of Paris into an entirely legible surface. The deceptive sign will be tamed and mastered by what, in *Splendeurs*, Balzac calls the 'signe infaillible' (p. 534) and, in *Illusions perdues*, 'cet indice . . . rarement trompeur' (p. 30). In a sense, the dream which animates the narrator's performance is the conversion of the arbitrary sign into the index, or the sign that does not lie (it is a dream we shall encounter elsewhere in the period, precisely in terms of a political anxiety concerning the fate of language and signification in a developing capitalist formation). This distinction is well illustrated by the dual status of that recurring Balzacian phrase 'laisser échapper'.[29] In *Splendeurs*, Vautrin warns Lucien against the perils of accidental disclosure of important information: 'ne dis pas un seul mot compremettant, ne laisse pas échapper un geste d'étonnement . . . ' (p. 281). It is certainly advice that the hapless Lucien needs, given what has ensued earlier in the narrative from the 'involuntary smile' which reveals that he is acquainted with Esther ('Lucien a laissé échapper', remarks Bianchon, 'un sourire qui me ferait croire qu'elle est de sa connaissance', p. 96). Esther, on the other hand, in her encounter with Nucingen, makes of the gesture 'laisser échapper' the occasion of a tour de force in deception: '[elle] regarda le banquier célèbre en laissant échapper un geste d'étonnement admirablement joué' (p. 200). Both gestures are signs that 'betray'. In the case of Lucien, the smile is that which betrays unconsciously, involuntarily; it has the causal status of the index, or what in earlier terminology is called a 'natural sign'. In the case of Esther, the gesture is one that betrays in another sense; it is an instance of the power of the arbitrary sign to deceive, to subvert the contract of communicative exchange by means of a forgery. In the social jungle of the *Comédie humaine*, the 'indexical' sign is, of course, more likely to be a liability than an asset (the consequences of Lucien's inadvertent disclosure are grave). At the level of the narrator's 'meta-language', however, it becomes, by analogy, something of an ideal model of representation, as the idea of a language of complete interpretative infallibility, a language with which it is not possible to make mistakes, that will not lie; a language for drawing inferences, furnishing explanations, for naming, identifying, classifying, finally covering the world in a 'clothing' quite different from the cosmetic deceptions of the Galeries-de-bois and the journalists' office; in its extreme form, it is the neo-Cratylist dream of *Louis Lambert*: 'Par leur seule physionomie, les mots raniment dans notre cerveau les créatures auxquelles ils servent de vêtement' (X, p. 356).

This is, of course, a linguistic and metaphysical pipe-dream. Louis Lambert may commune with the ineffable Absolute, but of this we necessarily know nothing, and the price that is paid is solitude and insanity, complete severance from the channels of human intercourse. In practice, Balzac's assumption of an authoritative language of representation depends on a social context of address, in which that assumption is confirmed and validated by his readers (his 'public'), by the public categories of discourse and meaning which shape the 'contractual' space of communication and exchange. No verbal sign in articulated language actually has the status of an 'index'; no sign *is* what it represents; no sign is an 'infallible' guide to the truth of things; nothing can be 'guaranteed' other than on the basis of agreements tacitly or explicitly posited. But this is precisely the area that *Illusions perdues* and *Splendeurs* problematise, even as the rhetoric of the narrator proclaims its confidence in the assent forthcoming from the reader. Both thematically and discursively, the problem of the 'public' and the 'reader' returns insistently in *Illusions perdues* and *Splendeurs*, as one of the terms of that heterogeneous social mix whose mapping by means of reliable conventions of recognition and identification can no longer be taken for granted.

From the point of view of the new literary and journalistic 'merchants' of *Illusions perdues*, the 'public' is simply an anonymous and amorphous mass of gullible consumers who can be made to believe anything (for Vignon the trick of journalism is that 'il peut . . . faire croire ce qu'il veut à des gens qui le lisent tous les jours', p. 35). Lousteau's recipe for the successful review is to throw the public a few 'maxims' which it will automatically absorb and uncritically repeat ('Lâche de ces sentences-là, le public les répète', p. 404). Balzac here places in critical perspective a new kind of cultural cynicism, as a speculative response to the forms of a rapidly changing society and reading public. Yet these are the very problems which return to haunt the Balzacian narrator at the level of his own discourse: one of the major forms of that discourse is, precisely, the 'maxim'; the discourse is like a textual machine for generating maxims on virtually every subject and on virtually every page. To whom are they addressed? Is it any longer possible to think the notion of the 'public' other than in terms of diversity and fragmentation, the terms which Balzac himself uses in *Splendeurs* ('les sept à huit publics qui forment le public', p. 384)? This is a view of the reality of the public as lying exactly parallel to the general fragmentation of the society into a collection of sectional groups and private interests, and is further mirrored, within the novels themselves, in that proliferation of private codes, sub-languages and secret sign systems, which it is the self-appointed task of the narrator's discourse to subjugate to the régime of a homogeneous order of interpretation.

This problem is paradoxically betrayed by what ostensibly seeks to mask it: the narrator's insistence on his own authority. That insistence may well be the symptom of a certain 'defensiveness'.[30] insisting in order to compensate for the absence, or fragility, of a shared normative discourse or common vocabulary. The implied reader of *Illusions perdues* and *Splendeurs* is characteristically perceived by the narrator as operating on a spectrum between insiders and outsiders, laymen and experts, the initiate and the ignorant. The outsider is treated to a massive exercise in pedagogic initiation: the master-plotter *of* the intrigue gives him access to the meanings of what the plotters *in* the intrigue are doing, gives 'les véritables motifs des événements que le public regarde passer bouche béante' (*Splendeurs*, p. 494). The assent of the outsider to what he is being told and the terms of its explanation is simply taken for granted. The initiate, however, constitutes more a court of appeal; his assent is also presumed, but in the form of an already established, shared framework of understanding, as a *point d'appui* for the narrator's interpretative efforts. A case in point is the interpretation in *Illusions perdues* of Cointet's 'blue-tinted spectacles': 'Enfin, pour peindre cet homme par un trait dont la valeur sera bien appréciée par des gens à traiter les affaires, il portait des conserves à verre bleu à l'aide desquelles il cachait son regard' (p. 566). The terms of the appeal here expose exactly the kind of problematic alignments and complicities between text and presumed reader which the assumption of a transcendent meta-language would otherwise conceal: the reader who will grasp and confirm the meaning (the semantic 'value') of the sign is precisely the reader who speaks the language of 'value' ('des gens à traiter les affaires'). But appeal to that kind of consensus is obviously fraught with difficulty, since it is the language of value, and its speakers, that are, in *Illusions perdues*, the object of merciless criticism. In other words, there is a problem of standpoint and perspective, and hence a problem of narrative 'reliability'.

Nowhere is this clearer than in the narrator's account of Lucien's early days in Paris. This period of dramatic revision of previous preconceptions includes a reassessment by Lucien of Anaïs (Madame de Bargeton). The syntax of the key sentence of that reassessment is worth noting: at the Opéra we are told that Lucien sees 'la pauvre Anaïs de Negrepelisse, la femme réelle, la femme que les gens de

Paris voyaient' (p. 181). The appositional syntax linking 'la femme réelle' and 'la femme que les gens de Paris voyaient' suggests an equation: 'Reality' is reality seen from the perspective of Paris. But all the moral energy of *Illusions perdues* is devoted to showing the perspective of Paris as the site of the false and the mendacious (two pages later we will find the narrator *denouncing* the triviality of the Parisian view of Anaïs: 'ce monde où les petites choses deviennent grandes', p. 183). The *point d'appui* has thus been shown to have rotten foundations, but at the same time is used as a basic support or reference point for the narrator's own comparative discriminations. Where, then, does the narrator actually stand? The more we read these two novels, the more difficult it becomes to answer that question. The hierarchical discursive model begins to crack; standards of interpretation and judgement become increasingly fluid and mobile; explanations take on more and more of an ad hoc air; the lines separating the language of characters on different sides of the moral divide and, more important, the language of the characters and that of the narrator, get obscured. Far from rescuing us from the 'perceptual panic' engendered by the multiform and changing nature of the modern social world, the narrator's performance only succeeds in compounding it.

Let us consider again, for example, the vexed question of the 'maxim', shifting ambivalently between being offered as an instrument of real cognitive power in the hands of the narrator, and being identified as an object of opportunistic exploitation in the hands of the journalistic practitioners of 'ce métier de spadassin des idées' (p. 272). To whom, if we have forgotten, might we be inclined to ascribe the following: 'L'impression est aux manuscrits ce que le théâtre est aux femmes' (p. 416)? Lousteau? Blondet? Vignon? (that is to any of those characters in *Illusions perdues* for whom the production of a text is analogous to the staging of an illusion or the sale of a cosmetic product). The speaker is in fact the narrator. Madame de Bargeton's homily to Lucien on the necessary martyrdom of the struggling writer is sardonically glossed by the narrator as a 'counterfeit' (p. 64) imitation of what is itself a flawed text (Madame de Staël's *Corinne*). But this is exactly the language that will be subsequently used in the homiletic disquisitions of both D'Arthez and the narrator on the theme of the aspirant artist (pp. 245ff). Lucien's generalisations, in the encounter with Vautrin, about nationalities and ethnic groups are described as 'vulgaire' (p. 722), but that has not prevented the narrator, in drawing the contrast between Lucien and the Cénacle, from adding a reference to Lucien's 'esprit méridional' (p. 249) to what is already a highly overdetermined account of the causes of Lucien's vacillating nature.

Most significantly of all, this crossing and coalescence of idioms tends to occur around utterances metaphorically constructed from the terms of money and gold, profit and loss. D'Arthez gives Lucien advice that is morally at the opposite pole to Lousteau's, but the clarity of that moral distinction is somewhat obscured by the nature of the language in which the advice is couched: 'On ne devient pas grand homme à bon marché' (p. 228). The discourse of moral exhortation is thus infected with that of exchange-value; even the road of virtue is a matter of 'investment', profit and prices. Again, it is surely appropriate, and ironic, that the already corrupted Lucien should thank his Cénacle friends for the intellectual and literary help they have given him in the following way: 'Vous avez changé mon billon en louis d'or' (p. 374). But the steadiness of the implied moral perspective is troubled by the terms of the narrator's own account, on the previous page, of the achievements of the Cénacle itself: 'De chapitre en chapitre, la plume habile et dévouée de ces grands hommes encore inconnus avait changé ses pauvretés en richesses' (p. 373).

The desire of the narrator to establish himself as a centre of authority within a discursive hierarchy is thus seriously compromised by a process of fluctuation in which the meanings and values of words appear to change from one context to another. The narrator does not so much stand apart, as himself get caught up in the continual raising and lowering of the semantic exchange-rate. In the end, perhaps the only utterance by the narrator in which we can place our trust is, paradoxically, his insistence on the relativity of things and the interchangeability of words and concepts: 'Enfin, changez les termes.' (p. 176). It may well be that the one article we would not find for sale in the Galeries-de-bois is Balzac's *Illusions perdues*.[31] but it does not follow from this that the language of its narrator is serenely exempt from the diagnosis of the fate of language in modern society *Illusions perdues* gives us.

'J'ai trop longtemps cru aux proverbes' (p. 258), remarks Esther, and it is important that the remark should be hers. Esther is the archetypal victim figure of the plot mounted in *Splendeurs*, the victim of the languages (supremely the 'patriarchal' language of Vautrin) which name and classify her as the 'harlot', as pure object of sexual exchange. It has been argued, in a psychoanalytical perspective, that *Illusions perdues*, as a typical example of the 'classic readable text', is predicated on a 'repression of the feminine'.[32] It is an argument that could be applied *a fortiori* to *Splendeurs*. Yet it is incomplete, in so far as that repression rebounds against its 'authors'. The one thing in the story of *Splendeurs* that cannot be fully controlled and manipulated is the desire of Esther and the only solution she can find for its impossible predicament. Her suicide marks the point of Vautrin's loss of control over events. It is also the point, as we have previously seen, at which Balzac's plot begins to thicken and proliferate at a quite astonishing pace. And, as the plot becomes more exotic, so the voice of the 'authoritative' narrator becomes more insistent, as if it too were seeking desperately to contain and subjugate what threatens to run out of control. Maxims, proverbs, generalisations, definitions, explanations start to pour off the discursive assembly line, in a continuous but unconvincing attempt to keep the story grounded within a normative framework of verisimilitude and intelligibility. The tautologous character of Balzac's 'explanations' has often been noted, that back-to-front logic whereby a universal 'law' is evoked as the causal explanation of a particular narrative state of affairs, when in fact the real determinations are the other way round, the desired 'effect' eliciting its explanatory 'cause' (what Genette calls the 'vraisemblable artificiel' of the *Comédie humaine*).[33] In the closing sequences of *Splendeurs*, the purely pragmatic function of these explanations, as *ex post facto* rationalisations of local and increasingly problematical narrative requirements, becomes entirely visible. Every twist and turn of the plot demands its justification, and gets it. But the explanatory apparatus is so transparently flexible, it involves so much internal inconsistency and contradiction that it is finally impossible to take it seriously.

This is above all the case with the different 'motivations' attributed to M. de Granville and Vautrin, in the attempt to account for their extraordinarily inconsistent conduct in the great negotiations of the Conciergerie. What must, however, be taken seriously are the implications of this confused and confusing *finale*. The bargain struck between Vautrin and the Attorney General is one of the most 'ténébreuse' of Balzac's many *ténébreuses affaires*. It is the deal made between 'crime' and 'justice' in order to keep the wheels of the State turning (what Vautrin has to swap, in return for a pardon and a post in the secret police, touches the political interests of the régime). I have argued elsewhere that this moment of *Splendeurs* represents a brilliant imaginative stroke on Balzac's part, on the grounds that the murky transaction of the Conciergerie is subversive of the moral imagery through which polite society distinguishes itself from the 'lower' orders and the 'dangerous' classes.[34] In that transaction, the images crack, 'identities' once more are blurred; the Law traduces and forges in order to do business with the Forger, the convict becomes a policeman, and we are left wondering who in fact is the greatest imposter, the Criminal, the Attorney General, the King.

These, of course, are provocatively bold implications. But one point which the argument overlooks is that they are also implications which the text, at other levels, seeks to evade or mask. Writing from the point of view of the State, Balzac works overtime to ensure that M. de Granville, the representative of the State, must come through it all somehow morally unscathed. Accordingly, the text returns once more to the use of schematic typologies in order to mark differences of identity. These range from abstract allegory ('Ces deux hommes, le CRIME et la JUSTICE, se regardèrent', p. 614) to the more concrete indicators drawn from the ever-available code of *physionomie*. Everything in the physical bearing of M.a de Granville suggests the 'majesty' of the Law: 'L'attitude, la physionomie, l'air de tête, le geste, le regard, firent en ce moment de ce grand Procureur-général une vivante image de la Magistrature, qui doit offrir les plus beaux exemples de courage civil'; everything in that of Vautrin suggests the 'savagery' of the Outlaw: 'Cette trompeuse attitude cachait la froide et terrible irritation des nerfs du sauvage. Les yeux de Jacques Collin couvaient une éruption volcanique, ses poings étaient crispés. C'était bien le tigre se ramassant pour bondir sur une proie' (p. 612). In these terms, the unfolding confrontation can be described as the domestication of the savage mind by the authority of the civilised. Vautrin capitulates entirely before the dignity and integrity of M. de Granville; he offers the compromising letters without conditions ('je n'en demande pas de rançon, je ne les vends pas', p. 644) and his own services in a spirit of fawning humility ('J'ai donc entrevu la possibilité . . . d'être utile au lieu d'être nuisible, et j'ai osé compter sur votre intelligence, votre bonté', p. 645). Impressed, M. de Granville softens, warms to the humanity of his captive; each gives his 'word' to the other, as if they were more in a gentlemen's club than in the Conciergerie. For these fantastic conversions, many 'explanations' are given, both by Vautrin and the narrator. It would be pointless to list them; improvised from one page to the next, they in fact explain nothing.

One reason why this is so is that, alongside the story of the taming of the criminal by the values of 'order', another, and quite incompatible, story is being told, but without any indication whatsoever that the text which houses them both is *aware* of the incompatibility. Thus, while Vautrin's surrender is presented *by the narrator* as being entirely in 'bonne foi' (p. 649), and hence with the implication that it is to be taken at face value, we are also told by the narrator that Vautrin 'jouait la Justice' (p. 619), that he is engaged in a 'game' involving subtle manoeuvres, wilful deception and implicit blackmail. So too is the otherwise exemplary M. de Granville; his attitude of benign paternalism conceals other, more cynical calculations ('il a plus à recevoir de moi qu'il ne me donne', remarks Granville to the Keeper of the Seals, p. 635). What at one moment is described as heartfelt magnanimity ('le magistrat qui fut pris d'une pitié divine pour ce malheureux', p. 614) becomes in the very next line mere masquerade ('Enfin, le magistrat (un magistrat est toujours un magistrat) . . . pensa qu'il pourrait se rendre maître de ce criminel').

What, here, is 'real' and what is 'feigned'? Balzac's authoritative' language offers us no reliable guide in coping with that question. It simply interleaves the two versions in a manner that veers towards incoherence, as a classic case of the left hand not appearing to know what the right hand is doing. Ordinarily, we might describe this as simply narrative incompetence, a careless despatch of an already exhausted plot (possibly exacerbated by the specific pressures of serial publication). But perhaps the surface disarray of the closing chapters of *Splendeurs* is the sign of a deeper malaise. It is as though, in taking us closer and closer to the heart of darkness of the modern city evoked by the transaction in the depths of the Conciergerie, the novel arrives at an impasse, faced with the image of a fraudulence so profound that its own conventions of explanation and representation cannot gain satisfactory purchase on it. The novel itself, hitherto so confident of its discriminating powers, no longer knows the distinction between the genuine and the fake.

Paper: Vautrin tells a story

Illusions perdues has been described as a truly 'materialist' book, in so far as that of which it is made is also what it is about: paper, its manufacture, its printing, its distribution, its fate in society.[35] Indeed the long sections on the changing technologies of printing and paper manufacture are partly justified in these very terms: 'David lui donna sur la papeterie des renseignements qui ne seront point déplacés dans une œuvre dont l'existence matérielle est due autant au Papier qu'à la Presse' (p. 116). As an inquiry into the material conditions of its own existence, *Illusions perdues* raises a set of questions deemed to be 'de la plus haute importance pour la littérature, pour les sciences et pour la politique' (p. 119). These questions concern the consequences for the whole society of a transformation in the material 'base'. Faced with these questions, Balzac's stance is an extremely uneasy one: what would make possible the large-scale production and distribution of *Illusions perdues* is seen as at once an exciting and menacing prospect. The old technologies are antiquated and expensive; rising demand requires cheap and efficient methods for a 'ten-fold' increase in the production of paper; David's efforts to develop the appropriate formula are seen, at least initially, as the creative energies of the inventor-hero rising to the challenge of the new age. Yet, as the 'genius' of invention is progressively annexed to commercial enterprise (in terms both of David's perception of its commercial possibilities and its final appropriation by the Cointet brothers), a more nervous view is registered. The mass production of blank paper and the mass circulation of printed paper obey only the laws of a 'théorème commercial': 'une rame de papier blanc vaut quinze francs, imprimée elle vaut, selon le succès, ou cent sous ou cent écus' (p. 413). From the manufacture of paper to the printed word there is a line of continuity; the Cointet brothers will use David's invention to service the publishing houses and, above all, the newspaper proprietors of Paris. The fate of paper (and of the products of paper) is to be caught up in the vast machine of capitalist production and consumption.

It is at this point of connection that Balzac's deep cultural and political conservatism comes into play. The commercial exploitation of the new modes of production means the disappearance of 'sound products': ('La solidité des produits s'en va de toutes parts', p. 119). The machine produces only for instant consumption, as with the *tartines* served up by the daily newspapers 'qui tous les matins en taille à ses abonnés de fort peu digérables, et que néanmoins ils avalent' (p. 45). Consumption as 'ingestion' is in fact a framing image in *Illusions perdues*. On the first page of the novel the new printing presses are described as 'ravenous' ('dévorantes'); on the penultimate page David's invention is presented as being assimilated 'dans la fabrication française comme la nourriture dans un grand corps' (p. 751). The metaphor of ingestion, with its corresponding connotations of waste and excess (the 'waste sheets of

print' which festoon the Galeries, the 'boutique de papier gâté' that
is Finot's office), might also give a clue to the interpretation of one
of the more curious features of *Illusions perdues*. Part of Vautrin's
strategy in seducing Lucien into signing the 'infernal pact' is to tell
him a story. It is a strange story, about a handsome young man
launched on a brilliant diplomatic career, but ruinously handi-
capped by an insatiable appetite for consuming paper – blank paper,
manuscripts ('qu'il trouve plus savoureux', p. 706), parchment,
financial receipts, political treaties; it is the story of a passion for
paper that is literally 'devouring'. This bizarre tale is normally construed as Vautrin's parable on the irresistibility of 'vice', designed to
persuade Lucien to see the futility of moral scruple.[36] But that still
leaves a considerable residue for interpretation: of all the vices
Vautrin could have chosen as illustrative examples, why one that is
so bizarre, why one that has to do with *paper*?

It is, of course, tempting to posit here some element of fantasy
identification on Balzac's part: Vautrin gratifies his own vice (the
seduction of Lucien) by means of a story about vice whose object is
paper, and it is on paper that Balzac will indulge his 'vice', namely
the writing of Vautrin, the irresistibility of his re-introduction to the
Comédie humaine. But perhaps a more plausible reading would be
to link Vautrin's story with the general logic of production and consumption articulated around the theme of paper in *Illusions perdues*
as a whole. In its peculiarly exotic way, it makes literal the informing
metaphor of the society as voraciously consuming and self-
consuming, in the sense both of a 'taking in' and a 'using up' (on the
principle of *usure* in the Balzacian philosophy of *énergie*). A society
based on the ceaseless production, circulation and 'consumption' of
bits of paper is a society that is fundamentally 'unsound', without a
stable centre, a society devoted to the dispersal and squandering of
vital substance, including supremely language. Its emblem is the
journalists' banquet or orgy,[37] the place where, as enormous
amounts of food and wine are engorged, the next issue of the newspaper is disgorged, in a frenetic production of language which, like
its speakers, is simultaneously subject to a process of rapid exhaus-
tion. The language of the journalists, remarks Vignon, is a language
that 'rots intelligence' ('ils [les journaux] dévorent nos intelligences
à vendre tous les matins leur trois-six cérébral', p. 359): it is a form
of 'mental fire water' that burns and consumes its users; or, in
Lousteau's image, it is like 'burning oil' ('absolument comme on
allume un quinquet . . . jusqu'à ce que l'huile manque', p. 337); or,
to complete the metaphorical configuration, it is like money that is

'frittered away' ('commerce où l'esprit s'amoindrit en se monnayant', p. 173).

For the form of paper that most completely resumes the circulating and self-dissipating energies of the society is paper money. The passing of bits of paper from hand to hand in connection with Lucien's forged bills of exchange is described by Balzac as generating 'capitaux fictifs' (p. 592), or, in yet another bodily image, circulating paper is the process of '*faire suer les écus*' (p. 592). Paper money is 'unsound' money. It is what, in the *pègre* section of *Splendeurs*, convict slang refers to as *fafiots*. The lexicographers assign to 'fafiot' a colourful, if somewhat eccentric, history. It appears in nineteenth-century *argot*, first, to denote 'paper', then 'paper money' or 'bank notes'. Robert lists 'faf-' as a root onomatopoeically evocative of the notion of 'un objet de peu de valeur'. How the onomatopoeic link is perceived is unclear, unless, as Balzac's own text suggests, it is with the sound of rustling paper ('Fafiot! n'entendez-vous pas le bruissement du papier de soie?', p. 526), a sound then associated with ideas of fragility and flimsiness (Heppenstall brilliantly translated 'fafiots' as 'flimsies').[38] Etymologies, let alone onomatopoeic ones, are notoriously untrustworthy guides in interpretation, and, in this case, may well be as 'unsound' as the object the word evokes. It does, however, provide the fetching paradox of an apparently natural (or 'motivated') sign being devised in popular speech to designate the purely arbitrary sign that is paper money. In any case, the distinction between the 'natural' and the 'arbitrary' is exactly the ground on which the analogy between money and language (as forms of 'representation' and standards of 'value') is characteristically deployed in the period as a whole. We do not have to wait for Saussure for the experience of an *angoisse fiduciaire* in relation to the contractual foundations of communication and exchange.[39] It is a recurring theme in a controversy that runs through the eighteenth century into the nineteenth. The debate about fiduciary currency is essentially a debate about the respective merits of coins and paper or, as Foucault puts it, between partisans of the theory of money-as-sign (as a token whose representative value is determined by consent) and supporters of the theory of money-as-merchandise (whose representative value is determined by its intrinsic material properties: the nature and amount of the metallic substance in the coin).[40]

In the post-Revolutionary period, the argument for the latter view is largely monopolised by the political Right, in particular in the writings of Bonald, de Maistre and Ballanche. Bonald, for example (one of Balzac's intellectual heroes), argues that paper money is economically and socially dangerous; its circulation promotes an expansion of the system of credit that is without secure foundations in 'real' property and wealth; it is an empty fiction ('fictitious capital'), a 'signe sans valeur', as distinct from coinage whose metallic substance guarantees that it is an 'expression réelle des valeurs parce qu'elle est valeur elle-même'. The same line of reasoning applies to language:

La parole est donc, dans le commerce des pensées, ce que l'argent est dans le commerce des marchandises, expression réelle des valeurs parce qu'elle est valeur elle-même. Et nos sophistes veulent en faire un signe de convention, à peu près comme le papier-monnaie, signe sans valeur, qui désigne tout ce qu'on veut, et qui n'exprime rien, qu'autant qu'il peut être échangé contre l'argent, expression réelle de toutes les valeurs.[41]

We recognise here a resurgence, in a specific political context, of the Adamic myth of the origins of language. Language, and hence human society, does not originate in humanly contrived pacts and contracts arbitrarily linking signifiers and signifieds. It is divinely installed as a union of the 'matériel' and the 'intellectuel', as a natural 'imaging', rather than a conventional signifying, of thoughts and objects.[42] This doctrine – essentially a kind of theocratic Cratylism that is the linguistic correlative of economic and political conservatism – must be understood in its historical context, as an articulation of a real anxiety in the face of the developing forms of a modern capitalist society. Like all conservative ideologies, it is based on a fear of inflation, the fear that, if values are not grounded in a God-given, natural order of things, the currencies of exchange, both monetary and semantic, will run out of control; the relations obtaining between money and goods, signifiers and signifieds, if based only upon the 'flimsiness' of contract, are at permanent risk of spiralling into an anarchic flux.

It is almost certainly in large measure from this worry that Balzac aligns himself with the positions of Bonald, Maistre and Ballanche. His own 'Cratylist' fantasies around the idea of a 'natural' condition of the sign, in which material form is consubstantial with what the sign expresses derive, as we have already seen, from a desire to arrest the proliferation and the adulteration of the sign, and the corresponding confusion of meanings and identities, as it is increasingly caught up in the market-place of 'free' exchange. It is around this nerve point of anxiety that the problematic signs of clothes, language and money converge, as the interrelated terms of an unstable semiotic. Clothes, no longer reliable markers of social identity, are compared in the *Traité de la vie élégante* to 'papier-monnaie' ('un des plus grands malheurs qui puissent affliger une nation');[43] in *Des mots à la mode* fashionable discourse is at once cosmetic ('vernis') and speculative capital ('alors le mot vole de bouche en bouche; il fait fortune').[44] The fullest incarnation of this speculative floating of linguistic currencies in *Illusions perdues* is, again, the language of the journalists, and, more particularly, what Balzac describes as the language of *esprit*. Wit, in the form of the pun, the *blague*, the *bon mot*, is that 'plus subtil des dissolvants' (p. 357). What it dissolves are firm standards of meaning, reference and truth, in the form of a generalised relativisation, and perversion, of values. 'Vous tenez à ce que vous écrivez?', Vignon asks Lucien, 'd'un air railleur' (p. 422). *Raillerie* is the name of the game, and its most visible object is the very instrument with which the game is played. In this game words can be made to mean virtually anything, anything 'peut devenir alternativement faux et vrai' (p. 346). Through the *bon mot*, whose function is 'de mettre tout en question' (p. 254), meanings are turned upside down, inverted, like the burlesque game of syntactic inversion which the journalists play with the book, *Le Solitaire* (p. 256).

The inversions and perversions of the journalistic *jeu d'esprit* Balzac cannot view with anything other than extreme alarm. It is the symptom of a moral disaster, whereby 'Tout s'excuse et se justifie à une époque où l'on a transformé la vertu en vice, comme on a érigé certains vices en vertus' (p. 500). Semantic instability brings with it the prospect of a menacing confusion and disorder at all levels; 'polysemy' is a potential social and political disaster area.[45] The most provocative case in point concerns Balzac's strictures, in *La Vieille fille*, on modern usages of the word *liberté* (IV, p. 276). Taking liberties with 'liberté', or with language in general (for example, in the name of liberty of expression or freedom of the press), is to unsettle both the lexicon and the order of social relationships. Again, we recognise the reactionary political stance, the longing for a regulative and legitimating centre, which in political terms is nothing other than Legitimism itself. This of course is the point at which we want to turn away, or to argue that Balzac's politics are so deeply repugnant that the only possible move is to detach Balzac the writer from them as much as possible, to argue that Balzac is great *despite* the politics.[46] This is an entirely understandable position, and moreover proceeds from the generally unexceptionable proposition that a writer's opinions are not the same thing as his writing. But this would be to fail to see the essential connections. Balzac's politics are not really an intellectually serious affair; what he took from Maistre, Bonald and Ballanche he took eclectically, at times even incoherently. But we do not redeem the *Comédie* by 'saving' it from the political views of its author. Seen in their historical context, they give, in however crude a form, a framework, a distanced perspective within which to develop a powerful understanding and analysis of real tendencies at work within the emerging economic and social formation. In *Illusions perdues* the paradigm of that formation is the journalistic 'intellectual brothel' ('ces mauvais lieux de la pensée appelés journalisme', p. 359), which, as Adorno reminds us, Balzac is among the first to identify as the masquerade behind which a 'false emancipation' disguises itself in the semblance of 'freedom of expression'.[47] To say that there is a 'repressive' force at work in Balzac's vision is absolutely right. But to say that there is a repressive force at work in that vision whereby he could not recognise polysemy, the pun and its 'perversions' in terms of the modernist notion of the liberation of the signifier, would be pointlessly anachronistic (indeed if anachronism is the order of the day, we might wish to reverse this perspective, and suggest that Balzac's text spells out some of the 'illusions' to which the liberationist aesthetic of today has perhaps fallen prey).

Balzac's conservatism is a response to the problem of 'individualism', both economic and linguistic, at a precise historical moment, and in terms that register the beginnings of a real crisis of representation. As signs multiply, meanings fluctuate, the 'public' fragments, the question that presses itself upon Balzac is how to gather up this heterogeneous, mobile and often deceptive material into a unified and coherent whole: what stands for what, what is the 'measure' of things, what might qualify as a 'common' language? It is in the encounter with these questions that some of Balzac's major novels experience that 'trouble de la représentation' which Barthes detects in *Sarrasine*. But they do not experience it as the euphorically attempted crossing of a 'limit', on the other side of which the text might liberate itself from the constraints of the narrative contract, and put its signs into a circulation untrammelled by the authority of the 'codes'. The experience is, precisely, an experience of *trouble* with regard to the phenomenon of 'circulation', arising from the disquieting sense of the frailty and fallibility of contracts. The political articulation of this worry, and its various accompanying fantasies about society, culture, language, are unambiguously reactionary; they speak of a desire to identify and order the heterogeneous according to systems of representation that are fixed and hierarchical, and geared to the interests of authority. That response was not the only available one in the period. Stendhal, for example, while engaging with similar sets of problems, will react in a quite different way. He too will question the 'contract', but not from a longing for a more securely grounded language of representation; on the contrary, he will do so from a position that, in many respects, is one of radical, iconoclastic individualism, taking on the myths of the age in terms of a dream of a hero, and a language, that might be genuinely 'free'. And that, in turn, will bring its own problems. This is why, in their respective engagements with the question of 'representation', it is ultimately pointless to 'modernise' either of them. If we do so, we are likely to overlook the specific historical determinations of the various kinds of uncertainty in their work, and, as a possible consequence, to overlook other kinds of issues of a more general character as well.

4

STENDHAL: THE ETHICS
OF VERISIMILITUDE

Writer and public

Balzac's novels show that the logic of mimesis is a 'socio-logic,[1] and that the 'fiduciary' conventions which support that logic reach deep into the language and culture of the age. But they also show that their most immediate and practical form turns on the relation between the writer and his public: in *Illusions perdues*, for whom you write is a question inseparable from what you write and how you write. The 'value' of the signs used to represent the world depends crucially on securing the agreement of the reader as to their 'worth'; the text is like a bill of exchange or a promissory note (promising among other things the pleasures of intelligibility, the *sens caché* of reality), the guarantee of which stems from a system of public 'confidence'. We have seen how Balzac's texts undermine that confidence at the very moment of apparently presupposing it. And that shifting, unstable stance brings us to the even more oblique relation to these matters maintained by Stendhal's novels. Stendhal is a writer who never takes his 'public' for granted. Indeed, as he himself was well aware (projecting utopically forward to an ideal readership in the late nineteenth century or dedicating his novels to the *happy few*), the response of his contemporary public appears to have been for the most part either bewildered or hostile. A naive reader of today, unencumbered by background knowledge or unalive to the ironies and ambiguities of the text, might be excused for thinking otherwise. For, through the voice of the narrator, Stendhal's fiction seems to institute and proclaim a concord with the values and attitudes of those very readers excluded elsewhere from the privileged band of true sympathisers. But this, as is now common knowledge, is misleading, part of the Stendhalian ruse, a cosy embrace concealing a dagger. Moreover, the historical facts suggest that the ruse may not have been entirely effective (despite Stendhal's own love of disguise), and lend support to

Georges Blin's thesis that Stendhal's ironic masks and subterfuges are almost wholly transparent.[2] The voice, it appears, did not deceive the nineteenth-century reader, who knew that many of his cherished assumptions were under attack, and who reacted with a corresponding counter-attack.

In itself this reaction is in no way remarkable, and belongs to a common pattern of writer-public relations in the nineteenth century. What is interesting, however, are the terms of that reaction, or rather the forms in which they can be seen to interconnect. The study of Stendhal's reputation in the nineteenth century reveals that two main themes stand out with monotonous, if instructive, regularity.[3] The first is the shrill repetition of the charge of immorality (the *Journal des débats* sets the tone and speaks for many in its account of 'une imagination délirante' whose sole objective is 'insulter aux principes de la plus saine morale').[4] The second is the recurrent accusation of the fundamental *invraisemblance* of many of Stendhal's major creations. Thus, the critic of *Le Globe* found Octave, the hero of *Armance*, to be not only 'un être prodigieuse-ment bizarre', but – introducing the critical theme of 'madness' – a being so bizarre as to resemble a character escaped from the lunatic asylum at Charenton.[5] Similarly, the critic for the *Revue des deux mondes* found that 'le caractère de Julien Sorel est donc faux, contradictoire, incompréhensible en certaines parties'.[6] The *Revue de Paris* commented on the relationship between Julien and Mathilde: 'on serait disposé surtout à lui demander raison de ses amants si étranges'.[7] In the *Journal des débats*, Jules Janin (again introducing the theme of 'madness') wrote of Mathilde de la Mole: 'Cette Mathilde est folle . . . on n'a jamais imaginé une fille comme cela.'[8] Even Mérimée, Stendhal's friend and colleague, remarked of Julien Sorel: 'Pourquoi avez-vous choisi un caractère qui a l'air si impossible . . . Je m'imaginais avoir compris Julien et il n'y a pas une seule de ses actions qui n'ait contredit le caractère que je lui supposais.'[9]

The list could be substantially extended, but the general shape of the predominant critical attitude should be clear. What has, I believe, gone unnoticed, however, are the important relations of overlap and interdependence between these two themes. For although normally proffered as distinct and discrete evaluations, the judgement of 'immorality' and the judgement of *invraisemblance* issue in large measure from the same ideological space, one in which the two are functionally inter-related, or, rather, where the latter often acts as a kind of cover for the former.

By means of a tacit strategy of transference, the moral critique is converted (and thereby strengthened) into a naturalistic critique, in terms of which transgressions of the moral order are seen as violations of the natural order. According to the class-bound morality of the nineteenth century, what could be more scandalous than that the aristocratic Mathilde should take the plebeian Julien as her lover? But what more effective way of rationalising that sense of scandal, and consolidating that morality, than by accusing her creator of stepping outside the limits of mimetic representation itself, by making of the moral scandal a scandal of representation itself? Émile Faguet remarked, imperturbably erecting prejudice into a criterion of literary realism, that it was 'dur à admettre' that Mathilde should have an affair with 'ce petit secrétaire, fils d'un scieur de bois'.[10] The irony is that he was probably right, but only by virtue of that self-fulfilling circularity through which prejudice is socially translated into 'fact'. The codes of nineteenth-century behaviour were indeed such as to make a love affair between an aristocratic woman and a man of lower rank appear exceedingly improbable, and could accordingly be appealed to with a good conscience as the empirical basis on which to judge the represen- tation of Mathilde's behaviour as a literary aberration. This is a classic instance of the recursive agency of Opinion in the social con- struction of reality and its representations; in a closed circuit, 'opinion' and 'reality' model each other, in such a way that the given 'facts' of the latter serve as the irrefutable proof of the legitimacy of the former.

At certain moments of his career, Stendhal appears to have believed that things might have been otherwise in the nineteenth century. In the *Vie de Rossini* he advances the argument that new 'democratic' conditions might lead to the emergence of a new kind of 'public', in which the ossified norms of the past might be broken by the pluralistic spirit of controversy and debate.[11] But as early as *Rome, Naples et Florence en 1817*, we find a quite different recogni- tion: 'Je désespère des arts depuis que nous marchions vers les gouvernements de l'opinion.'[12] Consensual politics entail the impoverishing prospect of consensual art, regulated by the con- formist pressures of Opinion and no less oppressive than the nor- mative culture of autocratic monarchy. To the extent that *Le Rouge et le Noir* works against those pressures, it reflects back an image to society in which the latter, or its critical spokesman, can see only a travesty and a perversion, a wilful secession from the 'common language' of an agreed way of seeing the world. In this respect, the author of the long review-essay on Stendhal in the *Revue des deux mondes* got, if only in a complacently unexamined way, the crucial emphasis absolutely right: 'Ici, nous devons l'avouer, l'auteur et nous ne parlons plus une *langue commune*, et nous ne pouvons comprendre celle qu'il parle.'[13] It is an emphasis, moreover, provocatively confirmed by Stendhal himself on those various occasions when he remarks that, from the point of view of that kind of definition of the 'common language', his own works will be read as if written in a 'foreign tongue'.[14]

The issue, it will be seen, is profound, and goes far beyond the ordinary scholarly concern with the history of critical reputations and reading publics. Fully elaborated, it touches on entrenched assumptions within early nineteenth-century culture and society (on the terms of what is construed as the 'common language'), and, in that context, on the relation of the internal economy of Stendhal's narrative to the theory and practice of mimesis. In particular, it returns us to the formal description of literary *vraisemblance* given in an earlier chapter,[15] to that reading of Aristotle's *Poetics* whereby the literary *eikos* is seen as a function of the *doxa*: what will be accepted as 'probable' or 'likely' in a literary representation will depend on presuppositions embedded in common opinion, in the 'common language', or – since relations of power and interests are importantly determining factors here – in a notion of the common language, as this is defined and protected by those groups and institutions with considerable investment in the ideological appropriation of that notion. One of the clearest examples of that appropriation we have already seen in the context of seventeenth-century poetics, especially the prescriptions, and proscriptions, brought to bear on Corneille's *Le Cid* (it is no accident that Stendhal's most vitriolic literary and cultural criticism is reserved for the Court culture of the seventeenth century). The clamour of nineteenth-century orthodoxy around Stendhal's representation of Mathilde de la Mole's behaviour reminds us of the close link between *vraisemblance* and *bienséance*, plausibility and propriety, in seventeenth-century judgements of *Le Cid*. In her affair with Julien, Mathilde crosses the threshold of intelligibility for the nineteenth-century conservative imagination in the same way that the seventeenth-century establishment found Chimène's marriage to Rodrigue to be unthinkable. In both cases, the application of criteria of *vraisemblance* in adverse judgement of the text reveals a strategy of censorship at work in the field of desire. Desires which are socially problematical, which threaten the social structure

(familial in *Le Cid*, class in *Le Rouge et le Noir*) are coped with by
querying or denying the 'plausibility' of the text which presents
them. They are removed from that area of society's classification
system which articulates the moral order (what is permitted and
what is forbidden) to that area which organises the division between
the normal and the abnormal, the typical and the aberrant; and,
following Aristotle's distinction between the contingently 'true' and
the poetically 'probable', although the aberrant may belong to life
and to history, it has no place in the representational project of literary mimesis. The seventeenth-century critic, Rapin, declared that
the *vraisemblable* rests on 'tout ce qui est conforme à l'opinion du
public'.[16] Nearly two hundred years later Balzac remarks, in *Lettres
sur la littérature*, that the verisimilitude of a fictional character 'doit
être appuyé par un consentement unanime'.[17] Changed historical
circumstances clearly redefine the terms on which that consent can
be solicited and given. But both cultures impose limits, the general
principle or logical form of which appears to be the same. *Le Rouge
et le Noir* is scandalous because it takes us to, and beyond, those
limits.

I do not propose to recapitulate here the complex web of cultural
and ideological relations engaged by the code of *vraisemblance*. But
a convenient shorthand for regaining purchase on them is through
John Bayley's unusual yet suggestive adaptation to the novel of the
notion of 'pastoral'. 'By pastoral', writes Bayley, 'I mean the principle of making everything in a work of art characteristic.'[18]
'Pastoral', in this account, falls therefore into the category of the
'typical', and hence of the *vraisemblable*; it answers to a system of
expectancies centred on likelihoods and predictabilities. As Bayley
remarks, taking Balzac's heroine, Eugénie Grandet, as an example
of pastoral characterisation, the mark of Eugénie's pastoral status is
her predictability, the knowledge that we 'will always find her doing
the right thing'.[19] Yet, like those other terms which aid and abet the
hidden transactions between *vraisemblance* and the *bienséances*,
the phrase 'the right thing' is suitably ambiguous. The 'right thing'
is the expected thing, but in two senses: in the sense of what is
logically appropriate, consistent with a given psychological model
of conduct; but beneath this sense there is also the sense of what is
morally 'right', proper rather than appropriate. 'Pastoral', in this
definition, responds simultaneously to, or rather gathers into one
convention, ideas concerning both what the world *is* and what it
should be; the fusion is brought out clearly in Bayley's discussion of
pastoral stereotypes in Socialist Realism, where the model of

'realistic' representation derives in part from moral assumptions about an ideal state of affairs.

In these terms, the most striking feature of Stendhal's narrative universe is its resolutely anti-pastoral character. The decisive moments of the narrative are, precisely, its 'a-typical' moments. Indeed, adapting a suggestion by Leo Bersani,[20] one might say that the mass of strictly 'mimetic' material in *Le Rouge et le Noir* (the representation of contemporary social reality by means of a series of interlocking types: the bourgeois of Verrières, the aristocrats of the de la Mole salon) exists mainly in order to focus, by way of contrast, those acts or experiences which subvert the models of 'reality' illustrated and endorsed by these various social types. These acts are, of course, primarily transgressions of moral codes, prompted by impulses and desires forbidden or unacknowledged by society: Julien's crime, Louise's adultery, Mathilde's passion. But the deeper meaning of these acts is in the way they are often received, within the novel itself, not just as defiances of the rules of morality but, more radically, as a departure from 'reality' itself. The rebellion against moral standards is also a rebellion against taken-for-granted standards of intelligibility. Julien not only offends, he also *surprises* his society, and the two are profoundly interconnected. Whence the importance in the text of the motif of the *imprévu*, the way Julien (like the other 'âmes nobles') repeatedly eludes and disturbs the 'internalised probability system' of the other characters, to whom he consequently appears, in the term that recurs throughout the novel to mark other people's perception of Julien, as *singulier*: strange, unplaceable, infinitely more complex and mysterious than the simple stereotype of the ambitious parvenu.

But it is not only the characters of *Le Rouge et le Noir* who view Julien as 'singulier'; as we have seen, this appears also to have been the case with many of its contemporary readers. And in terms of the relation of Stendhal's novel to nineteenth-century conventions of *vraisemblance* and their social context, the instructive perspective here is that opened up by this convergence between the reactions and judgements of character and reader (at least to the extent that those of the latter can be reliably inferred from the critical record of the period). Julien is, of course, the main focus for this overlap of 'internal' and 'external' viewpoint. But an equally notable example concerns the respective responses to the behaviour of Mathilde. I have already cited Jules Janin's remark, 'on n'a jamais imaginé une fille comme cela'. But Janin could arguably have taken his cue from what is said about Mathilde within the novel itself, from, for example, M. de la Mole. For, in a sense, he is only echoing the latter's opinion, according to which Mathilde's conduct in taking Julien as her lover is not only outrageous, but unthinkable, emphatically not the 'right thing', in both the prescriptive and the predictive senses of the term:

Qui l'eût pu prévoir? se disait-il. Une fille d'un caractère si altier, d'un génie si élevé, plus fière que moi du nom qu'elle porte! dont la main m'était demandée d'avance partout ce qu'il y a de plus illustre en France.   (p. 438)

Jules Janin and M. de la Mole speak in what is virtually the same voice from within a common framework of assumptions: what is threatening to both in Mathilde's desire is simply pushed off the map of the intelligible; it literally beggars the 'imagination'. Mathilde is thus the occasion of a double disturbance: for both character and critic (father and censor: two figures of the 'Law'), she disturbs a system of expectations, embedded at once in the novel and in the contemporary society (or at least in those sectors of the society exercising greatest influence over what will be admitted to the canon of the *vraisemblable*). That disturbance is a sign of the text pitting itself against the authority of the *doxa*, seen in its dual role as guardian of the moral order and source of what is naturalistically known as 'reality'.

Evidently there are many difficulties in proposing this type of parallelism between character and reader. There are difficulties of a theoretical kind (we have to avoid the crude reductionism of 'reflection' theory), and of an empirical kind (what is the status of the journalistic critical record as evidence of forms of understanding diffusely at work in society at large; on what grounds, for example, can we assume Janin's to be a representative voice?). Posed in empirical terms, the problem is identical to that which bedevils all attempts at an historical sociology of knowledge: 'opinion' is difficult to investigate, the evidence is often thin, and the temptation to spread it wide very great. Some of these difficulties can, however, be partly met by considering the implications of a third element in the equation – the position of the narrator. For the reactions of M. de la Mole and Jules Janin find a precise, although deceptive, echo in the magnificently ambiguous intervention of the narrator:

Le résultat de cette nuit de folie fût qu'elle crût être parvenue à triompher de son amour. Cette page nuira à plus d'une façon au malheureux auteur. Les âmes glacées l'accuseront d'indécence. Il ne fait point l'injure aux jeunes personnes qui brillent dans les salons de Paris, de supposer qu'une seule d'entre elles soit susceptible des mouvements de folie qui dégradent le caractère de Mathilde. Ce personnage est tout à fait d'imagination, et même imaginée en dehors des habitudes sociales qui parmi tous les siècles assureront un rang si distingué à la civilisation du XIXe siècle . . . Maintenant qu'il est bien convenu que le caractère de Mathilde est impossible dans notre siècle, non moins prudent que vertueux, je crains moins d'irriter en continuant le récit des folies de cette aimable fille.

(p. 356)

Everything in this famous passage is deeply equivocal, and I shall return to some of its more unsettled and unsettling features. In certain respects, however, it does suggest an apparent coincidence of view between character, critic and narrator. The narrator at once pre-empts and concedes the very criticisms of his creation that will be made by others inside and outside the novel. More exactly, it could be said that the narrator, in echoing his character and speaking to his reader, acts as a bridge between the value-systems of each. Of course, the narrator and his implied audience are problematical notions: who and what they stand for are complicated matters. Just as it would be wrong to confuse narrator with author, so it would be naive entirely to identify the implied audience with an actual public. At one level, the 'reader' here is every possible reader, not only those who have read Stendhal, but also those who will read him. We might say that the audience addressed by the narrator is an imaginary audience, a persona whose status is less referential than structural – in structuralist terms, a functional role corresponding to the category 'narrataire' and complementing the role 'narrateur'.

Yet the familiar criticism of the structuralist approach is pertinent here: that, in its insistent concern with abstract categories, it de-contextualises and de-historicises its object. That there is a specific historical basis both to the utterances of the Stendhalian narrator and the audience to which they are addressed is unmistakeable. The voice appeals to a set of public values and beliefs, rooted in the collective, or consecrated, 'wisdom' of the age. It draws upon attitudes represented, within the novel, by those characters who speak in the name of what the text calls 'l'opinion publique' (p. 148), and communicates with the reader outside the novel on the implicit assumption that these attitudes are shared by the reader. Thus, the empirical thinness of the evidence from the critical writings of the period are, as it were, compensated by the logically necessary implications of the narrator's role; the very act of appealing to the reader in this way carries with it the presumption of a correspondence between belief-systems within the novel and outside it. Or, to take up Stendhal's own analogy for the project of the mimetic novel, the narrator acts as a kind of 'mirror', reflecting 'doxic' images back and forth between reader and text; as a mediator of *doxai*, he opens a channel of communication, makes possible a 'contract' of intelligibility which, in its most important task, is the confirmation of the 'mimetic contract' itself. We of course know that, through submerged patterns of meaning, Stendhal secretly reneges on all the major clauses of that contract. But the question of the more guarded meanings of the novel is not, for the moment, the immediate point at issue. Rather it is a question of the intervention of certain *forms*, in both the technical sense of a form of discourse and the idiomatic sense of a series of purely formal gestures (without substantial content), designed to sustain the pretence of solidarity with the reader, of endorsing a system of shared meanings against which the 'bizarre' behaviour of Stendhal's heroes and heroines can then be adequately interpreted and assessed. That gesture of solidarity is an illusory and ironic construct, which throws into even sharper relief the forces which break the chain of exchange between writer and reader, and tear the contract of agreed meanings to pieces.

Recitations

Tearing up the contract and withdrawing from the *doxa* is not, however, a straightforward undertaking, and it is only a naive version of a particular romantic ideology of language that will pretend otherwise. That attempted secession is, on the contrary, one of the acutest difficulties faced by both Stendhal and his major characters, and it carries important implications for Stendhal's relation to mimetic notions of narrative, in particular those encapsulated in the conception of the novel as 'chronicle' or 'mirror'. Stendhal and his heroes and heroines often dream and speak of freedom. Freedom here, as Brombert shows,[21] means many things, but pre-eminently freedom from the prison-house of Opinion, even when, paradoxically, the condition of such freedom becomes literal incarceration: to be locked away, 'loin du regard des autres', is for Julien Sorel and Fabrice del Dongo the supreme mode of individual felicity, the habitat of the untouchable Self. This is, of course, a fantasy. Yet, however much Stendhal's critical intelligence surrounds it with equivocating irony, he was in some respects seduced by it, and it furnishes a coda to his novels (with the exception of *Lucien Leuwen*, which is one of the reasons why that novel remains unfinished, its essential predicament unresolved). The Stendhalian 'self', elusive and perhaps finally unknowable, can be located in at least one negative respect: its committed resistance to incorporation by the idioms of Opinion, or its progressive disengagement from the obsession with self-validation through others. How to outplay the Others is the name of the Stendhalian game.

That enterprise is to a considerable extent animated by what nowadays would be seen as a pure fiction: the notion – largely Rousseauist in its origins – of a unique and precious subjectivity which, in finding its own unique voice, a language fully present to self, will achieve true freedom, miraculously delivered from the social contract of meaning, discarding the currency, the 'well rubbed coins' – in Stendhal's quotation from Sterne[22] – of social exchange (the monetary image is as important for Stendhal as it is for Balzac). 'Mr. Myself', as Stendhal refers to himself in his private jottings, says it all: the paradox of securing the integrity of the self by speaking of it in a foreign tongue. It is the most revealing example of that effort of self-concealment manifested in Stendhal's passion for foreign languages and cryptic codes, and his heroes' frequent preference for secret sign systems and indirect modes of communication. The best, of course, is not to speak at all, and in *Le Rouge et le Noir* 'silence' of a sort will be an optimal, if fragile, solution for both hero and narrator alike. Stendhal himself knew at bottom that it was a fiction,[23] which is presumably one of the reasons why his two major heroes die young; beyond society and its languages there is nowhere else for them to go. But, even as fiction, it gives the terms for the tensions lived by his heroes within the fictions, as well as for some of the problems experienced by Stendhal in the writing of Fiction. How to speak to others, in the language of others, is at the heart of the Stendhalian dilemma.

The problem of living in society and of writing novels for a public is, then, the problem of the *doxa*, and it is primarily a problem of language. The *doxa*, as the sociologists remind us, is fundamentally a matter of language, a corpus of linguistic stereotypes through which a body of 'sedimented meanings' is deposited and maintained in the collective consciousness.[24] The sociological notion of 'sedimentation' corresponds exactly to a key emphasis in Stendhal's own reflections on language, as these have been summarised, in their specific bearing on the relation between writer and public, by Michel Crouzet in his magisterial *Stendhal et le langage*: 'La communication sociale, ou littéraire, quand elle est ajustée parfaitement au public, tend à se *sédimenter* en un répertoire de pure consommation, qui s'oppose absolument à la parole vive.'[25] In its most reduced and simplified form, Stendhal's linguistic imagination revolves around an opposition between two kinds of speech: *parole vive*, as the site of authentic subjectivity, versus *parole morte*, as the form of the 'pacte social'[26] of language, grasped precisely as a kind of mimesis whereby speech moulds itself, in a phrase which in varying guises recurs continually in Stendhal's writings, to what is 'appris, récité, su par cœur'.[27] Social discourse is a repetition of what has been learnt by heart, taken from elsewhere. It is a comedy of 'recitation'; its speakers do not so much speak as recite from a socially consecrated and socially memorised text; they are locked into a linguistic automatism, a petrified code of proprieties and commonplaces, subservient to the *convenu* and fearful of the *imprévu*.

Much of Stendhal's thinking about language turns on the notion of the *convenu*. Language, Stendhal frequently tells us, is a matter of agreements: in *Racine et Shakespeare*, language is 'une chose de convention';[28] in *Rome, Naples et Florence en 1817*, it is a system of 'signes convenus pour représenter les idées'.[29] In these remarks the status of the *convenu* is entirely neutral. It registers what Stendhal took from eighteenth-century accounts of the conventional basis of language (largely as encountered through his readings in the work of the *idéologues*). As such, the *convenu* merely states a theoretical fact of language: that linguistic agreements are a condition of mutually intelligible utterance (and hence with the implication that the idea of an autonomous subject exempting itself from those agreements is a myth). But in both his aesthetic and his political writings, the *convenu* also attracts emotionally and ideologically loaded meanings, and often becomes the object of unremitting attack. For something else that Stendhal may have inherited from the more anxious side of the eighteenth-century linguistic imagination – perhaps from Diderot, but more likely from Maine de Biran – is the sense of language as the site of self-alienation, along with the corresponding dream of a form beyond the arbitrarily coded linguistic sign, in which mind, body and sign will be at one. Music often presents itself as a candidate for this role (for Stendhal music is to the soul what for Diderot gesture and expression are to the body); and it is therefore not surprising that it is when Stendhal writes on music that his questioning of the linguistic contract is at its sharpest. In *Vie de Métastase*, for example, language is described once more in terms of the *convenu*, but this time in unequivocally negative vein: 'Il est tout simple que nos langages vulgaires qui ne sont qu'une suite de signes convenus pour exprimer des choses généralement connues, n'aient point de signes pour exprimer de tels mouvements que vingt personnes peut-être sur mille ont éprouvés.'[30] Language, in this account, is that which is shared by all, which ensures the circuit of exchange, but at a level of generality and commonplaceness from which the intimate and infinitely unpredictable inflections of Mr. Myself are wholly excluded. Stendhal, in short, engages critically with the notion of language-as-contract from an intellectual and political perspective quite different from that in which Balzac opposes it. The terms in which Balzac rejects the contractual basis of language derive from the theocratic doctrines of the political right, and in particular from Bonald's theory of the divine origins of language, as something God-given and therefore not dependent on merely human conventions. Stendhal's objections stem rather from the libertarian arguments of Maine de Biran, whereby the unique 'sensations' of the individual cannot find expression in the public stock of agreed forms.[31]

It is from that context that the *convenu* is regularly identified by Stendhal as pure ritual, as 'conventional' discourse in the disabling sense of the stereotyped, the mechanical and the inert. The paradigm of this discourse is Conversation. 'Conversation' is one of the section-headings of Stendhal's most sustained inquiry into the state of the language (*Racine et Shakespeare*), and he returns persistently to the idea that the quality of conversation is the index of the literary and political health of society. This emphasis forms the basis in *Racine et Shakespeare* of his rejection of the legacy of the seventeenth century, and of his attempt to promote an aesthetic of 'modernity'. Though doubtless of real polemical urgency in the early nineteenth century, Stendhal's battle with the neo-classical Academician is in some ways a side issue. For Stendhal's refusal of seventeenth-century literary forms is not just based on the familiar relativist arguments proposed by Romantic cultural historicism: what is right for the 'spirit of the age' in the seventeenth century cannot possibly be right for the culturally different circumstances of the nineteenth century. It stems rather from a deep intellectual and political hostility to the seventeenth century as such, and in particular to what Stendhal sees as the pernicious influence on literature exercised by the language of polite conversation at the Court of Versailles, the language of *le bon ton* and *le bel usage*. The conversation of the Court is pure *doxa*, the ceaseless imitation of a model autocratically imposed by the King as a means of political censorship and control. Hence the impossibility of Stendhal making up his mind properly about Racine: Racine is a great writer – indeed, on the relativist assumptions, a great 'Romantic' writer – but his work remains nevertheless vitiated by the severe constraints imposed by the norms of court exchange (Stendhal's true position is revealed in that bizarre throw-away remark, according to which Racine would have been an even greater tragedian if only he had had the good fortune to have lived in the nineteenth century).[32]

But what really matters in this provocative and often wayward account of the seventeenth century lies more in its bearing upon Stendhal's analysis of the position of the writer and his relation to language in the nineteenth century. 'Conversation' in the nineteenth century is in principle a very different affair; it has, at least potentially (if it were not blocked by the efforts of the Academicians and the salons), a certain vitality; it is linked to a 'torrent des passions' which 'menacent de renverser toutes les convenances et de disperser au loin les habitants du salon'.[33] The early nineteenth century offers, or offered, a possibility of healing the rift between public and private, language and action. It is the era ushered in by the Revolution, emancipated from the past, free of the dead weight of the stereotype and the model, and the language appropriate for the artistic representation of the decisive experiences of the age should be, precisely, a language suitable 'aux enfants de la Révolution'.[34] This is the context in which Stendhal tries to re-invent the notion of an authentic 'common language', notably through his interventions, in *Racine et Shakespeare* and elsewhere, in the contemporary debate about modern 'Italian'. Echoing the Jacobin argument that linguistic unity is a condition of political equality, Stendhal, in the Italian debate, sides with the 'modernists' against the 'purists', with the demand for a modern Italian projected as a rationalised 'public' language in which all its subjects will communicate as equal citizens of the republic.[35] *Racine et Shakespeare* also gives the social and political context for Stendhal's related attempt to rework the eighteenth-century concept of the *beau idéal* into what, in *Histoire de la peinture en Italie*, he calls the *beau idéal moderne*.[36] Modern literature will hold a 'mirror' up to the age, but in terms of what is most forceful, uplifting and energising in the age; its language will be that of the 'children of the Revolution' in that it will be consumed by the famous 'soif de l'énergie', the aesthetic equivalent, or indeed one of the very forms, of what Stendhal describes in *Racine et Shakespeare* as 'courage civil':[37] the spirit of innovation, liberty, independence, risk-taking, passionate action.

But by 1823 (the publication of the first part of *Racine et*

Shakespeare) this programme, although militantly argued for, is already perceived as in many ways a dead letter. It reflects more a nostalgic memory of possibilities seen as inherent in the heady and dangerous days of the Napoleonic campaigns, a cultural possibility where literature and action could conceivably be posed as mutually informing, where the former might mean something 'aux gens qui . . . ont fait la campagne de Moscou et vu de près les étranges transactions de 1814'.[38] By 1823 that possibility seems definitively lost. The return of the Bourbons, the restoration of the authority of the Church, the influence of the Académie and the salons, the proliferation of censors and spies, all conspire to re-imprison discourse within the orthodox grip of Opinion. Stendhal's career as a novelist, and that of his heroes within the novels, are indelibly marked by that loss. Their aversion from the idioms of the time is notorious: Stendhal's pronounced reluctance in *Le Rouge et le Noir* to recount the terms of provincial conversation (p. 19); Julien's disdain for the banalities of every milieu in which he finds himself. Yet for the author of *Le Rouge et le Noir*, the reproduction of these idioms is indispensable to the notion of the novel as a 'chronique du XIXe siècle', and their mastery a necessary condition of the hero's progress. The stake, and the ruse, of both author and hero in *Le Rouge et le Noir* is how to retain some vestige of freedom while negotiating what threatens that freedom: how Julien speaks to the other characters and how Stendhal speaks to his readers are two faces of the same dilemma and the same game.

One way of describing *Le Rouge et le Noir* is as an ensemble of discourses or, in Barthes's term, 'sociolectes',[39] each of which corresponds to a particular social group, and which together furnish the different 'scripts' with which Julien acts out his various roles. Leaving aside the more marginal forms – for example, the restricted code of the Congregation, that world of Jesuit conspiracy and high politics whose esoteric language strikes Julien as a source of immense power and influence – there are essentially three such forms: the discourse of Verrières and the provincial bourgeoisie, of the Church and the Besançon seminary, and of the aristocratic salon in Paris. Julien's 'journey' is a movement through this sociolectal universe in a determined, if somewhat discontinuous, process of adaptation and accommodation. For, contrary to his Napoleonic fantasy of a self realised in action, Julien makes his way in the world less through deeds than through words, and it is precisely his education in these terms that gives one of the novel's ironic comments on the fact that in the society of the Restoration significant forms of action are no longer available ('ce genre d'éloquence qui a remplacé la rapidité de l'action sous l'empire', p. 138). Most of the advice Julien receives (from Abbé Pirard, Prince Korasoff) centres not so much on what he should do as on what he should say (and not say), while many of his own self-admonitions are reflections on the importance of specifically verbal strategies ('Eh! bon Dieu! pour qui me prend-on, se dit-il, croit-on que je ne comprends pas *ce que parler veut dire?*', p. 175). His conquest of society consists largely in learning to manipulate social codes of speech, in acquiring arts of verbal dissimulation through which an accommodating and acceptable public self can be presented to the world ('Julien s'étant voué à ne jamais dire que des choses qui lui semblaient fausses à lui-même', p. 162). Through a series of studied verbal 'performances', modelled on the socially recognised idioms, he constantly seeks, though sometimes fails, to adjust his visible self to the expectations of others, and, in this way, to forge a secure place for himself in the world.

'Performance' can be taken here in a quite literal sense. Julien's basic relation to the standard discourses of his society is one of *recitation*, parodied in that grotesque recital from memory of long stretches of the Bible which so impresses the Valenod family. The emphasis of Julien's prowess in recital is usually discussed in moral and psychological terms (around the question of the 'hypocrisy' of Julien's conduct). But it can perhaps also be linked emblematically to the more general arguments about society, language and literature sketched in *Racine et Shakespeare*, and in particular to the connection Stendhal makes there between the doxal languages of society and exhausted forms of literary representation: namely, their character as pure repetition. Julien mechanically repeats, or mimes, what is itself already a language of repetition, and the success of the repetition is a condition of the convincingness (the *vraisemblance*) of the public self presented to others. I do not mean to suggest that there is here a conscious device of *mise-en-abyme* at work in the text of *Le Rouge et le Noir*. It is, however, arguable that, in the verbal mechanics of Julien's self-presentation to the social world of the novel, there is an implicit statement about the novel's own relation to the received idioms of narrative representation. That implication is at its strongest in the exchanges that take place in the salon of M. de la Mole. Of the salon conversations the narrator observes, in a rare moment of absolute candour:

Pourvu qu'on ne plaisantât ni de Dieu, ni des prêtres, ni du roi, ni des gens en place, ni des artistes protégés par la cour, ni de tout ce qui est établi; pourvu qu'on ne dît du bien ni de Béranger, ni de Voltaire, ni de Rousseau, ni de tout ce qui se permet un peu de franc-parler; pourvu surtout qu'on ne parlât jamais politique, on pouvait librement raisonner de tout.   (p. 251)

Embodied in figures such as le baron Bâton ('cet homme ne cause pas, il disserte', p. 256) and M. de Fervaques ('ne trouvant que des paroles élégantes au lieu d'idées', p. 294), the discourse of the salon is essentially a ritual discourse; it is composed largely of 'phatic' utterance, and devoted to the preservation of a social order by excluding all those other utterances which might threaten its closed system of meanings. It is the nineteenth-century equivalent of the language of seventeenth-century Versailles denounced as a form of cultural and moral death in *Racine et Shakespeare*. In contrast to the 'living' speech of the proscribed Comte Altamira (or the robust political dialogue between the occupants of the carriage in which Julien travels up to Paris), the salon discourse is a 'dead' language, a moribund code within which no real energy or individuality is possible. It is a language of pure 'pastoral' images, where everyone says what everyone expects to hear, always the 'right thing'. Even in matters of life and death, as in Mathilde's acerbic reflection on the conventions of the duel, the bland surface of discursive homogeneity is never ruffled: 'Tout est su d'avance, même ce que l'on doit dire en tombant' (p. 327). Confronted with the new, on the other hand, it reacts as if before an alien life form with which it simply cannot cope; the discourse turns in on itself, breaks the circuit of communication, retreats into mute resistance: 'si l'on se permet quelque chose de neuf et de vrai, ils sont étonnés, ne savent que répondre' (p. 277).

Nowhere is the grip of orthodoxy more powerful in *Le Rouge et le Noir* than in the conversation of the aristocrats. Conversation here is not simply a way of passing the time. It is a 'sociolecte' operating from a *vraisemblable* of speech, whose purpose is to ensure that all interchange acts as a continuous reproduction of the order of 'reality' consecrated by Opinion. As such, the language of the salon may be said to provide an analogue of one way of construing the task of mimesis: namely, the negative definition we have already encountered, whereby mimesis turns on a relation between the literary *eikos* and the public *doxa*, in which the former repeats and reinforces the versions of reality proposed by the latter. The discourse of the salon enacts a self-perpetuating cycle of repetitions in which all the participants appear, in the words of the text, as 'copies les uns des autres' (p. 355), as derivatives of a 'patron commun' (p. 328) that is itself the copy of another model (the idea of the pre-Revolutionary aristocracy). Reproducing in and through language forms of social interaction that are themselves already reproductions, they generate an unbroken chain of imitations and duplications that corresponds directly to the idea of mimesis as the imitation of a language that is itself an imitation; as, in Barthes's phrase, the 'copy of a copy'.[40]

It is therefore no surprise that the mode in which Julien engages with those discourses is that of 'recitation', his own interventions in them constituting, as it were, a mimesis at a triple remove, a copy of a copy of a copy. For Julien, mastering the speech of the salon is like mastering a 'competence' with zero generative power and total redundancy, with which the speaker simply recycles a fixed stock of learnt phrases and *idées reçues*. This theme is realised above all in the comic episode of Julien's attempted seduction of Madame de Fervaques by means of the collection of stock love letters lent to him by Prince Korasoff. The importance of Madame de Fervaques lies in her status as pure type, pure pastoral, as the character in whose eyes the aristocratic *bienséances* are identified with a natural and immutable order of things; for whom the 'imprévu' and the 'malséant' are synonyms. For Madame de Fervaques, the unexpected not only surprises, it scandalises, not only offends but induces a kind of existential terror; to depart from the norms of 'proper' behaviour is literally to take leave of one's senses, to succumb to an 'ivresse morale' ('Le moindre signe de sensibilité eût été à ses yeux comme une sorte d'*ivresse* morale', p. 403).

What more appropriate occasion, then, for illustrating, and parodying, a system of social relations based on a language of pure repetition? Julien faithfully copies out the text of the letters (which, in yet another image of the 'copy of a copy', have already been copied out from the originals), making only minor emendations at the level of circumstantial details. Madame de Fervaques replies, presumably in her own hand, but in exactly the same style. The exchange is, precisely, like a sustained formal recitation from a known, stereotyped text. So mechanical is the transaction, that inevitably certain discrepancies arise; literally copying out the Prince's letters in the prescribed sequence, Julien does not actually 'reply' to Madame de Fervaques. Yet the gap seems in no way to perturb the great lady: 'Peu à peu on prit la douce habitude d'écrire presque tous les jours. Julien répondait par des copies fidèles des lettres russes, et tel est l'avantage du style emphatique: Madame de Fervaques n'était point étonnée du peu de rapport des réponses avec ses lettres' (p. 416). Indeed at one point Julien's transcription of the letters is so mechanical that, through inadvertence, he forgets to emend the place names London and Richmond to Paris and Saint-Cloud. Madame de Fervaques raises the point, with a slightly puzzled air, but does not pursue it; Julien gives a hopelessly unsatisfactory reply, but, since the reply falls within the convention of the agreed discourse, does not blow his cover. The reason is clear: what matters is not the production of the message, but the reproduction of the code; since the code is 'empty', void of individual substance, discrepancies and inconsistencies which would otherwise betray the insincerity of the message, do not in fact matter; the general message is so strongly presupposed by the code that attention to its actual articulation becomes unnecessary.

Silences

Julien's slip in the correspondence with Madame de Fervaques is nevertheless symptomatic of a more general insecurity with regard to the demands of his various performances. Julien plays the required verbal game, but not in a manner that is uniformly successful. The slips, or interruptions, in the performances are fairly frequent, and what they evoke is a radical interior distance from the public forms of exchange with which he outwardly engages. Julien adopts, but unlike Madame de Fervaques, never internalises the role; Julien merely plays a part, whereas Madame de Fervaques *is* the part. At a critical level, Julien always stands back from the role, and it is one of the main functions of Stendhal's version of the interior monologue to bring out Julien's deeply estranged relation to his own dissimulating manoeuvres. Behind the discourse of the Other and the public self, there is another discourse and another self, at odds with what is being transacted by the socially presented persona. Many of the most important moments of *Le Rouge et le Noir* are built around the troubled co-existence in Julien of public and private. There is, for instance, the occasion of his first social invitation (the Valenod dinner party), at which Julien pursues an inner meditation not only cut off from, but actively opposed to the social patter in which he is outwardly involved. Conversation and monologue run concurrently, but in a relation of total antagonism; Julien 'performs' at the same time as inwardly despising the performance; the contradiction produces the potentially tell-tale sign of pain and protest (the tear induced by Valenod's suppression of the pauper's song in the adjoining debtors' prison); but it is hastily effaced in a violent recall to the required role: 'Julien fut violemment rappelé à son rôle. Ce n'était pas pour rêver et ne rien dire qu'on l'avait invité à diner, et en si bonne compagnie' (p. 140).

The gap between 'rêver' and 'dire', inwardness and speech, and the concomitant notion that to cross that gap is to do 'violence' to the self, is a recurring theme of the novel. In the salon of M. de la Mole there are moments when it cannot be crossed, when the game becomes impossible: 'Souvent il riait de grand cœur de ce qu'on disait dans ce petit groupe; mais il se sentait incapable de rien inventer de semblable' (p. 254). More dramatically still, there is the episode in the library with Mathilde (pp. 419–23), in which the stratagems of seducer's discourse enter into violent conflict with the intensities of concealed feelings. Here the experience of self-estrangement in language is complete, as Julien listens to himself speaking as if he were uttering a foreign tongue ('écoutant le son des vaines paroles que prononçait sa bouche, comme s'il eût fait un bruit étranger'). The whole episode works as a bewilderingly rapid shifting of vocal registers, whereby any sense of a unified speaking voice splinters into a series of heterogeneous and dissociated fragments: the inward voice ('Ah, s'écria-t-il intérieurement') becomes detached from the speaking voice ('Pendant ce temps sa voix disait'); the latter struggles against the force of the former ('les replis les plus intimes de son cœur'), but at a physical and emotional cost that threatens articulation itself ('d'une voix à peine formée', 'sa voix s'affaiblissait toujours'). The co-existence of the two competing voices is thus far from peaceful. Although for the most part of the novel Julien negotiates the contradictions, he lives in a state of acute tension in which the two voices perpetually threaten to clash with each other; the private voice is the object of continued repression and self-censorship ('le son de ma voix me trahirait', p. 424; 'Je puis tout perdre par un seul mot', p. 417); on the other hand, that repressed voice will not cease in its efforts to make itself heard. And, at the vital moments, it is of course the private voice which wins the contest: in the relationship with Louise, in the Besançon seminary, in the tortured affair with Mathilde, in the speech of denunciation to the court – all so many occasions when the pressures of the inward self lead Julien to say exactly the opposite of the 'expected' thing.

Yet perhaps the mode in which Julien most effectively transcends these self-traducing discourses lies less in the usurping of public performance by 'private' language than in the refusal of language as such, in the opting for silence. Criticism has commented extensively on the symbolism of the *prison heureuse* in *Le Rouge et le Noir*, on the paradox of incarceration as liberation, as the moment when Julien abandons the mask to be at one with himself. What has rarely been remarked upon, however, are the implications of that withdrawal for Julien's attitude to language itself. The refusal of the world is also in part a refusal of the word. The leave-taking from society is marked by a silence which provides the novel's own epitaph to the epigraph placed at the head of one of its chapters: 'La parole a été donnée à l'homme pour cacher sa pensée' (p. 136). From his prison cell Julien writes to Mathilde: 'Ne parlez jamais de moi, même à mon fils; le silence est la seule façon de m'honorer . . . je vais dire comme lui [Iago]: *From this time forth I never will speak word*. On ne me verra ni parler ni écrire; vous aurez eu mes dernières paroles comme mes dernières adorations.' (p. 453). That declaration will of course not in fact be Julien's last word. Yet, despite the theatrical quotation, it would be misleading to put this down to being just another instance of the kind of rhetorical bravado that so often intervenes in the relationship with Mathilde. For Julien the prison represents above all a withdrawal from the Other ('Que m'importe *les autres*? Mes relations avec les autres vont être tranchées brusquement', p. 475), a withdrawal from the communicative situation and hence from the language of social exchange. (The exception to this self-appointed exile is Louise, and it is significant that it is in the interchange with her that the 'true' discourse, the language of inwardness, finds its way for almost the first time into a genuine intersubjective encounter: 'je te parle comme je parle à moi-même', p. 442.)

The rule, however, is silence, and necessarily so, since the inner resources discovered by Julien in the prison are not communicable within the public forms which have hitherto mediated his relations with society. But perhaps the most important aspect of Julien's choice of silence concerns not so much our interpretation of the hero, as our interpretation of the position of the narrator and his relation to the given discourses of narrative representation. I have suggested that the deeper meaning of Julien's rebellion against the stereotyped morality and language of his society is the questioning by Stendhal of the order of mimesis and the conventions of *vraisemblance* which sustain that order. That connection is, I think, powerfully reinforced by the convergence of hero and narrator on the question of their respective attitudes to language. The parallel can be constructed on various levels. Both hero and narrator impose upon themselves a principle of self-censorship: the constraints

Julien places on himself are matched, for example, by the self-censoring footnotes through which, in the political passages of the novel, the narrator proclaims his orthodoxy. Both disguise themselves in the clothing of the *doxa*, the narrator donning a self-protective mask before the reader which corresponds to the mask displayed by Julien to the other characters of the novel. For both this produces various kinds of tension and contradiction, and calls into play various strategies for dealing with them.

In this respect, however, there is a major difference between them: whereas the hero is allowed to compensate for his outward social deceptions by means of the freedom of the interior monologue, the perpetually exposed narrator can cope with his duplicitous involvement with the codes of his readers only by displacing it into irony. The ironic reversals and pirouettes of the Stendhalian narrator, the masking of implicit negotiations in explicit affirmations, are already the subject of an extensive critical literature.[41] My point here concerns the way these ironic interventions produce a secret sabotaging of the 'contract' with the reader. That sabotaging gesture is nicely illustrated by returning to the example cited at the beginning of this chapter of the narrator's comment on Mathilde. The overt intention is to make a gesture of reassurance to the reader by endorsing those interpretations of her conduct issuing from a shared system of meanings and values. In these terms, not only is Mathilde 'immoral' (an immorality from which the narrator dissociates himself by disclaiming all 'responsibility' for it), but – a far more decisive gesture of recuperation – she is also 'a-typical': she is an 'exception', purely a creature of the 'imagination' (Janin went further in asserting that she was strictly 'unimaginable'); she is 'imaginée en dehors des habitudes sociales'; she is 'impossible dans notre siècle'; in short, her behaviour is not only unrepresentative, it is inexplicable, *invraisemblable*, except as a psychological aberration, as a moment of 'madness'.

It is, of course, the incongruity of the word 'folie' here (it occurs three times in the passage) that gives the game away. As Shoshana Felman has demonstrated in her remarkable study, the lexical adventures of the word 'folie' take us to the very heart of Stendhal's ironies and ambiguities.[42] 'Folie' is one of the most unstable terms in the constitutively unstable Stendhalian lexicon, the perfect example of a word whose meaning varies from one context to the next, which conjures up and brings into conflict rival systems of connotation in such a way as to play havoc with the *doxa*. Stendhal uses the term in order to show that, as a stable item in the vocabulary of a culture, 'madness' is always defined according to the prevailing norms of 'reason' and 'common sense', as the extreme form through which the consensus deals with what is outside and alien to its system of intelligibility; and that to de-stabilise the term by ironic means is therefore to place great pressure on that system. This is exactly what takes place in the passage about Mathilde, largely by means of the device (later exploited systematically by Flaubert) that Barthes has aptly called 'la citation sans guillemets'.[43] The narrator here does not so much repeat the commonplaces of the culture as self-consciously *quote* from them, thereby at once instituting an ironic distance and a perspective of negation. The underlying meaning of the commentary depends on a recognition of its 'citational' nature, of the way the narrator signals it as belonging to a discourse with which the narrator is by no means necessarily identified. The commentary thus subtly turns against its own source, provokes a reading that, in fundamental ways, reverses the received meanings (a reversal reinforced elsewhere in the novel by the appearance of the word 'folie' in contexts whose associations of contiguity directly challenge the conventional wisdom of society – 'c'était de la folie, de la grandeur d'âme', p. 304). Describing Mathilde's behaviour as a 'mouvement de folie' is not, therefore, the occasion of a negative interpretation. Underlining the fact that she is a-typical, that she acts outside the expectation system of society, and the probability system of the novel, is in no sense a classification of her as 'unnatural'. If anything, it is the contrary; it is the conformity to 'bon sens' that represents the denial of 'nature' (*le naturel*); it is the modelling of one's life on the *doxa*, adaptation of self to the dead forms of the stereotype, that is the mark of inner atrophy and impoverishment. In short, it is precisely the degree to which Stendhal allows his character to be 'mad' in society's terms and *invraisemblable* in the novel's terms, that Mathilde is at her most compelling as a fictional creation. It is at just these points that she becomes the incarnation of the energising force of 'moral courage', in contrast to the 'moral asphyxia' that dominates the salon (although that description of Mathilde has also to be tempered by the extent to which she too is caught in the 'mimetic trap', imitatively basing her desires and actions on heroic images of her sixteenth-century ancestors).

Irony, then, is one of the narrator's means for secretly withdrawing from the contract. The other, and more powerful, is simply silence, where the narrator joins with his hero in a common refusal of available forms of explanation and self-explanation. Stendhal's 'silences' are famous, and subject to varying interpretations. The most common sees them as deriving from Stendhal's innate *pudeur*, his extreme reluctance to expose the most cherished moments of his narrative to the gaze of the hostile Other (as in the example of the three year idyll between Fabrice and Clélia, passed over in a single sentence). The issue, however, may be less one of authorial psychology than one of language and discourse. Leo Bersani has suggested that Stendhal's reticence at key moments of his narrative springs from the hero's profound commitment to a fantasy of withdrawal and regression which is fundamentally incapable of verbal realisation, a condition 'about which, finally, there is very little to say',[44] and which therefore can exist in the text only as that which is missing, which can be evoked only through a perpetual deferral. In other words, its unsayability is a sign of its impossibility, its status as myth and illusion, the untenable dream of a return to an undifferentiated unity of self and world; it is the point at which Stendhal allows himself to be seduced, and hence paralysed, by the Rousseauist myth of a unique, pre-social, pre-linguistic self. Such an interpretation is by no means implausible, and would moreover connect with some of the themes we have seen at work in Stendhal's own reflections on the gap between language and subjectivity. My own claim here, however, would be not so much that the hero's interior distance from the world is, as it were, ontologically unsayable, as that it encounters a difficulty of representation that is social and historical in character; that it resists and exceeds nineteenth-century schemes of *vraisemblance* and intelligibility.

This surely is the sense of the most spectacular instance of Stendhalian silence, the episode of Julien's crime. For Julien's attempted murder of Louise is not an instance of regressive fantasy, but a concrete act, the sudden and unexpected surfacing of the energy and passion hitherto repressed beneath the role-playing performances. It is the moment at which we find him categorically not doing the 'right thing'. It is the triumph of spontaneity over calculation, of the immediacy of action over the mediations of language, through which Julien not only places himself outside society but, far more importantly, outside society's frame of meanings. Of all his unexpected acts, this is the most bewildering. Apart from an official insistence on the 'premeditated' nature of the deed, Julien himself says virtually nothing about it, rejects all invitation to self-explanation. While he remains detached and indifferent, everyone else rushes around in a frenzy of incomprehension; even the abbé de Frilair, that past master of worldly 'rationality', is entirely baffled

('Ce Julien est bien singulier, son action est inexplicable', p. 461). And this incomprehension on the part of the characters was matched by a similar failure of understanding on the part of many of Stendhal's nineteenth-century readers, who, as we have seen, on the whole could make sense of it only by claiming that it made no sense. Faguet, the high priest of the Establishment doctrine of 'realism', the equivalent figure of the official critics of the seventeenth-century Académie, described it as incomprehensible, quite beyond the logic of *vraisemblance*.[45] And Faguet's sense of bewilderment was doubtless accentuated by the fact of the narrator's studious silence. Just as Julien makes no attempt to explain his actions to the people around him, so the narrator makes no attempt to render it intelligible to his readers. The garrulous narrator simply shuts up shop, pulls the carpet from under the feet of the reader, abandons the *doxa* at the very moment it is most needed, for he knows that to make sense of it in these terms would be to betray its meaning.

This silence is, of course, the complete opposite of the silence of the *vraisemblable*. In the most highly developed systems of *vraisemblance*, the norms of the system remain tacit because the writer's confidence in their authority, and in the acceptance of that authority by the reader, is so strong that they do not need to be explicitly named. It is sometimes suggested that this is exactly the case with Stendhal's representation of Julien's crime. Richard Wollheim, for example, commenting on Merleau-Ponty's account of this episode, remarks: 'Merleau-Ponty suggests that much of the tension of Julien's return to Verrières arises from the suppression of the kinds of thoughts or interior detail that we could expect to find in such an account; we get in one page what might have taken up five. If this is so, then it would seem to follow that, for the understanding of this passage, the reader of *Le Rouge et le Noir* needs to come to the book with at any rate some acquaintance with the conventions of the early nineteenth-century novel.'[46] Knowledge of those conventions will not, however, help much in this particular case. Stendhal's silence signifies not the tacit acceptance but the disdainful refusal of given codes of *vraisemblance*.[47] It is not that the meaning of Julien's conduct is so obvious that it does not need to be named, but that, in these terms, it is unnameable, except – within a psychological code – as 'fou' or – within a literary code – as *invraisemblable*. This returns us finally to the ironies and paradoxes surrounding the use of the word 'folie' in Stendhal's text (and, moreover, opens on to some of the questions we will encounter in a much acuter form in the work of Nerval). 'Folie', as the construct of its opposite, the discourse of 'reason', is, by virtue of that very fact, strictly unnameable; it can be named, made intelligible, only through a discourse that comes from the other side of 'madness'. Thus, to maintain a certain silence on these matters is to begin to question the hegemony of that discourse; and thereby to pose questions about the foundations and constraints of representation, verisimilitude.

They are in fact exactly the sorts of questions implicit in Stendhal's own revealing remark about the endlessly problematic relations between narration and autobiography:

J'aurai grand'peine à faire une narration raisonnable de mon amour pour Angela Pietragrua. Comment faire un récit un peu raisonnable de tant de folies? Par où commencer? Comment rendre cela un peu intelligible? . . . En me réduisant aux formes raisonnables, je ferais trop d'injustice à ce que je veux raconter . . . Ma foi je ne puis continuer, le sujet surpasse le disant.[48]

This passage from *La Vie de Henri Brulard* could well stand as definitive witness to those points of stubborn resistance in Stendhal's writings to the given stereotypes of representation: the intimacies of the private self lie beyond the resources of narrative embodiment; 'rationality' cannot cope with what, in its own terms, it names as 'folie'; language fails when it is most needed; the authenticity of desire evades the 'injustices' of public discourse by taking flight into silence. *Le sujet surpasse le disant* . . . This remark, above all, is music to our *avantgardiste* ears, resonating with the distinctive tones of modernism, and in part explains why Stendhal, of all the nineteenth-century novelists, was so regularly exempted from the exhausted tradition of realism by the leading spokesmen of the early twentieth-century avant-garde, from the *Nouvelle Revue Française* to surrealism. Gide – always ready to invoke a model for the urgency of escaping the tyranny of the Model – annexes Stendhal to the libertarian individualism of *disponibilité* and the *acte gratuit*. Bataille includes *Le Rouge et le Noir* in his short list of privileged texts which transgress the 'limit' beyond which lies the fundamental incommunicability of 'experience'.[49] Breton, in a virulent attack on the language of rationality and the notion of representational art, remarks in the *Manifeste du surréalisme* that Stendhal's heroes can be seen as incarnations of active spontaneous life at those moments when the analytical Stendhalian narrator stops talking about them; we refind Stendhal's heroes when

Stendhal loses them ('où nous les retrouvons vraiment, c'est là où Stendhal les a perdus').[50]

Yet perhaps the modernist apotheosis of Stendhal brings with it other kinds of problem. And, before we turn the clock forward to place Stendhal in the century to which he truly belongs, we might pause to consider whether the aesthetics of 'silence' is an adequate response to the dilemmas Stendhal faced; whether, moreover, it does not itself also risk the very fate to which it is in principle opposed. For if 'le sujet surpasse le disant', what, as Bersani intimates, can we possibly *say* about that surpassing? Logically nothing (silence is uninspectable), but in practice a very great deal. The paradoxical outcome of Stendhal's silences has been to spawn critical and interpretative discourse on a large scale; around those gaps the languages of criticism have garrulously swarmed, usually in the mode of uncritical celebration. The value, the subversive force, of Silence has become one of the taken-for-granted stereotypes of our own age. Indeed it was already such in Stendhal's time. It is almost certainly the case that the local intellectual source of Stendhal's worry about language was the theory of Maine de Biran, in particular Biran's insistence on the impossibility of private 'sensations' obtaining passage into the public categories of language. But the idea of the excess of subjectivity over language, the notion of an ineffable 'privateness', deeply resistant to expression, is one of the great *poncifs* of the romantic period as a whole: the romantic subject speaks endlessly of his own incapacity to speak himself, or rather of the incapacity of language to speak him, to express his irreducible 'originality'.

We have seen some of the terms in which Stendhal is caught up in the romantic fictions of uniqueness and originality. But at the same time Stendhal's ironic consciousness of the complexities he faces was in many ways far more sophisticated than that of both many of his romantic contemporaries and his twentieth-century *avant-gardiste* admirers. As Barthes notes, in what was his last publication ('On échoue toujours à parler de ce qu'on aime'),[51] Stendhal repeatedly encounters a blockage in speaking of what is most important to him (his love affairs, Italy, his heroes' 'aberrations'). Yet that blockage assumes not one form (silence), but two: either Stendhal can write nothing, or he writes badly; in the latter case, the inability to speak is a linguistic impotence manifested as a 'fiasco' of style, whose name is nothing other than the platitude.[52] Silence and cliché are thus not in a simple relation of opposition, the one a capitulation to the received discourses, the other their negation.

Silence is the other side of the *idée reçue*, a symptom of the same malaise. The incommunicability of silence and the stupidity of the stereotype are sides of the same coin (in a logic whose paradoxical ramifications we will meet in a more developed form in Flaubert). This is an important realignment of the terms in which Stendhal perceived the predicament of self and language, and carries us well beyond the easy individualism which has uncritically informed so many other accounts. Barthes's argument, however, also takes another, and somewhat surprising, turn. It is not in fact true that 'on échoue toujours à parler de ce qu'on aime'. Stendhal finds a way out of the repetition of the linguistic and stylistic fiasco. The solution comes after much delay, *après-coup*: in the magnificent opening pages of *La Chartreuse de Parme*, or, as Barthes puts it, in the mediation of checked desire by the 'mythical' structures of narrative. The release of subjectivity into language, the literary consummation of the *chasse au bonheur*, occurs in a narrative structure which has a liberating hero (Napoleon) and a corresponding hierarchy of positive and negative terms:

Que faut-il pour faire un mythe? Il faut l'action de deux forces: d'abord un héros, une grande figure libératrice: c'est Bonaparte, qui entre dans Milan, pénètre l'Italie . . . ; ensuite une opposition, une antithèse, un paradigme, en somme, qui met en scène le combat du Bien et du Mal et produit ainsi ce qui manque à l'Album et appartient au livre, à savoir un sens: d'un côté, dans ces premières pages de *La Chartreuse*, l'ennui, la richesse, l'avarice, l'Autriche, la Police, Asciano, Grianta; de l'autre, l'ivresse, l'héroisme, la pauvreté, la République, Fabrice, Milan; et surtout, d'un côté le Père, de l'autre les Femmes.[53]

But this version of Stendhal's escape from the double bind of silence and the stereotype is at once puzzling and unsatisfactory. It is puzzling in that it does not really square with what Barthes has to say about narrative in many of his other writings; it is unsatisfactory, because it returns us, in its own way, to the limiting terms of an aesthetics of individualism. The impasse of desire before the public categories of language, forever waylaid and blocked by the fiasco of the platitude, achieves expression in the 'mythic' structure of narrative – that is, in precisely what elsewhere (notably in *S/Z*) has been exposed as one of the major cultural forms of the platitude (the 'nauseous' simplifications of the narrative stereotype). Narrative myth here, however, assumes a new and more positive function; it has become the occasion of a private therapy, a jubilatory release of otherwise linguistically blocked emotion. Whereas in *Le Rouge et le*

Noir, it is the complicities of narrative in the rejected terms of specific social representations of subjectivity and desire which lead to a breakdown and a retreat (into 'silence'), in *La Chartreuse de Parme* a miraculous fusion and exorcism are performed. This proposed conjunction of narrative *poncif* and the authentic subjectivity of Mr. Myself is odd to a degree. Yet perhaps it is a conjunction that can be used to push the argument in a different direction, and in particular away from the neo-romantic heroisation of Stendhal's 'silences', and also away from the perhaps equally neo-romantic notion of narrative as a kind of private catharsis. *La Chartreuse de Parme* certainly has its mythic structure (precisely of the kind that Barthes himself described in *Mythologies* as the narrative myths flowing from the republican-bonapartist versions of History).[54] But it is also a novel whose power remains unintelligible without reference to its encounter with the public scene of history. It would doubtless be misleading to talk of that encounter as the unproblematical passage of 'real history' into the novel (Napoleon's entry into Italy could be narrativised in a whole number of different, and ideologically determined, ways). But neither does it make much sense to transform the representation of that public scene into a purely private cure. The point about *La Chartreuse de Parme* is that, even as it continues to problematise the relations of 'public' and 'private' (like *Le Rouge et le Noir*, *La Chartreuse de Parme* has its silences), it also, for one brief extraordinary moment, brings the two together. In those opening pages, public event and private feeling are strictly indissociable. We may wish to say that an enabling condition of that connection is the creation of a myth, and certainly sentimental visions of Napoleon exporting the ideals of the French Revolution into Italy require rigorous 'ideological' unpacking. But we should also remember that it was the memory of the historical experience of the Revolution that inspired Stendhal's (short-lived) belief in an art and a language in which personal feelings and collective experience might be brought together (a language 'suitable to the children of the Revolution').

The argument of *Racine et Shakespeare*, it will be recalled, is for an art at once libertarian and modern. But just as the libertarian emphasis is not finally reducible to a code of purely individualist values (it engages a whole politics), so the 'modernist' emphasis does not entail a rejection of mimetic or representational notions of the function of art. What Stendhal rejects is not the idea of representation as such, but outworn forms of representation (the academicist 'imitation of the Model'), in the name of an art that should respond to the challenge of its age. For Stendhal responding to that challenge, holding out the promise of an art that would capture the 'spirit of the age', is directly linked to what he perceived as the dynamic promise of the Revolution. Although not formally systematised as such, *Racine et Shakespeare* proposes a complex representational aesthetic attuned to that dynamic; an idea of art which involves saying both how it is and how it might be, embodying both an actual and a potential within a whole social and historical process. The opening pages of *La Chartreuse de Parme* are a fulfilment, belated and partial, of that promise. We cannot, of course, abstract that beginning from what happens in the rest of the novel, and in particular from that tragic 'fading' effect produced by its strange ending: that rapid narrative despatch of broken lives into their respective 'silences', or indeed the rapid despatch of the narrative itself into its own silence. In the gap between the fluent expansiveness of its opening pages and the abrupt curtailment of its closing pages a profound disillusionment is registered; the novel cannot maintain its promise because the history it represents did not. Yet the initial energy of *La Chartreuse de Parme* may require us to be a little more reticent over proclaiming silence as an artistic *solution* to the problems and contradictions Stendhal encountered in the relations between history, language and narrative. It may in fact give an entirely different context for the meaning of silence: that which Stendhal himself evokes, in the words he puts into the mouth of his Academician adversary in *Racine et Shakespeare*: 'sachons ne répondre que par le silence du mépris à tous ces auteurs Romantiques écrivant pour les exigences d'un siècle révolutionnaire'.[55]

5
NERVAL:
THE MADNESS OF MIMESIS

Chuang Tzu dreamt he was a butterfly and, when he awoke, did not know if he was a man who had dreamt he was a butterfly, or a butterfly who was dreaming he was a man.　　　　Borges and Casares, *Extraordinary Tales*

Romanticism, realism

At first sight it might seem quite inappropriate to associate Nerval's fiction with the project of mimesis or, in the latter's characteristic nineteenth-century incarnation, the enterprise of 'realism' ('Je m'arrête – le métier de réaliste est trop dur à faire').[1] In terms of our ordinary classifications, Nerval belongs more properly to the romantic movement, not just in the superficial sense of his biographical affiliations, but also in the deeper sense of, for example, Hegel's account of the romantic mind as embodying a sustained retreat from the external world into a state of pure inwardness. Nerval's work can be described as primarily an exploration of a troubled 'subjectivity', one of the sources of that experience of trouble being precisely what Hegel diagnosed as the irremediable split, for the modern artist, between self and world, subject and object, desire and action. Indeed the narrator of *Sylvie* explicitly situates himself in terms that directly recall the Hegelian paradigm (and, although it is not a question of adducing here any notion of 'influence', we should remember that Nerval was probably more deeply versed in German romantic philosophy and literature than any other French writer of the period): in the opening pages of *Sylvie* the narrator describes a relation of antagonism between the inward self and the world of practical knowledge and action, a gulf between the 'sphères d'activités possibles' and the 'tour d'ivoire des poètes' (I, p. 266) that is reminiscent of Hegel's famous opposition between the 'poetry of the heart' and the 'opposing prose of circumstances'.[2]

Yet it is just this echo of Hegel that perhaps points the way to the relation of Nerval's *Sylvie* to the problematic of mimesis. For it is part of the significance of Hegel's use of the category 'romantic' that it erodes the standard distinctions of literary history. Thus, his account includes within its frame of reference the novel (the form whose development is routinely associated with the rise of 'realism'), and, more importantly, turns crucially on the general question of 'representation'. Indeed Hegel's notion, in the *Aesthetic Lectures*, of the clash between the 'poetry of the heart' and the 'prose of circumstances' arises in the context of a discussion of the patterns of the modern novel. Modern (i.e. romantic) narrative works from the irreparable loss of that immanent 'totality' unselfconsciously articulated by ancient epic, whereby mind and matter, private and public, 'inside' and 'outside' are welded together in a continuous unity of fully achieved artistic expression. That happy 'in-dwelling' of the spirit in the world, the miraculous coincidence of *Sein* and *Schein*, characteristic of classical art, is what is no longer available to the tormented soul of the romantic artist. For the latter the material world collapses into the degraded notion of material contingency (*Zufälligkeit*), from the shackles of which the ineffable Inwardness (*Innerlichkeit*) of the subject strives to free itself. Self and world divide according to a logic which propels the former towards the radically fugitive and the latter towards the radically fragmented. The outcome is a potential crisis of representation of virtually unmanageable proportions: desperate to bid farewell to the world in the search for its own transcendental essence, romantic art, in so far as it seeks to represent that search, must fatally return to the material forms and conditions whose degraded fragmentariness it would ideally negate. Hegel's impossible paradox is, of course, a purely theoretic construction of the romantic dilemma *in extremis*, and is moreover geared to his own opaque metaphysic of the world-historical itinerary of the *Geist*; as such, it takes very little account of the practical negotiations of this dilemma undertaken by actual romantic artists. But as a general emphasis, as distinct from a detailed description of a working programme, it directs us towards the area in which romantic narrative intersects, problematically, with some of the founding presuppositions of mimesis. For the experience of division which Hegel places at the heart of his diagnosis of the romantic condition disturbs exactly that anchored subject-object relation which, we have already seen in other terms, is posed as tacitly dominating the space of representation, that 'triangular geometry' at the apex of which lies the masterful gaze of the Subject.

In *Sylvie* the problem of the self, of self-knowledge, is inextricably bound to the problem of representation. The difficulty of ordering the self ('mettre de l'ordre dans mes sentiments', p. 293) is simultaneously a difficulty of ordering the world within a securely grounded system of coherence and intelligibility. The major symptoms of that unease in the text are those of a strange, even manic activity of mimesis, but a mimesis which runs counter to its socially sanctioned forms, and which threatens to spiral dangerously out of control. The 'mimesis' produced by *Sylvie* is an internalised one; it is internal to the text, to the mind of its narrator, and takes the form of a series of 'chains' in which part is constantly likened to part within a textual whole, which itself however, *as* whole, suspends all possibility of a direct 'referential' passage to a world beyond the text. *Sylvie* is haunted by the signs of likenesses, resemblances, simulacra, a text which tries to shape the world in terms of those signs, but which is bereft of any stable anchorage point for the multiple reproductive and associative chains along which it travels. The narrative is built around a journey.[3] One way of describing that journey is as a quest for an elusive point of reference, a lost (and unfindable) Referent, at once outside the network of perceived resemblances and, by virtue of that position, the guarantee that they are not merely the insubstantial imaginings of a mind that has lost touch with reality. 'Madness' will indeed be the term with which the natural attitude, the voice of common sense, will recuperate this transgression of consensual codes of recognition, as a failure to draw the line between what is real and what is fiction. But the meaning of 'madness' as construed by consensus is exactly what the text of *Sylvie* will not allow us to take for granted, just as, in the opposite emphasis, it will not allow us simply to invert that meaning. Where 'subject' and 'consensus' part company, where there is departure from the common-place, the site of agreed meanings, there is certainly a problem, and much of the interest of *Sylvie* lies in the way it acknowledges this problem in terms more sophisticated than those of reductive psychological categories. It is in fact the great problem of romantic idealism: the implications and consequences of the divorce of mind and world, the priority accorded to the noumenal over the phenomenal, the disconnection of the individual imagination from the social context of practical knowledge. The psychological and affective drama of *Sylvie* is also an epistemological drama; it operates what we might call an 'epistemological suspension',[4] whereby both the knowing subject and the object of knowledge remain irreducibly uncertain entities. The journey is like a journey undertaken without a reliable map, without

150

the reassuring cartography of consensus; in which the attempted charting of the relations between self and world takes place at an interface of memory, dream and imagination, whose indeterminate contours produce a blurring of the map of the 'real' itself. In short, far from being removed from the question of the economy of mimesis, *Sylvie* engages with it in quite profoundly important ways. Perhaps more than any other French nineteenth-century narrative text, it demonstrates how perplexities and uncertainties in the organising of 'subjectivity' ultimately disturb the efficient function-ing of that economy.

Another way of describing what Hegel saw as the romantic severance of subject and object, and its consequences for the idea of representation, might be in terms of the following equation, 'rep-resentation: desire and its objects'.[5] From that elliptical formula (in-telligible in fact only to those already well versed in psychoanalytical semiotics) can be extrapolated a whole transformation of the classic notion of mimesis. Instead of the stable field of 'model' and 'copy', there is the mobile topology of the desiring substratum of the mind in interaction with an object-world, and it is from that interaction that 'representations' are constructed. Or rather the 'objects' of the desiring imagination's interests are *already* representations, Freud's 'object-representations' behind which . . . lies what? An influential answer to that question is Nothing; instead of presence, absence; instead of plenitude, lack. The 'original' object of desire is/was never there; it is primordially lost, the 'objet primordialement perdu'.[6] Around that inaugural absence, desire circulates, forging its compensatory representations for what it can never know or have; necessarily condemned to incompletion, it operates in, and only in, the mode of substitution.

It is not my intention to rehearse the theory of the Lack, still less to attempt a 'Lacanian' reading of Nerval (since I am not sure what that might mean). What I want to take from this body of thought is, quite simply, the notion that representation is intimately linked to substitution. That notion is, moreover, by no means confined to Lacanian theory and its various offshoots. A more accessible (though less developed) version is to be found, for instance, in Gombrich's 'functional' account of the foundations of represen-tational art in *Meditations on a Hobby-Horse*. Imitation, argues Gombrich, originates less in techniques of 'formal' resemblance than in a strategy of 'functional' replacement of an absent object of desire: the stick can serve as a representation of a horse in so far as it provides, for the imagination of the child, phantasmatic gratification of the desire to ride a horse.[7] Gombrich, in other words, proposes that representation is an activity of substitution, originating in a relation between desire and a lack, in an impulse to forms of satisfaction that are frustrated or unavailable in the real world. There are various problems and deficiencies in this version: the reduction of the substitutive phenomenon to purely biological and psychological factors, with a corresponding neglect of social mediation; the assumption – deeply questioned by the more radical propositions of Lacan – that 'behind' the phantasmatic object there still remains the 'real' object (the founding 'referent'), in all its ontological security. The common emphases, however, are the ones to be retained here: the emphasis on substitution, replacement, on representation as bound to fantasy, as a kind of 'acting out' on a scene of absence, as *theatre*.

The chain, the origin and the primordially lost object

In a text so obsessively concerned with the problem of beginnings ('origins'), it is as well to attend closely to the way it itself begins: 'Je sortais d'un théâtre où tous les soirs je paraissais aux avant-scènes en grande tenue de soupirant' (p. 265). It begins (and, in a significantly circular movement, ends) in a theatre.[8] The initial moment of leaving the theatre ('je sortais') suggests the crossing of a threshold that separates the imaginary from the real ('sortant du théâtre avec l'amère tristesse que laisse un songe évanoui', p. 267), and, as such, could furnish a model for the text as embodying a movement from illusion to truth, from fantasy to recognition of the reality-principle. Such an implication is, however, checked by other elements, both in the opening sentence and in the rest of the chapter. Thus, the phrase 'où tous les soirs je paraissais aux avant-scènes' invokes a pattern of repetition that borders on the compulsive (the 'compulsion to repeat' which, in displaced and substitutive forms, gives one of the main axes of the text). More interesting still is the doubling of the theatrical image in the consciously ironic 'en grande tenue de soupirant'. The hero not only visits a theatre; within it he creates his own private theatre, in which he plays out a role of his own invention. Indifferent to both the auditorium ('indifférent au spectacle de la salle') and the performance on stage ('celui du théâtre ne m'arrêtait guère'), the hero effectively occupies a kind of play-within-a-play in which he is the 'soupirant' to the distant actress, Aurélie: 'Je me sentais vivre en elle et elle vivant pour moi seul' (p. 265).

As we learn in the next chapter, however, this identification is one that takes place, as it were, at a triple remove from the physical person before the hero's eyes. Aurélie is not directly an object of desire. She is less a figure than a figure of speech, a kind of metaphor; more precisely, a metaphorical substitution for the memory of the lost Adrienne (in particular, of the latter's appearance in the mystery play performed in the narrator's youth at Châalis). The imaginary relation between hero and actress is highly mediated, the product of a multi-layered system of images and representations. 'Aurélie', as the 'miroir magique qui me renvoyait son image', becomes the focus of a series of identifications and transferences in which what we ordinarily call the 'real' is out of focus. For in this palimpsest-like structure of reflections and doublings, what represents what, what refers to what, what founds the chain of associations? Not the woman in Aurélie ('vue de près, la femme réelle révoltait notre ingénuité', p. 266), not even the actress (in the sense of the part she is playing on the stage); both are entirely eclipsed by a private phantasm in which Aurélie functions as a substitute-representation for another woman, who herself has earlier appeared to the hero in a play, that is, in the form of an 'image'. The Nervalian theatre places us in a world of pure artifice, a veritable hall of mirrors, where the refraction of images, the relations of illusion and resemblance lack the solidity of a grounded and grounding origin.

The inaugural moment of *Sylvie* thus self-consciously marks the very problem of inauguration that will be its major preoccupation. The motif of the theatre does not behave here as it does, say, in Balzac to articulate the familiar opposition between error and truth (as in the contrast in *Illusions perdues* between the scintillating glitter of the *scène* and the sordid reality of the *coulisses*). The terms that inform the Nervalian version of the theatre are less those of error and truth than the more unsettling ones of presence and absence ('Quelquefois tout était plein, quelquefois tout était vide', p. 265). In the opening paragraph the theatre is described as an 'espace vide'; it is originally a blank space, the site of an original absence, that can be filled by a variety of 'presences' which are, however, but substitutions for something else that can itself never be grasped or named. Aurélie repressents Adrienne, Adrienne represents the world of childhood, childhood represents, or reproduces, the ancient rituals of a distant past, and so on into a movement or spiral of reproduction that is theoretically without end, or without an original founding term. In this turning of presence into absence, we might then say that the theatre is an allegory of the activity of the text itself, as the imaginary scene instituted by a narrator and into which we, as readers, are inserted, to discover that the orderings of reality it attempts are entirely circumscribed by the signs of artifice, behind or beyond which we are lead to an encounter only with a primordial emptiness. The theatre, as a place of substitutions, is thus at once the initial moment (*mise-en-scène*) of the text, and also its emblem (*mise-en-abyme*). The motif will recur throughout (its other incarnations will include the mystery play, the various childhood rituals, the mock-wedding episode with Sylvie); and, through its implicit reference to the work in which it figures, we can say of *Sylvie* that not only do we begin in a theatre, but also that in an important sense we never really leave it.

In immediate context, however, the hero will leave. The departure from Paris to Loisy, triggered by the chance reading of the newspaper announcement of the village archery festival, is the attempt to break out of the cycle of repetitions, the circularity of images reflecting other images, into a purposively organised quest. As, apparently, a movement from the 'artificial' to the 'natural', from derivative substitute to original model, the journey is the occasion of both a return and a resurrection: the physical journey is a return to the place of childhood, invested with the Edenesque connotations of the primal paradise;[9] secondly, the exterior journey is juxtaposed and interwoven with an interior journey through time, as, in the course of the nocturnal cab-ride, the narrator inwardly resurrects the past whose recapture is the object of the present quest ('Pendant que la voiture monte les côtes, recomposons les souvenirs du temps où j'y venais si souvent', p. 272). That imbrication of external and internal, event and memory, the crossing of linear narration with 'palimpsest' narration, supplies the basis for the unusually complex time-scheme of *Sylvie*, as an intricate overlay of memories and memories-within-memories, where each movement 'forwards' in narrative time is also a movement 'backwards' within the structure of recall; in Raymond Jean's striking phrase, the temporality of *Sylvie* is that of 'le temps à reculons'.[10] The details of this temporal design have been described many times, and there is little point in adding to them here. The more general problem to which they give rise turns on an ambiguity which informs the whole text: the recovery this regressive movement seeks to accomplish is exactly what that very movement thwarts, either in the mode of displacement or in the mode of deferral.[11] Within the structure of recollection, each memory is but the trace or catalyst of a further memory, in a descending trajectory from adulthood to adolescence to childhood, and from there into a vast temporal perspective that reaches far beyond the confines of the narrator's personal experience – the eighteenth century, the Renaissance, the Middle Ages, the pagan world of Druid ritual. In that vast opening out, there is in principle no reason why the temporal itinerary of the text should stop. The text assumes the shape of a 'chain', a series of linkages whose terminus (or rather *point de départ*), however, remains elusive, elsewhere, access to which is indefinitely postponed.

The imagery of the Origin and the Chain, like the cognate imagery of the Circle and the Centre (extensively analysed by Georges Poulet in *Les Métamorphoses du cercle*),[12] are ubiquitous features of the Nervalian corpus. At one level, they simply reflect the conventional *topoi* of romantic nostalgia, that fixation on the myth of the happy Beginning, the ceaselessly attempted reappropriation of a magical 'first' moment of harmony and completion prior to the experience of division and separation. Here, for example, is its wildly euphoric incarnation in that visionary re-ordering of space and time on the analogy of the 'chain', *Aurélia*:

Je me promenais le soir plein de sérénité aux rayons de la lune, et, en levant les yeux vers les arbres, il me semblait que les feuilles se roulaient capricieusement de manière à former des images de cavaliers et de dames, portés par des chevaux caparaçonnés. C'étaient pour moi les figures triomphantes des aïeux. Cette pensée me conduisit à celle qu'il y avait une vaste conspiration de tous les êtres animés pour rétablir le monde dans son harmonie première . . . qu'une *chaîne non interrompue* liait autour de la terre les intelligences dévouées à cette communication générale.

(I, pp. 407–7, my italics)

Tout vit, tout agit, tout se correspond; les rayons magnétiques émanés de moi-même ou des autres traversent sans obstacle la *chaîne infinie* des choses créés. (p. 407, my italics)

Comme si les murs de la salle fussent ouverts sur des perspectives infinies, il me semblait voir une *chaîne non interrompue* d'hommes et de femmes, en qui j'étais et qui étaient moi-même; les costumes de tous les peuples et de tous les pays apparaissaient distinctement à la fois, comme si mes facultés d'attention s'étaient multipliées sans se confondre, par un phénomène d'espace analogue à celui du temps qui concentre un siècle d'action dans une minute de rêve. (p. 382, my italics)

The dream of universal contact and communion, of trans-individual and supra-temporal identity recurs throughout *Aurélia*, as one of its major thematic configurations. But it is precisely because it recurs, because the fantasy is insistently *repeated* in different guises, that it remains destined to incompletion and, even in its most euphoric moments, shadowed by anxiety. For the logic of the fantasy is such as to exclude, as missing, unlocatable, its key term: the *origin* of the chain. How is one to assign a terminal or inaugural point to the great chain of being? The chain is, by definition, 'infinie'; the perspectives opened up are 'perspectives infinies', unbounded, unarrestable, caught in a process of infinite regress:

Il me semblait que mes pieds s'enfonçaient dans les couches successives des édifices des différentes âges. Ces fantômes de construction en découvraient toujours d'autres . . . (p. 472)

This, in a less dramatic key, is the vertiginous prospect faced by the narrator of *Sylvie*, in his effort to re-enter the lost paradise associated with the world of childhood. The people, places and rituals of that world form a chain, on which they themselves appear as but surrogate representations of something else beyond and behind them. Take the example of the village festival ('les fêtes naïves de la jeunesse', p. 268). In contrast to the Parisian world of the theatre (place of artifice, fiction), the country festival is posed as the embodiment of authentic, shared and permanent values. It signifies the reproduction of collective forms of experience through history, a 'chain' of continuities through which the past is renewed and revivified in the present. Thus, of the 'fête patronale' described in chapter IV we are told: 'on avait reproduit une image des galantes solemnités d'autrefois' (p. 274); of the archery festival, whose announcement generates the whole narrative, we learn: 'nous ne faisions que répéter d'âge en âge une fête druidique survivant aux monarchies et aux religions nouvelles' (p. 268). Yet the meaning of that link between the personal past of the narrator and an ancient past is ambiguous. On the one hand, it is imbued with strong positive meaning, as a sign of continuity in an otherwise changing world. On the other hand, that connection also implies a disconnection, an unhooking of the temporal chain from the security of a locatable origin. One level of the past (the narrator's remembered childhood) appears not as a fixed point in a tranquil scenario of paradise regained, but as continually collapsing back into other levels, and from there into that *recul infini* (for why stop at the Druids?) whose founding moment can never be satisfactorily retrieved. The *fons et origo* disappears into the *sans fond*, the fathomless *abîme* that terrifies the questing protagonist of 'Le

Christ aux Oliviers'.[13] The journey unfolds as if towards a constantly receding horizon, beyond which the original 'oasis' which memory seeks to grasp proves to be an unseizable 'mirage': 'Au-delà de l'horizon possible, je sens toujours l'éblouissement de ce *mirage* lointain qui flamboie et poudroie dans mon souvenir', writes Nerval, magnificently, in the *Voyage en Orient* (11, p. 437). The image of the 'mirage' is quintessentially Nervalian; it also occurs in *Sylvie*, in the context of another festival, and in connection with that figure on whom supremely the drama of desire, memory, representation converges: Adrienne.

A(d)rien(ne)

Adrienne is at once the most privileged and the most elusive (indeed the most privileged *because* the most elusive) figure in *Sylvie*. She appears on only two occasions (chapters II and VII), both highly fugitive appearances, filtered through the prism of memory, and in connection with one of these occasions there is even some uncertainty as to whether the events in question actually occurred at all. Evanescent and enigmatic, Adrienne nevertheless acts as the main focus of the narrator's anxious quest; it is the memory of her which produces the 'chain' that leads from the Loisy festival to the Paris theatre. Her first appearance in chapter II is preceded and heralded by a number of details that themselves call for comment. The process of recall is initiated by the evocation, in the narrator's half-dreaming mind, of a castle ('Je me représentais un château du temps de Henri IV', p. 269). The castle will in fact prove to be of ambiguous symbolic value, but at this juncture it functions primarily as an emblem of the old Valois world and culture with which the person of Adrienne will be so intimately associated, and at various points in the story will be the metonymic catalyst for further efforts at calling up the memory of Adrienne. Secondly, on the lawn in front of the castle there is the group of young girls singing and dancing: 'Des jeunes filles dansaient en rond sur la pelouse, en chantant de vieux airs transmis par leurs mères, et d'un français si naturellement pur que l'on se sentait bien exister dans ce vieux pays du Valois où, pendant plus de mille ans, a battu le cœur de la France' (p. 269). If Charles Mauron is right in his suggestion that the Nervalian search revolves around the loss of the 'mother',[14] we could not wish for a more condensed and ramified representation of that set of associations than this image of the girls singing the old Valois songs: the

Mother ('transmis par leurs mères'), the Mother-tongue ('un français si naturellement pur'), and the Motherland ('le cœur de la France').

Adrienne thus enters a scene already heavily laden with many of Nerval's most cherished motifs. In more schematic terms, she seems the living incarnation of the two most powerful themes of Nerval's universe: the Circle and the Origin. The narrator finds himself placed with her 'au milieu du cercle' (p. 269), while in her second appearance she wears a halo 'qui nous paraissait bien naturellement un cercle de lumière' (p. 281). More importantly, Adrienne bears the traces of a distant, and revered, past. She is reported to be a descendant of a family linked to the Valois kings ('C'était, nous dit-on, la petite fille d'une famille alliée aux anciens rois de France; le sang des Valois coulait dans ses veines', p. 270). At the first gathering she sings one of the Valois songs ('une de ces romances pleines de mélancolie et d'amour', p. 269); at the second, we see her taking part in an ancient mystery play which 'remontait aux premiers essais lyriques importés en France du temps des Valois. Ce que je vis jouer était comme un mystère des anciens temps' (p. 281). Not surprisingly, the spectacle of Adrienne arouses in the narrator the feeling of effecting a kind of magical re-entry into an original paradise, in one of the most famous, and most beautiful, passages of *Sylvie*:

A mesure qu'elle chantait, l'ombre descendait des grands arbres, et le clair de lune naissant tombait sur elle seule, isolée de notre cercle attentif. Elle se tut, et personne n'osa rompre le silence. La pelouse était couverte de faibles vapeurs condensées, qui déroulaient leurs blancs flocons sur la pointe des herbes. Nous pensions être en paradis. (p. 269)

It has often been remarked that this moment appears as an image of pure stasis in an otherwise frenziedly mobile narrative, like a fixed image that will indeed be forever fixed (fixated) in the imagination of the narrator. As narrative event, however, it is but a moment. The silence is broken, the paradisiac atmosphere dispelled, as Adrienne arises and departs:

Adrienne se leva. Développant sa taille élancée, elle nous fit un salut gracieux, et rentra en courant dans le château . . . Nous ne devions plus la revoir, car le lendemain elle repartit pour un couvent où elle était pensionnaire. (p. 270)

The disruption of the magical setting is both sudden and total. The castle now appears in a quite different light, joining with the convent as a symbol of claustration and seclusion. Adrienne disappears from the scene and disappears from the text, to become a figure, *the* figure of Absence, the permanently missing term around which the imagination of the narrator will be ceaselessly active, but which it can approach only by way of various substitutions or substitute-representations.

This process of substitution around an absent object of desire can be described in rhetorical terms, as a troping activity of the imagination whose major forms are those of metaphor and metonymy. The most striking instance of 'metaphorical' substitution is, of course, through the actress, Aurélie. The relation between the first chapter (where we first meet Aurélie) and the second (where we first meet Adrienne) is at once a relation of antithesis and of resemblance. There is opposition, between the city and the country, present and past, actress and nun, adulthood and childhood. But cutting across these polarities there are also complementarities, echoes, substitutions. The analogy drawn between Aurélie and Adrienne is both detailed (above all in the correspondences between the stage and its lighting and the 'pelouse verte' bathed in moonlight on which Adrienne appears), and made explicit, in the narrator's remark: 'Cet amour vague et sans espoir conçu pour une femme de théâtre . . . avait son germe dans le souvenir d'Adrienne' (p. 270). But as well as substitution by way of metaphorical similarity, there is also displacement by way of metonymy, or contextually associated detail. We first see Adrienne against the background of the castle, from which she emerges on to the 'pelouse verte'. Since these are items connected with Adrienne in a relation of contiguity, in the narrator's mind they can work metonymically to re-activate the memory of Adrienne. Either in the form of mental representations or of actual visits, these places will recur in the story as the means of conjuring up that lost presence: the walk to Châalis with Sylvie ('Je menai Sylvie dans la salle même du château où j'avais entendu chanter Adrienne', p. 289); or the planned visit with Aurélie ('j'avais projeté de conduire Aurélie au château, près d'Orry, sur la même place verte où pour la première fois j'avais vu Adrienne', p. 295).

This is the rhetoric from which the world of *Sylvie* appears to be composed, as a 'chain' of interlocking metaphors and metonymies, the originating term (the founding 'referent') of which is supplied by the dazzling, if transient, perception of Adrienne. Such a description of the text would be in many ways very neat, assigning to it a fixed point against which everything else could be placed and interpreted. But it would also be an interpretative mirage, recalling perhaps the 'mirage' of which the narrator himself speaks ('mirage de la gloire et de la beauté', p. 270). Although it is through Adrienne that we get closest to the Nervalian epiphany of the Origin, to the point where desire, object and representation ideally coincide, there is much else in the text which conspires to undo that consoling myth. For although a source of substitutions, Adrienne herself is also a substitution, caught up in a network of metaphors and metonymies whose ultimate 'source' remains unknown and inaccessible. Adrienne is in fact only presented in the mode of indirection. More important than the person of Adrienne is the *role* of Adrienne. In this respect, it is of capital importance that the two occasions on which we meet her are literally those of performances: the first when she sings the old Valois songs, the second in the mystery play. In that emphasis on performance, we refind the crucial opening motif of the theatre, reappearing in a new guise to trouble the set of meanings that initially attaches to Adrienne. Just as Aurélie plays a part, so the decisive encounter with Adrienne is not with Adrienne in her own person, but as someone else. She too mimes a part, engages in make-believe. She functions herself as 'reproduction', as surrogate reflection of a lost world; as a kind of metaphor, she 'resembles', through the line of descent, the noble families of a distant time and place; by virtue of contiguity, she evokes (as well as being evoked by) the castle and the convent, themselves the metonymic representations of the Valois culture of Church and King. In brief, Adrienne is pure sign or, more accurately, both *signifiant* and *signifié* (metaphorical *signifié* to Aurélie, but metaphorical *signifiant* to the eclipsed Valois forms of life, which themselves in turn contain the traces of prior forms). Adrienne does not so much actualise the point of Origin as operate as the focal point for its indefinite dispersal. She is inscribed within a chain of substitutions and reproductions of which she is not herself the founding moment, but only one (if a somewhat privileged) element in the chain; a chain that corresponds perfectly to what, in another context, Barthes has called the phenomenon of *disoriginated metaphor*: 'J'appelle métaphore inoriginée une chaîne de substitutions dans laquelle on s'obstient de repérer un terme premier, fondateur.'[15]

It is this experience of disorigination in the sequence of substitutions, whereby every point of desire for the narrator (Aurélie, Sylvie, Adrienne, the festivals and rituals of childhood, the places and objects of the Valois countryside) fades into the perspective of an indefinitely receding anteriority, that produces the most astonishing, and disturbing, effects of *Sylvie*. What, at the deepest level, it disturbs is the economy of Representation itself. If, in the classic view of the matter, the adequacy of representation depends on the support of a presumed referent outside and prior to the process of representation, then the force of *Sylvie* consists in removing the certainty of that support. *Sylvie* is densely packed with images of the phenomenon of 'representation', many of which can be seen as analogues of the workings of the text itself. People, places, objects are constantly described by the narrator as representations or reproductions, as if everything in the world existed in order to be compared with some other term. They form a system of resemblances, duplications, correspondences across space and time, life and art, in a manner that suggests a view of the world as conforming to some vast, if mysterious, analogical design. Of Adrienne the narrator remarks: 'elle ressemblait à la Béatrice de Dante qui sourit au poète errant sur la lisière des saintes demeures' (p. 270); of Sylvie that she is 'comme une statue souriante de la Sagesse antique' (p. 293), and that 'j'admirais cette physionomie digne de l'art antique' (p. 274); of the old aunt in the mock wedding episode: 'Cela me fit penser aux fées des Funambules qui cachent, sous leur masque ridé, un visage attrayant qu'elles révèlent au dénoûment' (p. 278); of the site of the Temple de la Philosophie that it is a 'réalisation pittoresque de l'*Anarchisis* et de l'*Émile*' (p. 285); of Ermenonville: 'Ermenonville! pays où fleurissait encore l'idylle antique – traduite une seconde fois d'après Gessner' (p. 296); of the outing at the village festival (the 'fête patronale'): 'La traversée du lac avait été imaginée peut-être pour rappeler le *Voyage à Cythère* de Watteau' (p. 273).

The list of examples could be greatly extended, but it will be noted that those I have given derive principally from the arts, from theatre, literature, sculpture, painting. One might be tempted to construe these allusions and comparisons along the lines of Barthes's account of the operations of the 'cultural code' and its involvement in the creation of the *vraisemblance* of the text (as an appeal to forms of knowledge and representation embodied in the tradition of the Great Works). That, however, would be to misconstrue their significance. The point is rather that *Sylvie* proposes a series of representations whose models are themselves representations, and for which, therefore, prior (but often unspecified) models must exist; a series, that is, subject to a logic at once regressive and recursive (life as art, art as life), and hence giving a system of doublings within which, yet again, it is the question of the 'origin' which reappears as problem, which cannot be located at some determinate point outside the interplay of representations. For if *everything* is 'representation', what happens to the distinction between representing and represented; to the clarity of the relation between 'model' and 'copy'; to the notion of the 'referent' in which that distinction and that relation are classically grounded?

It is here that we can return to the central importance of the figure of Adrienne. The most interesting example in *Sylvie* of representation of one thing in terms of another is the one which concerns the most basic metaphorical transaction of the text, that between Adrienne and Aurélie:

> Cet amour vague et sans espoir conçu pour une femme de théâtre . . . avait son germe dans le souvenir d'Adrienne . . . La ressemblance d'une figure oubliée depuis des années se dessinait désormais avec une netteté singulière; *c'était un crayon estompé par le temps qui se faisait peinture, comme ces vieux croquis de maître admirés dans un musée, dont on retrouve ailleurs l'original éblouissant.* (pp. 270–1, my italics)

This is a complex figurative structure, whose major terms are taken from the representational medium of painting and drawing, and which is built on the principle of a double articulation. A primary metaphorical relation (in the sense of the perceived resemblance between Aurélie and Adrienne) is represented by means of a further metaphor ('crayon'/'peinture'), which is itself further developed through a related simile ('vieux croquis'/'l'original éblouissant'). The interesting property of this sequence is that it constitutes an analogical chain whose origin ('l'original') is itself a participating element of the figurative construction, as distinct from being a reference point outside and controlling the construction. As substitution for Adrienne, Aurélie is compared to a painting; Aurélie is to Adrienne what 'peinture' is to 'crayon', or, more accurately, the drawing becomes painting as, through the mediation of Aurélie, the dimmed memory of Adrienne comes back into sharper focus. But, more important, Adrienne, the model or point of origin for the sequence, is herself contained entirely within the space of metaphor and analogy. Not only is she, in the metaphor, the drawing (a representation) on which the painting is modelled; she is also, in the simile, the original (the 'original éblouissant'), but in the sense of an original canvas or picture, that is, another representation. Indeed the analogical structure is even more complex, in so far as, closely considered, it appears to involve a possible reversal of logical and temporal relations, in which the order of past and present, perception and memory (what comes 'first') is obscured. In the metaphor, the old drawing *becomes* the painting, with an implied forwards movement from the faded to the bright, as the unconsciously deposited image of Adrienne surfaces into consciousness; in the simile, this movement is reversed: the old sketches are preceded by the dazzling original. Thus, quite what refers to what, or to whom, remains logically unclear. What the sequence does is to superimpose one representation on another representation, without, however, locking that structure of superimpositions into something external to the representational process itself; it is a perfect example of 'disoriginated' metaphor. Alternatively, it could be compared to a 'palimpsest', where one layer is inscribed upon another, in exactly the same way that Nerval himself uses the term in another of his stories (*Angélique*) to describe the act of reconstructing the past: 'Les souvenirs d'enfance se ravivent quand on a atteint la moîtié de la vie. – C'est comme un manuscrit palimpseste dont on fait reparaître les lignes par des procédés chimiques' (I, p. 215).

But if the writing of *Sylvie* resembles a palimpsest, it is one where the excavation of the different layers of imagery or inscription does not lead to the disclosure of some founding *Ur*-text. The narrative represents Aurélie, who represents Adrienne, who represents the lost world of the Valois, which in turn represents . . . Its structure is akin to what is sometimes called 'paradigmatic' narrative, a set of repetitions, variations, transformations organised entirely along the 'metaphoric axis'. Or, to change analogies (in the spirit of the constantly changing metaphorical landscape of *Sylvie* itself), reading *Sylvie* is like peeling off the layers of an onion, where there is no centre, no original core to be found.[16] Beneath the palimpsest, as at the heart of the onion, there is nothing, an empty space, the 'espace vide' of the theatre (scene of *représentations* par excellence) with which the story begins. And perhaps therefore it is not necessarily also a 'mirage' if we see the proper name, 'Adrienne' (that most securely 'referential' of terms), decompose anagramatically into the phrase 'A rien'.[17] The narrator's journey thus becomes finally a journey to nowhere, towards this primordial nothingness, which underlies, and from which is born, the chain of representations, the process of substitution and the experience of indefinite postponement of which the narrative consists. From the perspective of 'common sense', the perception of that anagram could, of course, be described as a misperception, an optical illusion, a reader's will-o'-the-wisp, reminiscent of the 'feu follet' to which the narrator alludes

at the beginning of his story, and the pursuit of which is seen as veer-
ing dangerously towards the unhappy condition of derangement ('Il
y a de quoi devenir fou', p. 271). If only we adjust our interpretative
sights to the perspective of common sense, the 'mirage' will simply
disappear, and our reading of *Sylvie* will be restored to the luminous
clarity which the narrator himself, suitably exorcised, offers us.
Except that he doesn't.

Losing one's way or losing one's mind

In the final moment of the story, the narrator returns once more to
that tantalising proper name. In the provincial theatre at
Dammartin where Aurélie is performing, the narrator asks Sylvie if
she sees any resemblance between the former and Adrienne. His
question is met with incredulous and derisive laughter ('Quelle
idée!', p. 297), in exactly the same way that, earlier, Aurélie herself
dismissively mocks the narrator's identification as an empty fixation
(and one moreover which has ethical implications in that it entails a
refusal or an inability to see the reality of others). The common
sense way of seeing thus sees nothing where the narrator sees
everything, it punctures and deflates, denies and censures the very
principle from which the narrator organises his mental life. The
implication, from the common sense point of view, is clear: to perceive the world in terms of an unanchored set of 'resemblances' is to
lose one's bearings, internal and external. Metaphor, disoriginated
or severed from a determinable relation to a referent, can produce
a double disorientation – in the map of reality and in the map of the
mind. The narrator's mind creates a ramified 'order', internally
coherent, but at odds with what passes for reality in other minds
more closely attuned to familiar and rooted models of perception.
Metaphor thus becomes an ambiguous, and potentially treacherous, ally. On the one hand, it governs that achieved poetic pattern-
ing of the text whose celebration is one of the standard commonplaces of Nerval criticism. On the other hand, it is an object of
suspicion and a source of anxiety in so far as its operations do not
appear to be grounded in any secure cognitive structure. If its
systematic deployment is testimony to the unifying power of the
imagination, it simultaneously draws attention to that power as
problem. Metaphor is the point at which desire and imagination
meet in a manner which throws doubt on the capacity of the subject
to produce a properly adequate 'representation' of the world.
'Aimer une religieuse sous la forme d'une actrice . . . Il y a de quoi

devenir fou' (p. 271). I shall return shortly to that famous line, and to some of the mismanagements to which it has given rise. For the moment it directs attention to one of the deepest configurations of *Sylvie*: the nexus of relations which connect, or oppose, metaphor, mimesis and madness.

In many traditional versions, mimesis and metaphor belong to the same conceptual space. 'La métaphore, effet de mimesis . . . ', so runs Derrida's gloss on Aristotle's *Poetics*: 'La définition de la métaphore est à sa place dans la *Poétique* qui s'ouvre comme un traité de la *mimesis*. La *mimesis* ne va pas sans la perception théorique de la ressemblance ou de la similitude, c'est-à-dire de ce qui sera toujours posé comme la condition de la métaphore.'[18] Indeed in some versions (notably in the eighteenth century) we find a concerted attempt to make metaphor the very foundation of the theory of literary imitation.[19] On the other hand, the analysis of metaphor, and of figurative language generally, has nearly always also included an awareness of its potential for exceeding and subverting the framework of the mimetic programme. Metaphor serves mimesis only for so long as it issues from a 'code de substitutions réglées'.[20] Once it escapes that system of checks and controls, once the substitutions and resemblances it proposes fall the other side of a recognised norm of 'propriety', metaphor can readily be seen as disreputable, dangerous or deranged. For, in the making of a metaphor, what motivates the relationship between compared object and comparing term? What validates a metaphoric likeness as true, real or even merely probable? Since, in theory, anything can be compared with anything else, what circumscribes the field of legitimate metaphor, or alternatively what prevents it from spilling over into uncontrolled 'catachresis' (in the negative sense of that term as the 'abuse' or 'perversion' of metaphor)?

In short, for metaphor to serve the cause of mimesis, it requires a licence. The licensing authority, in its traditional form, is Rhetoric. As the formal codification of tropes and figures, Rhetoric seeks to adjudicate and police the boundaries of metaphor, largely through the distinction between the 'proper' and the 'improper'. The abiding problem for the rhetorician, however, concerns the rationality of this distinction. Although at the deepest level the worry about metaphor touches the issue of its epistemological reliability, the final court of appeal in traditional rhetoric is social rather than logical. What is admitted to, or excluded from, the canon of proper metaphor seems to be essentially a matter of custom and consensus, of its relation to a culturally grounded 'system of associated commonplaces'.[21] In other words, the true legislator of metaphorical propriety is the very same institution we have seen to govern the conventions of the literary *eikos* (or *vraisemblance*), namely the *doxa*; a proper metaphorical likeness, however bold and inventive, must stand in some recognisable relation to public, socially consecrated perceptions of likeness. Conversely, private perceptions of likeness which diverge radically from public perceptions, which bypass the circuit of communicative exchange, can then be consigned to the area of 'catachresis', defined as a form of 'abuse' along a spectrum which includes the deviant, the grotesque, the fantastical, the unintelligible, and whose extreme point lies in the identification of unlicensed metaphor with the discourse of madness and delirium, where the subject is deemed to have lost all stable cognitive relationship with the world around him.

This potential coalescence of (unregulated) metaphor and madness has been an implicitly available theme of rhetorical theory since its inception. But it tends to come explicitly and strongly into the foreground at specific historical moments. Foucault has shown, for example, how the displacement of the analogical metaphysics of the Renaissance by the scientific episteme of the classical period brings the unlicensed perception of similitude increasingly within the syndrome of madness: the madman is 'celui qui s'est *aliéné* dans l'*analogie*', who 'n'est le Différent que dans la mesure où il ne connaît pas la Différence; il ne voit partout que ressemblances et signes de la ressemblance' (the key literary text for Foucault in this epistemic transition is *Don Quixote*).[22] The problem becomes even more acute in the romantic period, when, in turn, the hegemony of scientific method comes under pressure. The attitude of the romantic generation towards the institution of rhetoric and established modes of figurative language is notoriously ambivalent.[23] Rhetoric as normative regimentation of discourse is standardly opposed in the name of the values of individuality, spontaneity and originality. Just as the reifying procedures of science must be resisted, so the dead weight of codified metaphor must be overthrown for the autonomous creative self to come fully into its own. But the common emphasis on the constitutive power and sovereign authority of the individual imagination also brings with it once again the problem of limits. On this the romantics often sharply divide. A. W. Schlegel, for example, recognises no limits: 'But, strictly speaking, a metaphor can never be too bold. All things stand in relation to one another, and everything therefore signifies every other thing, each part of the universe mirrors the whole: these are just as much philosophic as poetic truths.'[24] Similarly, Shelley, committed to the view that the task of the artist is to seize 'the before unapprehended relations of things',[25] effectively transforms the negative sense of catachresis into the positive virtue of a continuous production of 'new' meanings from 'old' terms. Metaphoric excess is the royal road of the imagination; and, if that way madness lies, then it is the 'harmonious madness' announced at the end of 'To a Skylark' as the means of access to the higher unity of nature. The underpinning of metaphor will rest less on social agreements as to 'propriety' than on a quasi-mystical theology, whereby the language of 'true' metaphor reveals a divinely ordained design.

Other figures in the period however – supremely, Coleridge in England and, later, Baudelaire in France – will enter considered and considerable reservations with regard to the unregulated figuring activity of the imagination. Both writers, of course, argue for the supremacy of the imagination, and the artist's unique grasp of the hidden analogical structure of the world. But both are equally haunted by the problem of 'delirium', as precisely the dangerous confusion of the metaphoric with the real, the site of those artificial paradises 'où le premier objet venu devient symbole parlant'.[26] For Coleridge and Baudelaire the dilemma is acute. Where an earlier tradition could, by virtue of the authority of Rhetoric, more or less relaxedly take for granted the distinction between 'proper' and 'improper' metaphor, Coleridge and Baudelaire inhabit an historical moment in which an appeal to consensus is no longer possible, or indeed desirable. But, if the conventional writs of the *doxa* no longer automatically run, the ground on which the perceiving subject can confidently distinguish between fantasy and reality, where self ends and other begins, remains necessarily shifting and unstable. The complex meditations of Coleridge and Baudelaire embody a strenuous and scrupulous effort to negotiate this shifting terrain. But, given its terms, it is not surprising that it is permanently hedged by uncertainty and hesitation.

I take this kind of hesitation to be central to *Sylvie*, and if I have entered these brief remarks on romantic attitudes to metaphor and madness, it is because it is important to give a wider context to a question which, on other terms, it is very easy to handle in damagingly reductive ways. The question of 'madness' in *Sylvie* is an exceptionally delicate one. Although, as Proust observed[27] (in his decisive rejection of the received view of *Sylvie* as a piece of whimsical Arcadian nostalgia), madness shadows the text at every point, the word 'fou' appears only twice, and on one of these occasions merely in its weak idiomatic sense. That relative silence effectively withdraws from the reader any invitation to univocal interpretations. It will not do, for example, to make of Nerval the champion of 'madness' (as in the exceptionally foolish comments on Nerval by Breton in the *Manifeste du surréalisme*),[28] the writer for whom the strategy of proliferating resemblances and metaphorical transactions brings the victorious release of the subject from the tyrannical grip of Reason. Nerval was in fact extremely sensitive to the paradoxes of madness and reason ('ce qu'on appelle vulgairement la raison'), and at least one of his remarks, written while in confinement, might be said to pre-empt all the emphases of twentieth-century radical psychoanalysis and anti-psychiatry: 'J'ai peur d'être dans une maison de sages et que les fous soient au dehors' (I, p. 864). But provocative *ad hoc* remarks in the correspondence are not necessarily a reliable guide to a reading of the literary works. The text of *Sylvie* certainly equivocates and destabilises fixed categories, but not, as is sometimes suggested, in the form of a schematic, and ultimately facile, *reversal*.[29]

I shall come back to this (increasingly fashionable) way of seeing *Sylvie*. For the moment it is more important to focus on the inadequacies of the converse, though equally reductive, approach. Perhaps the greatest risk to interpretation of Nerval's work comes from interference, tacit or explicit, by the known facts of Nerval's biography (the record of hallucination, breakdown and confinement). From there it is but a step to a quasi-clinical, diagnostic view of what is at stake: 'madness' as illness or disorder, for which the act of writing is then seen as an attempted 'cure'. 'Aimer une religieuse sous la forme d'une actrice . . . Il y a de quoi devenir fou', remarks the narrator, and then continues: 'c'est un entraînement fatal où l'inconnu vous attire comme un feu follet sur les joncs d'une eau morte . . . Reprenons pied sur le réel' (p. 271). On the 'diagnostic' model, *Sylvie* both endorses and enacts that imperative, casts off the blandishments of the chimerical (the 'fou') to regain a foothold on the 'real'. It is the story of an exorcism and a conquest, in which what Mallarmé was to call the *démon de l'analogie* is finally tamed by the voice of normality and good sense.

To operate this reading successfully, however, one must make a number of assumptions which the actual practice of the text will not comfortably accommodate. In particular, the 'adaptive' reading requires that, within the 'je' of the story, we distinguish categorically between the hero and the narrator (or, in Benveniste's terms, between the 'je' of the *énoncé* and the 'je' of the *énonciation*).

The hero is confused, the victim of neurotic obsession and delusion; the narrator, on the other hand, is lucid, the figure who commands his retrospective view of experience from a position of untrammelled mastery. In these terms, *Sylvie* is the narrative of an education, whereby an initial disturbance (which threatens to play havoc with our customary category-systems) gives way to a finally restored equilibrium; the hero passes from error to truth, incipient madness to recovered sanity, a process at once confirmed and guaranteed by the untroubled clarity of the narrator's retrospective vision. In brief, to the extent that *Sylvie* is a text about madness, it is so reassuringly; if it puts in place initially a 'discours *de* la folie', it is for it to be usurped and domesticated by the serene rationality of a 'discours *sur* la folie'.[30]

To grasp what is seriously amiss in this account we need only turn to the last chapter, the 'Dernier feuillet'. This is generally adduced as conclusive evidence in support of the reading I have just described. It is certainly not difficult to interpret the 'Dernier feuillet' as a form of epilogue, a moment of closure that gives, as narrative, an affirmative answer to the great question of *Aurélia*: 'N'est-il pas possible de dompter cette chimère attrayante et redoutable, d'imposer une règle à ces esprits de nuit qui se jouent de notre raison?' (I, p. 406). It is saturated in images of tranquillity and repose, notably in the reference to Sylvie, her marriage and her children. It is written for the most part in the present tense, with the implication that hero and narrator are now one in a shared recognition of, and submission to, the authority of normality and common sense. Yet beneath that deceptively bland surface there are various signs which undermine that implication. I refer not just to the obviously destabilising effect of the final paragraph which returns us once more to the theatre and resurrects yet again the obsessional memory of Adrienne; nor to the oft-quoted remark by the narrator as he contemplates the picture of domestic harmony represented by Sylvie and her children: 'là était le bonheur peut-être; cependant . . . ' (p. 297). The latter is of course a characteristic piece of Nervalian equivocation: an assertion weakened by the qualifying 'peut-être' and then re-routed by 'cependant' towards an alternative, though unspecified, hypothesis. In what terms we might supply that unwritten sentence remains a necessarily open question (and possibly a futile one, since there is presumably meaning in the fact that, at this juncture, the text withholds meaning). But of the various possibilities – regret at the loss of Sylvie, nostalgia for the chimerical world of the imagination – none would, I think, cause us to query the received view of the narrator as working from a position of unclouded understanding. A residual emotional attachment to 'illusion' is not incompatible with intellectual distance from it; *value* may be problematical (the value of the respective claims of the 'illusory' and the 'real'), but *knowledge* (the cognitive security of our distinctions between the illusory and the real, error and truth, dream and fact, madness and sanity) remains intact.

Where those distinctions, and accordingly the position of the narrator, are truly problematised lies elsewhere in the 'Dernier feuillet', where we least expect it, at those moments when the writing appears at its most self-assured. For instance, the chapter begins with what seems to be a veritable litany of distilled Wisdom:

Telles sont les chimères qui charment et égarent au matin de la vie. J'ai essayé de les fixer sans beaucoup d'ordre, mais bien des cœurs me comprendront. Les illusions tombent l'une apres l'autre, comme les écorces d'un fruit, et le fruit, c'est l'expérience. Sa saveur est amère; elle a pourtant quelque chose d'âcre qui fortifie.   (p. 295)

That reads like an extended pedagogical maxim on the virtues of adult recognition of the reality-principle. These lines are reproduced in virtually every discussion of *Sylvie* as conclusive proof of an acquired poise and maturity. What always goes unremarked is, first, their sheer banality (their source in an entrenched *doxa* of stereotypes) and, second, the fact that the text *knows* this. For the regularity with which these lines are quoted is matched only by the equally regular omission of what immediately follows: 'qu'on me pardonne ce style vieilli' (p. 296). The narrator ironically apologises for his own recourse to the 'style' of the wise and weighty maxim, effectively places it in quotation marks, as belonging to a type of discourse with which he himself is far from being unequivocally aligned. This citational displacement and distancing of received positions we will find elsewhere in Nerval's writings, and most notably around the critical issue of 'reason' and 'madness' ('Or, maintenant, que . . . j'ai recouvré *ce qu'on appelle vulgairement* la raison, raisonnons', 1, p. 173, my italics; 'mes actions, insensées en apparence, étaient soumises à *ce que l'on appelle illusion, selon la raison humaine*', 1, p. 367, my italics). The status of key terms – *chimère, illusion, expérience, raison* – is thus revealed as inherently uncertain. The text which deploys them simultaneously turns back on them, and, in that paradoxical gesture, decisively removes all possibility of a stable discriminating framework for the narrating subject. The narrator of the 'Dernier feuillet' is in fact no more secure than the narrator of the 'Châalis' episode. This, it will be recalled, recounts what is symbolically the richest incident of the whole narrative: the appearance of Adrienne in the medieval mystery play. Heavy with meaning, its credentials as objective narrative are nevertheless drastically compromised when, at the end of the chapter, the narrator comments: 'En me retraçant ces détails, j'en suis à me demander s'ils sont réels ou bien si je les ai rêvés.' (p. 281). We should attend in particular to the disorientating force of that present tense. As Raymond Jean points out,[31] it must be distinguished from the use elsewhere in *Sylvie* of the conventional 'historic' present. This instance of the present is to be taken literally, as referring to the moment and act of narration itself. This is emphatically not a narrator recollecting emotion in tranquillity. It is rather a narrator for whom fundamental categories – dream/reality – have become blurred, for whom what belongs to one order and what to another is fraught with doubt and confusion. The narrative is abruptly deprived of an assured 'referent', its origin – in imagination or in fact? – radically obscured.

And that confusion in the present of narration is also a confusion in the present of reading. As we try to orientate ourselves in the shifting landscape of the text, we find that it plays strange linguistic tricks on us. There is, for example, the case of the view from Dammartin. The village inn at Dammartin is where, in the 'Dernier feuillet', the narrator stays on his visits to see Sylvie and her family. The view from the window of his room is described as follows:

Le matin, quand j'ouvre la fenêtre, encadrée de vigne et de roses, je découvre avec ravissement un horizon vert de dix lieues, où les peupliers s'alignent comme des armées. Quelques villages s'abritent çà et là sous leurs clochers aigus, construits, comme on dit là, en pointes d'ossements. On distingue d'abord Othys, – puis Ève, puis Ver; on distinguerait Ermenonville à travers le bois, s'il avait un clocher – mais dans ce lieu philosophique on a bien négligé l'église.   (p. 296)

Nearly everything here stands in sharp contrast to the terms in which the hero's relation to the Valois countryside has been previously depicted; against the 'pays brumeux', the labyrinth of tracks and forests, we have here the clarity of the sun-lit landscape; instead of the restless movements from one place to the next (a literal displacement of self in search of the unfindable), there is the restful gaze of the contemplative spectator, marking out the visual terrain in a way that might well serve as a paradigm of the commanding subject at the apex of Barthes's 'triangle of Representation'. Above all there is the apparent closing of the gap between place and place name. Much of the tension of *Sylvie* is in the disjunction of place names, invested with large affective meanings, and the reality of places actually encountered ('Othys, Montagny, Loisy, pauvres hameaux voisins, Châalis . . . vous n'avez rien gardé de tout ce passé', p. 296). In these terms, the 'Dernier feuillet' may be said to evacuate the signifier of its imaginary signified and to restore its everyday referential link; the view from Dammartin is the returning of the place name to the 'map' of reality.

Yet, as the eye moves through this passage, it may well halt at, and dwell upon, the names 'Ève' and 'Ver'. At one level they are, of course, simple geographical informants, and their referential status is easily checked by consulting any adequate map of the Ile-de-France region. At the level of their material form as signifiers, however, they are liable to resurrect, in the reader, the very *démon de l'analogie* whose exorcism is supposed to be the major function of the closing chapter. For, as 'Ève' and 'Ver' look at each other across the conjoining 'et', they produce a strange effect of reversed mirror images; the 'miroir magique' of the opening chapter becomes here a textual mirror in which the function of the names as topographical notations is lost in the play of phonemic doublings and inversions. As palindrome, 'Ève' is self-reversing, it mirrors itself in the sense that 'beginning' is end and 'end' is beginning. 'Ve(r)' produces (backwards) the whole of 'Èv(e)'. Moreover, in a highly over-determined way (both anagrammatically and palindromically), 'Ève' and 'Ver' are capable of generating the most ambiguous and charged word of the Nervalian vocabulary: a reader, in a state of reverie, might see here less the terms of a map than the word which denotes for Nerval the area of mergings and fusions, which lifts the barrier of difference and activates the principle of resemblance – *rêve*. Naturally, as with the example of A(d)rien(ne), such interpretative dispositions will bring in their wake the legitimate question: what authorises the reader's perception of these anagrammatic and palindromic combinations (a question exactly analogous to the question – what licenses the writer's perception of metaphorical likenesses?)? Are they 'there', in the text? What does it mean to say that they are, or are not, 'there'? How do we decide, in the terms of Saussure's worry about the anagram, between 'effet de hasard' and 'procédé conscient'?[32] Are they 'intended' by the author, or mere phonetic 'accident', or the 'dream' of a reader's mind going off the semantic rails, exceeding the limits of interpretative 'propriety', losing its way? But the nature of this text is such as to render that question strictly unanswerable. We are just left wondering, caught through our own reading process in constructing a set of 'resemblances' whose relation to what is 'real' is inherently undecidable.

The text here does to us what its landscape earlier does to the hero: it produces an *égarement* (in the double sense of physical and mental disorientation). The Valois countryside of *Sylvie* is a place where signs and perspectives are often literally blurred, where the hero is at risk of losing his way. In chapter V, he wanders from the main road into the forest of Ermenonville and is instantly lost in a maze of unmarked paths ('à droite et à gauche, des lisières de forêts sans routes tracées', p. 275). A similar experience is repeated in chapter IX ('Il me vint l'idée de me distraire par une promenade à Ermenonville . . . Un instant je risquai de me perdre, car les poteaux dont les palettes annoncent diverses routes n'offrent plus, par endroits, que des caractères effacés', p. 285). Absent or illegible signposts give rise to what the hero himself describes to Sylvie as 'mes courses égarées' (p. 276), with the strong implication of inward turmoil as well as external dislocation. For the literal 'unreadability' of the landscape is directly connected with a point of emotional and mental danger: the forest of Ermenonville is the site of the 'couvent de Saint S . . . ', the place of the inaccessible Adrienne, the absent centre around which the whole network of 'resemblances' converges, but on which it can never securely rest. Many critics (and notably Jean-Pierre Richard)[33] have argued that the quality of indistinction characteristic of landscape in *Sylvie* is an externalisation of the hero's inner disarray. What I wish to suggest here is that it also gives the terms for a kind of allegory of both the writing and the reading of the text. Getting lost is an experience that implicates the narrator and the reader as well as the hero. Of a crucial incident in the story, the narrator cannot tell whether what he narrates is dream or reality. Similarly, the reader strays across the boundaries of an apparently ordered landscape into anagrammatic reverie, while remaining deeply uncertain as to whether or not the 'signposts' to that semantic detour are entirely of his own imagining. The reader enters a zone of semantic indeterminacy which corresponds to that feeling of temporal indeterminacy in the unfolding of the narrative, whereby, as Proust again observes, 'on est obligé à tout moment de tourner les pages pour voir où on se trouve'.[34] Losing one's way, and struggling to refind it, is not, therefore, simply the predicament of a 'confused' hero, from which both narrator and reader are safely detached. Enshrouded in the mists and mysteries of the past, the 'géographie magique' of the Valois becomes a vortex drawing the attention of hero, narrator and reader alike, while simultaneously equivocating the perceptions and judgements invested in that attention.

Its essential form is not unlike what Nerval appears to have found in the paintings of his revered Watteau. The landscape and the rituals of the Valois, it will be recalled, are at one point in *Sylvie* explicitly modelled on Watteau's *L'Embarquement pour Cythère*, and it could be argued that Watteau's example is invisibly but actively present elsewhere in the text. This is not, of course, the place to unravel the exact nature of Nerval's interest in Watteau (it would in any case be a difficult undertaking, since the available evidence is somewhat thin and fragmentary). We do know that, as a member of the impasse du Doyenné group, Nerval was directly involved in the rehabilitation of Watteau's reputation in the romantic period. The publications by that group in their journal, *L'Artiste* – culminating in the famous piece by the brothers Goncourt – both assume and promote a distinctive mode of Watteau-writing: the mode of the *reverie*. As a form of art criticism, the reverie has little to tell us either about the technicalities of Watteau's work in particular or painting in general. Moreover in certain milieux (witness the enormous popularity of Watteau amongst the aristocracy of the Faubourg Saint-Germain during the Restoration and the July Monarchy), rhapsodising over Watteau has a highly visible political meaning: the appropriation of Watteau's imagery to accommodate a fantasy of return to the leisured elegance of the *ancien régime*.[35] Yet, as Norman Bryson shows, however uninformative or ideologically misapplied, this type of commentary symptomatically reveals something of major importance about the character of Watteau's paintings, and which it would not be unreasonable to assume that Nerval – perhaps alone in the period – intuitively recognised: the pictures generate the discourse of reverie because they are intrinsically incomplete; they invite – at the same time as they deflect – the effort of the imagination to fill a 'semantic vacuum'.[36] In its most interesting forms, the reverie they produce is quite different from the insipid 'charmantes fantaisies' which so many other nineteenth-century commentators read into the pictures. It is a reverie which disorientates, which raises questions about limits and boundaries, identities and origins. In the 'theatrical' paintings, for example, are the figures actors (in costume but not in performance) or ordinary people (in masquerade)? Are they on-stage or off-stage, just as in Nerval's 'fête patronale' the characters are half inside the 'frame' of Watteau's painting and half outside it ('La traversée du lac avait été imaginée peut-être pour rappeler le *Voyage à Cythère* de Watteau. Nos costumes modernes dérangeaient seuls l'illusion', p. 273)? Is the Watteau landscape inspired by the real landscape of Northern France and Belgium (as Nerval occasionally insists),[37] or is it of strictly painterly, or even literary, origins, analogous to the passing of Nerval's own Valois through the filter of Watteau's paintings? What, here, is 'model' and what is 'copy'; what is 'imitating' what, and where are the grounds of the relations of 'resemblance'? The paradox of the Watteau-Nerval relationship is that the former's pictures give a model for the latter's world, precisely in so far as they problematise the very notion of 'model'. Cultivatedly ambiguous and enigmatic, they open on to a space of indeterminacy within which the spectator's gaze wanders restlessly over the canvas without ever obtaining any secure interpretative or referential foothold. Watteau's world is the world of indefinite contour, of ellipsis and blending; it is a world which the eye cannot confidently 'map', and in which, as in Nerval's Valois, we are liable to lose our way, confronted with questions to which we cannot supply the answers; in Bryson's formula, 'Watteau's form is the *koan* – the question without closure.'[38]

Betwixt and between

The form of the *koan* may well not only figure what Nerval found in the pictures of Watteau, but also clarify why they enter so importantly into the inspiration of *Sylvie*. All the major themes of the latter, and supremely the theme of madness, are 'framed' by the logic of the question without closure. The questions it implicitly poses include the following: what is madness, what is the dividing line between madness and sanity; does madness have its reasons of which Reason knows nothing; or is it but a disabling affliction demanding a cure by way of a re-centering of the subject in the reality-principle? The questions are posed, but the answers are left suspended. This strategy of suspensiveness informs the whole text, to make of it a meeting-place of divergent and competing discourses in which none is allowed to exercise unqualified sway over the others.[39] Its ambiguities deflect all reductive readings, whether as celebration of madness as liberating force or as endorsement of the proprieties of common sense. The voice of common sense is in fact given an ample and serious hearing in *Sylvie*, and only a reading geared to a particular *parti pris* could overlook the strength of its claims. Thus, Aurélie gives the hero's 'metaphorical' transformations of her exceedingly short shrift, and in so doing specifically underlines the ethical dangers of untempered imagination (as extension of self at the cost of obliterating the reality of others): 'Vous ne m'aimez pas! Vous voulez que je vous dise: "La comédienne est la même que la religieuse"; vous cherchez un drame, voilà tout, et le dénoûment vous échappe' (p. 295). Less trenchant, but equally firm, is Sylvie's call to the imperatives of practical living: 'Il faut songer au solide' (p. 290). The difficulty, however, lies in determining the ground of the 'solide'. For what is taken-for-granted within the common sense attitude is, precisely, what the activity of *Sylvie* de-solidifies. Common sense represents one order of knowledge, but the text also brings into play other possible orders, which clash violently with the presuppositions of common sense constructions of reality, as in the narrator's enigmatic remark: 'J'ai mangé du tambour et de la cymbale, comme dit la phrase dénuée de sens apparent des initiés d'Eleusis. Elle signifie sans doute qu'il faut au besoin passer par les bornes du non-sens et de l'absurdité: la raison pour moi, c'était de conquérir et de fixer mon idéal' (p. 294). Yet again the writing shifts ambiguously between the citational, the equivocal and the paradoxical, recasting the notions of 'raison' and 'sens' in terms which the language of common sense could only describe as belonging to the domain of 'non-sens', 'absurdité', and – by implicit extension – 'folie'.

This refusal to take up an unambiguous position, or, more actively, the concerted de-positioning and re-positioning of the terms of a certain vocabulary, and of the narrating subject within that vocabulary, returns us to the wider question of the relation of *Sylvie* to the economy of mimesis. Julia Kristeva has argued that the modes of closure associated with the mimetic project (or the 'classic readable text') can be formally represented in terms of a 'disjunctive' theory of signification, the logic of 'either/or', of the proposition that is decidably true or not true with regard to states of affairs in the world.[40] The suspensiveness and mobility of Nerval's text, its refusal to adjudicate competing claims, mean that it comes down on neither side of the disjunctive opposition. If it can be seen as taking up a 'position' anywhere, it is rather *between* different disjunctive possibilities. *Sylvie* is a work that we might describe as a text of the borderland, which both hesitantly situates itself at, and equivocates, the frontiers and transitions between different categories of thought and experience. Indeed the theme of the transition point is crucial to the structure of the narrative, and is articulated primarily across a number of basic oppositions (past/ present, night/day, sleep/waking). Thus, the inner 'awakening' triggered by reading the newspaper announcement of the archery festival ('Ces mots fort simples réveillèrent en moi toute une nouvelle série d'impressions', p. 268) is immediately followed by a falling asleep. Or rather by a 'demi-somnolence', and it is at this interface of sleeping and waking that the most important image of the narrator's past first appears: the memory (or dream?) of Adrienne ('Plongé dans une demi-somnolence, toute ma jeunesse reparaissait dans mes souvenirs,' p. 268). The same motif of the transition, or mid-point, reappears at the moment of the narrator's arrival at the Loisy festival, as just that uncertain, crepuscular point on the threshold of daybreak: 'Je suis entré au bal de Loisy à cette heure mélancolique et douce où les lumières pâlissent et tremblent aux approches du jour' (p. 282). It is in these intermediate or inter-stitial zones, neither sleep nor waking, night nor day, *betwixt and between*, that the dissolutions operated by the text take place; where the signs with which we delineate our normal constructions of reality and identity are attenuated or effaced. The 'trembling' of the light is also a 'trembling' of categories, a vacillation in the 'codes' of narrative representation, a disturbance of the 'solid' foundations of mimesis.

How the famous five might look when applied to *Sylvie* would require a textual analysis as extensive as that of *S/Z* itself. But most of the remarks in this chapter on *Sylvie* could well be reassembled and classified in terms of a relation to the five major codes described by Barthes as controlling the order of mimesis. That relation is essentially one of resistance or uncertainty. Thus, the *proairetic code* (or logic of actions): the plot of *Sylvie* does not dispose of its elements such that we can readily combine and name them as sequences corresponding to our ordinary notions of the empirical world; instead the wilful scrambling of empirical time bypasses linear codings and chronological expectations in a way that creates doubt not only in the reader's mind as to what happened in what order, but also in the narrator's mind as to what actually happened as such. The *hermeneutic code* (the posing and unravelling of mysteries): *Sylvie* is centred on an unresolved enigma (who or what exactly is Adrienne?); as a quest around an absent figure, it issues not in a discovery but in the permanent deferral of a discovery (the final disclosure of Adrienne's death is less the consummation of the hermeneutic drive, the terminus of Truth, than its suspension; it leaves entirely open critical questions of meaning and knowledge). The *semic code* (the code for the construction of 'realistic' character and atmosphere): the semic energies of the text are paradoxically at their most vivid and intense in just those episodes which have the strange, unreal clarity of the dream (Adrienne bathed in moonlight in chapter II); conversely, markers of everyday reality are nudged by the play of the signifier from factual notation towards oneiric association, from landscape to dreamscape (as in the view from Dammartin). The *cultural code*: artistic and literary references are foregrounded in their status as fabrication and reproduction, as a relation between modelling and modelled in which the 'model' itself is seen as construct, artifice; while the forms of 'gnomic wisdom' (such as the maxim and the proverb) are removed from their naturalised self-evidence, ironised, inverted, placed as quotations. Finally, and above all, the *symbolic code*: the symbolic code works, formally, as a hierarchy of binary oppositions. But when, crucially, the narrator finds himself incapable of deciding whether what he relates is fact or fiction, memory or dream, a primary antithesis is disturbed, and its repercussions are enormous. Antithesis is the basic figure in the symbolic codes we use to order the world. And, as Barthes remarks, to disturb an antithesis (either by redistributing its terms or by raising the barrier of difference which separates those terms) is to disturb nothing less than the economy of the Real itself.[41] The subversive power of *Sylvie* – its subversion of the programme of mimesis – lies in the way it dislocates and confuses the boundary lines which separate the great cultural opposites. The motif of the 'middle-point' does not function here, in the way it does in other literary forms, as mediator, reinforcing a structure of separation and difference, confirming the validity of our customary antithetical orderings of reality. The 'middle' is not so much a fixed point in a stable mental geography as an indeterminate area in which the divisions and distinctions with which we make sense of self and world have become problematical.

Situated at the borderland, *Sylvie* (along with *Aurélia*) is one of the purest nineteenth-century examples we have of what Bataille called the 'limit-text'. Its dynamic consists not in the confident march towards the revelation of a final truth or wisdom, the re-establishment of a happy equilibrium between self and world. Rather its movement is that of a constant metaphorical circling around a notional centre of meaning to which access is forever barred, which is forever deferred across the play of images, representations, superimpositions of which the text consists. The hero's journey is like the attempt to travel down a spiral or to break into a circle. We have already noted the importance attaching to the metaphor of the circle, and its connection with the prestigious theme of the Origin. But, like the motif of the middle point, that of the circle is equally troublesome. Just as the middle is less a point of division than a point where oppositions merge and identities are lost, so the circle is less a figure of completion and centredness (as in conventional romantic mythology) than the space of a perpetually fugitive centre, compulsively sought for, but never found, in a series of displacements, repetitions, substitutions which, in the end, are but 'tant de portes ouvertes sur le néant' (11, p. 1186).

6

FLAUBERT:
THE STUPIDITY OF MIMESIS

Je me sens démesurément stupide . . . Écrire, ne pas écrire. Publier est une
idée reçue.   G. Flaubert, *Correspondance*

I imagined Loulou sitting on the other side of Flaubert's desk and staring
back at him like some taunting reflection from a funfair mirror. No wonder
three weeks of its parodic presence caused irritation. Is the writer much
more than a sophisticated parrot?   J. Barnes, *Flaubert's Parrot*

Quotation and modernity

The narrator of *Flaubert's Parrot*, while amiably disposed towards
the articulacy of parrots, is laceratingly severe with the inept chatter
of Flaubert's critics (pointing out, for example, that when Dr.
Starkie took Flaubert to task for inconsistency in describing the
colour of Emma Bovary's eyes, she must have been reading with her
own eyes half-shut). But, beyond the contingent frailties of
scholarly attention, there is the abiding problem of the intrinsic
bêtise of discourse itself. When we open our mouths to pronounce
on Flaubert, we perforce declare our eligibility for an entry in the
Dictionnaire des idées reçues. Or we all behave like parrots (without
the saving grace of actually being one), religiously intoning our
acquired critical catechisms as if we were bringers of important
news. Indeed, as Shoshana Felman remarks, *perroquet* derives from
Italian *parrocchetto*, from *parroco* meaning a parish priest, a *curé*.[1]
From there, by a perverse yet compelling logic, it is perhaps but a
step to one of Flaubert's most extraordinary narrative *coups*: the
delirium of the 'simple' Félicité's dying moments in which she
hallucinates the parrot Loulou as the Holy Ghost. If the parrot can
image the divine bringer of news and giver of tongues, what chance
of 'originality' can there be for mere mortal utterance? – for
Flaubert's critics, for the narrator of *Flaubert's Parrot*, for Flaubert
himself: 'Is the writer much more than a sophisticated parrot?'
   In the course of this book I have repeated on various occasions

the oft-repeated view that mimesis is basically a matter of repetition; its discourse 'parrots' the *doxa*. The question posed by Flaubert's work is whether there is any way out of the impasse of repetition. One answer which, with increasing regularity, modern criticism has seen Flaubert's work as giving to this question takes a somewhat paradoxical form: Flaubert outwits the *doxa* by 'miming' it, by adopting a form of 'parrotting' as provocative in its implications as the last incarnation of Loulou in *Un Cœur simple*. In Flaubert's text, the inertia of repetition is met and subverted by a counter-strategy of repetition that Barthes describes as the technique of *la citation sans guillemets*.[2] This technique operates deviously, as an ironic montage of 'quotations' in which the fabric of *bêtise* is taken apart while apparently remaining intact. But perhaps the deviousness of the technique is subtler and more paradoxical than even this extremely subtle description implies. It is also important to note that the description itself has not escaped the fate of its adversary. In the body of work largely inspired by Barthes's mainly fragmentary remarks on Flaubert (from *Mythologies* to *Le Plaisir du texte*), it has now established itself as such a familiar point in the critical landscape that, by a strange yet appropriate irony, it risks itself becoming another *idée reçue*, a constitutive element of a new *doxa* of 'Flaubert'.

One of the claims I wish to argue in this chapter is that, in very many respects, we are still only at the threshold of grasping the peculiar tensions and ambiguities generated by this citational mode; and, moreover, that the terms in which a great deal of modern criticism has pursued these matters are not only incomplete, but also potentially misleading. In fact, it may well be that the strategy is destined to remain irreducibly enigmatic, deeply resistant to 'interpretation'. Since it is closely linked to the project of disorientating the reader ('ahurir le lecteur'),[3] it would certainly be presumptuous – a major instance of *bêtise* – for any particular reading of this disconcerting method to assume privileged credentials. If it does so, then it is likely to be caught in a paradoxical net from which it will be quite unable to extricate itself. The paradox in question has an ancient lineage; in its original form, it is Epimenides's Cretan Liar paradox (the Cretan who says 'All Cretans are liars': true or false?; if true, then false).[4] I have already suggested, in my opening chapter, how this paradox can be seen as relevant to general arguments about mimesis, and in particular the ways in which the effort to 'deconstruct' mimesis can find itself haplessly dependent on the categories it rejects. This paradox is inscribed at the very heart of

Flaubert's writing, and, in its detailed workings, one of the things it requires us to think about again is the exact nature of Flaubert's relation to the question of mimesis.

In contemporary approaches to Flaubert this relation has become somewhat obscured. The long process of detaching Flaubert from nineteenth-century doctrines of 'naive' realism (unnecessarily prolonged since we were earnestly pressed to do so by Flaubert himself) has resulted in an *avantgardiste* version of Flaubert, in whose novels we hear the death-knell of mimetic conceptions of narrative. Flaubert, in retrospect, is now seen as one of the first exemplars of the Modern. According to Nathalie Sarraute, Flaubert 'est le précurseur du roman moderne';[5] and Jean Rousset makes the alignment more precise in describing Flaubert as 'le premier en date des *non-figuratifs* du roman moderne'.[6] Rolling back the historical frontiers of the 'modern' has become, as Samuel Weber observes,[7] a game with exceptionally flexible and even arbitrary rules. Why fix the frontier at Flaubert? Do not the preceding chapters of this book themselves imply that, from certain versions of the 'modern', Balzac, Stendhal and Nerval might also qualify? But, if that is so, then the 'modern' as a term of *historical* location, begins to lose all intellectual credibility; if it cannot serve moderately precise historical argument (if, the further we go back in the past, the more we find the 'modern'), there seems little point to the term in the first place.

But conducting battles with what seems a straw literary history is not really the issue. What matters, in this assimilation of Flaubert to the 'modern', is the view of his art as resolutely 'non-figurative', or indeed as actively anti-figurative in the sense of injecting into the fictions a powerfully corrosive dissolvent of any attempt to read them according to representational or mimetic expectations. The Copy, or the Simulacrum, is often inserted into Flaubert's novels as a caricature or ironic *mise-en-abyme* of the absurdity (the 'stupidity') of the mimetic enterprise: in *Madame Bovary*, Emma's grotesque wedding cake, Monsieur Binet's lathe endlessly replicating copies of copies, things that are no-things;[8] in *L'Éducation sentimentale*, Pellerin, the 'idealist' painter who ends up as the artist of mechanical reproduction, the professional photographer; the manic copying of the two clerks projected as the ending of *Bouvard et Pécuchet*. The Copy is the emblem of spiritual and artistic death, and its incorporation into Flaubert's text is presumably intended as an indirect warning that to read his own novels as 'copies' is to skirt a similar death.

The reproduction of the *idée reçue*, or the cliché, invites a similar interpretation. The *idée reçue* is the site of the entombment of language, the symptom of a dead culture (a culture of mindless 'copying'); and hence to 'quote' it is to operate a kind of autopsy, to insert the knife of irony into a death-in-life, 'dissecting' (one of Flaubert's favourite metaphors) the corpus of commonplaces in order to bring us to greater consciousness of both the limits and the possibilities of language. Yet, as the incisions are made, the hand falters. For what authorises the doctor-novelist's diagnosis and operation? Where is the 'living' language in the name of which the ironic incisions into the dead language are justified; what are the conditions of linguistic 'health'? The problem, although by no means confined to the period, is one of the great historical problems of the nineteenth century. For, as Amossy and Rosen point out, in *Les Discours du cliché*, the notion of 'cliché' is rooted in the etymology which connects it with modern printing processes.[9] The figurative sense of cliché is not active before the era and the technologies of mass reproduction, and it characteristically emerges in the context of the romantic opposition between banality and originality, public and private, along with the corresponding desire for a uniquely 'individual' language within, or beyond, the terms of public and social discourse.

In previous chapters I have alluded to the nature of this predicament. As we have seen, both Stendhal and Nerval use quasi-citational methods to place themselves at an ironic distance from what are perceived as cliché-laden vocabularies and discursive forms. Both, moreover, by temperament and artistic ideology, are wedded to the romantic ideal of 'originality', Stendhal in the mode of iconoclastic individualism, Nerval in the mode of poetic reverie. But in the pursuit of that chimerical ideal, both encounter, in different ways, major blockages and crises: Stendhal's resistance to cliché drives him towards the (non-)solution of silence, Nerval's towards the *abîme* of 'madness'. It is sometimes said that Flaubert embraces, or rather adapts, both these consequences to forge the terms of his own response to the problem of the literary and linguistic commonplace: the 'silences de Flaubert', argues Genette, contest the commonplaceness of the 'fonction narrative, jusqu'alors essentielle au roman';[10] while according to Shoshana Felman, Flaubert liberates himself from the tyranny of the *lieu commun* by way of a paroxysmic 'intoxication' in which the sheer reiteration and accumulation of cliché engenders its transformation into a special kind of 'madness' ('la folie du cliché'); the 'modernity' of Flaubert lies in his undoing of the cliché through a process of systematic exacerbation, whereby it finally becomes its opposite, a form of literary *délire*.[11]

On their respective assumptions, both these arguments are powerful, and take us well beyond the terms in which the topic is ordinarily discussed. But the assumptions are restrictive by virtue of the general *parti pris* they embody, the prior decision that the perspective in which to read Flaubert is that of *modernité*. However elusive Flaubert's writing proves, it remains, in this view, unshakeably 'modern' in its basic commitments. And whatever the unstable meanings which attend the term (Felman is exceptionally alert to these instabilities), 'modernité' retains at least one stable feature: its outright rejection of the aesthetics of mimesis; in Felman's words, Flaubert's writing is 'modern' in so far as it 'décompose . . . l'idéologie de la représentation mimétique'.[12] But in this character-isation of Flaubert, much depends on what is understood by 'ideology'. If it is taken as meaning the unexamined assumption whereby the language of mimesis taken-for-grantedly proposes itself as situated beyond convention and constraint, as giving an unmediated picture of the Truth of the world, then Flaubert's work is indeed correctly seen as a work of 'decomposition' on the ossified forms of representation buttressed by that ideology. From the intimate sphere of private relationships to the public stage of history and politics, 'mediation' – the mediated nature of our desires and actions – is the continuing theme of Flaubert's novels. Nothing in these texts is allowed a space that is not made relative to a mediating framework, or to what Flaubert himself called 'une manière de voir' ('Il n'y a pas de Vrai, il n'y a que des manières de voir', VIII, p. 370). On the other hand, if by 'ideology' is simply meant the notion of 'representation' itself, we are brought face to face with the difficult paradox which the modernist appropriation of Flaubert so often side-steps: the sense of the relativity of representations requires a representation of relativity, a form – a 'perspective' – within which the multiplicity of partial and shifting perspectives can be juxta-posed and combined. In decomposing the discourses it 'quotes', the writing has to compose, to put its quotations into its own structure of intelligibility and coherence. But then does not that requirement entail an even deeper incoherence, sending the mind into an uncon-trollable epistemological spin? How Flaubert tries to negotiate this vertiginous paradox is the main theme of this chapter. In my con-cluding chapter I shall also maintain that it has wider implications for many of the arguments and positions concerning mimesis described in this book as a whole.

Let us, however, stay provisionally within the terms of the new orthodoxies. On this view, the ceaseless miming of the *idée reçue* (not only in the direct or reported speech of the characters, but more pervasively, and more disconcertingly, in the whole texture of the narrative) marks the point at which Flaubert's novels engage critically with the nineteenth-century *doxa*. Or in Flaubert's own terms, the strategy of quotation represents a way of insinuating a criticism of the forms and effects of *bêtise*. The definitions and descriptions of the Flaubertian notion of *bêtise* are, of course, legion, and there is no need to rehearse these here in any detail.[13] Essentially, *bêtise* is Flaubert's shorthand for defining what he sees as the basic relation between language and society, and the location of the individual subject (including, though in problematic ways, the artistic subject) within that relation. It is the name given to that routinised language which seeks to confer on what passes for 'knowledge' in society the aura of Knowledge *tout court*. It is the source of the stereotypes through which a society furnishes itself with a stable economy of meaning. Or, to recall the definition given by Barthes's *Mythologies* (where, it will be recalled, *Bouvard et Pécuchet* occupies a very special place), *bêtise* corresponds to the processes whereby cultural meanings are converted into natural or self-evident ones; it is 'culture made nature'.

In these terms, and as Barthes suggests, quotation in Flaubert represents a way of taking up a critical position against *bêtise* from within the structure of *bêtise* itself; quotation is the instrument of a peculiarly oblique mode of self-conscious irony. By assiduously transcribing the discourse of *bêtise*, Flaubert transforms it into the object of an impassive yet unmistakably ironic scrutiny. Although for the most part formally unmarked ('sans guillemets'), the citations are none the less instantly recognisable as such, and it is largely in and through such recognitions that the realisation of Flaubert's ironic project is guaranteed. The text foregrounds what is normally backgrounded in the surrounding linguistic culture. As Sartre argues,[14] it signals the radical 'alterity' of the discourse it reproduces. It 'makes strange', defamiliarises what in practical life is taken for granted, divests the language of everyday exchange of its innocence by a kind of ironic petrification of that language (whence, perhaps, one of the meanings of what Proust saw as the 'monotony' of Flaubert's style). Flaubert's novels are thus organised as a huge, mobile network of citations drawn from a diffuse corpus of other texts, but which, as they enter the space of the Flaubert text, are ironically displayed as, precisely, citations, or, at a further self-reflexive move, as instances of the activity of Quotation itself. They constitute a series of discursive fragments deliberately placed on exhibition as the alien, often exotic specimens of that doxographic science announted in the *Dictionnaire des idées reçues*, but of which the true archives are furnished by the novels themselves.

The stupidity of beginnings

From the perspective of *bêtise* we can read the adventures of Flaubert's heroes and heroines as a tragi-comic adventure of language. The journey they make is primarily a textual journey through the 'doxal' mausoleum of the nineteenth century, whose exhibits include the discourses of Art, Love, Science, Progress and Revolution. The world they both discover and construct for themselves is a world made of quotations; in the heading given by Flaubert to one of the projected sections of *Bouvard et Pécuchet*, it is a world made by 'des citations empruntées à toute espèce de littérature'[15] (understanding 'littérature' here in the broad sense of the discourses issuing from the 'innumerable centres of culture').[16] Yet pre-eminent amongst these multiple discourses, and of immediate implication for Flaubert's own position as a writer, is the discourse of the Novel itself. Flaubert, so it is argued, is one of the first to understand, and to live the consequences of that understanding, what in the twentieth century has become (paradoxically enough) commonplace: that the novel embodies a whole social way of seeing; and that the insertion of the novel into the circuit of communication forming the 'natural attitude' of society is one of the major facts of modern cultural history. This proposition rests on the argument that in the course of the nineteenth century the novel rapidly becomes the Novel, a literary institution congealing into a fixed system of conventions and expectations which, by virtue of their special mimetic claims, are actively involved in both reproducing and reinforcing standardised ways of seeing the world. In brief, through its progressive absorption into the forms of 'doxal' knowledge, the Novel becomes a capital manifestation of *bêtise*.

As such it presents itself to Flaubert as a highly eligible candidate for 'citational' treatment. Or, more accurately, since it is the form Flaubert himself is using, it provides the ideal ground not only for illustrating Flaubert's citational method, but also for grasping some of its more ambiguous aspects. The 'modernist' view, as we have seen, has it that Flaubert employs the medium in order to undermine the mimetic claims of the Novel; that he deconstructs mimesis by ironically 'miming' (quoting) mimetic procedures in such a way that they fall apart or are dissolved back into the social knowledge from which they derive and which they serve to legitimate. As examples of this obliquely deconstructive enterprise, we could begin by considering the question of 'beginnings', by looking at two roughly parallel sentences from the two versions of *L'Éducation sentimentale*. The first is the opening sentence from the *Éducation sentimentale* of 1845: 'Le héros de ce livre, un matin d'octobre, arriva à Paris avec un cœur de dix-huit ans et un diplôme de bachelier ès lettres.'[17] The second sentence comes from the first page of the definitive *Éducation* of 1869: 'Un jeune homme de dix-huit ans, à longs cheveux et qui tenait un album sous les bras, restait auprès d'un gouvernail, immobile.'[18] It is probably reasonable to say that most readers will experience these sentences with a strong sense of 'déjà-vu' or, in Barthes's term, of the 'déjà-lu'. If we come to them armed with a foreknowledge of the nineteenth-century narrative tradition, they send out all sorts of recognition signals. In the case of the first sentence, the verb 'arriva' not only speaks of a literal arrival, but evokes the moral and social theme of 'arrivisme', reinforced by the destination 'Paris', the great Mecca of the novels of Stendhal and Balzac; 'un cœur de dix-huit ans' connotes innocence, naivety and the imminent testing of illusions against reality (recalling Balzac's archetypal title, *Illusions perdues*); 'un diplôme de bachelier ès lettres' suggests perhaps the model of the struggling student (Rastignac) or, as professional qualification, the themes of ambition and advancement. In short, the sentence organises a network of connotations that points unmistakeably to the way the text inscribed itself within a familiar narrative code: what Lionel Trilling has called the novel of the young-man-up-from-the-provinces,[19] that convention which pervades the nineteenth-century European novel, and which is generalised elsewhere by Lukács under the heading of the Novel of Apprenticeship.[20]

It is, however, much more than simply a repeat performance of that convention, and to read it exclusively in this way would be to miss another level of connotation, at which one can detect a strong element of self-reflexive irony. For beneath the apparent innocence and simplicity of the sentence there is a certain oddness and ambiguity. For example, the conjunction 'un cœur de dix-huit ans' and 'un diplôme de bachelier ès lettres' may strike us as slightly incongruous; the prosaic quality of the latter sits uneasily with the more elevated quality of the former, and thus hints at its possible status as stereotype, sentimental cliché; the expression 'le héros de ce livre' directly signals the bookishness of the book; the phrase 'un matin d'octobre' probably denotes the beginning of the academic year, but also contains an element of temporal indeterminacy which displays a certain indifference to the very precise temporal specifications characteristic of earlier novels written within this convention. In other words, the sentence produces connotations of a sort that institute an ironic distance from the very code within which the text ostensibly situates itself. They furnish the points at which the convention self-consciously identifies itself as convention, directs attention to its specifically literary origins. As such there is an important sense in which we can read the sentence as a kind of quotation, as a generalised quotation that at once refers back to, summarises and ironises, under the sign of *bêtise*, an inherited body of narrative texts. More specifically, since it is the opening sentence of the novel, one could say that it is less a beginning than a quotation from a code of Beginnings, a condensed and ironic paradigm of the way novels typically (or stereotypically) set about representing the manner in which young men negotiate the social world.

This citational quality of the writing comes across even more powerfully in our second sentence, indeed right down to its tiniest details (the comma separating 'gouvernail' and 'immobile' is already a warning sign of a type I shall return to later). In this sentence Frédéric Moreau initially appears before our eyes as if transplanted from a book, or as a composite stereotype fashioned from a series of books: 'dix-huit ans' repeats the opening sentence of the earlier version: 'longs cheveux' connotes the 'romantic' style; 'restait auprès du gouvernail, immobile' evokes the pose of Contemplation (the overarching model here being possibly Chateaubriand, who is to Frédéric roughly what Balzac is to Deslauriers). But perhaps the most interesting element of the sentence, or at least the one that lends itself to a rather more complex form of analysis, is the phrase 'tenait un album sous les bras'. It is, of course, easily read as pure denotation, introducing a fact about the immediate situation of the hero which has no significance beyond its pure presence as 'fact'. It corresponds to what we have previously seen Barthes describe as one of the primary functions of mimetic writing: the creation of the 'effet de réel', or what Georges Blin has termed the 'détail significativement non-significatif',[21] the detail which stands for the Real *tout court*. This apparent innocence is, however, quite deceptive. If it has been noted, it is because it is 'notable', and if it is notable, it is precisely because it possesses a secondary semantic function at the level of connotation, or rather at various levels of connotation. For example, 'tenir un album' connotes the idea that Frédéric is interested in drawing because it is the done thing; it is, within the system of received ideas, a sign of the young man of taste and sensibility; it proposes a cultural model, possibly diffused throughout middle-class society at large, but whose major source is undoubtedly literary and novelistic. In other words, it is once again an example of a citational discourse, an index of the way Flaubert's representation of his hero is ironically modelled on the clichés and platitudes that form the inherited 'romantic' *doxa*. In sum, the first sentence works from a model derived chiefly from Balzac, essentially a model of engagement and action in the social world. The second sentence works from a model derived from the romantics, essentially a model of inwardness and sensibility. Together they ironically resume two of the main strands of the combined narrative tradition whose combined 'doxal' weight it is one of Flaubert's purposes to overturn.

The ostensible target of this irony is, of course, the hero himself, and, by implication, the reader (or rather a certain kind of reader). The citations evoke an imaginary order of reference for the hero's projects and expectations that will be cruelly outplayed and undone by the derisory order of 'reality'. The reader is potentially implicated in so far as he shares the expectations of the hero. Or, more accurately, the sentences play ambiguously on different levels of readerly 'recognition'. A 'naive' reader will (mis-)recognise, and possibly identify with, a literary stereotype; his attitude to the hero will parallel the hero's attitude to his own literary models, and will thus be caught in the same trap of taking a purely textual construction for reality. A 'clever' reader, on the other hand, will recognise the models *as* stereotypes, take the requisite distance from them, and so join the narrator in his privileged position of ironic detachment. Yet these convenient distinctions are too convenient by half, and leave entirely on one side a question of capital importance. For the ironic interpretation takes for granted what is deeply problematic, namely the relation of Flaubert's own narrative discourse to the citational mode it employs. We can say that the two sentences are concealed quotations, an instance of free indirect discourse in which what is cited, metonymically and ironically, is a whole narrative genre. But the question then arises as to whether Flaubert's novels are themselves members of the genre whose conventions they ironically stage. The general implications of that question are somewhat startling, and have been provocatively formulated by

Derrida in 'Living On: Border Lines':

What are we doing when, to practise a 'genre', we quote a genre, represent it, stage it, expose its *generic law*, analyse it practically? Are we still practising the genre? Does the 'work' still belong to the genre it re-cites? But inversely, how could we make a genre work without referring to it (quasi-) quotationally, indicating at some point 'See, this is a work of such-and-such a genre'? Such an indication does not belong to the genre, and makes the statement of belonging an ironical exercise. It interrupts the very belonging of which it is a necessary condition. I must abandon this question for the moment; it's capable of disrupting more than one system of poetics, more than one literary pact.[22]

It is a pity that Derrida is here in such a hurry, for, although there is of course only so much that can be said within a given 'frame', what is condensed into this impromptu aside merits extended analysis. His remarks are yet another dazzling example of the deconstructive turn, transgressing the disjunctive logic of either/or, insisting that something is what it isn't and isn't what it is, belongs and yet does not belong to a class of which it is/is not a member. They do, however, capture the essential ambiguity in the act of self-reflexive quotation. For reasons to do with his own interests Derrida prefers to stress the aspect of 'ironical exercise', the interruptive and disruptive effects on 'belonging' which indirect citation creates. But the question remains: 'does the "work" still belong to the genre it re-cites?', and one possible answer to that question pushes the argument in a quite different direction. We have become accustomed to associating free indirect discourse with the desire of the reporting discourse to dissociate itself from what it reports. This, however (unlike the phenomenon of free indirect discourse itself), is a relatively late development, linked to the emergence of the modern ironic literary consciousness. But, as Lyotard reminds us, in its 'original' manifestations, the free indirect reporting of somebody else's speech in narrative acts more as a sign of solidarity between the reporting and the reported discourses; it is a marker of a continuity, a common 'belonging' to a shared world of language and knowledge.[23]

I do not of course mean that, from these considerations, we should proceed to evacuate Flaubert's citational technique of all ironic connotations. It does mean, however, that we can return to the problem of quotation in an enlarged and more complex context. We could, for example, reverse – indeed it is the very reversibility of Flaubert's writing that is the source of many of its deepest ambiguities – an earlier statement about the opening sentence of the first *Éducation sentimentale*. It is not just an ironic reference to a paradigm of narrative Beginnings; it is itself a beginning, it 'belongs' to a narrative repertoire. In a quite straightforward way, it is a functional component of the novel before us, not just a reflection on how novels are typically inaugurated, but itself inaugurating the space of the narrative we are about to read. Thus, if Beginnings are stereotyped, examples of *bêtise*, if the desire to begin is as stupid as the desire to conclude ('la bêtise consiste à vouloir conclure', II, p. 239), how are we to respond to the fact that Flaubert's own novels must themselves necessarily begin (and end)? Another way of putting this would be to remark on the extent to which the ironic effect of that opening sentence depends on Flaubert's use of the rhetorical figure of zeugma ('un cœur de dix-huit ans et un diplôme de bachelier ès lettres'). Once again we encounter a nice paradox: a traditional narrative beginning is ironised by means of an even more traditional figure of speech. On what legitimate grounds, therefore, can we distinguish hierarchically between the instrument and the object of ironic attack? Is the figure of speech accorded neutral status because of its instrumental function, or does the ironic self-consciousness of the text extend to the figure as well, as metonymic representation of the tired institution of Rhetoric; but, in that case, what is the status of the figure of metonymy?

This infuriatingly recessive or circular logic (the delight of Derrideans) brings us to the heart of Flaubert's predicament. In very general terms that predicament can be formulated in the following way: if having citational recourse to bookish models in the construction of versions of the world is to be inescapably ensnared in the net of *bêtise*, then what are we to make of the book itself which advances such a claim? Is it simply that a certain *class* of books is complicit in stupidity, or a certain way of reading books (one of the possible implications of *Madame Bovary*), from which other books (such as Flaubert's) are exempt, secure in the possession of their own ironic knowledge and self-consciousness? Alternatively, and more radically, is it the case that *all* books, all texts, all orders of discourse are fatally contaminated by *bêtise* (one of the possible implications of the multiple scenarios for the second volume of *Bouvard et Pécuchet*)? Recast in the form of a (rather deceptive) syllogism, the latter alternative produces the following, somewhat disconcerting, propositions: recourse to books is stupid; the source of this claim is a book; it is therefore stupid; therefore the claim that all books are stupid is itself stupid (applied to the *Dictionnaire des idées reçues*, for example, this line of reasoning would compel us to reflect on the 'sottise' of compiling a 'sottisier'). It will be seen that we are entering the dizzying regress and insane proliferations of the Cretan Liar paradox. Applied to Flaubert, this paradox produces a series of extremely awkward questions. Does the text, which shows us characters compulsively quoting, itself 'quote'? Is the claim that people always quote in trying to make sense of their lives itself a quotation (from, for example, a *doxa* of Cynicism), and therefore also open to critical 'deconstruction'? Is the text which seeks to display idiots itself idiotic by that very act? If so, does it not then follow that the idiots are not necessarily idiots at all? Does the text show a certain awareness of these difficulties, and what might be both the forms and implications of such an awareness? What, for example, are its implications for the vexed question of 'irony'? Is it (can it be) ironic about irony, and thus entertain the possibility of non-ironic readings? Within the infernal logic and infinite self-referentiality of the Cretan Liar paradox, the questions are theoretically almost endless, and, on those terms, their answers almost certainly inconclusive ('la bêtise consiste à vouloir conclure'; but, in its closed and conclusive form, is not this statement itself an example of what it denounces?). Indeed, the perverse logic of the paradox is such that, in a kind of frenzied paroxysm, it must in the end turn against its own terms: in a happily mindless phonetic coincidence our Cretan turns out to be a cretin.

Doubtless some would argue that these endlessly regressive displacements and equivocations are sterile rather than vertiginous, mere games for the jaded academic mind. Certainly, they can easily become that, but the case I wish to argue here is that it is just such an experience of irreducible perversity that underlies much of what is most crucial in Flaubert's literary enterprise. It produces a radical hesitation or ambiguity in his texts, a hesitation that can be resolved, and an ambiguity that can be collapsed, according to various strategies of reading, but which not only re-emerge intact on the other side of such readings, but which are also somehow self-referential, hesitant about hesitation, ambiguous about ambiguity. The key point at which to enter into this paradoxical maze is through a recognition of the insidious scope and, more important, the uncertain status of *bêtise*. Flaubert's ambivalent attitude to *bêtise* is well known, that curious mixture of revulsion and fascination which appears as a constant leitmotiv of the *Correspondance*. But this psychological ambivalence corresponds to something much deeper, to a profound uncertainty concerning the relation between the individual subject and language. The real problem for Flaubert, as

Leslie Hill points out,[24] is the apparent impossibility of delimiting and circumscribing *bêtise* in order to be able to take up an unequivocal stand against it. For *bêtise*, rigorously defined, is not simply an accidental or local feature of human discourse, the mark of a particular intellectual or moral deficiency, and against which one can set the magisterial authority of Intelligence: 'La bêtise n'est pas d'un côté et l'esprit de l'autre. C'est comme le vice et la vertu; malin qui les distingue' (IV, p. 83). *Bêtise* is not fundamentally a matter of intellectual competence or personal morality, but a matter of language as such, of the inescapable entry of the subject into an inherited system of categories and meanings. It is a constitutive feature of utterance, in the sense that all utterance (and therefore all intelligibility) is in some way derivative or 'citational', articulated from a system that is socially established and maintained by means of convention, habit and repetition.[25]

This gives a deeper meaning to Flaubert's otherwise rather trivial remark à propos of the *Dictionnaire* that, after reading it, no-one would be able to speak 'de peur de dire tout naturellement une des phrases qui s'y trouveraient' (III, p. 67). Such is the universal catchment area of *bêtise* that its ultimate victory is to engender the paralysis of silence. Yet even the response of silence is problematic. For to say nothing is also flawed, or tarred with the same brush. To be silent is to be dumb, and, as everybody knows, to be dumb is to be stupid. In other words, such is the insidious logic and tentacular reach of *bêtise* that it ends by assimilating and devouring what is ostensibly opposed to it. Thus, the discourse of Wisdom which assumes its own serene detachment from *bêtise*, is, by virtue of that assumption, exceedingly stupid, displaying the complacent idiocy of a presumed innocence. A similar paradoxical fate awaits the discourse of Denunciation. One cannot simply *attack* stupidity, since, as Barthes observes, the rhetoric of contestation can rapidly develop its own *doxa*, its own baggage of stereotypes and *idées reçues*.[26] Flaubert once compared *bêtise* to a rock of granite, hard, resistant, indestructible ('la bêtise est quelque chose d'inébranlable; rien ne l'attaque sans se briser contre elle. Elle est de la nature du granit, dure et résistante', II, p. 243). It would perhaps be more appropriate, however, to describe it as a kind of monstrous sponge, ceaselessly absorbing and appropriating all those orders of discourse which seek to reject or subvert it. In short, any discourse which opposes stupidity from the premiss of its own transcendent rationality, which implicitly proffers itself as an instrument of Truth exposing Error, is fatally implicated in what it appears to challenge.

The essential stress falls therefore on the ubiquity of *bêtise*, and on the corresponding impossibility of any position of transcendence (except as an act of bad faith that would constitute the ultimate form of *bêtise* itself). There is literally nothing one can say that is not already caught in the trammels of *bêtise*; as Flaubert puts it in one of his letters: 'Quelle forme faut-il prendre pour exprimer parfois son opinion sur les choses de ce monde, sans risquer de passer plus tard pour un imbécile? Cela est un rude problème' (V, p. 347). *Bêtise* is everywhere and inescapable. One is inside it as if inside a prison from which there is no possible escape; Nietzsche's 'prison-house of language' becomes, in its Flaubertian incarnation, the prison-house of stupidity. It is the circle of culture and language which one can attempt to query and equivocate, contest and disrupt, but which one cannot break. The writing subject, as well as the reading subject, does not stand outside the framework of *bêtise*, but is held within the play of its forms, its system of representations and intelligibility. Thus, if, as Sartre maintained, Flaubert distances and negates the taken-for-granted languages of his culture by presenting them as an alien object, as something radically 'other', he does not, and cannot, approach that otherness from a position of non-problematic detachment. The subject who speaks (ironically) of the discourse of the other can only do so *through* that discourse, since as a speaking subject he is constituted by its very categories.[27]

Clearly, this is a perspective which alters and complicates, in major ways, the terms of Flaubert's encounter with the phenomenon of *bêtise*. For it implies that the very decision to write, and to publish, is necessarily to be directly and deeply caught in the web of what in theory it seeks to expose.[28] Indeed an inventory of such complicities might make for an interesting appendix to the *Dictionnaire des idées reçues*. Thibaudet wryly suggested that many of Flaubert's remarks in the *Correspondance* could readily find a place in the *Dictionnaire*.[29] More pertinently, the same argument could be applied to the discourse of the novels themselves. I have already hinted at the peculiarly unsettled logic of reading and writing this might entail, in the example of the paradoxical 'beginning' of the early *Éducation sentimental* as itself a member of the class of narrative conventions it ironises. This blurring of the distinction between 'meta-language' and 'object-language' in fact permeates the definitive *Éducation* (the text I now want to consider in more detail), and nowhere more so than in that central theme of the novel which seems most securely held within the grip of irony: the theme of the 'mimetic' nature of love. As with the ambiguous question of 'beginnings', the articulation of this theme touches on the relations of language and representation to the issues of both origins and originality, and, through that set of relations, opens once more on to the whole problematics of mimesis itself.

Reading 'Marie'

Elle l'appelait 'Frédéric', il l'appelait 'Marie', adorant ce nom-là, fait exprès, disait-il, pour être soupiré dans l'extase, et qui semblait contenir des images d'encens, des jonchées de roses. (p. 273)

This is one of the rare occasions in the novel on which Madame Arnoux is referred to by her Christian name. It is of course that most Christian of Christian names, and the allusion to the Virgin Mary (through the association in Frédéric's mind with religious notions of purity and innocence) will be clear from the 'imagery' of roses and incense Frédéric invests in the name. We are, however, not told (since the episode involves an exchange of names) what, if any, are the equivalent connotations of the name 'Frédéric' for Madame Arnoux; indeed it is difficult to see what they could be (although a mischievously speculative mind might see distinct possibilities in the surname 'Moreau'). The reciprocity of the exchange reveals a disjunction, between an 'empty' name and a 'full' name. It suggests an ironic gap which is not unlike the ambiguous effect produced by Flaubert's own practice with proper names (for a reader bent on interpretative games, a practice at once alluring and frustrating). Moreover, to the interpretative asymmetry of 'Marie' and 'Frédéric' is added another ironic perspective: the gap between the prospective and the postponed. The exchange of names holds out the promise of an intimacy, an achieved communion, whose realisation in the narrative, however, is permanently deferred, and finally lost. It is a deferral whose permanence is captured in that curiously indeterminate future perfect with which Madame Arnoux sums up their love in her final meeting with Frédéric: 'Nous nous serons bien aimés' (p. 421), at once a celebration of what has been and an acknowledgement of the inherent incompletion, the element of irreducible futurity in what has been.

I shall return shortly to some of the further implications of Frédéric's use of Madame Arnoux's Christian name. For the moment the implicit ironic relation it establishes between desire and deferral points to the central pattern of the love affair. As lover, Frédéric is not just a paradigm case of delayed gratification. He is the lover in whom the strategy of delay wholly usurps the movement towards gratification, and for whom, as a consequence (or perhaps as a condition), the object of desire exists almost entirely in the mode of absence; 'Marie' will characteristically appear to Frédéric as a veiled being, surrounded by an ambience of shadows and darkness, a mysterious, penumbral figure around which Frédéric's imagination will weave its designs without ever attempting the decisive move which would translate those designs into action. This state of affairs is partly a reflection of purely local and contingent matters: of external circumstances which impede his amorous progress, or unconscious psychological choices arising from an innate timidity which prefers distance to closeness, looking to touching. But these local narrative considerations are also elements of a larger and more impersonal conception, which has to do finally with Flaubert's sense of the genesis and structure of desire itself. For Flaubert's novels carry out as a systematic programme what René Girard has identified as the self-appointed task of narrative in general: the unmasking of 'ce mensonge qu'est le désir spontané',[30] the myth that desire comes directly from its subject and moves directly to its object. In Girard's terms, Flaubert's recognition is that, in its very constitution, desire is always mediated or 'mimetic'; it is 'désir selon un Autre';[31] it occupies a 'triangular' structure within which subject and object are related, and divided, by the force of a third term. This third term is the 'model' or the 'mediator' (the rival, the book or, in the more radical psychoanalytical version of this theory, language itself), from the conscious or unconscious copying of which both the desire of the subject and the desirability of the object are installed within inescapable alterity and division. Any belief we have in the spontaneous, unmediated nature of our desires disguises the deflected and substitutive forms of desire. Similarly, any feeling we have of immediate and abiding union with another is but a fixation on a set of 'signifiers', whose true form is that of the fetish (that which arrests the movement of desire and reifies the object of desire).

It is in these basically derivative and substitutive guises that Frédéric's sentimental education unfolds. The most striking feature of the narrative of Frédéric's love is the way the latter lives it as if it were itself narrative. This is not just a question of Frédéric's attempts to convert experience into literature, as in his abortive project of writing the historical romance *Sylvio*, in which hero and heroine are to be transpositions of himself and Madame Arnoux. More important is the reverse process whereby literature is constantly converted into (or rather made constitutive of) 'experi-ence'. Flaubert's choice of terms in presenting the discourse through which Frédéric seeks to woo Madame Arnoux deliberately underlines its character as narration. Thus, in the first 'serious' con-versation Frédéric has with her ('la première fois qu'ils ne parlaient pas de choses insignifiantes'), we are told that 'il entama le chapitre des aventures sentimentales' (p. 84). The bookish metaphor laconi-cally marks what later will be more explicitly registered as the liter-ary filter through which Frédéric's emotions typically pass: 'Il lui *conta* ses mélancolies au collège, et comment dans son ciel poétique resplendissait un visage de femme, si bien qu'en la voyant pour la première fois il l'avait reconnue' (p. 272, my italics).

What Frédéric narrates is a further 'chapter' (or an extended quotation) from the story that has been told innumerable times before, the Love Story or, as Barthes puts it, the *'histoire d'amour asservie à ce grand Autre narratif'*.[32] Frédéric lives his life through the conventions of that story, as if, in loving, he were re-reading or re-telling it. Madame Arnoux is cast as a figure in a time-honoured plot, adored not so much for what she is (whatever that might be) as for what she *resembles* ('Elle ressemblait aux femmes des livres romantiques', p. 9). The moment of actual encounter is thus always transformed or displaced by the 'otherness' of the prior narrative model Frédéric brings to it. The present is referred to a past ('ses mélancolies au collège'), which is in turn referred to another past: the literary tradition from which Frédéric's interior 'ciel poétique' is fashioned. Madame Arnoux is thus never 'there', as an immediate, fully present object of desire, because within the dialectic of desire she is herself a substitute; she is the image of what is already an image ('un visage de femme'), a face which belongs to no-one, whose origins are essentially literary, and whose appear-ance in Frédéric's consciousness long precedes the arrival of Madame Arnoux on the scene of his life. She is a substitute-representation for what are themselves the substitute-representations with which the stereotyped linguistic and cultural models of desire have furnished Frédéric's imagination.

It is in this context that we can return to Frédéric's use of Madame Arnoux's Christian name. 'Marie' is a fetishised term in the fiction-making process through which Frédéric attempts to fill the vacancy at the centre of his desires: ' . . . et les délires de la chair et de l'âme étaient contenues pour moi dans votre nom que je me répétais, en tâchant de la baiser sur mes lèvres' (p. 422). Flaubert here antici-pates the Proustian theme of the 'magic' of proper names. As with the narrator's fantastication of 'Gilberte' in *À la recherche*, the magical transformation wrought on 'Marie' is the construction of an imaginary fable. In semiological terms, it is the operation whereby the signifier is separated from its referent (the actual person of Madame Arnoux) only to be returned to it laden with a collection of literary and cultural signifieds (such as the various connotations of 'incense' and 'roses'). Naturally, the name cannot support the fiction erected upon it, and nowhere is the gap between the two more clearly seen than on that much earlier, and very different, occasion when Frédéric utters Madame Arnoux's Christian name: 'A Bray, il n'attendit pas qu'on eût donné de l'avoine, il alla devant, sur la route, tout seul. Arnoux l'avait appelé "Marie!". Il cria très haut "Marie!". Sa voix se perdit dans l'air' (p. 9). In this passage (which occurs shortly after Frédéric has met Madame Arnoux for the first time on the boat), 'Marie' takes exactly the form of a magical incantation, whose purpose is to conjure up in imagination the presence of the absent loved one. The ironic effect is situated in the gap between the intensity of Frédéric's cry and the narrative flatness of the sentence which succeeds it. No sooner is the name uttered than it simply expires, a mere puff of breath lost on the wind; literally a *signifiant flottant*, or better, a signifier adrift which (not unlike the hero of the novel) simply fades and disperses because there is nowhere in particular for it to go, or nothing substantial to which it might attach itself.

Flaubert's *L'Éducation sentimentale* is thus written as a critical assessment of the vacuousness of Frédéric's sentimental projects. In this respect, the strictly pedagogical implication of the title needs to be taken seriously, although it is characteristically double-edged. Basically, the hero learns nothing. We, however, are presumably meant to learn from his failure to learn. The 'education' *L'Éducation sentimentale* offers the reader is the negative one of unlearning the myths and stereotypes with which Frédéric fills and frames his desire. More schematically, the discourse of the novel undermines the discourse of the love story; the text of Sentiment is taken apart by the corrosive rhetorical force of irony. This is doubtless the 'safe' way of reading *L'Éducation sentimentale*, and one which unproblematically accommodates that predominantly critical function which has so often been seen (notably by Lukács) as the very essence of the novel form since its inception.

The security of this reading is, however, troubled if we ask the question, where, or what, is the *language* which makes this programme possible? This is not just a question of the familiar issue of 'point of view' (where do we see Madame Arnoux other than through Frédéric's eyes?), although technically it is closely bound up with the use of *style indirect libre*. Nor is it simply a matter of the oft-rehearsed ambiguities of Flaubert's personal attitudes (that oscillation between irony and sympathy ostensibly inspired by Flaubert's own obsession with Madame Schlésinger). The essential question is whether there is in the text a viable language of representation that transcends the received discourses through which Frédéric thinks and feels. If the ironic effect of the text depends on the reader seeing the gap between the imaginary 'Marie' and the real Madame Arnoux, how is this 'reality' constituted in the text? What, for example, are we to make of her first appearance in the novel? That appearance is the famous 'apparition': 'Ce fut comme une apparition' (p. 4). But an 'apparition' to, and for, whom? Obviously, to Frédéric, as a dramatic rupture in the continuum of dırab ugliness he sees around him on the boat, and he will immediately proceed to fabulate this initial perception in the standardised exotic ways. But the sentence in which it is couched is not Frédéric's; as the verb tense makes clear, this is not an example of *style indirect libre*. The voice that speaks here is the voice of the narrator. It is the narrator who presents her in that most commonplace of romantic clichés, 'comme une apparition'. How, then, are we to distinguish between Frédéric and narrator, between Irony and Sentiment? From the very beginning, Madame Arnoux 'appears' as a construct of language, in relation to which it is exceptionally difficult for the reader to decide where to apportion responsibility for the cliché, or to decide whether 'cliché' (and the ironic distance it implies) is the correct description, or, finally, to decide whether what we call cliché is an object worthy only of ironic treatment.

This uncertainty, both as to who is speaking and the quality of what is being said, saturates *L'Éducation sentimentale*. But its peculiarly disorientating force can be illustrated by the following passage, which deals explicitly, though in irreducibly equivocal fashion, with the question of language itself:

Elle ne s'exaltait point pour la littérature, mais son esprit charmait par des mots simples et pénétrants. Elle aimait les voyages, le bruit du vent dans les bois, et à se promener tête nue sous la pluie. Frédéric écoutait ces choses délicieusement. (p. 145)

On the face of it, this looks straightforward enough. It is 'lovers' discourse', rendered in the form of free indirect speech and ironised by means of a simple rhetorical trick. The apparent opposition between 'littérature' and 'mots simples' is ironically cancelled by means of the actual examples given of the latter: 'les voyages', 'le bruit du vent dans les bois', 'se promener tête nue dans la pluie'. Nothing could in fact be more stereotypically 'literary'; it is exactly the sort of phraseology we will find in the books that turn Emma's head. But matters are not as 'simple' as they appear. It is not just that Marie and Frédéric are incapable of distinguishing between the 'literary' and the 'simple', perpetually confusing the one with the other. It is rather that the distinction itself is inherently unclear. The complication arises with the opening clause: 'Elle ne s'exaltait point pour la littérature.' Who is responsible for this claim? Is it Madame Arnoux (in the form of *style indirect libre*)? Is it Frédéric recasting her talk in his own head? Or is it the Narrator? The question is both crucial and unanswerable, or crucial *because* unanswerable. The blurring of the source of enunciation blurs everything else. Perhaps the real snare lies in assuming that the content of Madame Arnoux's utterances and the prior claim made on their behalf are discrepant; perhaps they are 'simple' after all. In any case, the confusion as to who is speaking and the value of what is being said fulfils admirably Flaubert's declared project of dislocating the reader's frames of reference. From the initial question as to who is responsible for the discourse, the reader is lost in a veritable proliferation of questions: what is 'literary' and what is 'simple'; does the distinction hold; and, if so, to which category do Madame Arnoux's words belong; if to the latter, are they still nevertheless clichés; what, then, is the difference between a 'literary' cliché and a 'simple' cliché; what, in fact, is the status of the cliché as such? Are the 'simplest', as well as the strongest, of our feelings incapable of expression without clichés? And is 'irony' simply the hollow pretence that we can escape them?

The closest Flaubert ever comes to giving his own answer to these questions is in the famous passage in *Madame Bovary* where he resumes human discourse in the simile of the 'chaudron fêlé'. All manifestations of human speech are flawed, but some, it would appear, less flawed than others. In the exchange between Emma and Rodolphe, from which the simile of the 'chaudron fêlé' is drawn, the two lovers speak to each other in the 'empty' language ('les métaphores les plus vides') of romantic love, but the exchange is not one of pure equivalence. They use the 'same' language ('le même langage') but 'mean' different things. Rodolphe mechanically repeats the formulae he has used in similar circumstances countless times before. He is merely posturing, reproducing a

discourse that is empty by virtue of the inner emptiness which motivates its utterance. Emma's relation to the 'same' language, however, is at once more paradoxical and pathetic. In passing through
that language her desires and feelings undergo an inevitable
deformation and alienation. Her tragedy lies in the permanent
absence of fit between her intense, inchoate subjectivity and its
attempted articulation in language. Yet, for all their 'stupidity',
there is a decisive sense in which her words express the truth of her
being. Cliché is all that she has, and perhaps because it is all that,
in analogous circumstances, any of us has. Leo Bersani is, of course,
right when he argues that Emma turns to the language of 'literature'
to make sense of her desires, only to find she cannot return from
literature to life.[33] Yet, for all his ironic exploitation of that gulf,
Flaubert here emphatically underlines – it is one of the few absolute
statements in the otherwise endlessly shifting and unstable reality of
the text – what Rodolphe's cynicism (the *reductio* of irony) prevents
him from seeing:

la dissemblance des sentiments sous la parité des expressions . . . comme si
la plénitude de l'âme ne débordait quelquefois par les métaphores les plus
vides, puisque *personne, jamais*, ne peut donner l'exacte mesure de ses
besoins, ni de ses conceptions, ni de ses douleurs, et que la parole humaine
est comme un chaudron fêlé où nous battons les mélodies à faire danser les
ours, quand on voudrait attendrir les étoiles.[34]

The central proposition is thus categorical: *no-one* can
adequately express in language his 'conceptions', including presumably the person who tries to express his 'conception' of language in
the (cumbersome) simile of the 'chaudron fêlé'. This is not exactly
a rehabilitation of the *idée reçue*. But the sensitivity it shows towards
the dilemma of human utterance is infinitely richer than that
afforded by an exclusively ironic perspective. Moreover, to the
extent that the logic of the statement implicitly includes its author
within its frame of reference, that the propositions it asserts about
language apply to the assertion itself, it calls upon us to re-assess
Flaubert's own relation to the *idée reçue*. It means not only that
Flaubert is as capable of being commonplace as his characters, but
that the value we should attribute to such commonplaces is not
unequivocally negative. The commonplace, however flawed
('cracked') is, precisely, the common-place; if it blocks and traduces
the communication of what we feel and believe, it is, in many fundamental respects, the only space in which any kind of communication
at all can occur. And ironic contempt for that space (in the name, for

example, of 'originality') may simply be a recipe for falling back into another set of clichés, infested with a form of bad faith that is even more contemptible.

The examples I have given are, of course, a condensed illustration of an argument that properly requires a far more intricate textual analysis. The essential point lies not so much in extracting individual instances from any given novel as in showing how, from within the logic of Flaubert's position, the discourse of received ideas can be said to invade the whole texture of the writing, and what the necessary consequences of that invasion are for interpreting Flaubert's citational method. The major consequence is to destabilise the ironic perspectives of the writing, to problematise the question of 'point of view', in that there no longer appears to be any fixed position to which we can refer in order to evaluate the 'quotations' circulating within the text. As with the relative disappearance in Flaubert's novels of what Jonathan Culler has called the 'characterisable narrator',[35] there is here no secure hierarchy of discourse, no master language that will assume responsibility for what is said, that will provide the reference points by which we can interpret, measure, judge. The citational play of the text swallows up narrator and character alike, immerses both in the *doxa*, and radically obscures any firm evaluative distinction between them.

This evidently places a large question mark against the precise function and meaning of quotation in Flaubert. On the one hand, quotation signifies a borrowing; it is a way of acknowledging a 'debt', of recognising an 'authority' that supports and guarantees the truth or plausibility of what is being affirmed. In this sense, to quote is to accept and to endorse, to submit to the words of the Other. On the other hand, quotation can have the opposite function: it represents the insertion of a certain distance between the speaker and what is being said, and thus opens up the possibility of ironic negation. Flaubert's text plays systematically on and across these two contradictory functions, but at the same time immeasurably complicates and refines that play by the device of *dropping the quotation marks*. Whereas quotation marks (like the use of italics) explicitly identify the utterance as quotation, the effect of dispensing with the marks is, as it were, to disguise the citational origins of the utterance. But the significance of that disguise is suitably ambiguous. On one interpretation, the disguise is a kind of mask, serving the purposes of an ironic unmasking. The absence of inverted commas maintains the *illusion* of the innocence or 'naturalness' of the writing. It superficially disguises its derivative character in order to proffer itself as pure 'representation', in accordance with an aesthetic of naive realism. It tacitly proclaims a position taken up unproblematically within the circle of *bêtise*, sustaining with its discourse a relation of pure repetition. The key purpose of this tactic, however, depends on the reader moving from surface appearance to recognition of a deeper reality. As he becomes aware of the cliché-ridden nature of the language, the appearance of a non-problematic innocence gives way to the sense of an underlying ironic intent. In this way, the text operates a simultaneous dialectic of simulation and subversion, in which paradoxically the force of the latter depends crucially on the efficacy of the former. The more effectively the text reproduces the inherited linguistic and literary forms, the sharper our recognition of the ironic force of what is 'really' going on behind the bland, poker-faced simulation; as Barthes summarises it, it is a strategy which maintains 'un état très subtil, presque intenable, du discours: la narrativité est déconstruite et l'histoire reste cependant lisible'.[36]

That is an elegant summary of a now very influential way of reading Flaubert. It does, however, have an implication which (unless I have misunderstood him)[37] Barthes seems to have missed: the point of view it expresses is strictly *reversible*. That is, one can equally argue that the story does not 'remain readable' (i.e. representational) as a ruse designed to throw into sharper relief the ironic deconstruction of the conventions of narrative representation; it does not masquerade as a novel in order to operate obliquely as an 'anti-novel'. Rather, if the story remains readable, this would simply be because, at one level, it *is* readable, profoundly complicit in the classic discourse of representation. If, therefore, it can be described as 'citational', it is precisely because it is doing the same sort of thing as the other books from which it 'quotes', because it shares (rather than refuses) the same order of discourse. In other words, *la citation sans guillemets* could be construed in direct relation to the primary function of unmarked quotation: the function of plagiarism (of unacknowledged quotation, where the 'borrowing' becomes, as it were, a 'theft'). Of course, in the ordinary ethical sense, such a claim would be quite preposterous. Indeed, in accordance with the theory of intertextuality, one of the meanings we could assign to Flaubert's citational method would be the dissolution of the ordinary sense of the term 'plagiarism', the loss, within the anonymous space of the *doxa*, of any notion of a 'proprietorial' source. The important inference, however, is that if, as Flaubert himself asserts, *bêtise* is everywhere and inescapable, then Flaubert's own text cannot be exempted. Accordingly, the absence of quotation marks is not wholly interpretable as the sign of a tongue-in-cheek game played by the narrator with the reader. Rather it could be seen as the sign of a certain modesty, an implicit concession of the equality of writer and reader before the ubiquitous text of *bêtise*. The dropping of the commas would thus be an indirect acknowledgement of the impossibility of transcendence, a refusal of the disingenuous ironic distance implied by the retention of the marks; it is a way of signalling what one could call, although in a non-proprietorial sense, the necessary 'plagiarism' of any activity of writing. In this way, we could begin to reverse the Barthesian description of reading Flaubert as the movement from the surface appearance of innocence to the deeper recognition of irony. We might say that the expectation of irony created by our sense of cliché is blocked and reversed by the possibility of accepting the writing in its pure literality. The elimination of the commas thus troubles standard assumptions and raises searching questions about Flaubert's literary practice. Are the sentences before us really ironic? How, in good faith, could they be unequivocally so? Is it not possible, for example, to read the sentence 'Un jeune homme de dix-huit ans, à longs cheveux et qui tenait un album sous les bras, restait auprès du gouvernail, immobile' as a purely 'innocent' narrative statement of a particular state of affairs, akin to a hundred other such sentences that we will have already encountered elsewhere?

Ambiguous adverbs

This oscillation between irony and literalness in fact confronts the reader at almost every point in the Flaubert text. But it could be further illustrated by briefly considering Flaubert's unusual handling of a specific grammatical category (his use of adverbs and adverbial phrases), since here the relation between discourse and quotation can be seen at work at the most basic level of language itself. In his comments on the relationship between style and grammar in Flaubert, Proust remarked on the peculiar awkwardness or 'heaviness' of a great deal of the former's adverbial usage ('les adverbes, les locutions adverbiales, ils sont toujours placés dans Flaubert de la façon à la fois la plus laide, la plus inattendue, la plus lourde').[38] What Proust had in mind was Flaubert's tendency to emphasise the presence of the adverb by the insertion of commas, coupled with its unusual positioning in terms of customary word order (frequently placed at the end of the sentence). The example given by Proust is the famous 'alternativement' of *Hérodias*, which not only comes at the end of the sentence but at the end of the story itself, and which may be described as the stylistic equivalent of the 'heaviness' of the head which its bearers alternately carry. The purpose of the device is not, however, solely impressionistic. As Culler observes, the isolation of the adverb disrupts the smooth linear flow of the sentence.[39] And these checks and halts in the phrasal rhythm of narration serve above all to remind us that what we are experiencing is, precisely, narration, writing, text. It is another instance of 'foregrounding', of what Sartre describes as the self-consciousness of language in Flaubert. Separated off from the rest of the sentence by means of the commas, the adverb appears as a kind of grotesque, almost free-standing object, which displaces attention from its referential function to its autonomy as a pure linguistic form: it says 'I am an Adverb'. In other words, it is a 'quotation', from the institution of Language or the text of Grammar; it tells us something about the strangeness, even the absurdity, of the business of putting a sentence together.

It can, moreover, be seen as a quotation from a literary and social text, a citation from the corpus of *bêtise*. 'Il la rencontra, pourtant' is the deceptively 'simple' sentence which tells of Frédéric's meeting with Madame Arnoux after numerous delays and obstructions. Verb and adverb together evoke a standard romantic paradigm: that of the Obstacle and the Encounter, the obstacle here finally overcome to make the encounter between the two 'lovers' possible. But the positioning of the adverb subtly weakens the paradigm; the adverb appears almost as an afterthought, gives to the episode an almost casual air. It is further weakened by what follows, in a sequence which also ends with a similar use of an adverbial phrase: 'La première fois, il y avait trois dames avec elles; une autre après-midi, le maître d'écriture de Mademoiselle Marthe survint. D'ailleurs, les hommes que recevaient Madame Arnoux ne lui faisaient point de visites. Il n'y retourna plus, par discrétion' (p. 55). The promise of the encounter is thus yet again deferred by a series of further 'obstacles', whose common characteristic is their absolute ordinariness; these are not the grand obstacles typically faced by the heroic romantic lover; they are rather obstructions emanating from the trivially perverse circumstantiality of everyday life. The final adverbial phrase ('par discrétion') completes the devaluing perspective, at once evoking and undermining the stereotype of the Gentleman (Frédéric's 'discrétion' is in fact but an alibi for his hopeless timidity). The two adverbs, each made prominent by virtue of their

terminal position in the sentence, frame a movement from assertion
('Il la rencontra') to negation ('Il n'y retourna plus'), in which the
whole theme of the lover's pursuit dwindles to a point where it is no
longer possible for the reader to take it seriously.

Indeed, whether or not we can take Frédéric 'seriously' is the
implicit question of Flaubert's own use of that adverb. When we
are told of Frédéric that 'il se demanda, sérieusement, s'il serait
un grand peintre ou un grand poète' (p. 50), we do not have to wait
for subsequent information to assess the absurdity of Frédéric's
aspirations. It is already indicated by the commas which separate
the adverb from the two clauses of the sentence. They mark the fact
that, in the question he solemnly puts to himself, Frédéric is once
more 'quoting' (from the code of the Artistic Vocation), and that
consequently the reader cannot possibly take this 'sérieusement',
seriously. Similarly, there is the interesting example of the adverbial
phrase used to describe Frédéric's manner of walking about the
streets of Paris after his first ecstatic encounter with Madame
Arnoux at her Paris home: 'Il n'avait plus conscience du milieu, de
l'espace, de rien: et, battant le sol du talon, en frappant avec sa
canne les volets des boutiques, il allait toujours devant lui, *au
hasard, éperdu, entraîné*' (p. 52, my italics). The notorious commas
of the adverbial phrase again underline it as self-conscious
quotation. Indeed we may say of the commas that they are a kind of
downwards displacement of the eliminated quotation marks:
Frédéric is miming a text; he has so strongly internalised the stereotyped language of Love that it even organises his physical responses
to emotion; he walks in this way because this is what the Romantic
code of 'passion' pescribes; in brief, he is quite literally a walking
idée reçue.

Yet – and this is why this particular example is especially instructive – the potential for ironic interpretation is checked, or at least
equivocated, by the later recurrence of the same or very similar
adverbial expression, in at once analogous yet utterly different circumstances. Much later in the novel we again find Frédéric leaving
Madame Arnoux's salon to wander the streets of Paris, but this time
in a condition of complete despair: 'Il marchait cependant, mais sans
rien voir, *au hasard*' (p. 200, my italics). It is, of course, possible to
read this as being also ironic and parodic. But the supporting context of quite genuine suffering might well require a very different
interpretation: namely, that we take this representation of his
manner of walking literally and seriously. In other words, Frédéric
may walk in this way because the models of romantic literature

demand it (as a sign of Ecstasy or Despair). But it may also be quite simply the 'natural' way to walk in those circumstances, and the endless repetition ('mimesis') of the same gesture by countless individuals both in real life and in literary representations may be founded on its inherent 'rightness'; it may derive from the patrimony of the 'déjà-lu, déjà-dit, déjà-fait', but perhaps because the 'déjà' has in fact a certain authenticating authority. If doubts remain, we might turn to that other instance in the text of the adverbial phrase 'au hasard'. It comes in the context of the treatment by père Roque and his colleagues in the National Guard of the political prisoners arrested during the uprising of 1848: 'Quand les prisonniers s'approchaient d'un soupirail, les gardes nationaux qui étaient de faction . . . fourraient des coups de baïonnette, *au hasard*, dans le tas' (p. 337, my italics). It would be difficult to construe the isolating commas here as just an exercise in self-conscious irony. Or, at least, if the random brutality of the National Guard is perceived by Flaubert as simply an occasion for playing a linguistic game around the self-advertising adverbiality of adverbs, then that would make of *L'Éducation sentimentale* a deeply trivial novel indeed.

Madame Dambreuse speaks

The implications of this potential for non-ironic, literal readings are very far-reaching, and touch ultimately on the foundations of the theory and practice of mimesis itself. For if it is possible to take the literal sense seriously (as distinct from being merely hoodwinked by it, which would imply the absolute priority of the ironic sense), if a literal interpretation of Flaubert's most banal phrases and sentences can be proposed *in good faith*, then this in turn implies the legitimacy of a strictly mimetic reading of the text, in which the sceptical and ironic positions are usurped. Routine representations are not perforce unacceptable for being routine, just as truisms may nonetheless be true for being 'stupid'. Thus, if, as Leslie Hill suggests, *bêtise* originates in the 'desire to convince'[40] and is expressed through an order of discourse, a rhetoric that promotes itself as a persuasively 'true' or 'realistic' account of the world, it does not follow that there are no reasonable grounds for accepting some accounts as more plausible than others. Flaubert could have written of Frédéric that he walked in a quite different way (shall we say, in a jolly way), but the question would then arise as to whether it would have *made any sense* to do so. It would certainly have 'defeated expectations', produced 'déception' and enabled us to continue mumbling happily about 'anti-novels' and the like, but probably only in the way that non-sense can enable this sort of thing. In other words, it may be that many of our *lieux communs* are commonplace precisely because they possess a certain 'appropriateness'. If they are subject to repetition, become routinised formulae, it is because they are in some way 'right' for the situations and states of the world to which they refer. This does not necessarily mean a return to crude positivist fantasies about language. The meanings in question are products of culture and creations of habit; in the language of the sociologists they are the 'sedimented meanings' which habit and stupidity bequeath to us. But Habit, as Proust (ostensibly the arch-enemy of habit) remarked, is one of our vital means for making the world habitable,[41] of rendering the world intelligible; and the systems of intelligibility it produces and maintains are not necessarily to be ascribed merely to collective mental laziness or ideological conspiracy. Habit, in Beckett's sardonic phrase, is the 'grande sourdine',[42] but then a certain deafness may be a necessary condition of warding off an intolerable chaos, and the 'stupidities' it consecrates a way of keeping reality this side of the dividing line between information and mere noise. Or, to adapt George Eliot's celebrated metaphor from *Middlemarch* – one which furnishes a quite different context to Flaubert's obsession with *bêtise* – it is perhaps best 'to walk about well wadded with stupidity' lest 'we should die of that roar which lies on the other side of silence'.[43]

In its bearing on Flaubert, this represents, of course, an exceedingly large, controversial and, in some quarters, quite heretical claim. It raises complex issues, many of which have been short-circuited here. I am not arguing that Flaubert was actually committed to this conservative or 'naive' position, but only that he understood its possibility as a necessary element in the ambiguous configuration of possibilities generated from the paradoxical logic of his conception of language and literature. I am, moreover, suggesting that, since it is semiotics that has done most to put key aspects of this logic on the critical map, it is also an implication inherent in semiological criticism, but which for various reasons has been neglected. For one of the major difficulties with semiological theory – although this is often vigorously denied – is the problem of Relativism. Relativism has powerful fists, but a perilously exposed jaw, to which it itself perversely delivers the fatal upper-cut; as Flaubert knew only too well, it has a sting in its tail which bites the head. If, as the semiologist typically asserts, all statements about the world are culture-dependent, issue from the 'cultural codes', then what of the statement itself which puts forward that proposition? If it is deemed to be 'true', it must therefore both assume and meet criteria that are culture-independent, and, as such, provides the exception which devastates the rule that it asserts (we know the delight taken by Flaubert in the paradoxes of the Exception and the Rule).[44] On the other hand, if it is deemed self-referential, it is perforce caught up in a reflexive process in which it in turn becomes the critical object of a new meta-language which 'deconstructs' it. This is the position most radically developed in the work of Jacques Derrida, those astonishing books simultaneously wedded to and divorced from a system of categories they use as 'operational necessities' and yet which at the same time are under perpetual 'erasure'. But if the tortured and self-conscious contradictions of the Derridean text bear witness to the dilemma, they hardly resolve it.[45] If the proposition is self-referential and therefore open to displacement, it can be displaced, and replaced, only by its opposite: namely, the statement that not all statements are culture-bound. Either way, it is a position that inevitably turns back on itself; like all relativist and sceptical positions, it is an enterprise self-defeating from its own premises; which, from the logic of those premises, engenders its own negation.

We are of course back with the maddening circularities and regressions of our ancient friend, the Cretan Liar, as well as with the paradoxes surrounding the 'deconstructionist' approach to mimesis which I briefly sketched in my opening chapter. But it should now be clear that this is not simply a matter of frivolous dalliance in the footnotes of the Greek Sceptics. On the contrary, it is of major consequence for our understanding of Flaubert's literary project. Like Beckett's perverse scholasticism which obstinately chases its own tail, conscious that the 'I' which speaks of the impossibility of the 'I' presupposes the very thing that it contests, Flaubert's work is based on a peculiarly radical form of the uncertainty principle: one that, in defiance of ordinary logic, is somehow uncertain about uncertainty, and which therefore entertains the possibility of certainty (on the grounds that to say categorically everything is uncertain is to claim that at least one thing is certain). Put in more banal terms – but it is precisely the meaning of 'banality' that is in question here – the text implicitly accepts that it may be non-problematic (i.e. uncomplicated by submerged ironic purpose) to represent Frédéric's reaction to falling in love with Madame Arnoux in the way it does, simply because it makes perfect sense to do so. One final implication of such an approach might be a more complex interpretation of Flaubert's *boutade* about the *Dictionnaire des idées reçues*, that it was written 'de sorte que le lecteur ne sache pas si on se fout de lui, oui ou non' (II, p. 238). Conventional exegesis of this remark implicitly poses both a manipulative author playing mystifying tricks on his readers and, as a necessary corollary, a division of these readers into those who are taken in (stupid) and those who see through the ruse (intelligent). A more radical reading, inspired by the problematic of *bêtise*, would rather emphasise the utter impossibility of deciding exactly who, or what, is fooling whom; it would stress how everybody and everything – author, reader, and all possible assumptions made by either about the other or themselves – are called into question by the text. On this interpretation, it would then follow that it is not necessarily those who read the *lieux communs* 'naively' who are being fooled, but, just as plausibly, those who take refuge (and thereby confirm their own sense of superiority) in irony and paradox, ambiguity and equivocation.

That Flaubert was perfectly aware of this seems clear from that astonishing moment in *L'Éducation sentimentale* – at once a displacement of and a critical reflection on his own strategies of equivocation – when he describes the style of speech of none other than Madame Dambreuse in the following terms: 's'il lui échappait des lieux communs, c'était dans une formule tellement convenue que sa phrase pouvait passer pour une déférence ou une ironie' (p. 362). In a limited but important sense, Madame Dambreuse speaks to her interlocutor 'de sorte qu'on ne sache pas si on se fout de lui, oui ou non', disguises commonplaces in a cultivatedly ambiguous discourse. But since no exemplary value can conceivably attach to her, the principle of 'equivocation' appears here in just as stereotyped and stupid a light as the society lady who exploits it. It hardens into convention ('une formule toute convenue'), develops its own *doxa*. And perhaps the same could be said of one dimension to Flaubert's attitude to the paradoxes of relativism, indeed to paradox as such. For, as the classicists have pointed out, it is not the least of the paradoxes that para-dox is in fact subsumed under the general class of the *doxa*. Like the animal classification system of the Borges story which includes as one of its classes all the animals 'included in the present classification', the *doxa* is a generic concept that includes both itself and paradox as the sub-classes of which it is the overarching class. Once again we stray dangerously towards the intellectual quicksands of the Cretan Liar. But it is difficult to resist the feeling that this tantalising creation of Epimenides was at the back of Flaubert's mind when, in his ultimate, maniacally self-negating gesture of paradoxicality, he gave to Paradox a place in the *Dictionnaire des idées reçues*: 'Paradoxe. Se dit toujours sur le boulevard des Italiens, entre deux bouffées de cigarette.'[46]

7

CONCLUSION: MIMESIS, A MATTER FOR THE POLICE?

'Last words'

Is mimesis possible, or is it just an 'illusion' and, if so, at what cost (at the cost, for example, of the repression of difference in a call to identification with uniform images of reality, or human nature)? Conversely, is the rejection of mimesis possible, and, if so, at what cost (at the cost, for example, of another illusion: the escape from the mediations of history and society into the 'free' play of the signifier)? Posed in terms of these questions, the issue of mimesis seems to touch a highly sensitive intellectual and psychic nerve, and presumably explains why, roughly since the appearance of *S/Z*, it has reappeared with such regularity on the agenda of contemporary literary theory and philosophy, at least in France. On mimesis nearly everyone has their say, *must* have their say. Why this has been so is a matter we might be tempted to leave for future historians of ideas, but that would be to duck the contentious nature of the agenda *hic et nunc*. Equally we might wish to recall that the kind and degree of intellectual combativeness that have informed recent debate on the subject have not always been the case. Auerbach's magisterial *Mimesis* is magisterial precisely because for him the concept of 'mimesis' as such was intrinsically non-problematical; the task in hand was to plot the vast panorama of its changing embodiments over a period of three thousand years from Homer to Virginia Woolf, broadly as a form of literary and cultural history centred on changing relations between different 'levels of style'. *Mimesis* is a monumental work, not just because of its extraordinary erudition, but because the conceptual foundation-stone on which the monument is built is always assumed to be entirely intact. Auerbach's history, moreover, both has an ideal addressee ('those whose love for our Western history has serenely persevered'), and discloses an over-all design and purpose: a movement in Western representational literary art away from division and conflict towards the 'elementary things which our lives have in common'.[1] These last words were written towards the end of the Second World War, and the first shortly afterwards. From the scholar removed from his post at Marburg University by the Nazis in 1935, they are words which betoken a courageously humanist *profession de foi*, and only the most foolish and superficial 'anti-humanism' will treat them with anything other than respect.

Yet, if the humanist monumentality of *Mimesis* at one time lent it the air of being the 'last word' on the subject (although there is no book less imperialist, less 'fascist' than this), it is no longer possible to take for granted what Auerbach assumed. Mimesis is back on the agenda as *problem*, and in large measure because of the 'crisis of humanism' that has so deeply marked contemporary thought. Crisis led to demise, and with the death of 'humanism', most loudly proclaimed in post-1968 Paris, went the burial of mimesis, as we entered into full recognition of our truly 'modern', and now 'postmodern', condition. But the burial has been exceedingly prolonged, indeed repeatedly performed. The corpse keeps springing back to life in order to be put to death again; it has become something of an obsession (it has of course become one of my own). What then is at stake in this constantly renewed debate about mimesis, what is the *enjeu de la mimesis*?[2] This is the question to which this final chapter is addressed. One possible answer is, quite simply, everything. Consult or compile a thematic index for any of the major recent works concerned with mimesis and related matters, and you will find yourself reading or making entries for 'related matters' under such headings as 'reality', 'knowledge','language', 'sign', 'code', 'reference', 'subject', 'culture', 'society', 'ideology', 'power'; you will find most of the '-isms' (Marxism, Freudianism, Structuralism, etc.) and most of the '-ologies' (epistemology, ontology, etc.); in short, you will find yourself tracing our most of the overlapping epistemic configurations of our time. As such, the answer is, therefore, fairly useless. As the proliferating contexts encroach upon mimesis, or mimesis encroaches upon them, the topic begins to look fundamentally unmanageable. If plotting the modern story of mimesis is the plotting of everything in the epistemic labyrinth, it becomes an endeavour inspired, and undone, by a special kind of madness, a combination of hubris and paranoia.

But if it is madness to say that *everything* is at stake, it is reasonable to say that much is at stake. In the preceding chapters I have outlined some of the different claims about, and conflicting approaches to, the question of mimesis. In doing that, it has not been my primary purpose to adjudicate. There is no 'last word'. Just as mimesis can be described as a 'language game' with flexible rules (with different ways of positioning its 'referents'), so the discourses *on* mimesis can be seen as a heterogeneous series of language games, each positioning its referent (mimesis) in different ways. perhaps, as Lyotard might put it, in the quarrel about mimesis what we have is an object not so much of a *litige* (before a tribunal authorised to pass judgement) as of a *différend* (a conflict for the resolution of which there is no rule of adjudication). My purpose has been rather to show what it is about the inherently ambiguous and unstable character of the idea of mimesis that attracts such divergent descriptions and evaluations, and, more importantly, how these tensions are acted out, in different forms, in a number of major nineteenth-century literary texts. On the other hand, my manner of presenting the issues has followed, and reproduced, a certain direction: its movement has been essentially from stating the terms of the various critiques of mimesis towards the terms of a possible rehabilitation (in the last sections of each of the three main parts of the book: the section on Aristotle in chapter 1; the section on 'reference' in chapter 2; and in the second half of the chapter on Flaubert). The chronology is neither accidental nor a matter of simple expository convenience. It reflects the desire to give my own 'last word', though not without considerable hesitations, to the effort to salvage something of the notion of mimesis from the intellectual hammering it has received in the transition from traditional ('humanist') culture to modern and postmodern culture.

In the face of the very powerful tide which has threatened to engulf it, this may seem a feeble, and even pointless gesture. It is also liable to misinterpretation. Rehabilitation jobs can easily take the form that all this polemical jousting was never really necessary in the first place (basically a burst of '68 spring fever subsequently degenerating into jaundice). All that is required to cure those of us stricken by this unfortunate malady is a dose of brisk common sense. But brisk appeals to the commonsensical self-evidence of things tend to leave their advocates like Canute before the incoming tide; the spectacle is absurd. Thus, while it is true that the 'bracketing' of common sense or, as A. D. Nuttall puts it in *A New Mimesis*, the use of 'stock apologetic inverted commas' around all the basic terms of our vocabulary, has itself become something of an *idée reçue* (at its worst in the ritual intonings of *le roland-barthes sans peine*), to describe that bracketing as 'nakedly counter-intuitive', appropriately dealt with by a breezy removal of the quotation marks, does little to advance the argument in any substantial cognitive sense. 'My own position', writes Nuttall, 'is that the word *reality* can legitimately be used without apologetic inverted commas.'[3] The prospect of an end to the inverted commas is indeed a fetching one, but there is here much question-begging. What, for instance, is the difference between putting the word 'reality' in italics or inverted commas (for Flaubert there is certainly none)? Are we to infer that an intuitively grounded defence of mimesis against the 'nakedly counter-intuitive' is one which argues that forms of language (such as the word 'reality') correspond, in some unmediated relation, with forms of nature (reality)? If not, then *whose* 'reality' is the one privileged to dispense with the quotation marks? Is it simply Nuttall's, in a gesture where self-confidence collapses into solipsism? But solipsism is one of the charges he himself occasionally levels against his post-structuralist adversary. Is it, then, 'our' reality? But who are 'we'? Does 'we' designate the collective guardianship of healthy common sense, alongside which the 'others', who challenge the legitimacy of that 'we', are but a band of aberrant deviants? Or is the discourse of common sense a 'genre de discours' (in Lyotard's sense) which refuses to acknowledge its own specific generic constitution in the interests of imposing a *pax culturalis* on the war of meanings, and engendering a paralysis of the critical will before the forms of the given? Unexamined assertions of the 'intuitive' are simply not equipped to deal with this sort of question, and may indeed be construed as actively seeking to evade it. On the other hand, if common sense is what should always be in the dock, it may be that it is now only common sense to say so. But that returns us to our *circulus vitiosus* with a vengeance, in which language goes not merely on holiday but on permanent vacation, agreeable to crazed philosophers and presumably commendable to them as a perfectly commonsensical way of passing the time, but conceivably of little use to anybody else.

Where does this leave us with regard to the question of mimesis? Perhaps travelling forever around the vicious circle, with or without inverted commas. Having used the dilemma of the paradoxical circle to describe some of the difficulties associated with other positions, it is by no means clear that there is in fact any exit from it. It would certainly be disingenuous to try and break the circle through a Johnsonian kick at the proverbial stone, or a simple invocation of what 'we' self-evidently have in common. Yet, as Flaubert's play with the presence/absence of quotation marks shows, the *lieu commun* cannot be made unambiguously an object of derisive scorn (without that attitude becoming as *bête* as its object). Where the *lieu commun* offers itself as the 'last word' on any given matter, it is rightly attacked and exposed. On the other hand, in a basic but strong sense, the *lieu commun* may be the indispensable place in which 'individuals' assemble as in a commonplace; and the ironic knowingness which would transcend it may well entail a blindness to what are fundamental forms of (common) knowledge.

Plots and paranoia

The etymology of 'narrative' is closely tied to notions of 'knowledge'. To 'narrate', Victor Turner reminds us,[4] is from Latin *narrare*, which is akin to *gnarus* ('knowing', 'acquainted with', 'expert in'), both derivative from the Indo-European root *gna* ('to know'), from which comes that vast family of words variously related to Latin *cognoscere*, Greek *gignoskein* (whence *gnosis*) and Old English *geenawwan*. For Aristotle, it will be recalled, mimetic fictions are also embodiments, or realisations, of forms of knowledge; the pleasures of mimesis, according to the *Poetics*, are the pleasures of learning, of cognitive mastery of the world. In Aristotle's account there is, however, some uncertainty as to what kind of knowledge mimesis supplies. In places it is seen as being on a par with philosophical knowledge; in the distinction drawn in the *Poetics* (1451b 5) between the necessary or general truths of philosophy and the merely contingent truths of history, mimesis is unambiguously aligned with the former. Linked to certain arguments in the *Physics* and *Metaphysics*, mimesis discloses the fundamental laws of Nature, as the doubling or completion of processes (*entelechy*) inscribed in *physis*. But at other moments of the Aristotelian argument – especially those where the interpretation of the *Poetics* requires reference to the *Rhetoric* – the 'knowledge' informing and reproduced by the mimetic work of art is seen as being more of a social and cultural kind. The main support of the mimetic plot is the 'probable' (*eikos*), and the 'probable' is distinguished from both the 'necessary' and the 'accidental', as an essentially rhetorical category. Its (ideo-)logical form is that of the *enthymeme* (the 'probable' syllogism), which rests more on persuasive strategy than on formal proof, and whose corresponding artistic forms depend entirely on a social context of custom, belief and expectation shared by artist and audience.

This shift in the ground of mimetic knowledge – from the laws of philosophy and metaphysics to a generalised social rhetoric – evidently represents a point of instability in the Aristotelian system, and it is on what is implied by that instability that a great deal of the modern debate about mimesis turns. For Turner, narrative knowledge is indeed social knowledge; it is knowledge emerging from action and practice, or what he calls 'experiential knowledge'. Its main function is a reparative and healing one; within the 'agonistics' of social life, narrative remakes cultural sense in a world threatened by division and conflict; it 're-articulates a social group broken by sectional or self-serving interests'.[5] The configurational act of binding together the elements of a plot is the formal equivalent of a social binding or 'gathering together'. Narrative knowledge is the knowledge through which ('even in certain industrial societies') a sense of collective identity is affirmed and maintained. On the other side of the argument, however, it is precisely the function of narrative as the articulation of collective identity that renders it radically suspect. In this version, narrative (except in its 'deviant' forms) legislates a repressive orthodoxy; as Lyotard puts it, the great official forms of narrative do not so much repair as 'pacify', gathering up the heterogeneous character of social life (the indefinite heterogeneity of 'language games') into an imaginary, yet highly exploitative, homogeneity.[6] Thus, the 'binding' effect of narrative becomes a bind of a far alarming sort, whereby we are bound over to keep the peace, caught in the grip of law and order; or in Derrida's notorious emphasis, the 'knowing' entailed by 'narrating' is one that *polices*: 'The narratorial voice is the voice of a subject recounting . . . knowing who he is, where he is, what he is and what he is talking about . . . In this sense, all organised narration is a 'matter for the police . . . '.[7] Narrative tracks, tames, frames the world under the aegis of the Law (in its various incarnations as the Father, the Censor, the Institution, the State, and ultimately, the Word). The plots of fiction, and of culture, appear as another kind of Plot, deeply 'paranoid' in its structure and effects, fearful of deviance and excess, imposing silence on oppositional voices, editing the multifariousness of reality into a tyrannically ordered pattern; the great narratives of legitimation are basically 'fascist'.

Mimesis as a matter for the police, a regulative symbolic system for keeping a check on our collective *carte d'identité* or, alternatively, as one of the crucial symbolic forms through which collective sense is forged, and without which there is always the risk of collapse into trivial individualism or a sliding off the map of intelligibility altogether? Collective paranoia or collective wisdom? This may appear an absurdly reductive polarisation of the issue, but, whatever the simplifications, these are the two faces of the essential argument about mimesis, the area in which the *enjeu de la mimesis* is situated. There are many ways of drawing out the implications of that confrontation, but the imperative starting point lies once again in a return to Aristotle. The purpose of this return is not, of course, to attempt a summary of exegetical work on the Aristotelian canon; still less is it to recover what Aristotle himself 'meant' (quite apart from considerations of varying exegetical competence, it may well be, for reasons familiar to hermeneutic theory, that what Aristotle 'meant' is irrecoverable). It is rather a question of attending to a range of quite different modern 'readings' of Aristotle, in particular the various extended meanings given to, and the arguments derived from, some of the basic categories of the *Poetics*: crucially, *mythos*, *dianoia*, *anagnorisis*.

One of the first important attempts in modern times to re-work – in what is acknowledgedly a free interpretation of Aristotle's text – the interrelations of these three categories in terms of a general theory of fictional representation is Northrop Frye's *Anatomy of Criticism* and, subsequently, *Fables of Identity*. For Frye the significance of the poetic *mythos* (the plot or 'imitation of an action') resides in its disclosure of an otherwise hidden structure of intelligibility in events. The *mythos* shows us the connection and shape, and hence the meaning, of human actions. In this function, the *mythos* is supplemented by *dianoia*. The latter term covers a variety of meanings in ancient Greek (in Liddell-Scott-Jones: 'intention', 'thought', 'intelligence', 'rational discourse'). In the *Poetics*, *dianoia* is primarily a property of dramatic speech ('the power of saying whatever can be said, or what is appropriate to the occasion', 1450b 5–6); it is linked to reason and to rhetoric, and is 'shown in all they (the characters) say when proving or disproving some particular point, or enunciating some universal proposition' (1450b 11–12). In Frye's extended sense, *dianoia* is rendered as 'theme', and is transferred from the speech of characters to a work of interpretation effected by the reader. It designates an act of conceptualisation on the part of the reader or audience, whereby an order of meaning is abstracted from the *mythos*; it represents a shift of attention from following the sequence of events to a reflection on what the events are 'about'; in brief, *dianoia* completes the conceptual structure immanent in *mythos*.[8]

But more important still in the process of conceptual completion is the role played by the *anagnorisis* or 'recognition'. For Aristotle *anagnorisis* is a key constituent of the structure of beginning, middle and end that forms the mimetic plot. In general terms, the *anagnorisis* brings about a 'change from ignorance to knowledge' (1452a 30). In more specific terms, it concerns the knowledge of identities, recognition of a person or persons previously unknown, but usually related by kin to the subject of recognition ('the recognition, then, being of persons', 1452b 2). Frye's approach to *anagnorisis* (possibly influenced by F. J. Lucas's account of the *Poetics*)[9] is again to extend the sense of the term towards the notion of an intelligible design retrospectively seized by the reader; reader recognition is the 'bringing of the end into line with the beginning', the intellectual operation through which the 'unifying shape of the whole design becomes visible'.[10] *Mythos*, *dianoia* and *anagnorisis* are thus all connected as the terms of a mode of understanding, a form of knowledge, in which what is finally revealed is a general truth of the reader's own experience; what the reader ultimately recognises is himself or, more precisely, his connection with a continuing community of meaningful life. In its widest sense, 'recognition' is an artistic mechanism for the cultural transmission of the past into the living present: 'The culture of the past is not only the memory of mankind, but our own buried life, and study of it leads to a recognition scene, a discovery in which we see, not our past lives, but the total cultural form of our present life.'[11]

Frye's reading of Aristotle is at once 'rationalist' (in the emphasis on intelligible structure) and 'conservative' (in the emphasis on continuities, deep-laid 'archetypes' of collective experience). It is a reading that has fertilised many subsequent commentaries, notably Peter Brooks's remarkable psychoanalytical account of the recognition-scene (as repetition of the 'life-plot' illustrated by Freud's *Beyond the Pleasure Principle*)[12] and, above all, the exemplary case for the significance of mimesis developed in the work of Paul Ricœur (to which I shall return). There is, however, another way with the Aristotelian categories, which strikes a far less reassuring note, where mimesis is indeed tied to 'fables of identity', but where the fables are suspect because it is the very notion of identity itself that is the object of critical interrogation. This alternative stance derives in part, as we have already seen, from misgivings over the invasion of rhetoric into the mimetic system. In Plato's *Republic* (511d), for example, *dianoia* denotes a form of understanding hovering uncertainly somewhere between the despised rhetorical category 'opinion' (*doxa*) and pure cognition (*nous*). In

Poetics Aristotle explicitly refers us to the *Rhetoric* for further discussion of the context of *dianoia* (1450b 8). But proving that something is the case ('proving or disproving some particular point'), and
persuading that something is the case, are not necessarily the same.
The latter (especially in the hands of the sophist) may well draw on
rhetorical strategies involving false inference, and hence misrecognition. And the possibility of misrecognition is precisely one of the
main anxieties tacitly registered in the *Poetics*. That *anagnorisis*, in
the restricted sense of 'recognition of persons', can misfire is made
clear in the controversial chapter XVI of the *Poetics*. The chief
interest of chapter XVI concerns what Aristotle seeks to exclude
from the mimetic plot as potentially threatening to the integrity of
the knowledge it supposedly embodies. There are various kinds of
'recognition' based on various kinds of inference, and organised
hierarchically from the 'best' to the 'least artistic'. The latter
includes 'recognition by signs', material traces, bodily marks,
physical tokens (1454b 19–25). Inferences from the latter may be
false, they may entail instances of mistaken identity, in particular
errors with regard to kinship relations, and implicitly even the possibility of forgery, or the arrival on the scene of an impostor.

Quite what is to be made of the anxiety expressed in chapter XVI,
and its more general implications for the security of the mimetic
work of art, is a question that has a long exegetical history. One of
the most interesting recent attempts to make sense of this somewhat
murky area is Terence Cave's adaptation[13] to the *Poetics* of Carlo
Ginzburg's influential notion of the *paradigme cynégétique*.[14] The
cynegetic paradigm (or, in the English translation, the 'conjectural
paradigm') designates a primitive form of understanding based on
inference from the material trace, the 'clue' (in Peirce's typology it
corresponds to what he calls 'abductive reasoning'),[15] and which has
its origins in the tracking activity of the Hunter. Knowledge thus
'begins' with hunting, and so too, Ginzburg suggests, does
narrative:

Il se peut que l'idée même de narration . . . ait vu le jour dans une société
de chasseurs, à partir de l'expérience du déchiffrement des traces . . . Le
chasseur aurait été le premier à 'raconter une histoire' parce que lui seul
était en mesure de lire une série d'événements cohérente dans les traces
muettes (sinon imperceptibles) laissées par les proies.[16]

Ginzburg also assigns a specific and varied history to the cynegetic
paradigm. As a form of 'popular' knowledge, it lies alongside the
higher forms of logic and science, and is characteristically despised

by the latter as saturated with prejudice and superstition. On the other hand, it can, at certain moments, penetrate into the established intellectual and institutional culture, where it is appropriated and refined as a means of social monitoring and control. Such is the case, argues Ginzburg,[17] in the late nineteenth century, especially in connection with the growth of those human sciences – such as medicine and criminology – that are institutionally harnessed to the *policing* of an increasingly complex and mobile urban population (the prime example of this appropriation is Galton's text on the uses and techniques of finger-printing, although the 'tracking' model is already in evidence in the emergence of early nineteenth-century 'statistical' sociology).

Ginzburg's observations are, of course, highly speculative, and they may seem very far removed from the business of interpreting the Aristotelian *anagnorisis*. But it must not be forgotten that for Aristotle the recognition-scene literally concerns the 'recognition of persons', and that the plots he uses as illustrative examples are concerned with the identity of individuals within a network of familial relationships (supremely *Oedipus*, where catastrophe arises from a confusion of identities and resolution from their subsequent clarification). In that regard, the recognitive order of mimesis could be described as a system for keeping tabs on identities, and the exclusions of chapter XVI of the *Poetics* as a worry about a potential flaw in the system – basically Aristotle's covering of the traces over the problem of the 'trace', in the potential drift from the solid ground of inductive and deductive reasoning to the less secure ground of abductive reasoning. This, of course, is roughly the direction in which Freud will take the argument, in his reading of the *Oedipus*, its generalisation into the notion of the Family Romance, and his speculations on the origins of patriarchal society.[18] 'Identity' is intrinsically uncertain, because what by definition can never be 'tracked' is the origin of paternity. The great family plots turn on the implicit knowledge that *pater semper incertus est*, and are formal mechanisms for managing the sexual and social tensions of that uncertainty; as Barthes puts it, the law of narrative is inseparable from the 'law of the Father'.[19] Narrative 'plots' family ties, legislates positions within the sexual order, determines who belongs to whom, who lies with whom, who the father is. It constitutes and consecrates a nomenclature. In 'primitive' narrative that function is highly visible; thus in the example of Cashinahua narrative analysed by Lyotard, everything revolves around the enunciation of names; both the parties *in* the narrative (usually the ancestors) and the parties *to* the narrative (tellers and listeners) are obligatorily named, and hence positioned, according to three variables: 'les sexes, les générations et les moitiés exogamiques'; through the controlled distribution of names around marriage, kinship and paternity, Cashinahua narrative proclaims and reinforces a communal identity.[20]

From these 'primitive' origins, one can then begin to trace out the development of the novel as the transformation of the 'basic nucleus' of the Family Romance from individual to social plot, from family unit to whole society.[21] Whence the recurring preoccupation, described by Tony Tanner, in the eighteenth- and nineteenth-century novel with the theme of marriage and adultery, its ramification into the whole fabric of bourgeois society, and the radical 'category-confusion',[22] the loss of social cohesion when the juridical rights of the institution of *pater familias* are infringed by the transgressing adulterous woman. Whence also, as in Ginzburg's argument, the extension of this basic tracking model to whole sections of the population, the systematic classification of the 'deviant' and 'criminal' classes, their separation from the rest of society, and the symbolic representation of that endeavour in the emerging form of the detective novel. Adultery and crime are recurring themes of nineteenth-century fiction. If one of the main concerns of the serious 'bourgeois' novel is with the disorder caused by female adultery, the major preoccupation of the 'popular' novel is with avenging the disorder caused by the criminal transgressor. Sherlock Holmes, suggests Ginzburg, is the great Hunter of nineteenth-century fiction, the hunter at work in the modern metropolis, reading everywhere the trace of the criminal and finally tracking him down to his lair. He is, moreover, the product of a development in popular fiction that goes back to the early nineteenth century, and in which the figure of the Hunter is ubiquitous. As Benjamin points out, the formation of the crime and mystery novel in the first half of the nineteenth century commonly involves the analogical transfer of a specific literary motif: the adaptation to an urban context of Fenimore Cooper's Mohican.[23] The title of Dumas's *Les Mohicans de Paris* resumes the genre, the analogy is active in Sue's *Les Mystères de Paris*, while in the *Comédie humaine* (above all in *Splendeurs et misères des courtisanes*) the reference to Cooper is endemic: Balzac's Paris is the urban equivalent of Cooper's forest, the place of the hunter and the hunted ('ce qu'est la forêt vierge pour les animaux féroces'); and such is the apparent complicity of Balzac's narrative enterprise as a whole in strategies of tracking and detection that one nineteenth-century critic was led to remark of Balzac's imaginative interests:

Quand Balzac découvre les toits ou perce les murs pour donner un champ libre à l'observation, vous parlez insidieusement au portier, vous vous glissez le long des clôtures, vous pratiquez de petits trous dans les cloisons, vous écoutez aux portes, vous braquez votre lunette d'approche, la nuit, sur les ombres chinoises qui dansent au loin derrière les vitres éclairées; vous faites, en un mot, . . . ce que nos voisins les Anglais appellent dans leur pruderie le *police detective*.[24]

But perhaps the late nineteenth-century literary detective is also the culmination and transformation of a model that is far more remote in time. Ginzburg says that the detective novel 'prenait appui sur un modèle cognitif à la fois très ancien et moderne'.[25] What is new derives from the developing sciences of criminological theory and criminal detection. But the reference to antiquity suggests a deep, if intermittent, line of continuity: from the Greek obsession with feet and footprints to the nineteenth-century techniques of finger-printing, from the primal law of the Father to the authority of the Policeman, or from the *Oedipus* (the first literary 'policeman', turning the whole of Thebes into a court-room) to the nineteenth-century detective novel, we see different articulations of an abiding preoccupation with systems of identification and control.

It is against that wider background that we may construe Derrida's description of narrative ('a matter for the police') as being more than just a fanciful provocative metaphor. It is also from the notion of the policing functions of the *paradigme cynégétique* that we can understand various aspects of the critical re-working of the terms of mimesis in modern literary practice; in particular, the implied relation proposed by the modern novel between fictional 'plotting' and the syndrome of 'paranoia'. That implication is especially prominent in the texts of those modern novelists who question the forms of the traditional ('classic realist') novel from an inversion of the procedures of the detective novel. Thus, Oedipa Maas, in Pynchon's *The Crying of Lot 49*, acts as a kind of private investigator uncovering what she sees as the Tristero plot in the communicative labyrinth beneath the surface of contemporary California; Jacques Revel, in Butor's *L'Emploi du temps*, seeks out what he believes to be the true story transposed in George Burton's detective story *Le Meurtre de Bleston*. But the more they seek, the more they find, and the less they confirm. In the perceptions of Oedipa and Revel, the respective realities of California and Bleston become infinitely porous to signification, caught in an indiscriminate semiosis in which everything is available for conversion into sign, and hence where the process of interpretation is theoretically unstoppable. The revelation of a final truth ('l'explosion de la vérité') in the conventional thriller, remarks Burton (Butor?), is a kind of second murder, an act of violence not only on the first murderer (in the bringing to justice and punishment), but also on reality itself.[26] If the Court lays down the judicial law, the Detective lays down the semiotic and narrative law; he provides the 'end', from the perspective of which reality and truth fall into place; and, as Lyotard says, narrative finality, the end which gives retrospective sense to what precedes, is an act of violence, the violence of assuming and exploiting a right to a 'last word'.[27] In the novels of Pynchon and Butor, however, there is no last word. Plot is everywhere, but resolution nowhere; inhabiting their worlds is like being in a detective story without the hermeneutic consolations proffered by the detective. Once the process of perceiving and decoding clues has been launched, there is no possibility of 'arresting' it. The signs proliferate, but are resistant to totalisation and closure; the plot refuses to cohere. The consequence is pandemonium, a crisis of representation turning on the absolute uncertainty as to whether, in the case of *The Crying of Lot 49*, there is a 'real Tristero' or 'the orbiting ecstasy of a true paranoia';[28] or, in the case of *L'Emploi du temps*, on the studied ambiguities of the preposition in 'Le Meurtre *de* Bleston' (who, or what, is menacing whom?). In other words, the security of *dianoia* (in the sense of 'rational thought') gives way to the disorders of *paranoia*, in the form of a flow of signs and meanings in excess of the sanctioned protocols of rationality and interpretation.

Our response to this disturbing situation can vary. Either we follow Sartre's recommendation and abandon the idea of 'plot' altogether, as a myth infested with bad faith ('Il faut choisir: vivre ou raconter').[29] Or we call in the narrative police to restore order, to install a legality of the sign, to affirm the ancient rights of responsible representation. But if this is our response, we may have failed to grasp the lesson of the experiments of Pynchon and Butor. Oedipa Maas and Jacques Revel are not simply 'cases', safely recuperated by a psychiatric description of their condition (the consequences of that move we have already seen in connection with Nerval). The original 'para' of paranoia implies, of course, the notion of 'deviance'.[30] But, if the condition of Oedipa Maas and Jacques Revel can be described as deviant or diseased, this is only

so from the perspective of an official culture ignoring its own intimate relation to what it censors. The point of the novels of Pynchon
and Butor is to overturn the simple relation of opposition between
dianoia and *paranoia*, whereby true cognition and mental health are
to the former what miscognition and disease are to the latter. What
their impossible narratives show is that the structure of *paranoia* is
already inscribed in *dianoia*, but that it remains hidden, repressed
and domesticated by the force of customary sanction and
institutionalised plots. The real choice is not between plots (some
healthy, others mad). It is between plot and pure randomness. But
once the transformation of randomness into plot gets under way, it
is only the arbitrary conventions of closure, Vaihinger's provisional
'as if',[31] that stop the business of plotting from going on for ever.
Query or remove those conventions, and interpretative mayhem
breaks out.

Or, as Deleuze and Guattari argue in *Mille Plateaux*, interpretation ('normal hermeneutic activity')[32] carries within it from its
beginnings the traces of disease, the malady of *interpretosis*;[33] man
the maker of signs, *homo significans*, is already perniciously sick.
Paranoia is not a 'deviation' from the interpretative norm, it is
inherent in the norm itself. From the moment of the installation of
the sign, and hence of the world as an object of 'rational' decipherment, the structure of paranoia is already in place. This paradox
Deleuze and Guattari explain through the related notions of
'territorialisation' and the 'régime'. All signs come into being and
are organised under the auspices of a (despotic) 'régime' ('le régime
despotique paranoïaque').[34] The régime of the sign is the expression
of a desire for mastery and control, a symbolic tracking or 'territorialisation' of the world through the institution of fixed and hierarchical taxonomies. But the desire for control is itself predicated
on the fear of an absence of control, the anxiety that there will
always be something that eludes the net of the régime's surveillance.
To institute the régime of the sign is necessarily to produce and
encounter what threatens the régime. The sign, once positioned,
will not stay in position; any sign, variously interpretable, calls for
another sign; the mechanism of semiosis, by its own logic, generates
a movement of 'déterritorialisation' and hence, on the part of the
régime, a panic before the deterritorialising energies the régime
itself has set in motion; it gives rise to the 'opération paranoïaque du
despote installé dans son monde de signifiance . . . le délire
paranoïaque interprétateur'.[35] The semiotisation of the world is
basically an affair of State, guarded by its various orders of priests

and policemen.[36] The *locus classicus* of the 'régime paranoïaque' is, again, the *Oedipus*, from which can be read the whole nightmarish history of the 'oedipianisation' of Western representations of the body, the psyche and society, culminating in the emergence of psychoanalysis; for Deleuze and Guattari (as for Ginzburg), the psychoanalyst is the interpreter-detective-priest par excellence.[37]

Mille Plateaux is unquestionably the most radical and far-reaching adaptation of the model of paranoia in critique of the idea of 'representation' and the social, cultural and artistic formations which sustain it. Although it visibly belongs to a certain 'genre' (crudely, contemporary 'Paris'), it is also an extremely unusual book, quite beyond the resources of ordinary exposition. Indeed its authors deny that it is a 'book' at all (the unifying structure of the Book is seen as a cultural form cognate with the centralised authority of the State-Apparatus: 'le livre-appareil d'Etat').[38] The textual strategy of *Mille Plateaux* is based on its own favourite metaphor: the Rhizome.[39] The rhizome is a plant (bulbs and tubers) that has no roots; its stem grows underground, in a complex and ceaselessly mobile network of criss-crossing and divergent relations that are without linear direction, hierarchical structure or teleological finality. The rhizomic economy (of feeling, living, writing) demands the complete disarticulation of all structured representation, in favour of a free-wheeling, uncensored (uncastrated) movement of desiring energy, a polymorphous *devenir* ('devenir-animal', 'devenir-femme')[40] released from the territorialising grip of 'la forme paranoïaque virile'[41] of the dominant patriarchal culture. Thus, to the extent that the writing of *Mille Plateaux* remains faithful to its informing analogy, it cannot possibly be 'summarised' (that would be to attempt a summary gesture of the most despicably repressive kind). Reading it is like wandering through an underground bulbous labyrinth, an inter-systemic maze in which numerous discourses cross, but can never be gathered up into an overarching System or global Theory. But from this tangled maze, we can perhaps carry away something that vaguely resembles a set of general 'propositions', and they bear directly upon the specific question of mimesis. The hero of the rhizomic scenario is the Nomad ('les nomades . . . les Déterritorialisés par excellence').[42] There is a nomadic society, occupying 'un espace sans frontière ni clôture',[43] in opposition to the 'sedentary' society commanded by the State, the Imperium, the *Polis*; there is a nomadic politics based on maximum decentralisation away from the authority of the State; a nomadic culture, exacerbating marginality, opening up 'lignes de fuite' from the cultural norm; a nomadic art, refusing symmetry and unity in favour of 'une progression infinie', an art of the 'intermezzo' where what counts in the moves from A to B are not the points but the movements between them;[44] a nomadic literature which dissolves the notion of a 'standard' language into a 'concours de dialectes, de patois, d'argots, de langues spéciales',[45] and whose most radical moment is the disintegration of articulated speech altogether into grunts, cries, murmurs in tune with the pulsional 'intensités' of the body (the exemplary figures here are Kafka, Artaud and late Beckett).

Naturally, in the rhizomic/nomadic purview, mimesis is exceedingly bad news. Deleuze and Guattari make no bones about the matter; 'Le concept de mimésis n'est pas seulement insuffisant, mais radicalement faux.'[46] Mimesis is on the side of what they call the culture of the *calque* (the copy), as distinct from the culture of the *carte*. The *carte* denotes no ordinary topography, it does not map the world, fixing divisions, frontiers, identities. The topography of the Deleuzian *carte*, is, again, rhizomic: 'la carte est ouverte, elle est connectable dans toutes ses dimensions, démontable, renversable, susceptible de recevoir constamment des modifications'.[47] The *calque*, on the other hand, is the absolute mode of sedentarity, fixity, hierarchy, the mechanism for the reproduction of the forms authorised by the régime. The *calque* is the instrument of socialisation, the construction and control of 'identity', first within the family, and finally in the hands of the State.[48] Mimetic art is profoundly complicit in these despotic, and paranoiac, arrangements. Mimesis is that which 'arrests', in the double sense of halting (the flux of *devenir*) and incarceration (imprisoning mobile energy according to a strategy of territorialisation). The Aristotelian *mythos* is the founding fiction of the appropriating power of the State, in the mythical disguise of a rational 'pacte ou contrat', a consensus whereby all 'subjects' are led to believe that they are assenting partners in a shared universe of knowledge: 'Le sens commun, l'unité de toutes les facultés comme centre du Cogito, c'est le consensus d'État porté à l'absolu.'[49] The *mythos* is thus pure myth, the plot a *com-plot*.

In the light of these considerations, we could return briefly to the four major nineteenth-century writers with whom I have been chiefly concerned. It would not be difficult to describe the varying tensions and contradictions of their work, and of critical reaction to it, in terms of the relation between representation and paranoia. On this view, Balzac would be the most spectacularly paranoid, creating a universe subject to a super-saturation of meaning, and dreaming of a master-discourse with which to take it in charge. The endeavour of the *Comédie humaine* is to subjugate that inflow of meaning from a position of despotic transcendence. In the *Comédie* everything signifies; there is no surface without depth, no exterior without interior, no 'token' without 'type', nothing that escapes the net of identification. Physical appearances – clothes, physiognomies (for Deleuze the face, *visagéité*, is the privileged site of paranoia)[50] – are crucial to the Balzacian enterprise of tracking identities and classifying social types. But, as Balzac seeks an authoritative language with which to map the social landscape of the early nineteenth century, he encounters everywhere a *problem* of identification, an anxiety about the scrambling of signs and meanings produced by the figure of the impostor, the charlatan, the false 'salesman'. The 'paranoid' anxiety is not just the reactionary reflex of the novelist-despot. The drive towards interpretative 'order' and 'unity' also reflects a desire to integrate elements in the face of the disintegrative forces of a society based on private interests. The circulation of signs, energies, desires which Deleuze and Guattari wish to see released from the bondage of the territorialising apparatus (and which, in the closing pages of *Mille Plateaux*, entails also the notion of a 'nomadic' economics linked to the libidinal possibilities of 'late' capitalism and the mobile liquidities of the multinational)[51] is exactly what worries Balzac in his own account of the developing forms of 'early' capitalism.

On the other hand, Stendhal, enamoured of *imposture* (in the obsession with pseudonymity), creates a hero acutely sensitive to the sign, especially in the play of *le regard* (no hero more sensitive to *visagéité* than Julien Sorel); who sees plots everywhere, but who meets the 'plot' of society in the mode of systematic transgression: rejecting the father (while dreaming of another paternity), masking identity, transgressing codes of behaviour, social, sexual, legal; and who, at the critical moment of the narrative, becomes virtually 'unrecognisable' to everyone, including, it would seem, many of the nineteenth-century readers of *Le Rouge et le Noir*. For, although the relations of the Stendhalian narrator to the hero are complex and equivocal, the former finally joins forces with the latter's transgressive energies, in a corresponding subversion of received models of narrative representation. If, from the decisive turning-point of the novel (the attempted murder of Louise de Rênal), Julien becomes unrecognisable, it is largely because the narrator refuses to supply a *vraisemblable* (motivations and explanations) for his actions. In the famous 'silences' of *Le Rouge et le Noir*, there is a refusal to interpret. But, if Stendhal says nothing, it does not follow that there is nothing to be said; the urge to interpret has proved irresistible, and into the hermeneutic gaps of *Le Rouge et le Noir* modern critical discourses have swarmed, if only to inquire what the 'significance' of that silence is. The refusal of one *vraisemblable*, as Todorov has pointed out,[52] is always accommodated in another, and if the nineteenth century was baffled by Julien Sorel, we seemingly are not, or at least are no longer baffled by bafflement. We have simply produced a new *vraisemblable* according to which 'life' is properly grasped in terms of the disruptive and aleatory movements of the *imprévu*.

The narrator of *Sylvie* is without parents and forges substitutes (the 'maternal' symbolism that surrounds the young girls at Loisy, the affection for the traditions and customs of the Valois as an attachment to 'ce pays patriarcal', p. 274). But the substitution never works, the hero remains outside the community, locked in a visionary world of dream and fantasy which is divorced from the 'reality principle', and which entails deep uncertainty as to 'identities' (of both self and other). Here we find perhaps a specific transformation of one of the fundamental types that Marthe Robert has extrapolated from her account of the 'primal novel', Freud's *Familienroman*: the figure of the Foundling. The Foundling, according to Robert, is 'le phantaste fasciné par ses rêves et ses métamorphoses, créant à l'écart du monde et contre le monde un peuple de chimères sans proportion avec l'expérience . . . captif de l'univers pré-œdipéen dont la seule loi est encore la toute-puissance de la pensée'.[53] The Nervalian narrator recomposes time and place in a manner that bypasses social codes of recognition; the imagination discovers another 'plot' beyond those of everyday practical reason. But that twilight zone, where the connection-making play of the imagination is given free reign, is fraught with anxiety and danger; categories get blurred, identities are threatened; pastoral nostalgia dissolves into panic and restless agitation. And the text ends with the narrator ambiguously poised between the siren-call of the imagination (in the obsession with the 'memory' of Adrienne) and the call to sociality (the domesticity of Sylvie's household, Sylvie and the narrator playing ironically with the roles of Goethe's *Werther*, in what seems to be an ironic farewell to the genre of which *Sylvie* is a member). It ends, we might say, with the narrator caught between two kinds of 'plot'.[54]

Finally, there is the supremely equivocating example of Flaubert, who writes a novel which contests the novel, but which also contests the contestation of the novel. The ending of *L'Éducation senti-mentale* looks like a definitive leave-taking from traditional forms of emplotment; in Frédéric Moreau's summary of his meandering life as the outcome of a 'défaut de ligne droite' (p. 426), we can also read Flaubert's negation of the purposive movements of narrative, its dispersal into the fragmentary and the indeterminate, its refusal of the 'secret signs and omens'[55] with which the narrative present announces its already pre-formed future. On the other hand, that future is in fact there from the very 'beginning': the 'end' sheds light on all that has preceded it, in that looping backformation whereby a concluding retrospect gathers up and assesses the whole of the story in terms of a remembered incident – the bordello episode – which predates the narrative proper ('C'est là ce que nous avons eu de meilleur', p. 427). Perhaps the deepest irony of *L'Éducation sentimentale* is that it turns out to be one of the most 'closed' novels of the nineteenth century, inviting our deconstructive gambits while at the same time tripping us up as we perform them. Similarly, it is a novel which restores the world to its non-interpreted contingency, but which is also threaded with 'symbolic' connections; which wilfully obstructs and insistently solicits interpretation; where, for example, clothes, faces, furnishings are anchored in meaningful pattern, or are just pretexts for the activity of the fetishising imagin-ation of the hero (Madame Arnoux's dress, the silver box sold at the auction). For the terms of the unsettling position in which this situates the reader of *L'Éducation sentimentale*, we might turn to the example of *Madame Bovary*: either, like Emma, we over-interpret (see 'plot' everywhere), or, like Charles, we under-interpret. The text thrusts upon us the responsibility of interpret-ation, but also places large obstacles in the path of discharging that responsibility.

But, if the obstacles serve to remind us of the problematics of 'reading', Flaubert's text also shows that to abrogate the responsi-bility is simply to cease being a reader altogether. Or is that claim merely a paranoid reflex, possibly commensurate with the furious paranoia of Flaubert's search for the *mot juste* (the 'last word')? With that question we can return not only to what Deleuze and Guattari have to say, but also to how they say it. *Mille Plateaux* is a full-frontal assault on the categories of interpretation, represen-tation and mimesis (alongside which the more 'ludic' tone of Derrida's critique seems positively genteel). It is also a book that is vexingly disarming of its potential adversaries. For to question it, even to 'interpret' it, is to show the symptoms of the very malady they diagnose. On the other hand, the compliment can be returned. For the forms of knowledge and discourse it condemns, it also deploys (again the paradoxes that beset 'deconstruction'): the apodictic statement ('le mimétisme est un très mauvais concept');[56] the emphatic prescriptive utterance ('le multiple, *il faut le faire*');[57] the grammatically well-formed sentence (including that which says 'une règle de grammaire est un marqueur de pouvoir avant d'être un marqueur syntaxique');[58] structured sets of binary oppositions ('nomade'/'sédentaire'; 'carte'/'calque'), despite the explicit rejection of the logic of binarism; rhetorical questions ('N'est-ce pas le propre d'une carte de pouvoir être décalquée?'),[59] implicitly positioning the addressor as a source of knowledge and the addressee as the subject of unquestioning assent; the give-away recurrence of the familiar phrase 'ce n'est pas un hasard si . . . ', prime marker of 'story-telling', of a narrator engaged in the 'paranoid' activity of emplotment.

But perhaps the most pressing question arising from the account of Deleuze and Guattari concerns where exactly, in all this, *is* the area of paranoia? Is it in the culture they describe, or is it in the description they give? Similar difficulties arise elsewhere. It is not impossible to hear in the text of *Mille Plateaux* residual echoes of earlier existentialism (and perhaps even more than a residue of primitivist romanticism).[60] Sartre, we recall, asks us to relinquish plot as a form of bad faith, as the alibi which saves us from having to live the contingency and randomness of the world ('Il faut choisir: vivre ou raconter'). But, in a sense, there is no story more paranoid than this all-encompassing version of bad faith, whereby moral guilt and dishonesty are seen as intrinsically attaching to our collective need for story. What also of the perspective of the demystifying mythologist? 'Combien, dans une journée, de champs véritablement *insignifiants* parcourons-nous?' asks Barthes in *Mythologies*.[61] The answer is none, nothing is 'innocent', everything signifies (dishonestly), the whole of modern bourgeois culture is a plot, but not just as narrative, an organised system of signs and meanings, but also as conspiracy, a *ruse* (one of Barthes's favourite terms) to keep the unsuspecting victims of the plot in a state of hypnotic thrall to the 'myths' of the age. But who is playing detective here: the culture or the semiologist? (Is it an 'accident' that the most distinguished semiologist of our time, Umberto Eco, is also the author of a bestselling detective story?)

On these matters the novelists are often subtler than the critics and theoreticians. The narrator of *L'Emploi du temps* may be sick, deliriously imagining what is simply not there (for where, other than in a very strange, or estranged, mental world, can a town be personified as a potential 'murderer'?). But it is equally possible, within the terms of the novel, that he is entirely sane, and that the struggle to map through writing the labyrinth of Bleston embodies the humanly necessary attempt to carve meaning from a menacing chaos. In Pynchon's novels, plot equals paranoia. But the alternative is certainly grimmer than Sartre would have us believe. In *Gravity's Rainbow* the area of randomness, the radically contingent, is called the Zone (that of plot, the System). The Zone (akin in some respects to Deleuze's nomadic space) is the place of anti-paranoia, where there is no order, no connections, no narratives, where 'categories have been blurred badly'. But being in the Zone ('where nothing is connected') is a 'condition not many of us can bear for very long'.[62] A normal reaction might be to leave the Zone as quickly as possible, and walk back into a plot. Pynchon's novels do not, of course, offer this as a straightforwardly available option. The Plot, as pre-programmed, encompassing system of signs and meanings policed by an all-powerful, if unlocatable, 'They', is the place of absolute paranoia. In *Gravity's Rainbow*, however, the possibilities of a third term are hinted at: in the débris of the Zone one of the characters speculates that there might be 'somewhere inside the waste of it a single set of coordinates from which to proceed'.[63] The coordinates are not fixed, they involve the indeterminate, the unforeseen, the uncertainties of 'probability'. But, just as *Gravity's Rainbow* itself provides – in however dispersed, fragmentary and provisional a form – the 'coordinates' for its own reading, so the coordinates of which its character speaks might lead us back towards the idea of 'plot', not as a surrender to a waiting policeman, but because it is only through some set of connections and recognitions that we can deal with the need to make sense of how we live.

Plots, praxis and consensus

Plot as a fulcrum of sense-making is the theme of Paul Ricœur's reflections on mimesis. Where Deleuze sees in the *mythos* the founding rationale of the paranoia of the *régime*, Ricœur sees the communal work of constructing an intelligible world ('By plot, I mean the intelligible whole which governs a succession of events in any story').[64] Where Lyotard sees in narrative finality a coercive imposition of a 'last word' on a potentially limitless heterogeneity, Ricœur takes a far calmer, even existentially cheerful view of the teleological structure of narrative. Where Sartre claims that narrative is the casting of life in the form of an 'obituary',[65] Ricœur proposes that 'story' is the mode of our living in the world. Where Barthes perceives the inertia of *doxa*, Ricœur perceives active practical knowledge. Where Lacoue-Labarthe argues that mimesis embodies 'la force identificatoire' of myth, whose epistemological and historical point of no return is the Nazi narrative of the *Volk*,[66] Ricœur sees the very 'structure of care'.[67] In Ricœur's vocabulary, *mythos* is emphatically not a dirty word. 'Emplotment', fictional or historical, is a form of human knowledge, perhaps *the* form of human knowledge. Knowledge, in this account, is inextricably linked to time. More specifically, it is the product of human work *upon* time, the active shaping of the otherwise formless character of pure succession: 'the plots we invent help us to shape our confused, formless and, in the last resort, mute temporal experience'.[68] Here Ricœur echoes Kermode's view of narrative as a 'concord' of beginnings and endings, but whereas for the latter such concords are but pragmatic fictions serving humanly necessary ends and, in his later work, subject only to 'institutional control', Ricœur's claim is epistemologically more daring: the fictional shapes with which we shape our lives have real cognitive power (although he does remain somewhat cagey on the question of the 'truth values' of narrative). Apprehending and explaining the world (that is, our experience in time) requires an act of narrative representation. Time is meaningless until it becomes 'temporality', and temporality is 'that structure of existence that reaches language in narrativity'.[69] To the objection that all such representations are mere arbitrary 'codings', Ricœur's reply is that the objection is so much wasted breath. For the mind there is no access to the world, no 'route to the referent', no explanatory endeavour, that is not in some way or other tied to the operations of story-telling. Human rationality and narrative emplotment are inseparable, and, in that fundamental connection, 'we are brought back to the link between *mythos* and *mimesis* in Aristotle's *Poetics*'.[70]

The terms of Ricœur's reading of Aristotle I have already sketched in a previous chapter.[71] The emphasis there, it will be recalled, was to extricate the idea of mimesis from the impasse of the 'closure of representation', to displace the Aristotelian theory of mimesis from its traditional association with the notion of 'the reduplication of presence' towards the notion of dynamic *praxis*.

Aristotle breaks with Plato's negative use of the term mimesis to signify the illusion of 'redoubled presence' or 'weakened copies of things', to relocate it in the area of 'action' or 'production'. Mimesis belongs to *poiesis*, and the shared suffix '*-sis*' points to Aristotle's sense of the productive, creative energies of the mimetic project. As the 'imitation of an action', the *mythos* is less a copy than a synthesis (*synthesis ton pragmaton* is the definition of *mythos* in chapter VI of the *Poetics*, 1450a 4–5). Where Plato sees in mimetic fiction mere 'feigning', Aristotle sees 'figuring', or what Ricœur calls 'configuration'.[72]

Mimetic configuration is a complex literary and cultural process, involving the interaction of various levels and stages of human practice, various forms of 'doings'. These doings include the social world of everyday actions (what Ricœur calls 'prefiguration'), the artistic making of the fictional plot ('configuration') and the act of reading ('transfiguration' or 'refiguration'). Prefiguration, configuration and transfiguration are three modes of *praxis*. Although each enjoys a certain autonomy, they interlock with each other in ways at once mutually enabling and constraining, and the phenomenon of mimesis is not properly understood without some account of that complex process of interaction. Prefiguration is what takes place in the sphere of everyday practical knowledge; it is the area of 'pre-understanding', and manifests itself (in Wolfgang Iser's term) as a 'repertory' of social competences. From the point of view of its role in the formation of the mimetic fiction, prefiguration possesses three major characteristics: it involves 'knowing how to do something' (mastery of a whole 'network of practical categories'); secondly, it denotes actions already symbolically mediated, and hence which 'confer a basic readability upon action'; thirdly, it has a temporal structure already removed from the simple succession of 'nows'; it is socially constructed time, the 'time with which we count and measure . . . the time for doing this or that . . . the time "in" which we live and act'.[73] Configuration is the crossing of the threshold from pre-understanding into the world of the literary fiction, in which the knowledge of action is made the object of a conscious and systematic synthesis (the organised 'plot'). Its relations to the domain of prefiguration are various. On the one hand, it can be seen as a completion, a 'purified' version of the intelligibility tacitly and informally deposited in the modes of pre-understanding. In this respect, the artistic plot is 'parasitic' upon a 'first order intelligibility', but not as a simple replica. If the sense of 'imitation' still holds, it is not as inert copy, but as 'synthetic comprehension': 'Far from producing a weakened image of pre-existing things, *mimesis* brings about an augmentation of meaning in the field of action, which is its privileged field. It does not equate itself with something already given. Rather it produces what it imitates, if we continue to translate *mimesis* by "imitation".'[74]

The emphasis is thus resolutely dynamic. The configuring action of the plot gives rise to what, in an earlier work, Ricœur calls a 'dynamic redescription' of experience, governed by the principle of 'productive reference' to the world.[75] On the other hand – or rather by the same token – configuration can stand in a relation of contestation to the forms of the prefigured world. Ricœur concedes the notion of basic narrative 'typologies', a 'schematism' given either in the inherited literary corpus or, more diffusely, in the social repertory of pre-understanding.[76] But the relation between 'type' and 'token', schematism and manifestation, is not one of static reproduction. Although at certain points Ricœur steers close to a brand of 'universalism' ('no symbolic creation which is not in the final analysis rooted in the common symbolical ground of humanity'),[77] he is wholly opposed to the notion of an ahistorical 'grammar' of narrative typologies favoured by early structuralism (just as the principle of 'schematism' has little in common with Gombrich's perceptualist account of 'schemata' somehow getting closer and closer to full adequation to Reality). Crucial to Ricœur's argument is the importance attached to *history*.[78] Narratives are not only orderings of time, they are also ordered by time; 'about' time, they are also 'in' time. It is history which determines the conditions for (as well as the checks on) dynamic redescription, productive imagination and productive reference.

One of the advantages of Ricœur's approach, therefore, is that it can deal with change and 'deviation'. In these terms, we could return to, say, the plot of *Illusions perdues*, and read it as the productive grafting of an old schematism on to a new social experience: the ancient *topos* of the questing hero, the wandering poet, brought into relation with the nineteenth-century realities of urban commerce, the new reading public, modern forms of circulation and exchange. The meeting of the two in the Balzacian plot works as a kind of *montage*, a strategy of ironic juxtaposition, from which a new relation of 'reference' to the world is generated. What needs to be stressed here, however, is that it is not just a question of incorporating into a traditional narrative framework a new social and historical 'content'. It is also, and more importantly, a matter of forms, of configurations of time: the combining of the archetypal time of the Quest and the specific time of the modern City (whence the particular temporal rhythms of *Illusions perdues*, its alternation between nervous pace – Lucien's first week in Paris – and relative torpor). Similarly, we could read the plot of *L'Éducation sentimentale* as a re-writing of the 'Balzacian' paradigm, again in the terms of ironic montage: the contrast between the desired 'Paris' of the *Comédie humaine* ('Rappelle-toi Rastignac dans la *Comédie humaine*, tu réussiras, j'en suis sûr', p. 17) and the actual Paris of *L'Éducation*; Frédéric Moreau's fantasy of repeating the 'time' of Balzac's Paris in juxtaposition with the 'real' time of Flaubert's novel, configured, or perhaps dis-figured, in the idiom of evasion, dispersal and vacancy.

Yet, if Ricœur's location of mimesis in the dynamics of history enables him to account for change and, more radically, for subversion of the pre-given paradigms, that very same location is also what sets constraints on subversive play with the paradigms. Narrative deviations work in terms of 'rule-governed deformations'.[79] Thus, even in those twentieth-century fictions which, in accordance with the modern sense of time as fragmentation, most drastically undo the inherited plottings of temporality, the paradigm, although it often becomes virtually invisible, does not do so entirely. The constructions of time we make in time, in time break into pieces, often irreparably, and it has been an essential part of the work of the modern novel to show us why this is both inevitable and desirable. But not only does deconstruction presuppose construction (and is therefore intelligible only by reference to a prior 'norm'); it itself – except when purely trivial – discloses new patterns (of 'readability') from the ruins of what it demolishes. Reality and art, as Nelson Goodman argues, are about makings and remakings.[80] The process necessarily demands un-makings, but there is a major error in isolating the latter from the total historical process to which they belong, and holding them up as the only object worthy of serious attention. Un-making has its context, and also its limit. Art cannot cross that limit without effecting its own negation. What lies beyond the limit is pure hypothesis (or pure noise); it is the strictly *illisible*. The *illisible* has had a good run for its money in the service of contemporary polemical ends. Severed from polemic and more soberly considered, the *illisible* cannot be anything other than an entirely imaginary category; unless geared to a particular social context ('illisible' to *whom*?), it tells us nothing whatsoever about any known (or conceivable) form of human practice (such as writing and reading). And what is long overdue is vigorous rejection of the view that to object to this impossible notion is to object to the 'modern' as such, either from the ground of a totalitarian Stalinist aesthetics or from that of a traditionalist Arnoldian defence of 'culture' against the despoliations of 'anarchy'.

In the terms of Ricœur's argument, however, the objection does require invoking the notion of a Tradition. If history is what makes change possible (and recognisable), it is also what acts as a check on change, what keeps it this side of the line of intelligibility. Ricœur's history is therefore a 'history that has all the characteristics of a *tradition*. By this, I do not mean the inert transmission of some dead deposit but the living transmission of an innovation that is always capable of being reactivated through a return to the most creative moments of poetic making'[81] (we recognise here Ricœur's debt to Northrop Frye). 'Tradition', as the interplay of 'innovation and sedimentation', is thus not the mortal enemy of the Artist, as Harold Bloom would have it;[82] it is not the stage of the Oedipal drama of the son slaying the father in order to carve out a terrain of independence and originality (Bloom's model, as Norman Bryson suggests,[83] perhaps works more satisfactorily with painting, and its special problems of medium, style and 'belatedness' with regard to the painterly traditions). The cultural and historical context of literary fictions is different (perhaps in part because of the porousness of literature to the vernacular). In any case, while it would be right to describe the plot of *L'Éducation sentimentale* as a dis-emplotment of *Illusions perdues*, Flaubert's text remains in part unrecognisable if we do not 'recognise' Balzac in it. Flaubert equivocates the terms, but there *are* terms, and they are not of Flaubert's choosing.

But if history supplies the terms, who carries out the act of recognition? Obviously, the reader, and it is the notion of the Reader (and its extended context in the 'reception theory' of Iser and Ingarden) which occupies the key place in the 'third' stage of Ricœur's account of mimesis as *praxis*. The reader is the agent of a 'transfiguration'. Readerly transfiguration 'intersects' with artistic configuration in ways that constitute 'a very complex problematic'.[84] Most neutrally, the operations of reading are an 'actualisation'; the act of reading is 'what accompanies the configuration of the narrative and what actualises its capacity for being followed. To follow a story is to actualise it by reading it.'[85] But the dialectic of configuration and transfiguration is far richer than a relation of simple 'accompaniment' of the one by the other. In many cases, it is the former which acts upon and modifies the latter (the reader's encounter with an artistic configuration after which things can never be the 'same again'). On the whole, however, transfiguration exerts constraints on configuration; it is basically a 'conservative' force, especially in connection with highly experimental narrative forms. Transfiguration most often works in the form of a 'return upon pre-figuration'.[86] The reader draws upon the 'repertory' of practical knowledge, the tacit resources of pre-understanding, in order to make sense of those fictions which have virtually deserted the paradigms. In such cases (Ricœur's example is Joyce's *Ulysses*) the 'written work' is but a 'sketch for the reader', which the latter then fleshes out by means of what he knows of the tactics of 'emplot-ment': 'the written text may involve holes, lacunae, and indeter-minate zones which, as in Joyce's *Ulysses*, defy the reader's capacity to configure the work which the author seemingly finds a mischiev-ous pleasure in defiguring. In this extreme case, it is the reader, whom the work almost abandons, who bears the burden of emplot-ment.'[87]

The reading subject could then be described (with the obvious problems to which such a description gives rise) as a repository of the 'tradition'. But whatever else he is, he is certainly not an indi-vidualist subject. The whole burden of Ricœur's effort to join pre-figuration, configuration and transfiguration in a general theory of mimesis is in the refusal of an aesthetics and an ideology of indi-vidualism. As historical products, the orderings of, and modifi-cations to, the human experience of time produced by mimesis are irreducibly social and collective in character. Narrative time is 'public time'; it is 'from the outset, the time of our "being-with-others".' Plot discloses a 'structure of care', and its teleology a 'narrative of preoccupation', a caring about how we make sense of a common world through projections towards and retrospections from common 'ends'. Here, for Ricœur, is the significance of Aristotle's *mythos*, *dianoia* and *anagnorisis*; they are the means for creating 'significant wholes out of scattered events'. Mimesis is thus integrative; the configurational act is a 'grasping together' that has, as for Victor Turner, social implications as well as purely 'aesthetic' ones: 'through its recitation, a story is incorporated into a com-munity which it "gathers together" '.[88]

The problems raised by Ricœur's defence of mimesis are manifold, and spread out along different levels of inquiry. There are acute epistemological difficulties in the attempt to marry an historical account of mimesis (with its implicit relativism) and the special cognitive values Ricœur invests in mimesis. There is an apparent conflation of the social context of oral story-telling and that of the diffusion of the written text (thus passing over the vital cultural and existential differences between the two described by Benjamin in 'The Storyteller').[89] But, in terms of the counter-argument I have outlined in the previous section, the most urgent question is: where, in this account, have all the policemen gone? In the retreat from the terrifying formlessness of the Zone into the more articulated, and therefore habitable, space of the System (the mimetic plot, says Ricœur, 'makes the world one that can be inhabited'),[90] do we not have to pick up our *carte d'identité* in order to be admitted? In the System, where are the systems, discursive and institutional, that speak, write, track, classify, programme us? In the emphasis on public time, social integration, commonalities, where is there any acknowledgement of the forces of domination and coercion? Alternatively, where is the Consensus through which, as Deleuze and Guattari argue, the paranoiac State Apparatus acquires the necessary legitimations for the enforcement of its authority? 'Consensus' is not a term that Ricoeur uses, but it is tacitly there all the time as the logically necessary accompaniment of the other major terms of his vocabulary.

But 'consensus' is, of course, one of the great problem-laden terms of our time. Its misuses and abuses are legion, such that it is now virtually impossible to use the term in good faith. The philosophically most determined attempt to retrieve it from the enchanted precincts of ideology (Habermas's notion of 'rational consensus') poses it as an ideal future goal, in the project of human emancipation from the actualities of 'distorted communication'. For Habermas, rational consensus, as the meeting of 'cognitive' discourse and human 'interest', is possible only under certain, as yet unrealised, conditions: it must be 'non-neurotic', 'non-ideological'; above all, it requires that all parties to the dialogue participate as full and equal partners.[91] It is therefore an illicit move to appropriate Habermas's 'rational consensus' for the description of current institutional arrangements, where dialogue occurs within a hierarchical structure of 'seniors' and 'juniors', expert and lay, initiates and novices. This may be how things actually operate (in the Church, the University), but this has nothing whatsoever to do with what Habermas understands by rational consensus. The move in question occurs in two of Frank Kermode's essays,[92] although in a manner so subtly self-equivocating that they instantly problematise everything they assert (in this respect they are quite unlike the *reductio* of that argument, in which one apologia for literary 'realism' tries to persuade us of the '*charm* of institutions').[93] Kermode refers to an 'institutional competence' as an enabling condition of interpretative work getting done (so that if institutions do not actually have 'charm', they may nevertheless be an occasion for 'moderate rejoicing'). On the other hand, the institution can make 'mistakes'; it is not 'infallible' – which must then mean that there is an order of judgement which transcends the competence of the institution. Again, the argument does not 'offer an opinion' as to whether institutional jurisdictions are 'right or wrong' ('I am describing the world as it is'), but concludes by remarking that 'it is only by recognising the tacit authority of the institution that we achieve the measure of liberty that we have in interpreting. It is a price to pay, but it purchases an incalculable boon.'[94]

There is here an uneasy sliding between the descriptive and the prescriptive, saying how it is and how it should be, and the account also seems to allow little space for the ways in which forms of practical knowledge and experience can effectively challenge or bypass systems of 'institutional' control. But in so far as there is prescriptive implication, this is very far removed from Habermas's project of human emancipation. As we strive for that emancipation (or dismiss it as an impossible utopia), the question therefore arises as to what positions in the meantime we can plausibly adopt, and where these leave us with the matter of mimesis. If Ricœur's account stumbles at the crucial hurdle of difference, conflict, inequality, what are the alternatives? A radically alternative prescription is Lyotard's demand, in his more recent work, that we smash 'consensus' (and the narrative myths which sustain it), in favour of a systematic aggravation of 'heterogeneity'. I have already referred, on several occasions but only in passing, to Lyotard's writings. And it is with some more extended remarks on this very important body of work that I should like to conclude, for where Lyotard puts us on all these issues is perhaps, at the present juncture, the most challenging place to be. The work is complex, and there can be no question of trying to summarise it here. If Deleuze and Guattari's *Mille Plateaux* is perhaps the wildest book to come lately out of Paris, Lyotard's *Le Différend* (preceded by *La Condition postmoderne*) is arguably the toughest. It is certainly not wild; on the contrary it is characterised by an analytical rigour (self-consciously advertised in the opening pages as the deliberate choice of a certain 'tone')[95] which could get him into trouble with those for whom playing figuratively with the figures– in order to uncover what is 'repressed' by the analytical – is stragetically *de rigueur*. Lyotard takes analytical philosophy very seriously indeed (nearly everything in his later work can be read as a development of his encounter with the work of Wittgenstein). But on many of the substantive issues, he tells a 'story' (while being deeply critical of Story) which is not dissimilar to that recounted by Deleuze and Guattari. It is suspicious of the traditions of Western 'rationality' and science, whose cognitive claims Lyotard links to a paranoid tactics of domination and exclusion (the text of *La Condition postmoderne* refers us approvingly to Horkheimer's pioneering essay, 'The Paranoia of Reason').[96] It also posits narrative ('le récit') as complicit in these repressive tactics, as a neutralisation of *différend*, and mimesis as a call to identification with politically manipulative images of 'community', legitimised as universal images of Man.[97]

Against these repressively homogenising forms, Lyotard proposes the domain of the indefinitely heterogeneous. This too resembles the insistence of Deleuze and Guattari on maximal dispersal into multiplicity ('le multiple, *il faut le faire*'). But whereas for the latter the extreme point of the multiple is the disarticulation of language into cries, murmurs, 'intensités', Lyotard's commitment to heterogeneity always remains this side of articulated language, and is based (at least in its initial form) on a radical interpretation of Wittgenstein's notion of the 'language game'. What Lyotard takes from the *Philosophical Investigations* is the emphasis on the irreducibly various nature of language games; each game is *sui generis*; there is no 'meta-game' which can gather up all the others into a totalising description; to the argument that to *define* language as a series of games is to effect just such a totalising move, the reply is that 'definitions' constitute simply one specific game in the plural, heterogeneous field. The point of Lyotard's adaptation of the language game is to halt and subvert the drive of any discourse towards hegemony. A major casualty of that undertaking is the idea of 'consensus' (along with Wittgenstein, the other philosopher repeatedly discussed in *Le Différend* is Kant: Wittgenstein's 'language game' is in part deployed to reject Kant's *sensus communis*). In the argument of *La Condition postmoderne*, consensus is either a utopian 'horizon' (Habermas) or an ideological-institutional trap locking us into the stratagems of 'la légitimation politique-étatique'.[98] From the closed world of consensus, Lyotard seeks to propel us into an open community based on local encounter, on the pragmatics of 'dissentiment', into a society grasped as a mobile, heteromorphous, non-formalisable flow of language games. The complicated detail of what that argument entails (especially its elaboration and refinement in *Le Différend*) cannot possibly be rehearsed here. But one way of catching its general drift, and also some of its problems, is through two of the motifs most actively at work in the text of *La Condition postmoderne*: the agon and the city.

The playing of language games takes place in a conflictual space, as an 'agonistique générale'.[99] Lyotard's version of heterogeneity is tough, not only because it refuses consensus, but also because it will not allow the heterogeneous to be consigned to the safer terrain of the ludic playground or the happy condition of peaceful co-existence. Lyotard's postmodern *agon* is a rough-house of radically dissenting voices, a place where languages are at war, an adversarial world in which players compete and clash. Yet the image of the *agon* raises a severe difficulty, which turns conceptually on the question of the 'rules'. Rule, for Lyotard, is a very tricky category. The rules of the game do not pre-exist the game; they are not eternal 'laws'; they can be re-negotiated, even broken. On the other hand, they are both constitutive and regulative of any given game played at any given time. Playing the game presupposes agreement between the players as to what the rules are, even if such agreements are purely provisional ones: what Lyotard calls the 'contrat temporaire' as opposed to the 'institution permanente'.[100] Another name he gives to these provisional and local arrangements is the 'minimum de consensus'.[101] Minimal consensus is the precondition of the language game. But this minimalism represents, in its larger implications, a major concession. For the return of consensus in its minimalist guise, if it is not to be just a tautologous naming of a component of the game, raises the question as to how minimal is the 'minimum'. By this I mean not what lies below the threshold of the minimum ('private languages', nonsense), but what lies *above* it. At what point does minimum become non-minimum, and start to move in the direction of the wider kinds of consensus to which Lyotard is so vehemently opposed?

That difficulty presents itself with even greater force when we consider the implications of the second analogy, that of the city. This Lyotard takes directly from Wittgenstein, in order to illustrate the heterogeneous character of language games:[102] in the city of language, there are many *quartiers*, side-streets, possible suburban additions; or in Wittgenstein's words: 'Our language can be seen as an ancient city: a maze of little streets, of old and new houses, and of houses with additions from other periods; and this surrounded by a multitude of new boroughs with straight regular streets and uniform houses.'[103] But the analogy of the city finally turns against the emphasis on indefinite heterogeneity Lyotard wishes to attribute to the notion of the language game. First, and as Wittgenstein was well aware, the city has its limits; they are not indefinitely extendable (the city cannot be indefinitely expanded by way of the addition of suburbs, 'territorialising' arrangements mean that you run out of space). Secondly, a city may be internally much differentiated, but in the naming of it *as* a city, an 'identity' is conferred upon it (the city and its citi-zens). It is perhaps engaged in agonistic transactions with other cities, but from the moment that the 'space' in question is named as a 'city', the notion of possible consensus instantly shifts from the purely local level of the 'quartier' and the 'ruelle' to a larger context. And, once that move has occurred, there can no longer be any criteria for stopping the shift at that level; the 'minimum', on this analogy, becomes a category so fluid that it can be geographically and politically demarcated in a whole number of different ways.

Le Différend is in part an attempt to deal with these complicating implications, but whether it does so satisfactorily is an open question. The argument of *Le Différend* is even tougher than that of *La Condition postmoderne*. The *agon* is recast as *différend*. According to the logistics of *différend*, there are no longer any players, no commonly agreed rules, only disputes in which the presuppositions of the respective parties are so fundamentally divergent that there is no possibility whatsoever of resolving the disputes on equitable grounds. *Différend* is a point in conflictual space where no consensus (however 'minimal') can hold, where there is dispute deprived of a rationale of negotiation and resolution, without available rules of adjudication:

A la différence d'un litige, un différend serait un cas de conflit entre deux parties (au moins) qui ne pourrait pas être tranché équitablement faute d'une règle de jugement applicable aux deux arguments.[104]

Similarly, Wittgenstein's language game (now adjudged to be too 'anthropocentric') is re-worked in terms of the more precise, and more unyielding, notions of the 'régime de phrases' and the 'genre de discours'. A 'régime de phrases' is a class of sentences grouped according to a specific function ('raisonner, connaître, décrire, raconter, interroger, montrer, ordonner, etc.'). *Régimes* are heterogeneous and strictly non-translatable into each other. They can, however, be combined ('enchaînés') to form a *genre de discours*. The latter is constituted according to a specific end or objective ('savoir, enseigner, être juste, séduire, justifier, évaluer, émouvoir, contrôler . . . ').[105] 'Genres de discours' are *absolutely* incommensurable. There are no bridges leading from one to the other; there is no overarching 'meta-genre', either cognitive or ethical, for resolving the differences stemming from that unconditional incommensurability. What happens when two 'genres' meet and clash is simply a power struggle, in which the victor wins only at the cost of inflicting an injustice (a 'tort') on the terms of the other, either by neutralising it or, more violently, by silencing it. In the world of *différend*, there is no place left for rational dialogue, or 'fair play'.

But the impossibility of fair play (in the sense of common rules and agreed outcomes) twists paradoxically in Lyotard's argument to produce the only possible recommendation in this grievous situation: being fair. In the absence of valid rules of adjudication holding across the heterogeneity of 'genres de discours', all we can do – but it is also what, from the fact of that absence, we are required to do – is to be fair to 'genres de discours' in their relations of difference, of *différend*. Since there are no justifiable reasons for elevating any one discourse above the others (a 'totalitarian' move), we must be fair to them all; acknowledge, and even actively intensify, the proliferation of incommensurables. But the paradox then twists viciously, and in several directions. First, in order to situate discourses in a conflictual relation (as *différends*), the argument must assume a point external to those discourses from which they can be thus situated. Even as agonistic multiplicity, they are perforce the object of a 'totalising' description, of a cognitive utterance (but the argument from heterogeneity has stipulated that the cognitive game cannot encroach upon the non-cognitive; the descriptive game can describe only descriptions). Secondly, the requirement that we 'respect' heterogeneity is necessarily a universal prescription brought to bear on all games (not just the purely prescriptive), thus contradicting the principle of heterogeneity itself. Conversely, withdrawal of this prescription, on the grounds that it violates the requirements of respect, means that we can no longer respect. In brief, the argument is suspended hopelessly between the denial of 'meta' and its indispensability (if only as a condition of that denial).

To offer this as a criticism of Lyotard's work is in some ways a trivial response to a text of quite remarkable complexity, and in which it is precisely these impossible twists and turns that are presented as an object of continuous and self-conscious scrutiny. They are indeed announced from the opening pages of *Le Différend*. Caught on the horns of an intractable dilemma, Lyotard asks the vital question (but why is it vital?): 'Comment sauver l'honneur de penser?' The question clearly matters, and the answer is: 'témoigner du différend'.[106] But here the paradoxical net becomes exceedingly tight. Who is the witness, what are his credentials, what point does he occupy in relation to the conflicting discourses whose conflicts he witnesses? The *témoignage* demands what its object denies, a discourse in the position of making both cognitive and ethical judgements. It demands bearing witness to the 'truth' of *différend*; hence, the one thing, in terms of the argument of *Le Différend*, about which there can be no *différend* is the truth of *différend*. It also demands bearing witness to the 'injustice' of the neutralisation or annihilation of a differing discourse by another; saving the honour of thought entails a morality, a notion of justice. But on what *authority*? For if, as Geoff Bennington has argued in an essay on Lyotard's work,[107] it is true that the author of *A Theory of Justice* (John Rawls) is unjust to justice in his very title, it is by no means clear where the attempt to expel the 'theoretical' (the 'meta') dimension puts us, or whether it is possible to expel it at all. We have here a further instance of a contradiction which Vincent Descombes has shown to be endemic to modern French thought in general: a critique of authority in which, from the terms of the critique itself, what is at once presumed and indefensible is the authority of the critique.[108] Lyotard's work is a rigorous confrontation with a problematic, whose possible outcome, however, is to leave us stranded on an island of total undecidability. In an entirely undecidable universe, you cannot do anything, or rather, since there can be no 'legitimating' rationale for any particular position, what you do might as well be anything, a matter of private intuitions or desires. But, on that claim, there can be no particular claim to our attention by the descriptive and prescriptive propositions of *Le Différend*.

This is, of course, to stray once more into the destructive circle of the Paradoxes, and moreover leaves unanswered the question – unaddressed by Ricœur – as to how to construct an account of 'commonality' in a world marked by inequity and division. In such a world, art, as a specific kind of language game, remarks Lyotard, takes us (should take us) across the limit of the 'tolerable' towards the domain of the 'intolerable'.[109] Instead of Kant's politics of the *sensus communis* (the most dangerous myth of our age), we should embrace that emphasis in Kant's aesthetics on 'agitation', on disturbance, that which shocks and shakes the System (nervous, political). But if we assent to this proposition, what does such assenting presuppose? What makes assent possible? Does it matter if I (you, he, she, we, they) disagree? Either the questions are posed in such a way as to block in advance all possible answers to them (in which case it is futile to pose them), or there are answers, however incomplete and provisional. But, if there are, this can only be because, in order to tolerate difference, including the 'intolerable' (both to endure it and be fair to it), there is a shared vocabulary in which these sorts of things can be done.

Public and private, frames and sentences

Soyons païens is another of the – logically complex – prescriptions enjoined upon us by Lyotard (in *Au juste*), in defence of the heterogeneous and the agonistic against the 'pious' constitution of orthodoxies.[110] But, as with so many other appeals to the ancient Greeks, it is doubtful if Lyotard's notion of 'paganism' is wholly compatible with the cause of radical dispersal into multiplicity it is designed to serve. We could just as well describe the ancient *agon*, and the ancient amphitheatre, as places in which differences were acted out, but also settled: the outcome of the contest, the resolution of the play, as 'ends' conferring meaning on what precedes. They could also be described as *public* places, in which persons (other than women and slaves) foregathered as 'citizens' participating in a public scheme of things. But that too is a somewhat idealised view of the 'pagan', and is certainly difficult to transplant in good faith to the conditions of the late twentieth century. From the perspective of the splintered and antagonistic postmodern *agon*, such retrospects will seem derisory. Nostalgia for the city state, the tradition of civic humanism, the idea of art as 'public' event have long since been caught up in quite different narratives of legitimitation; converted, and perverted (roughly from the end of the eighteenth century), into the myths of 'national' identity whereby the notion of the 'public', as resistance to the increasing encroachment of the 'private', also functioned to mask realities of division and inequality.

In the nineteenth century the myths crack wide open, in the growingly visible split between 'public' and 'private', and the corresponding mistrust on the part of the writer of the idea of a 'common language'. We have seen how for certain nineteenth-century writers the question of the 'public' is encountered as problem. Balzac looks for a 'public', but finds only fragments, and retreats into theocratic fantasies of an originally uncorrupted language. Stendhal goes abroad, not only literally but metaphorically, remarking that, from the point of view of the official culture, his own works will be read as if written in a 'foreign tongue'. Nerval takes his public on what appears to be an innocent pleasure trip to Cythera, and then abandons them to what turns out to be a more disquieting place. Flaubert brings 'public' and 'publication' together under the sign of *bêtise* ('publier . . . est une idée reçue'), then scandalises the public with the publication of *Madame Bovary*, whereupon public response is articulated through the voice of the public prosecutor. Here, in the trial of *Madame Bovary*, there appears to be a veritable case of *différend* (masquerading as a *litige*). The work of narrative representation is wholly at odds with that of a given social representation (around the sexuality of the woman-wife-adulteress). The presuppositions on either side of the dock are so fundamentally divergent that there is no possibility of rational accommodation. The terms – the 'genre de discours' – are chosen by the prosecutor; they are not Flaubert's terms, but are the ground on which his case must be presented. In the event, Flaubert is acquitted, but he is not given a proper 'hearing'; and moreover his text, already bowdlerised by the editors of the *Revue de Paris*, does not escape unscathed: the famous sentence 'Elle retrouvait dans l'adultère toutes les platitudes du mariage' is weakened to 'toutes les platitudes de *son* mariage' (the 'du' was not restored until the 1873 edition).

We are once again back with narrative as a matter for the 'police', although this time with narrative as the object rather than the subject of the policing operation. We can rest assured that, however the limits of what is permitted and forbidden are redefined, the policing, both institutional and symbolic, will continue. Whence the continuing validity of the aesthetics of 'shock', agitation, estrangement. But the latter will not mean much (outside the restricted circle of connoisseurs of the avant-garde) if it is severed from a public space of 'recognitions', or if the marriage of the 'signifier' and 'signified' is dissolved in the name of a libertarian ideology ceding to the former unlimited freedom of movement. What that space is, or might be, cannot be defined. There is no fixed lexicon of the 'common' vocabulary. It emerges only in ever-changing forms of social practice, themselves constrained by relations of force and conflict; and it is always vulnerable to ideological take-over by those who wish to pass off their particular vocabulary as a universal discourse. The case for mimesis I have been exploring here does not, or should not, assume some actually or potentially available canonic vocabulary furnishing the meta-sentences which could act as a final court of appeal for all other sentences. There is no timeless or wholly disinterested vocabulary, just as there is no universal story in which 'we' are all members of a quarrelsome but ultimately united family. And, if I have questioned Sartre's view that the need for 'story' *tout court* is intrinsically plagued by bad faith, it must be acknowledged that any notion of a narrative told by a naturalising 'we' about a naturalised 'us' is highly exposed to that specific form of bad faith in which self-deception is animated by the cunning stratagems of self-interest. What is historically and culturally authorised as the agenda of mimesis is not cosily negotiated; it takes place within situations where some have more negotiating power than others, or indeed the power to deprive others from participating in the negotiations altogether. Flaubert's alteration of 'du' to 'de son' was not the agreed outcome of an equal debate, but the consequence of a confrontation in which the court possessed coercive authority (either alteration or the risk of suppression).[111] Similarly, what is included on, or excluded from, the agenda of mimesis is to a very great extent determined by relations of power and differential access to resource (both material and symbolic). No debate on mimesis will get very far if it does not tackle the problem of which stories get told and which get repressed, whose interests are represented and whose are neglected.

The strength of Lyotard's argument – and of the 'deconstructionist' enterprise in general – is to have reminded us that the aesthetics of mimesis also entail a politics, and more particularly that there are important connections between the political and literary meanings of the idea of 'representation'. It is not clear that Ricœur's approach can deal satisfactorily with the implications of that linkage. Arguably his view of mimesis as dynamic *praxis* within history could accommodate these considerations; in theory, the notions of 'configuration' and 'refiguration' allow for possibilities of reflexiveness and change whereby the story can be indefinitely reshaped and the terms of recognition altered. On the other hand, this potential flexibility is severely constrained by the placing of *praxis* within the framework of what Ricœur calls the 'common symbolical ground of humanity'. Lyotard's model of the *agon* puts any such attempt at a universalist grounding under great pressure, by showing the ways in which the notion of a 'common symbolical ground' has been so regularly appropriated at once to conceal and to perpetuate divisions and conflicts of interests (as in the great narrative of the 'national interest' or the complex history of the use of the phrase the 'common people' largely by persons other than those to whom it is deemed to refer).

But if Lyotard's argument demands a certain kind of politically critical awareness concerning what gets – and does not get – represented or recognised, it is conspicuously unable to give any 'grounds' of its own for the specific forms which that awareness might take, and what specific requirements it might make. Drawing our attention to the 'editing' operations of narrative is in itself to utter nothing more than an uninteresting truism, to which the ordinary reply might be by way of Henry James's remark, 'really, universally, relations stop nowhere'.[112] When we talk of what narrative has edited out, we are not talking of *everything* that has been excluded. We are making an implicit appeal, from within particular historical and cultural situations, to a set of priorities, to a principle of 'rights' of representation. The problem with Lyotard's stress on the radical incommensurability of discourses is that it leaves us with no vocabulary in which to argue for that principle. The hypothesis of incommensurability implies that conflicting ways of looking at and describing the world are mutually unintelligible; they are unrecognisable to each other. But the task of a politically critical articulation of the issues is not to show that, in the terms of one representation, another is *unrecognisable*, but that, for reasons to do with interests and bad faith, it goes *unrecognised*.

Evidently, if it is refused recognition, dialogue ends and other things begin. In that situation the idea of a 'common' vocabulary will look invidiously disingenuous, and the theory of incommensurability correspondingly attractive. To many its attractions have been directly political, offering an escape from the myth-infested system of consensus into the liberationist zone of the permanent deconstructive turn, where the critical commitment has been to release from the bondage of 'we' a repressed 'other'; to release groups of people, bodies of thought and belief, or just bodies, desires, which are unseen or mis-seen by the discourses and representations commanded by the norms of Western 'rationality' and its narratives of self-legitimation. There are, however, other possible outcomes. In endlessly performing the 'turn', we may find ourselves at risk of rebounding into a new form of individualism, for example, into the do-it-yourself textualism described by Richard Rorty in *Consequences of Pragmatism*. In the latter Rorty proposes a blending of pragmatism and deconstruction as the recipe for our entry into what he calls the 'post-Philosophical culture'. The post-

Philosophical culture will, it appears, be an extremely agreeable place. In it there will be no privileged vocabulary, because we will have learnt to recognise the 'mortal' nature of all vocabularies. It will be conflict-free because, although there will be differences of opinion, these will be expressed without feelings of 'exasperation' on the part of any of the disputants. Above all, it will be 'fun'. Whereas Lyotard's postmodern condition resembles an *agon*, Rorty's post-Philosophical culture resembles a pleasure garden, in which we will play with our textualist toys until we get 'bored' with them and look around for others. Occasionally there will appear a genius 'inventing a new vocabulary which enables us to do a lot of new and marvellous things'. Otherwise it is likely to be dominated by the glamorous figure of 'the "strong" textualist' who 'has his own vocabulary and doesn't worry about whether anybody shares it'. In short, in this free enterprise version of the textualist paradise, anything goes, or, as Rorty revealingly puts it, everything is 'up for grabs'.[113]

In the grubby world of grabbing, 'sentences' compete not in the *agon*, but in the market-place, where presumably the successful entrepreneur takes all. In this scenario, the gap between 'private' and 'public' spheres becomes absolute. But if there is nothing between non-negotiable private vocabularies (strong or weak) and a public sphere in which we are merely 'spoken' (where 'Power' speaks), the implications of that polarisation are either deeply frivolous (a transformation of the world into a ludic toy-town) or deeply despairing. Barthes, for instance, was tempted to give up in despair, going in search of a space beyond the restrictive 'frame' of representation and the oppressive 'hierarchy' of the sentence. In *S/Z* there are moments when he suggests that the ultimate prop of the ideologically closed system of representation (the 'classic readable text') is the subject-predicate structure of the sentence itself.[114] In *Le Plaisir du texte*, these suggestions become categorical propositions: 'La Phrase est hiérarchique: elle implique des sujétions, des subordinations, des rections internes . . . La représentation, c'est cela: quand rien ne sort, rien ne saute hors du cadre.'[115] The closest Barthes gets in *Le Plaisir du texte* to giving us some sense of what his alternative space might look like is in the poetically alluring dream of the unframed, non-sentential *souk*:

Un soir, à moitié endormi sur une banquette de bar, j'essayais de dénombrer tous les langages qui entraient dans mon écoute: musiques, conversations, bruits de chaises, des verres, toute une stéréophonie dont une place de Tanger (décrite par Severo Sarduy) est le lieu exemplaire. En moi aussi cela parlait (c'est bien connu), et cette parole dite 'intérieure' ressemblait beaucoup au bruit de la place, à cet échelonnement de petites voix qui me venaient de l'extérieur: j'étais moi-même un lieu public, un souk: en moi passaient les mots, les menus syntagmes, les bouts de formules, et *aucune phrase ne se formait* . . . [116]

In the image of the stereophonic bazaar of fragmentary sounds and voices, where *aucune phrase ne se formait*, we arrive at a limit point of the attack on representation. From Derrida's 'police station' and 'juridical framing' of culture and narrative, we have moved on to a desire to dissolve the 'frames' of syntax itself (the repressive order of linguistic *ordo* will later be described in *Leçon* as basically 'fascist' in its dispositions).[117]

This is indeed a despairing view of the matter. The 'common sense' view within the academy will, of course, see it as an absurd, unnecessarily self-inflicted despair. But the appointed defenders of the realm of common sense are not conspicuous for knowing what it is in the name of which they speak, and in particular how arduous a task it is to make intellectual and moral sense of the notion of *common* sense. My own view is that Barthes went badly wrong here, but, if so, the conclusions to be drawn are not such as to give comfort to the respectable citizenry (for whom the question 'how we are represented' is more or less settled), or to the partisans of so-called 'hard' radicalism (for whom the swerve into reverie was a 'subjectivist' retreat from the front-line of the 'war' of sentences). I have argued, in a previous chapter, that the complex figures in the work of 'late' Barthes are not to be interpreted as a licence for a new individualism (while acknowledging that, in other hands, they have been adapted to precisely this end). Similarly, Barthes's internalised *souk* is not reducible to an other-evacuating fantasy of ego. It is exactly the reverse: 'les mots, les menus syntagmes, les bouts de formules' which make up this 'subjective' space are of collective origins; the 'moi' is a 'lieu public'.

Nevertheless, the fragmentary stereophony of a half-dream in a bar (transplanted to Tangiers) can no more do service for the idea of the 'public sphere' than can the enlightened discourse of the Addisonian coffee-house in eighteenth-century London.[118] In like manner, the notion that we can step outside the containing 'frames' of representation by slipping below the threshold of the sentence cannot be of much use to us for transactions with the world in our waking lives. The classifying and subordinating structure of the sentence is certainly a model of 'closure, and, as such, has been a major preoccupation of modern writers of fiction from Proust and Céline to Beckett and Butor. Proust's polyphonic sentence, with its 'losing' of the subject, its inversions of identity, its metaphorical scattering of predicates across the boundaries of logical space, is a sentence transgressive of the orders consecrated by 'normal' sentences. Butor's hypotactic monsters, ceaselessly self-qualifying and self-revising, look as if they have no particular reason ever to end ('relations stop nowhere'). But they do end, even if (as in *Finnegans Wake*), by 'a commodius vicus of recirculation', they take us back to our point of departure. We do not escape the tyrannical work of the Sentence by abandoning sentences, just as we do not escape the rigidities of Representation by forsaking representations. The dialogue and the arguments have to take place within, and not outside, them. The frame may be enlarged, complicated, democratised, strained to breaking point, but it does not crack. Or, if it does, we are more likely to find ourselves in Pynchon's intolerable Zone than in Barthes's non-sentential Utopia.

In the terms of Barthes's argument, what, for instance, are we to make of the following sentence: 'Pendant un demi-siècle, les bourgeoises de Pont-L'Évêque envièrent à Mme Aubain sa servante Félicité'? If we were to take Barthes at his word, this sentence – the opening sentence of *Un Cœur simple*[119] – could be read as a pure example of the imprisoning hierarchies of syntax. In the disposition of its elements, it 'mimes' a social structure of class relations: the servant comes appropriately at the end, in her right place (with her name as an appendage to her designated role in the labour force); she is the direct object of a verb ('envièrent') whose subject ('les bourgeoises') and indirect object ('Mme Aubain') 'frame' her in a relation of ownership. What is the status of this sentence? Is it an instance of the mimetic syntax of 'le langage "réaliste"' which in being 'respectueux de l'ordre des mots', declares its respect for 'une structure d'autorité?[120] Or is it a mimesis which implicitly mocks and criticises that order of social relations, foreshadowing the 'syntax' of the whole story, as the tale of the progressive reduction of Félicité, the person who always comes 'last'? Is it that the sentence itself imprisons its 'object', which can then only be freed either by dismantling the sentence (all sentences) or by replacing it with another, 'incommensurable' sentence from the phrasal *agon*? Or does it *expose* an imprisonment, demanding a 'recognition' that is not an ideological endorsement of what is recognised?

It seems to me that the consequence of a wholesale rejection of the idea of mimesis is that these sorts of questions cannot even be pursued. We are here at risk of throwing the baby out with the bath water, largely because we are allowing ourselves to be bewitched by only the negative senses of the term 'order'. In this regard, we might pause to reflect once more on the trial of *Madame Bovary*,[121] and in particular on the sentence which the prosecutor deemed so offensive to 'public order': 'Elle retrouvait dans l'adultère toutes les platitudes du mariage.' In ironic echo of the book mentioned in the narrator's guided tour of the church at Yonville (*La Sainte Famille, envoi du ministre de l'Intérieur*),[122] Flaubert's sentence implies a provocative question: is the institution of marriage bankrupt? The *ministère de l'Intérieur* takes its revenge by placing Flaubert's troublesome sentence under threat of another kind of 'sentence'. But, beyond the hypocrisies and absurdities of the trial, Flaubert's sentence opens on to another debate, another *litige*: *Madame Bovary* shows either the failure of *the* marriage (with Charles) or the failure of Marriage. Flaubert's original 'du' does not legislate which choice we make, and we certainly do not need trials to do so on our behalf. But any debate on that question (and all its related matters: sexuality, society, narrative) can only proceed meaningfully from some area of common terms of reference. I choose *the* marriage, you choose Marriage (or vice-versa). But we make our choices because we have both followed a story, within the terms of a larger cultural and historical story which encompasses us both, and in which the question of Marriage, and its representations, is still a question of common concern. Mimesis, it has been said, originates with family matters. Families may be more trouble than they are worth. But, for the purposes of this argument, that is not the point (still less if its consequence is the enjoyment of avant-garde art in the atomistic privacy of our own homes). The point has to do with what remains on the historical agenda and in public view. If there is any case for the continuing relevance of the 'order' of mimesis, it is because it provides forms for engaging with what remains the order of the day.

NOTES

1 The order of mimesis: poison, nausea, health

1 J.-F. Lyotard, *La Condition postmoderne*, Paris, 1979; *Le Différend*, Paris, 1983.
2 M. Abrams, *The Mirror and the Lamp*, New York, 1958, pp. 6ff.
3 'A Conversation with Roland Barthes' in *Signs of the Times, Introductory Readings in Textual Semiotics* (ed. S. Heath, C. McCabe and C. Prendergast), Cambridge, 1971, p. 42.
4 G. Genette, *Figures*, Paris, 1966, pp. 16ff.
5 R. Jakobson, *Essais de linguistique générale*, Paris, 1963, p. 218.
6 J. Derrida, 'Economimesis' in *Mimesis. Des articulations*, ed. S. Agacinski *et al.*, Paris, 1975.
7 J.-F. Lyotard, *Le Différend*, p. 10.
8 *Ibid.*, p. 206.
9 L. Althusser, *Positions*, 1976, pp. 110ff.
10 P. Bourdieu, *Outline of a Theory of Practice*, Cambridge, 1977, p. 27.
11 *Ibid.*, p. 2.
12 For an interesting recent application of Wittgenstein's notion of 'form of life' to the analysis of fiction, see M. Price, *Forms of Life, Character and Moral Imagination in Literature*, New Haven and London, 1983.
13 R. Barthes, *Leçon*, Paris, 1978, p. 16.
14 J.-P. Vernant, 'Image et apparence dans la théorie platonicienne de la *mimesis*' in *Journal de psychologie*, April–June, 1975, 133–60.
15 Cf. J.-F. Lyotard, *Le Différend*, p. 42: 'Socrate se sert de ce même artefact à *Rép.* VII. Ayant à expliquer que le soleil est aux objets comme le bien aux idées, il redouble l'analogie par un analogon on ne peut plus mimétique: et comme le feu, dit-il, placé à l'entrée de la caverne, est aux objets fabriqués dont il projette des ombres.'
16 J. Derrida, 'La Pharmacie de Platon' in *La Dissémination*, Paris, 1972.
17 Cit. P. Lacoue-Labarthe, 'Typographie' in *Mimesis. Des articulations*, p. 263.
18 P. Lacoue-Labarthe, *ibid.*, p. 249.
19 R. Barthes, *S/Z*, Paris, 1970, p. 145.
20 *Ibid.*, p. 89.

21 *Ibid.*, p. 61.
22 *Ibid.*, p. 145.
23 *Ibid.*, p. 211.
24 *Ibid.*, p. 222.
25 For a discussion of this aspect of Barthes's thinking, cf. A. Lavers, *Roland Barthes, Structuralism and After*, London, 1982.
26 R. Barthes, 'From Work to Text' in *Image-Music-Text*, ed. S. Heath, London, 1977, p. 156.
27 Cf. F. Kermode, 'The Use of the Codes' in *Essays on Fiction 1971–82*, London, 1983.
28 G. Bataille, *La Littérature et le Mal*, Paris, 1957, pp. 199ff.
29 M. Blanchot, *La Part du feu*, Paris, 1949.
30 Cf. R. Barthes, *S/Z*, p. 133, p. 160; J. Kristeva, *Semiotiké*, Paris, 1969, 212ff.
31 R. Barthes, *Leçon*, p. 14.
32 J. Derrida, *L'Écriture et la différence*, Paris, 1967, p. 412: 'Or tous ces discours destructeurs et tous leurs analogues sont pris dans une sorte de cercle. Ce cercle est unique et il décrit la forme du rapport entre l'histoire de la métaphysique et la destruction de l'histoire de la métaphysique: *il n'y a aucun sens* à se passer des concepts de la métaphysique pour ébranler la métaphysique; nous ne disposons d'aucun langage – d'aucune syntaxe et d'aucun lexique – qui soit étranger à cette histoire; nous ne pouvons énoncer aucune proposition destructrice qui n'ait déjà dû se glisser dans la forme, dans la logique et les postulations implicites de cela même qu'elle voudrait contester.'
33 All references to Aristotle are to *Works*, Revised Oxford Translation, ed. J. Barnes, 2 vols., Princeton, 1984, and are given in brackets after the quotation.
34 R. Barthes, *Le Plaisir du texte*, Paris, 1973, p. 25.
35 S. Freud, *Jokes and Their Relation to the Unconscious*, London, 1976, p. 178.
36 R. Barthes, 'L'Ancienne rhétorique (aide-mémoire)' in *Communications*, no. 16, 1970, 179.
37 My reconstruction of Ricœur's account of mimesis is based on the following publications: *La Métaphore vive*, Paris, 1975; 'Narrative Time' in *Critical Inquiry*, vol. 7, no. I, autumn 1980; 'Mimesis and Representation' in *Annals of Scholarship*, vol. II, no. 3, 1981; 'On Interpretation' in *Philosophy in France Today* (ed. A. Montefiore), Cambridge, 1983. The arguments sketched in the last three papers have been gathered up and expanded in *Temps et récit*, Paris, 1983. The latter, however, was unavailable to me at the time of writing.
38 P. Ricœur, *La Métaphore vive*, pp. 311ff.
39 Aristotle, *Metaphysics*, 1045b 33; 1050a 22.
40 P. Ricœur, *La Métaphore vive*, p. 301.
41 *Ibid.*, p. 308.

42 P. Ricœur, 'On Interpretation', p. 193.

2 The economy of mimesis

1 J.-P. Sartre, *La Nausée*, Paris, 1938, p. 60.

2 P. Sollers, *Logiques*, Paris, 1968, p. 228.

3 J. Kristeva, *Semiotiké*, p. 146: 'A la place de la notion d'inter-subjectivité s'installe celle d'*intertextualité*.'

4 I. Watt, *The Rise of the Novel*, London, 1970, pp. 12ff.

5 E. Auerbach, *Mimesis, The Representation of Reality in Western Literature*, New York, 1957; G. Lukács, *Studies in European Realism*, New York, 1964.

6 G. Lukács, *History and Class Consciousness*, London, 1971, p. 8.

7 G. Hegel, *Äesthetik* (ed. Glockner), Stuttgart, 1928 (trans. Knox, Oxford, 1975).

8 *Ibid.*, pp. 229, 355, 226.

9 *Ibid.*, p. 358: 'In this respect, the highest action of the spirit would be world-history itself, and one might wish to work up this universal deed on the battle-field of the general spirit to the absolute epic . . . but, precisely because of this universality, this subject would be insufficiently individualisable for art.'

10 J.-P. Stern, *On Realism*, London, 1973, p. 31, p. 54.

11 M. Foucault, *Les Mots et les choses*, Paris, 1966, p. 31.

12 *Ibid.*, p. 21.

13 *Ibid.*, p. 25.

14 R. Barthes, 'Diderot, Brecht, Eisenstein' in *Revue d'esthétique*, 1973, 185–6.

15 Cf. C. McCabe, *James Joyce and the Revolution of the Word*, London, 1978, pp. 13ff; R. Coward and J. Ellis, *Language and Materialism, Developments in Semiology and the Theory of the Subject*, London, 1977, p. 51.

16 R. Barthes, *S/Z*, p. 146.

17 A. Giddens, *New Rules of Sociological Method*, London, 1976, p. 89.

18 R. Barthes, *S/Z*, p. 16.

19 P. Berger and T. Luckmann, *The Social Construction of Reality*, London, 1971, p. 46.

20 J.-P. Stern, *On Realism*, pp. 113ff.

21 R. Williams (summarising Lukács), *Marxism and Literature*, Oxford, 1977, p. 101.

22 C. Prendergast, *Balzac: Fiction and Melodrama*, London, 1978.

23 Cf. B. O'Shaughnessy, 'The Picture Theory of Meaning' in *Essays on Wittgenstein's Tractatus* (ed. Copi and Beard), London, 1966.

24 H. James, 'The Art of Fiction', in *Literary Criticism: Essays, American and English Writers*, New York, 1984, p. 48.

25 G. Lukács, 'Erzählen oder beschreiben' in *Kunst und objektive Wahrheit*, Leipzig, 1977, pp. 113–65.

26 Cf. R. Barthes, *S/Z*, p. 69: 'Ainsi, un doigt, de son mouvement désignateur et muet, accompagne toujours le texte classique.'

27 L. Wittgenstein, *Philosophical Investigations*, no. 28.

28 R. Jakobson, *Essais de linguistique générale*, pp. 41–2.

29 U. Eco, *A Theory of Semiotics*, Bloomington, 1976, p. 225.

30 L. Wittgenstein, *Philosophical Investigations*, nos. 28–30.

31 E. Durkheim and M. Mauss, *Primitive Classification*, Chicago, 1963.

32 For an extended discussion of the model of 'contract' in the analysis of narrative, cf. Tony Tanner, *Adultery in the Novel, Contract and Transgression*, Baltimore and London, 1979; M. Price, 'The Fictional Contract' in *Forms of Life, Character and Moral Imagination in Literature*, New Haven and London, 1983.

33 R. Barthes, *Roland Barthes par Roland Barthes*, Paris, 1975, p. 63.

34 P. Sollers, *Logiques*, p. 236.

35 J. Kristeva, *Semiotiké*, p. 208.

36 F. de Saussure, *Cours de linguistique générale*, Paris, 1968, p. 108.

37 P. Sollers, *Logiques*, p. 236.

38 R. Barthes, 'Diderot, Brecht, Eisenstein', pp. 188, 186, 187, 190–1.

39 J. Derrida, 'Living On: Border Lines' in *Deconstruction and Criticism*, ed. Bloom *et al.*, New York, 1979, pp. 88, 104.

40 'A Conversation with Roland Barthes', p. 42.

41 *Réquisitoire* in G. Flaubert, *Madame Bovary*, ed. E. Maynial (Classiques Garnier), Paris, 1961, p. 337.

42 B. Brecht, 'A Small Contribution to the Theme of Realism' in *Screen*, Summer 1974, vol. 15, no. 2, 47.

43 Cf. G. Lloyd, *Science, Folklore and Ideology, Studies in the Life Sciences in Ancient Greece*, Cambridge, 1983.

44 This area of research is perhaps best represented by the various articles published under the heading 'Recherches sur le vraisemblable' in *Communications* II, 1968. A useful summary is given by J. Culler, *Structuralist Poetics*, London, 1975, ch. 7.

45 The interest of the detective story for the theory of literary *vraisemblance* has been stressed by T. Todorov, *Poétique de la prose*, Paris, 1971, pp. 96–7.

46 The expression 'internalised probability system' is used by L. Meyer in connection with music (*Music, the Arts and Ideas*, Chicago, 1967, p. 47). In the context of literary criticism, it has been adopted by F. Kermode, *The Classic*, London, 1975, p. 119.

47 T. Todorov, *Les Genres du discours*, Paris, 1978, p. 47.

48 It is briefly touched on by U. Eco, *The Role of the Reader*, London, 1981, p. 216.

49 E. Leach, *Culture and Communication*, Cambridge, 1976, pp. 23–4.

50 M. Foucault, *Naissance de la clinique*, Paris, 1963.

51 C. S. Peirce, *Collected Papers*, Cambridge, Mass., 1931–58, *cit.* U. Eco, *A Theory of Semiotics*, p. 17.

52 U. Eco, *A Theory of Semiotics*, p. 287.

53 R. Barthes, *Mythologies*, Paris, 1957, pp. 50–3; pp. 102–5.

54 For a discussion of this distinction, cf. J. Redfield, *Nature and Culture in the Iliad*, Chicago, 1975, pp. 57ff.

55 Connections, in terms of the theory of *vraisemblance*, between the *Poetics* and the *Rhetoric* have been suggested by T. Todorov, *Poétique de la prose*, p. 94; cf. also U. Eco, *A Theory of Semiotics*, p. 145: 'The *Poetics* cannot be understood without recourse to the *Rhetoric*; the functions of plot acquire value only when measured against the value system of a given group. A fact cannot be defined as "unexpected" if we do not know the *systems of expectation* of the addressee. Thus even researches into the structure of narration refer to a socio-historical definition of semantic systems.'

56 G. Genette, *Figures II*, Paris, 1969, pp. 74–5.

57 A fairly persuasive account of the possible relations between *eikos* and *doxa* in Aristotle's thought is given by Leslie Hill, 'Flaubert and the Rhetoric of Stupidity', in *Critical Inquiry*, winter 1976, vol. 3, no. 2, 336–7.

58 A. Schütz, *Collected Papers: I. The Problem of Social Reality*, Nighoff, 1962, p. 61.

59 O. Burgelin, 'Échange et déflation dans le système culturel' in *Communications* no. II, 1968, 123ff.

60 L. Hill, *art. cit.*, 336.

61 O. Burgelin, *art. cit.*, 134–5.

62 M. Douglas, *Implicit Meanings*, London, 1975, p. 5.

63 M. Douglas (ed.), *Rules and Meanings*, London, 1973, p. 15.

64 R. Bray, *La Formation de la doctrine classique en France*, Paris, 1927.

65 B. Wilson, 'A Sociologist's Introduction' in *Rationality* (ed. B. Wilson), Oxford, 1974, p. xvi.

66 E. Gellner, 'Concepts and Society', in *Rationality*, p. 42.

67 G. Genette, *Figures II*, p. 72.

68 *Ibid.*, p. 73.

69 G. Deleuze and F. Guattari, *Mille Plateaux*, Paris, 1980.

70 M. Foucault, *La Volonté de savoir*, Paris, 1976.

71 *Ibid.*, p. 111.

72 G. Genette, 'Frontières du récit' in *Figures II*, pp. 53–4.

73 R. Rorty, *Philosophy and the Mirror of Nature*, Princeton, 1980, p. 38.

74 J.-P. Sartre, *Qu'est-ce que la littérature?*, Paris, 1948, p. 18.

75 G. Frege, 'Sense and Reference' in the *Philosophical Writings of Gottlob Frege*, ed. P. Geach and M. Black (Oxford, 1970), pp. 62–3.

76 J. Searle, 'The Logical Status of Fictional Discourse' in *Expression and Meaning* (Cambridge, 1979). For an argument that the existential presupposition is not a necessary condition of linguistic reference, cf. T.

Parson, 'A Meinongian Analysis of Fictional Objects', *Grazer Philosophische Studien* (1974), 73–80.

77 On the issues raised by a change of proper name, cf. M. Dummett, *Frege: Philosophy of Language* (London, 1973).

78 H. de Balzac, *Comédie humaine*, Pléiade, vol. II, p. 851.

79 G. Flaubert, 'Un Cœur simple' in *Œuvres*, vol. 11, Pléiade (Paris, 1952), p. 591.

80 R. Barthes, 'L'Effet de réel' in *Communications* 11 (1968), 84–9.

81 If we have any doubts as to the thematic potential of 'baromètre', we might profitably turn to its appearance in the agronomic experiments of Bouvard and Pécuchet: 'Le baromètre les trompa . . . ', *Bouvard et Pécuchet*, *Oeuvres*, Pléiade, vol. II, p. 741.

82 R. Barthes, 'L'Effet de réel', p. 88.

83 J. Searle, 'The Logical Status of Fictional Discourse', p. 71.

84 R. Barthes, *S/Z*, p. 82.

85 Cf. Hayden White, *Metahistory*, Baltimore and London, 1973.

86 J. Derrida, *Positions*, Paris, 1972, p. 126.

87 E. Benveniste, 'The Nature of the Linguistic Sign' in *Problems in General Linguistics*, Florida, 1971, p. 44.

88 C. S. Peirce, *Collected Papers* 1, 229, 2, 230.

89 U. Eco, *A Theory of Semiotics*, p. 67.

90 U. Eco, *The Role of the Reader*, p. 222.

91 F. Jameson, *Marxism and Form*, Princeton, 1971, p. 402.

92 J. Kristeva, *Semiotiké*, p. 211.

93 M. Ron, 'Free Indirect Discourse, Mimetic Language Games and the Subject of Fiction', in *Poetics Today*, vol. 2, no. 2 (winter, 1981), 18.

94 R. Barthes, *S/Z*, p. 129.

95 A. Giddens, *Central Problems in Social Theory*, London, 1979, p. 37.

96 Cf. T. S. Seung, *Structuralism and Hermeneutics*, New York, 1982; V. Descombes, *Modern French Philosophy*, Cambridge, 1980, and *Grammaire des objets de tous genres*, Paris, 1983, esp. pp. 218–23.

97 By these remarks I do not mean to imply that there is such a thing as a 'pure' analytical discourse entirely free of the figurative (although many philosophers have sought to promote their own discourse as being such); nor do I mean to imply a hierarchical opposition between the analytical (serious, responsible) and the figurative (non-serious, irresponsible). My point here is a purely local one: that, *in this particular case*, Barthes's use of metaphor doesn't appear to be working in any intellectually helpful way.

98 Cf. L. Wittgenstein, *Philosophical Investigations*, no. 40.

99 B. Williams, 'Wittgenstein and Idealism', in *Moral Luck*, Cambridge, 1981.

100 J. Bouveresse, 'Why I am so very unFrench' in *Philosophy in France Today*, ed. A. Montefiore, Cambridge, 1983.

101 L. Wittgenstein, *Philosophical Investigations*, no. 29.

102 C. S. Peirce, *Collected Papers*, 4, 536; 5, 473–92.

103 P. Bourdieu, *Outline of a Theory of Practice*, Cambridge, 1977, p. 218.

104 M. Ron, art. cit., p. 18.

105 Cf. P. de Man, *Allegories of Reading*, New Haven, 1979, pp. 204–5: 'The innumerable writings that dominate our lives are made intelligible by a preordained agreement as to their referential authority; this agreement however is merely contractual, never constitutive. It can be broken at all times and every piece of writing can be questioned as to its rhetorical mode.'

106 P. Sollers, 'Overscan/Relations (Blocks)/Conflict' in *Signs of the Times*, p. 81.

107 F. Kermode, *The Sense of an Ending*, Oxford, 1968, p. 124.

108 G. Frege, *Posthumous Writings*, Oxford, 1979, p. 255.

109 R. Barthes, *Le Plaisir du texte*, pp. 98–9.

110 P. Ricoeur, 'Mimesis and Representation', pp. 18–19.

111 *Ibid.*, p. 20; cf. also 'On Interpretation' in *Philosophy in France Today*, p. 180: 'To say that fiction does not lack a reference is to reject an overly narrow conception of reference, which would relegate fiction to a purely emotional role. In one way or another, all symbol systems contribute to *shaping* reality. More particularly, the plots that we invent help us to shape our confused, formless and in the last resort mute temporal experience . . . The plot's referential function lies in the capacity of fiction to shape this mute temporal experience. We are here brought back to the link between *muthos* and *mimesis* in Aristotle's *Poetics*.'

112 J.-F. Lyotard, *La Condition postmoderne*, pp. 66, 99, 107.

113 Cf. *Naming, Necessity and Natural Kinds*, ed. S. P. Schwartz, Ithaca and London, 1977.

114 G. Frege, 'Sense and Reference', p. 58.

115 H. Putnam, 'Meaning and Reference', in Schwartz (ed.), p. 125.

116 Cf. *Glyph* I and II, Baltimore, 1977.

117 R. Barthes, *S/Z*, p. 14.

3 Balzac: narrative contracts

1 H. de Balzac, *Splendeurs et misères des courtisanes* (Classiques Garnier), Paris, 1964, p. 454. All references to *Splendeurs* are to this edition; all references to *Illusions perdues* are also to the Classiques Garnier edition, Paris, 1961. All other references to the *Comédie humaine* are to the Pléiade edition, Paris, 1951–65. Volume and page numbers are given in brackets immediately after the quotation.

2 Cf. F. Engels: 'His (Balzac's) great work was one long elegy deploring the inevitable decline of "good society" ', *cit.* G. Lukács, *Studies in European Realism*, p. 24.

3 R. Barthes, *S/Z*, p. 95.
4 Cf. especially the work of R. Finnegan, *Limba Stories and Story-Telling*, Oxford, 1967; *Oral Literature in Africa*, Oxford, 1970; *Oral Poetry, Its Nature, Significance and Social Context*, Cambridge, 1977.
5 T. Tanner, *Adultery in the Novel*, ch. I.
6 L. Mazet, 'Récit(s) dans le récit: l'échange du récit chez Balzac' in *L'Année balzacienne*, 1976, p. 135.
7 *Cit.* Mazet, p. 129.
8 R. Barthes, *S/Z*, p. 95.
9 H. de Balzac, 'Préface de la deuxième partie', *Illusions perdues*, p. 761.
10 G. Lukács, *Studies in European Realism*, pp. 49ff.
11 T. Tanner, *op. cit.*, p. 375.
12 Cf. Plato, *The Sophist*, where the sophist is named as the 'salesman', the 'merchant of learning' and 'is grouped with artists, the painter, the musician, the puppet-showman'. F. M. Cornford, *Plato's Theory of Knowledge*, London, 1935, p. 174.
13 Cf. T. Clark, 'The Bar at the Folies-Bergère' in *Popular Culture in France*, ed. J. Beauroy, M. Bertrand, E. Gargan, Sarratoga, 1977, p. 245, n. 26.
14 For a discussion of this genre, and its intellectual and social context, cf. J. Wechsler, *A Human Comedy: Physiognomy and Caricature in Nineteenth-Century Paris*, London, 1982; cf. also the interesting review of Wechsler's book by N. McWilliam, 'Making Faces' in *Art History*, vol. 7, no. I, March 1984, pp. 115–19.
15 Cf. R. Terdiman, 'Structures of Initiation: On Semiotic Education and its Contradictions in Balzac', *Yale French Studies*, no. 63, 1982, 198–226; cf. also M. Kanes, *Balzac's Comedy of Words*, Princeton, 1975. Although we diverge on a number of commonly posed issues, the general indebtedness of this chapter to Kanes's remarkable study is very considerable.
16 H. de Balzac, *Physiologie de la toilette in Œuvres diverses*, vol. II, p.47.
17 *Ibid.*, p. 50.
18 *Ibid.*, p. 47.
19 H. de Balzac, *Traité de la vie élégante*, Paris, 1922, p. 36.
20 *Physiologie de la toilette*, p. 47.
21 *Traité de la vie élégante*, p. 57.
22 Cf. R. Kempf, *Sur le corps romanesque*, Paris, 1968, pp. 94–6.
23 M. Bardèche, *Une Lecture de Balzac*, Paris, 1964, pp. 145–6.
24 I am indebted to one of my students, Ann Barnett, for drawing my attention to the possible significance of this remark.
25 W. Benjamin, *Charles Baudelaire: A Lyric Poet in the Era of High Capitalism*, London, 1972, p. 43.
26 H. de Balzac, *Lettres à Mme Hanska*, Paris, 1967–9, vol. II, p. 229.
27 C. Ginzburg, 'Signes, Pistes, Traces' in *Le Débat*, November 1980

(English trans., 'Morelli, Freud and Sherlock Holmes: Clues and Scientific Method' in *History Workshop*, issue 9, spring, 1980).

28 Balzac often compares his writings to the 'children' of which he is the 'father'; cf. *Lettres à Madame Hanska*, Paris, 1967–9.

29 On the ambiguities of the expression 'laisser échapper' in Balzac, cf. M. Kanes, *op. cit.* p. 8, p. 159.

30 *Ibid.*, p. 194.

31 *Ibid.*, p. 247.

32 C. McCabe, *James Joyce and the Revolution of the Word*, p. 50.

33 G. Genette, *Figures II*, p. 79.

34 C. Prendergast, *Balzac: Fiction and Melodrama*, ch. 4.

35 G. Lukács, *Studies in European Realism*, p. 51.

36 Cf. R. Kempf, *op. cit.*, p. 139. Kempf sees Vautrin's parable as specifically linked to a strategy of homosexual seduction.

37 On the significance of this motif, cf. S. Weber, *Unwrapping Balzac*, Toronto, 1979, p. 54.

38 R. Heppenstall, *A Harlot High and Low*, London (Penguin), 1970, p. 442.

39 Cf. R. Barthes, 'Saussure, le signe, la démocratie' in *Le Discours social*, nos. 3–4, 1973.

40 M. Foucault, *Les Mots et les choses*, p. 193.

41 L. de Bonald, *Législation primitive* (4th edition), Paris, 1847, p. 36.

42 *Ibid.*, pp. 118–19.

43 *Traité de la vie élégante*, p. 47: 'Tout à coup la Révolution, ayant pris d'une main puissante toute cette garde-robe inventée par quatorze siècles, et l'ayant réduite en papier-monnaie, amena follement un des plus grands malheurs qui puissent affliger une nation.'

44 H. de Balzac, *Des mots à la mode* in *Œuvres diverses*, vol. II, p. 36.

45 Balzac's attitude to 'polysemy' is in fact deeply ambivalent. Against his conservative views (discussed by Kanes, *op. cit.*, p, 132) should be set the following statement: 'Les mots sont susceptibles de prendre plusieurs significations; et leur en donner de nouvelles est ce que j'appelle *créer*, c'est enrichir une langue . . . ' *Correspondance* (ed. Pierrot), Paris, 1960–9, vol. IV, p. 690.

46 Cf. G. Lukács, *Studies in European Realism*, p. 21: 'It is precisely this discrepancy between . . . Balzac the political thinker and Balzac the author of *La Comédie humaine* that constitutes Balzac's greatness.'

47 T. Adorno, *Prisms*, London, 1967, p. 20.

4 Stendhal: the ethics of verisimilitude

1 I borrow the term 'socio-logic' from R. Barthes, 'A propos de deux ouvrages de Cl. Lévi-Strauss: sociologie et socio-logique' in R. Bellour and C. Clément (eds.), *Claude Lévi-Strauss, Textes de et sur Cl. Lévi-Strauss*, Paris, 1971.

2 G. Blin, *Stendhal et les problèmes de la personnalité*, Paris, 1958, vol. I, p. 299.

3 Cf. J. Mélia, *Stendhal et ses commentateurs*, Paris, 1911.

4 *Le Journal des débats*, March, 1818.

5 *Le Globe*, August, 1827.

6 *La Revue des deux mondes*, January, 1843.

7 *La Revue de Paris*, June, 1830.

8 *Le Journal des débats*, December, 1830.

9 P. Mérimée, *cit.* Mélia, *op. cit.*, p. 138.

10 E. Faguet, *Politiques et moralistes*, Paris, 1903, vol. II, p. 49.

11 Stendhal, *Vie de Rossini* (ed. Divan), vol. I, p. 284. Except where indicated, all references to Stendhal's works are to the Divan edition, ed. H. Martineau, Paris, 1927–37. References to the autobiographical writings are to the *Œuvres intimes*, Pléiade, Paris, 1955. References to *Le Rouge et le Noir* are to the Classiques Garnier edition, Paris, 1960, and page numbers are given in brackets after the quotation.

12 *Rome, Naples et Florence en 1817* (ed. Divan, 1956), vol. II, p. 285.

13 *La Revue des deux mondes*, January, 1843.

14 Cf. *Racine et Shakespeare*, p. 88.

15 Cf. supra pp. 41–57.

16 Rapin, *Réflexions sur la poétique*, *cit.* Genette, *Figures* II, p. 73.

17 H. de Balzac, 'Lettres sur la littérature' in *Oeuvres diverses*, Paris, 1940, vol. II, p. 278.

18 J. Bayley, *Tolstoy and the Novel*, London, 1968, p. 147.

19 *Ibid.*, p. 150.

20 L. Bersani, *From Balzac to Beckett*, New York, 1970, p. 98.

21 V. Brombert, *Stendhal, Fiction and the Themes of Freedom*, New York, 1968.

22 *Racine et Shakespeare*, p. 318: 'Sterne avait trop raison: nous ne sommes que des *pièces de monnaie effacées*.' On the relation between money and language in Stendhal's thinking, cf. M. Crouzet, 'Stendhal et les signes' in *Romantisme*, 3, 1972.

23 Cf. *Racine et Shakespeare*, p. 210: 'Le premier instrument du génie d'un peuple, c'est sa langue. Que sert à un muet d'avoir beaucoup d'esprit? Or l'homme qui ne parle qu'une langue entendue de lui seul est-il si différent d'un muet?'

24 P. Berger and T. Luckmann, *The Social Construction of Reality*, p. 87.

25 M. Crouzet, *Stendhal et le langage*, Paris, 1981, p. 22.

26 *Ibid.*, p. 18.

27 *Œuvres intimes*, pp. 395, 667.

28 *Racine et Shakespeare*, p. 364.

29 *Rome, Naples et Florence en 1817* (ed. Divan, 1956), p. 89n, p. 224.

30 *Vie de Métastase*, p. 357.

31 Maine de Biran, 'L'Origine du langage' in *Défense de la philosophie*, *Œuvres*, vol. XII, Paris, 1939, pp. 167–203.

32 *Racine et Shakespeare*, p. 24.
33 *Ibid.*, p. 297.
34 *Ibid.*, p. 88.
35 M. Crouzet, *op. cit.* pp. 288ff.
36 *Histoire de la peinture en Italie*, vol. II, pp. 132ff.
37 *Racine et Shakespeare*, p. 165, p. 318.
38 *Ibid.*, p. 88.
39 R. Barthes, *Le Plaisir du texte*, p. 46: 'Chaque fiction est soutenue par un parler social, un sociolecte, auquel elle s'identifie: la fiction, c'est ce degré de consistance où atteint un langage lorsqu'il a exceptionnelle-ment *pris* et trouvé une classe sacerdotale . . . pour le parler communément et le diffuser.'
40 R. Barthes, *S/Z*, p. 61.
41 Cf. V. Brombert, *Stendhal ou la voie oblique*, New Haven and London, 1954.
42 S. Felman, *La 'Folie' dans l'œuvre romanesque de Stendhal*, Paris, 1971.
43 R. Barthes, *Le Plaisir du texte*, p. 51.
44 L. Bersani, *op. cit.* p. 121.
45 E. Faguet, *op. cit.* p. 51.
46 R. Wollheim, *Art and its Objects*, London, 1980, p. 147.
47 G. Genette, *op. cit.* p. 78.
48 *La Vie de Henri Brulard* in *Oeuvres intimes*, pp. 393–4.
49 G. Bataille, 'Avant-propos', *Le Bleu du ciel*, Paris, 1957, p. 7.
50 A. Breton, *Manifeste du surréalisme*, Paris, 1972, p. 18.
51 R. Barthes, 'On échoue toujours à parler de ce qu'on aime' in *Tel Quel*, no. 85, autumn, 1980.
52 *Ibid.*, p. 35.
53 *Ibid.*, p. 38.
54 R. Barthes, *Mythologies*, pp. 188–90.
55 *Racine et Shakespeare*, p. 71.

5 Nerval: the madness of mimesis

1 All references to Nerval's works are to the *Œuvres complètes*, ed. Pléiade, Paris, 2 vols., 1956. Volume and page numbers are given in brackets immediately after the quotation.
2 G. Hegel, *Äesthetik* (trans. Knox), p. 1092.
3 Cf. R. Chambers, *G. de Nerval et la poétique du voyage*, Paris, 1969.
4 I borrow the expression 'epistemological suspension' from D. Simpson, *Irony and Authority in Romantic Poetry*, London, 1979, p. 15.
5 J. Kristeva, *Pouvoirs de l'horreur, Essai sur l'abjection*, Paris, 1980, p. 44.

6 J. Lacan, *Séminaire*, 1957/8, Compte rendu, J. B. Pontalis, *Bulletin de psychologie*, vol. XI, 4/5, January 1958, nos. 141–2, 293.

7 E. Gombrich, *Meditations on a Hobby Horse*, London, 1963, pp. 4–5.

8 On the importance of the theatre-motif in *Sylvie*, cf. R. Chambers, *L'Ange et l'Automate, Variations sur le mythe de l'actrice de Nerval à Proust*, Paris, 1971; M. Jeanneret, *La Lettre perdue, Écriture et folie dans l'œuvre de Nerval*, Paris, 1978.

9 On the 'paradise' theme in *Sylvie*, cf. U. Eisenzweig, *L'Espace imaginaire d'un récit: 'Sylvie' de Gérard de Nerval*, Neuchatel, 1976.

10 R. Jean, 'Lecture de *Sylvie*' in *La Poétique du désir*, Paris, 1974, p. 132.

11 S. Kofman describes *Sylvie* as a 'construction en écho', a structure of temporal and textual repetitions that is without origin, that is itself 'répétition originaire', *Nerval: Le charme de la répétition*, Lausanne, 1979, pp. 41–2. Whether 'charme' is the appropriate term for this experience is, however, another matter.

12 G. Poulet, *Les Métamorphoses du cercle*, Paris, 1961.

13 On the relations between 'abîme' and 'sans fond' in Nerval's poetry, cf. S. Felman, *La Folie et la chose littéraire*, Paris, 1978, pp. 93–4: 'le poème s'engloutit dans un *sans fond*, dans l'infini de la répétition non originaire, non-référentielle. L'abîme, c'est l'abîme de la ressemblance, l'engloutissement de la métaphore dans une répétition infinie.'

14 C. Mauron, *Des Métaphores obsédantes au mythe personnel*, Paris, 1962, p. 151.

15 R. Barthes, 'Digressions' in *Promesse*, spring, 1971, no. 29, 19n.

16 Cf. R. Barthes: ' . . . if up until now we have looked at the text as a species of fruit with a kernel (as an apricot, for example), the flesh being the form and the pit content, it would be better to see it as an onion, a construction of layers (or levels or systems) whose body contains, finally, no heart, no kernel, no secret, no irreducible principle, nothing except the infinity of its own envelopes.' 'Style and its Image' in *Literary Style: A Symposium*, ed. S. Chatman, New York and London, 1971, p. 10.

17 I am indebted for the suggestion of this anagram to R. B. Gordon, 'Dentelle: Métaphore du texte dans *Sylvie*', in *Romanic Review*, no. 73, I, 1982, 64.

18 J. Derrida, 'La Mythologie blanche' in *Poétique*, no. 5, 1971, p. 24.

19 T. Todorov, *Théories du symbole*, Paris, 1977, pp. 173ff. For the alternative view that attention to metaphor in eighteenth-century linguistic thought gives the grounds for breaking away from mimetic or representational theories of language, cf. S. Land, *From Signs to Propositions: The Concept of Form in Eighteenth-Century Linguistic Theory*, London, 1974.

20 J. Derrida, *art. cit.* p. 30.

21 M. Black, 'Metaphor' in *Proceedings of the Aristotelian Society*, 1954–5, London, 287.

22 M. Foucault, *Let Mots et les choses*, p. 63.

23 Cf. D. Simpson, *op. cit.* ch. 5.

24 A. W. Schlegel, *Kritische Schriften und Briefe*, Stuttgart, 1962–74, vol. II, p. 251.

25 P. Shelley, *The Complete Works*, New York and London, 1965, vol. VII, iii.

26 C. Baudelaire, *Les Paradis artificiels* in *Œuvres complètes*, Pléiade, Paris, 1961, p. 376.

27 M. Proust, 'Gérard de Nerval' in *Contre Sainte-Beuve*, Paris, 1954, p. 158.

28 A. Breton, *Manifeste du surréalisme*, Paris, 1972, p. 36. For a counter-view, cf. M. Leiris, *Fibrilles*, Paris, 1966, p. 251: 'De même, ce que j'ai pu croire de Nerval trouvant sa solution dans une sorte de folie volontaire – fusion de la vie et du rêve – m'apparaît aujourd'hui puéril: quelles affres ont dû être les siennes quand, homme qui vivait de sa plume, il était empêché de travailler par ses crises et, durant les répits qu'elles lui laissaient, en faisait le récit ou exploitait les matériaux fournis par son délire, à la fois pour essayer de s'en sortir et pour produire la copie qui était son gagne-pain.'

29 A tendency in R. Chamber's otherwise exemplary *G. de Nerval et la poétique du voyage* (cf. p. 316).

30 The notion that in *Sylvie* the discourse of 'madness' is finally mastered by the discourse of 'reason' is the one substantive issue on which I would disagree with M. Jeanneret's brilliant reading; cf. *La Lettre perdue*, p. 83.

31 R. Jean, *op. cit.*, p. 130.

32 J. Starobinski, *Les Mots sous les mots: les anagrammes de Ferdinand de Saussure*, Paris, 1971, p. 153.

33 J.-P. Richard, 'Géographie magique de Nerval' in *Poésie et profondeur*, Paris, 1955, p. 72.

34 M. Proust, *op. cit.*, p. 166.

35 Cf. S. Simches, *Le Romantisme et le goût esthétique du XVIIIè siècle*, Paris, 1964, pp. 121ff.

36 N. Bryson, *Word and Image*, Cambridge, 1983, p. 65.

37 Cf. G. de Nerval, *Angélique*, Pléiade, vol. II, p. 213.

38 N. Bryson, *op. cit.*, p. 75.

39 On *Sylvie* as narrative marked by irreducible semantic indeterminacy, cf. U. Eco, *Semiotics and the Philosophy of Language*, London, 1984, pp. 159–61.

40 J. Kristeva, *Le Texte du roman: approche sémiologique d'une structure discursive transformationnelle*, The Hague, 1970, p. 190.

41 R. Barthes, *S/Z*, p. 221.

6 Flaubert: the stupidity of mimesis

1 S. Felman, *La Folie et la chose littéraire*, p. 164.
2 R. Barthes, *Le Plaisir du texte*, p. 51.
3 G. Flaubert, *Correspondance* (ed. Conard), Paris, 1926–33, VIII, p. 175. All references to the *Correspondance* are to this edition; volume and page numbers are given in brackets immediately after the quotation.
4 For a succinct account of the sources and history of the Cretan Liar paradox, cf. I. Copi, *The Theory of Logical Types*, London, 1971, p. 12. It entails primarily a semantic paradox revolving around the simultaneous relation of overlap and division between, in Benveniste's terms, the subject of the *énoncé* and the subject of the *énonciation* (a purer representation of the difficulty might be found in the paradoxical truth-conditions of the statement 'I am lying'). The relevance of this ancient paradox to modern thought has assumed various forms, but for my present purpose the difficulty in question bears chiefly on the intellectual dilemmas generated from the positions of Relativism – a set of dilemmas whose recognition I take to be fundamental to the peculiar relation to paradox maintained by Flaubert's work. For a brief suggestion of the potential usefulness of the Cretan Liar paradox for understanding Flaubert, cf. C. Gothot-Mersch, *Préface* to *Bouvard et Pécuchet* (Collection Folio), Paris, 1979. Gothot-Mersch, however, sees the paradox as relevant only to the dialogue of the characters, and does not consider its possible extension to the narrative discourse as well.
5 N. Sarraute, 'Flaubert le précurseur' in *Preuves*, XV, 1965, pp. 3–11.
6 J. Rousset, *Forme et signification*, Paris, 1962, p. III.
7 S. Weber, *Unwrapping Balzac*, pp. 3ff.
8 On the reflexive significance of M. Binet's lathe, cf. T. Tanner, *Adultery in the Novel*, pp. 244ff.
9 R. Amossy and E. Rosen, *Les Discours du cliché*, Paris, 1982.
10 G. Genette, 'Silences de Flaubert' in *Figures*, p. 243.
11 S. Felman, *op. cit.*, pp. 191–213.
12 *Ibid.*, p. 166.
13 For a review of Flaubert's approach to *bêtise*, cf. G. Bollème, 'Flaubert et la bêtise' in *Le second volume de Bouvard et Pécuchet*, Paris, 1966.
14 J.-P. Sartre, *L'Idiot de la famille*, Paris, 1971, vol. II, pp. 1977–81.
15 G. Bollème, *op. cit.*, p. 200.
16 R. Barthes, 'La Mort de l'auteur' in *Mantéia*, no. V, 1968, p. 15: ' . . . le texte est un tissu de citations, issues des mille foyers de la culture. Pareil à Bouvard et Pécuchet, ces éternels copistes, à la fois sublimes et comiques et dont le profond ridicule désigne *précisément* la

vérité de l'écriture, l'écrivain ne peut qu'imiter un geste toujours antérieur, jamais originel.'

17 G. Flaubert, *La 'première' Éducation sentimentale*, Paris, 1963, p. 15.

18 G. Flaubert, *L'Éducation sentimentale* (Classiques Garnier), Paris, 1964, p. 1. All subsequent references to *L'Éducation sentimentale* are to this edition, and are given in brackets immediately after the quotation.

19 L. Trilling, *The Liberal Imagination*, London, 1951, p. 61.

20 G. Lukács, *The Theory of the Novel*, London, 1978.

21 G. Blin, *Stendhal et les problèmes du roman*, Paris, 1954, p. 146.

22 J. Derrida, 'Living On: Border Lines', p. 86.

23 J.-F. Lyotard, *Le Différend*, p. 222.

24 L. Hill, 'Flaubert and the Rhetoric of Stupidity', p. 337.

25 Whether in fact the different modes whereby one utterance can relate to another (allusion, reference, connotation, iteration, recursiveness, etc.) can all be collapsed into the notion of a general 'citationality' is a matter of some contention; cf. the controversial exchange between J. Derrida and J. Searle, *Glyph* I and II, Baltimore and London, 1977.

26 R. Barthes, 'Changer l'objet lui-même' in *Esprit*, April, 1971, 614: ' . . . autrement dit, il s'est créé une *doxa* mythologique: la dénonciation, la démystification (ou démythification) est devenue elle-même discours, corpus de phrases, énoncé catéchistique'.

27 Cf. V. Descombes, *L'Inconscient malgré lui*, Paris, 1977, p. 115: 'Le problème posé par Flaubert est le suivant: comment y aurait-il la possibilité d'une parole propre au sujet, dès lors que le langage est langage de l'Autre? Comment faire autre chose que répéter, citer, c'est-à-dire en définitive ressasser et radoter?'

28 G. Flaubert, *Correspondance*, vol. II, p. 5: 'Je me sens démesurément stupide . . . Écrire, ne pas écrire. Publier est une idée reçue.'

29 A. Thibaudet, *Gustave Flaubert*, Paris, 1935, p. 211.

30 R. Girard, *Mensonge romantique et vérité romanesque*, Paris, 1961, p. 29.

31 *Ibid.*, p. 13.

32 R. Barthes, *Fragments d'un discours amoureux*, Paris, 1977, p. 11.

33 L. Bersani, 'Emma Bovary and The Sense of Sex' in *A Future for Astyanax*, London, 1978, p. 211.

34 G. Flaubert, *Madame Bovary* (Classiques Garnier), Paris, pp. 178–9.

35 J. Culler, *Flaubert, The Uses of Uncertainty*, London, 1974, p. 110.

36 R. Barthes, *Le Plaisir du texte*, p. 18.

37 As Diana Knight forcefully points out (*Flaubert's Characters*, Cambridge, 1985), I may well here be simplifying Barthes's position on Flaubert. In *S/Z*, for example, Barthes explicitly identifies Flaubert's irony as deeply equivocal and uncertain in its effects ('une ironie frappée d'incertitude', p. 146). On the other hand, even if marked by 'incertitude', the writing is still perceived as governed by the figure of

irony, and hence by a predominantly critical attitude towards given forms of language.

38 M. Proust, 'A propos du "style" de Flaubert', *Chroniques*, Paris, 1927, p. 202.

39 J. Culler, *op. cit.*, p. 203.

40 L. Hill, *art. cit.*, p. 343.

41 M. Proust, *A la recherche du temps perdu*, Pléiade, Paris, 1954, vol. I, p. 8.

42 S. Beckett, *En attendant Godot*, Paris, 1952, p. 157.

43 G. Eliot, *Middlemarch*, London, 1965, p. 226.

44 Cf. *Correspondance*, IX, pp. 29, 31–2.

45 Derrida's position on truth is notoriously difficult, essentially by virtue of being subject to a double imperative. On the one hand, as a hypostasized category of discourse, it is to be the object of a programme of systematic 'deconstruction' – a programme of which the very discourse (Derrida's own) which announces it is to be an integral part (no privileged 'meta-language'). On the other hand, 'truth' is not thereby abandoned to the clutches of relativism, but is rather reinstated as that which can be grasped only in dialectical fashion, in terms of temporal process rather than static categories. 'Truth' cannot be formalised according to the procedures of propositional logic, but seized only in the ceaseless movement of affirmation and negation, as that which is never fully there, 'in position'. Clearly this represents a quite different way of construing 'truth' from that represented by 'traditional' philosophy, but it does not necessarily meet the difficulty embodied in the Cretan Liar Paradox. Either the formal statement that 'truth is non-formalisable' is true (in which case it forms the exception to the rule it puts forward), or, alternatively, it is untrue, on the grounds that it fails to satisfy the condition of the proposition it enunciates. Either way, it thus seems to be fatally caught in the grip of irreducible paradox.

46 G. Flaubert, *Dictionnaire des idées reçues*, in G. Bollème, *op. cit.*, p. 299.

7 Conclusion: mimesis, a matter for the police?

1 E. Auerbach, *Mimesis, The Representation of Reality in Western Literature*, pp. 492, 488.

2 The question posed (though never answered) in the 'Préface' to *Mimesis, Des articulations*, pp. 5–14.

3 A. D. Nuttall, *A New Mimesis*, London, 1983, p. viii.

4 V. Turner, 'Social Dramas and Stories about Them', *Critical Inquiry*, autumn 1980, vol. 7, no. I, p. 167.

5 *Ibid.*, p. 168.

6 J.-F. Lyotard, *Le Différend*, p. 218.

7 J. Derrida, 'Living On: Border Lines', p. 104, p. 102.

8 N. Frye, *Anatomy of Criticism*, New York, 1965, p. 52; *Fables of Identity*, New York, 1963, p. 24.

9 F. L. Lucas, *Tragedy: Serious Drama in Relation to Aristotle's Poetics*, London, 1981.

10 N. Frye, *Fables of Identity*, p. 25.

11 N. Frye, *Anatomy of Criticism*, p. 346.

12 P. Brooks, 'Freud's Master-Plot', *Yale French Studies*, 55/56, 1977.

13 T. Cave,'What is a Recognition-Scene?', a paper read to the Cambridge Modern Language Society, spring, 1984.

14 C. Ginzburg, 'Signes, Pistes, Traces' in *Le Débat*, November 1980 (trans. 'Morelli, Freud and Sherlock Holmes: Clues and Scientific Method', *History Workshop*, issue 9, spring 1980).

15 On Peirce's notion of 'abductive reasoning', cf. U. Eco, *Semiotics and the Philosophy of Language*, pp. 39ff.

16 C. Ginzburg, *art. cit.*, p. 14.

17 *Ibid.*, pp. 41–2.

18 S. Freud, 'Family Romances', Standard Edition, IX, London, 1959.

19 R. Barthes, *Le Plaisir du texte*, p. 20.

20 J.-F. Lyotard, *Le Différend*, p. 220.

21 Cf. M. Robert, *Roman des origines et origines du roman*, Paris, 1972; S. Heath, 'Family Plots' in *Comparative Criticism*, no. 5, 1983, 328.

22 T. Tanner, *Adultery in the Novel, Contract and Transgression*, p. 12.

23 W. Benjamin, *Charles Baudelaire*, p. 43.

24 H. Babou, *La Vérité sur le cas Champfleury*, Paris, 1857, p. 30.

25 C. Ginzburg, *art. cit.*, p. 23.

26 M. Butor, *L'Emploi du temps*, Paris, 1957, p. 47.

27 J.-F. Lyotard, *Le Différend*, p. 218: 'D'une part le récit raconte un ou des différends, et il lui ou leur impose une fin, un achèvement qui est son propre terme . . . Elle (sa finalité) fait comme si l'occurrence, avec sa puissance de différends, pouvait s'achever, comme s'il y avait un dernier mot.'

28 T. Pynchon, *The Crying of Lot 49*, London, 1963, p. 126.

29 J.-P. Sartre, *La Nausée*, p. 60.

30 Cf. Plato's use of the verb *paranoeō* (*Theatetos*, 1950) to mean 'misthinking'; cf. also Plotinus (6.8.13) where *paranoeō* signifies 'deviating from accurate thought' (Liddell-Scott-Jones).

31 For an extended discussion of Vaihinger's 'as if' in relation to conventions of narrative closure, cf. F. Kermode, *The Sense of an Ending*, Oxford, 1966.

32 F. Kermode, 'The Uses of Codes' in *Essays on Fiction 1971–82*, p. 84.

33 G. Deleuze and F. Guattari, *Mille Plateaux*, Paris, 1980, p. 144.

34 *Ibid.*, p. 142.

35 *Ibid.*, pp. 143–4.

36 *Ibid.*, p. 494.

37 *Ibid.*, pp. 156ff.

38 *Ibid.*, p. 15.
39 *Ibid.*, pp. 13ff.
40 *Ibid.*, pp. 336ff.
41 *Ibid.*, p. 353.
42 *Ibid.*, p. 473.
43 *Ibid.*, p. 472.
44 *Ibid.*, p. 471.
45 *Ibid.*, p. 14.
46 *Ibid.*, p. 374.
47 *Ibid.*, p. 20.
48 *Ibid.*, pp. 21ff.
49 *Ibid.*, p. 466.
50 *Ibid.*, pp. 144–5.
51 *Ibid.*, p. 614.
52 T. Todorov, *Poétique de la prose*, p. 99.
53 M. Robert, *Roman des origines, origines du roman*, p. 73.
54 On this ambiguity in the narrative of *Sylvie*, cf. R. Chambers, 'Seduction Renounced: *Sylvie* as Narrative Act' in *Story and Situation: Narrative Seduction and the Power of Fiction*, Manchester, 1984, p. 121.
55 V. Brombert, *The Novels of Flaubert*, Princeton, 1966, p. 184.
56 G. Deleuze and F. Guttari, *op. cit.*, p. 18.
57 *Ibid.*, p. 15.
58 *Ibid.*, p. 96.
59 *Ibid.*, p. 21.
60 V. Descombes points to the 'Rousseauist' assumptions in much of Deleuze's thinking, *Modern French Philosophy*, p. 178.
61 R. Barthes, *Mythologies*, p. 197.
62 T. Pynchon, *Gravity's Rainbow*, New York, 1973, p. 304, p. 305.
63 *Ibid.*, p. 556.
64 P. Ricoeur, 'Narrative Time', p. 171.
65 J.-P. Sartre, *Les Mots*, Paris, 1971, p. 171.
66 P. Lacoue-Labarthe, 'Le Mythe nazi', *cit.* Lyotard, *Le Différend*, p. 219.
67 P. Ricœur, 'Narrative Time', p. 181.
68 P. Ricœur, 'On Interpretation', p. 180.
69 'Narrative Time', p. 169.
70 'On Interpretation', p. 181.
71 Cf. *supra*, pp. 20–3.
72 P. Ricœur, 'Mimesis and Representation', pp. 15–32.
73 *Ibid.*, pp. 19–20.
74 *Ibid.*, p. 16.
75 P. Ricœur, *La Métaphore vive*, pp. 308ff.
76 'Mimesis and Representation', pp. 24–5.
77 'On Interpretation', p. 193.

78 'Mimesis and Representation', p. 24.
79 *Ibid.*, p. 27.
80 N. Goodman, *Languages of Art*, Indianapolis, 1976.
81 'Mimesis and Representation', p. 24.
82 H. Bloom, *The Anxiety of Influence*, New York, 1973.
83 N. Bryson, *Tradition and Desire, From David to Delacroix*, Cambridge, 1984, p. xviii.
84 'Mimesis and Representation', p. 26.
85 *Ibid.*, p. 29.
86 *Ibid.*, p. 28.
87 *Ibid.*, p. 29.
88 'Narrative Time', pp. 175, 188, 177, 176.
89 W. Benjamin, 'The Storyteller' in *Illuminations*, London, 1973.
90 'On Interpretation', p. 186.
91 J. Habermas, *Knowledge and Human Interests*, Boston, 1972.
92 F. Kermode, 'Can We Say Absolutely Anything We Like', and 'The Institutional Control of Interpretation' in *Essays on Fiction 1972–82*.
93 J. P. Stern, *On Realism*, pp. 92ff.
94 F. Kermode, *op. cit.*, pp. 158, 164, 183, 169, 184.
95 J.-F. Lyotard, *Le Différend*, p. 13.
96 J.-F. Lyotard, *La Condition postmoderne*, p. 27.
97 *Le Différend*, pp. 218ff.
98 *La Condition postmoderne*, p. 57.
99 *Ibid.*, p. 23.
100 *Ibid.*, p. 107.
101 *Ibid.*, p. 32.
102 *Ibid.*, p. 66.
103 L. Wittgenstein, *Philosophical Investigations*, no. 18.
104 *Le Différend*, p. 9.
105 *Ibid.*, p. 10.
106 *Ibid.*, pp. 10–11.
107 G. Bennington, 'August: Double Justice' in *Diacritics*, Fall, 1984, pp. 64–71.
108 V. Descombes, *Modern French Philosophy*, p. 183.
109 J.-F. Lyotard, 'Presentations' in *Philosophy in France Today*, p. 125.
110 J.-F. Lyotard and J.-L. Thébaud, *Au Juste*, Paris, 1979, p. 37.
111 The Court did not of course demand, as a condition of acquittal, that the text be so emended. But since a great deal of the prosecutor's case turned on this sentence, it is reasonable to infer that the experience of the trial was the main reason why Flaubert suppressed the offending 'du' and did not restore it until the 1873 edition. In this connection, the advice of Louis Bouilhet – especially when Flaubert was revising the text for the 1862 edition – proved decisive: 'Tu as rétabli *les platitudes du mariage*, moi j'aime ça parbleu! mais est-ce bien prudent? tu attaques la société par une de ses bases – tu reliras avec soin ton

édition corrigée, prends garde – tu vas rire – mais je dois te dire tout ce qui me passe par la cervelle.' *Cit.* R. Dumesnil and D. L. Demorest, *Bibliographie de G. Flaubert*, Paris, 1939.

112 H. James, *The Art of the Novel*, New York, 1934, p. 5.

113 R. Rorty, *Consequences of Pragmatism*, Minneapolis, 1982, pp. xii, 108, 153, 152, 229.

114 R. Barthes, *S/Z*, pp. 133, 160.

115 R. Barthes, *Le Plaisir du texte*, pp. 80, 90.

116 *Ibid.*, p. 79.

117 R. Barthes, *Leçon*, p. 14.

118 Cf. T. Eagleton, *The Function of Criticism: From 'The Spectator' to Post-structuralism*, London, 1984. Eagleton's argument is for aligning literary criticism with the concerns of what – citing Habermas – he calls the 'public sphere'. But, as P. Parrinder has pointed out (*London Review of Books*, vol. 7, no. 7, February 1985, pp. 16–17), Eagleton's historical model of such an alignment – eighteenth-century literary London – is extremely problematic.

119 G. Flaubert, *Un Cœur simple*, Pléiade, vol. II, p. 591.

120 S. Felman, *La Folie et la chose littéraire*, p. 161.

121 For an interesting discussion of some of the larger issues raised by the trial of *Madame Bovary*, cf. Dominick LaCapra, *'Madame Bovary' on Trial*, Ithaca and London, 1982.

122 G. Flaubert, *Madame Bovary* (ed. Classiques Garnier), p. 67.

TRANSLATIONS

The following include translations of only the longer or more complex passages of French cited in the main text. Where possible I give an already published translation; otherwise the translations are my own.

pp. 5–6   J.-F. Lyotard, *Le Différend*: 'Authority is not something which can be deduced. Efforts to legitimate authority lead to the vicious circle (I have authority over you because you authorise me to have it), to question-begging (authorisation authorises authority), to the infinite regress (x is authorised by y, who is authorised by z), to the paradox of the idiolect (God, Life, etc. designates me to exercise authority, only I am the witness of this revelation).'

p. 28   R. Barthes, 'Diderot, Brecht, Eisenstein': 'Representation is not defined directly by imitation: even if one gets rid of notions of the "real", of the "vraisemblable", or the "copy", there will still be representation for so long as a subject (author, reader, spectator or voyeur) casts his *gaze* towards a horizon on which he cuts out the base of a triangle, his eye (or his mind) forming the apex. The "Organon of Representation" (which it is today becoming possible to write because there are intimations of *something else*) will have as its dual foundation the sovereignty of the act of cutting out (*découpage*) and the unity of the subject of that action. The substance of the various arts will therefore be of little importance; certainly, theatre and cinema are direct expressions of geometry . . . but classic (readable) literary discourse . . . is also a representational, geometrical discourse in that it cuts out segments in order to depict them: to

274

discourse (the classics would have said) is simply "to depict the tableau one has in one's mind".' (Trans. S. Heath)

p. 31   R. Barthes, *S/Z*: '*Objectivity* and *subjectivity* are of course forces which can take over the text, but they are forces which have no affinity with it. Subjectivity is a plenary image, with which I may be thought to encounter the text, but whose deceptive plenitude is merely the wake of all the codes which constitute me, so that my subjectivity has ultimately the generality of stereotypes. Objectivity is the same type of replenishment; it is an imaginary system like the rest . . . an image which serves to name me advantageously, to make myself known, "misknown", even to myself.' (Trans. R. Miller)

pp. 36–7   P. Sollers, *Logiques*: 'realism . . . that prejudice which consists in believing that a piece of writing must express something that is not given in the writing, something on which unanimity can be immediately realised. But it is necessary to see that this agreement can only rest on pre-established conventions, the notion of *reality* being itself a convention and a mode of conformism, a sort of tacit contract passes between the individual and his social group.'

p. 50   G. Genette, *Figures II*: 'What defines the *vraisemblable* is the formal respect for the principle of the norm, that is, the existence of an implied relation between the particular conduct attributed to a given character and an accepted, implicit general maxim.'

p. 57   M. Foucault, *La Volonté de savoir*: 'The logic of *censorship*. This interdiction is thought to take three forms: affirming that such a thing is not permitted, preventing it from being said, denying that it exists. Forms that are difficult to reconcile. But it is here that one imagines a sort of logical sequence that characterizes censorship mechanisms: it links the inexistent, the illicit and the inexpressible in such a way that each is at the same time the principle and the effect of the others: one must not talk about what is forbidden until it is annulled in reality; what is inexistent has no right to show itself, even in the order of speech where its existence is declared; and that which one must keep silent about is banished from reality as the thing that is tabooed above all else. The logic of power exerted on sex is the paradoxical logic of a law that might be expressed as an injunction of nonexistence, non-manifestation, and silence.' (Trans. R. Hurley)

p. 65 R. Barthes, 'L'Effet de réel': 'Semiotically, the "concrete detail" is constituted by the *direct* collusion of a referent and a signifier; the signified is expelled from the sign, and along with it, of course, there is eliminated the possibility of developing a *form of the signified* . . . This is what might be called the *referential illusion*. The truth behind this illusion is this: eliminated from the realist utterance as a signified of denotation, the 'real' slips back in as a signified of connotation; for at the very moment when these details are supposed to denote reality directly, all they do, tacitly, is to signify it. Flaubert's barometer, Michelet's little door, say, in the last analysis, only this: *we are the real*. It is the category of the 'real', and not its various contents, which is being signified; in other words, the very absence of the signified, to the advantage of the referent, standing alone, becomes the true signifier of realism. A reality effect is produced . . . ' (Trans. R. Carter)

p. 83 H. de Balzac, *Splendeurs et misères des courtisanes*: 'It is to the glory of Royer-Collard that he proclaimed the regular victory of natural over dictated feelings, to have maintained the cause of the anteriority of oaths by insisting that the law of hospitality, for instance, was binding on a man to the point of annulling the virtue of a juridical oath.' (Trans. R. Heppenstall)

p. 91 H. de Balzac, *Illusions perdues*: 'This sinister accumulation of refuse, these windows grimy with rain and dust, these squat huts with rags and tatters heaped around them, the filthy condition of the half-built walls, this agglomeration reminiscent of a gypsy camp or the booths on a fairground – the sort of temporary constructions which Paris heaps about the monuments it fails to build – this contorted physiognomy was wonderfully in keeping with the teeming variety of trades carried on beneath these brazenly indecent hutments, noisy with babble and hectic with gaiety, and where an enormous amount of business has been transacted between the Revolutions of 1789 and 1830. For twenty years the Stock Exchange stood opposite, on the ground-floor of the Palais-Royal. There then public opinion was formed, reputations were made and unmade, political and financial affairs discussed. People met in these galleries before and after Stock Exchange hours. The Paris of bankers and merchants often encumbered the court-yard of the Palais-Royal and swarmed inside the building for shelter in rainy weather . . . It was the home ground of publishers, poets, pedlars of prose, politicians, milliners and lastly the prostitutes who roamed about it in the evenings. There news buzzed and books by both young and established authors abounded. There Parliamentary conspiracies were hatched and publishers concocted their mendacities.' (Trans. H. J. Hunt)

p. 96   H. de Balzac, *Illusions perdues*: 'In France then, in politics as well as ethics, all and sundry reached a goal which gave the lie to their beginnings: their opinions belied their behaviour, or else their behaviour belied their opinions . . . hence, young man, another precept: put up a fine outward show! Hide the reverse of the coin, but keep the obverse bright and shining . . . From then on you'll no longer be guilty of tarnishing the back-cloth in the great theatre which we call the world. Napoleon had a phrase for this: "Wash your dirty linen in private." There is a corollary to this second precept: *form* is all-important.' (Trans. Hunt)

p. 115   L. de Bonald, *Législation primitive*: 'Speech is therefore, in the commerce of ideas, what money is in the commerce of goods, the real expression of values because it is value itself. And our sophists would like to make of it a conventional sign, roughly like paper money, a sign without value, which designates anything and everything, and expresses nothing, in so far as it can be exchanged for money, the real expression of all values.'

pp. 125–6   Stendhal, *Le Rouge et le Noir*: 'The result of this night of love was that she imagined she had succeeded in

conquering her love. (This page will damage its author in more ways than one. Ice-cold hearts will accuse him of impropriety. He does not attempt to insult those young persons who shine in Parisian drawing-rooms by supposing a single one of them to be susceptible to mad impulses such as degrade Mathilde's character. This character is wholly drawn from imagination, and conceived as being well outside those social habits which will assure the nineteenth century so distinguished a place amongst all other centuries . . . Now that we are quite agreed that a character like Mathilde's is impossible in our virtuous, and no less prudent age, I am less afraid of vexing you by continuing my account of the follies of this charming girl).'
(Trans. M. Shaw)

pp. 129–30   Stendhal, *Vie de Métastase*: 'It is quite simply the fact that our vulgar languages, which are but a series of conventional signs for expressing things that are generally known, do not at all possess any signs for expressing those movements of the soul which perhaps but twenty people out of a thousand have felt.'

pp. 133–4   Stendhal, *Le Rouge et le Noir*: 'Provided you did not treat God, the clergy, the King, or anyone holding public office as a matter for jest; provided you did not speak in praise of Béranger, the newspapers of the opposite party, Voltaire, Rousseau, or anyone allowing himself any freedom of speech; provided above all you never mentioned politics – then you were free to discuss anything you pleased.' (Trans. M. Shaw)

p. 143   Stendhal, *La Vie de Henri Brulard*: 'I shall find it very hard to give a rational account of my love for Angela Pietragrua. How can I give an account of so many follies that is at all rational? Where should I begin? How could I make it all understandable? By confining myself to rational forms of explanation I should do too great an injustice to what I want to tell . . . I declare I cannot go on, the tale is too great for the teller.' (Trans. J. Stewart and B. Knight)

p. 145   R. Barthes, 'On échoue toujours à parler de ce qu'on aime': 'What is necessary in order to construct a myth? What is necessary is the working of two forces: first, a hero, a great liberating figure: that's Bonaparte, who

enters into Milan, penetrates Italy . . . ; next, an
opposition, an antithesis, in brief a paradigm which
stages the combat of Good and Evil and thus produces
what is lacking in the Album and what belongs to the
Book, that is, a sense: on the one hand, in those opening pages of the *Chartreuse*, boredom, wealth,
avarice, Austria, the Police, Asciano, Grianta; on the
other hand, intoxication, heroism, poverty, the
Republic, Fabrice, Milan; and above all, on the one
hand, the Father, on the other, Women.'

p. 155   G. de Nerval, *Aurélia*: 'I walked in the evening,
full of serenity in the moonlight, and, as I lifted my
eyes to the trees, it seemed to me that the leaves
moved capriciously, in such a way as to form the
images of knights and ladies borne on caparisoned
steeds. To me they were the triumphant figures of
ancestors. This thought led me to think that there was
a vast conspiracy of all animate beings to re-establish
the world in its first harmony . . . that an uninterrupted
chain linked around the earth all the intelligences
devoted to this general communication . . . ' (Trans.
R. Aldington)

p. 155   *Aurélia*: 'Everything lives, everything acts, everything
corresponds; the magnetic rays emanating from
myself or others traverse unimpeded the infinite chain
of created things.' (Trans. R. Aldington)

p. 155   *Aurélia*: 'The walls of the room seemed to open on to
infinite distances, I seemed to see an uninterrupted
chain of men and women, in whom I was and who were
myself. The costumes of all nations, the images of all
lands appeared distinctly at the same time, as if my
faculties of attention had been multiplied without falling into confusion, through a phenomenon of space
similar to that of time, whereby a century of action is
concentrated in a minute's dreaming.' (Trans.
R. Aldington)

p. 156   *Aurélia*: 'It seemed as if my feet sank into successive
layers of buildings of different epochs. These phan-
toms of buildings kept opening into others . . . '
(Trans. R. Aldington)

p. 158   G. de Nerval, *Sylvie*: 'As she sang, the shadows fell
from the great trees, and the early moonlight touched

her as she stood alone in our listening circle. She ended, and no one dared to break the silence. The lawn was covered with light, condensed vapours, which unrolled their white curls on the tips of the grasses. We felt we were in paradise.' (Trans. R. Aldington)

p. 162   *Sylvie*: 'This vague and unhoping love for an actress . . . had its germ in the memory of Adrienne . . . The resemblance to a face forgotten for years was henceforth outlined with curious clarity; it was a pencil drawing marked by time which became a picture, like those old drawings of the masters admired in museums when we find the dazzling original.' (Trans. R. Aldington)

p. 165   J. Derrida, 'La Mythologie blanche': 'The definition of metaphor has its place in the *Poetics*, a work which starts off as a study of *mimesis*. Now *mimesis* does not occur without theoretical awareness of resemblance or likeness, that is, of what will always be taken to be the condition of metaphor.' (Trans. F. C. T. Moore)

p. 170   *Sylvie*: 'Such are the delusions which charm and lead us astray in the morning of life. I have tried to set them down in no particular order, but there are many hearts which will understand me. Illusions fall one by one, like the husks of a fruit, and the fruit is experience. Its taste is bitter, yet there is something sharp about it which is tonic.' (Trans. R. Aldington)

p. 171   *Sylvie*: 'In the morning when I open the window, framed with roses and grapevines, I discover with delight a green horizon of ten leagues where the poplars are aligned like armies. Here and there a few villages shelter under their pointed spires, built, as they say there, in bony points. First of all there is Othys – then Eve, then Ver; I could distinguish Ermenonville through the woods if it had a spire; but in that philosophical spot they quite neglected the church. After I have filled my lungs with the pure air you breathe on those high plains, I go gaily downstairs, and take a turn to the pastry-cook's.' (Trans. R. Aldington)

p. 195   G. Flaubert, *L'Éducation sentimentale*: 'She gave him her gloves, and a week later her handkerchief. She called him Frederic and he called her Marie, worshipping that name, which he said was made specially to be breathed in ecstasy, and which seemed to contain clouds of incense and trails of roses.' (Trans. R. Baldick)

p. 199   *L'Éducation sentimentale*: 'She did not wax enthusiastic about literature, but she made simple penetrating remarks which showed a charming intelligence. She liked travelling, listening to the sound of the wind in the woods, and walking bare-headed in the rain. Frederic listened to these confidences with delight . . . ' (Trans. R. Baldick)

p. 229   M. Robert, *Roman des origines et origines du roman*: 'the visionary bewitched by his visions and transformations, creating in isolation and against reality a dream world unrelated to experience . . . , imprisoned in the pre-Oedipal universe whose only law is still the omnipotence of thought'. (Trans. S. Rabinovitch)

p. 243   J.-F. Lyotard, *Le Différend*: 'As distinct from a dispute, a *différend* would be a case of conflict between two parties (at least) which could not be resolved equitably, in the absence of a rule of adjudication applicable to the two arguments.' (N.B. Lyotard's specialised use of the term 'différend' is such as to make it untranslatable.)

pp. 250–1   R. Barthes, *Le Plaisir du texte*: 'One evening, half-asleep on the banquette in a bar, just for fun, I tried to enumerate all the languages within earshot: music, conversations, the sounds of chairs, glasses, a whole stereophony of which a square in Tangiers (as described by Severo Sarduy) is the exemplary site. That too spoke within me, and this so-called "interior" speech was very like the noise of the square, like that amassing of minor voices coming to me from the outside: I myself was a public square, a *sook*: through me passed words, tiny syntagms, bits of formulae, and *no sentence formed* . . . ' (Trans. R. Miller)

SELECT BIBLIOGRAPHY

Abrams, M. *The Mirror and the Lamp*, New York, 1958
Adorno, T. *Prisms*, London, 1967
Agacinski, S. *et al. Mimesis. Des articulations*, Paris, 1975
Amossy, R. and Rosen, E. *Les Discours du cliché*, Paris, 1982
Auerbach, E. *Mimesis, The Representation of Reality in Western Literature*, New York, 1957
Barthes, R. *Mythologies*, Paris, 1957
  'L'Effet de réel', *Communications* 11, 1968
  S/Z, Paris, 1970
  Le Plaisir du texte, Paris, 1973
  'Diderot, Brecht, Eisenstein', *Revue d'esthétique*, Paris, 1973
  Leçon, Paris, 1978
  'On échoue toujours à parler de ce qu'on aime', *Tel Quel*, no. 85, 1980
Bataille, G. *La Littérature et le Mal*, Paris, 1957
Benjamin, W. *Charles Baudelaire: A Lyric Poet in the Era of High Capitalism*, London, 1972
Benveniste, E. *Problèmes de linguistique générale*, Paris, 1966
Berger, P. and Luckmann, T. *The Social Construction of Reality*, London, 1971
Bersani, L. *From Balzac to Beckett*, New York, 1970
  A Future for Astyanax, London, 1978
Bryson, N. *Tradition and Desire. From David to Delacroix*, Cambridge, 1984
Chambers, R. *Story and Situation: Narrative Seduction and the Power of Fiction*, Manchester, 1984
Coward, R. and Ellis, J. *Language and Materialism, Developments in Semiology and the Theory of the Subject*, London, 1977
Crouzet, M. *Stendhal et le langage*, Paris, 1981
Culler, J. *Structuralist Poetics*, London, 1975
Deleuze, G. and Guattari, F. *Mille Plateaux*, Paris, 1980
Derrida, J. *L'Écriture et la différence*, Paris, 1967
  Positions, Paris, 1972
  La Dissémination, Paris, 1972
  'La Mythologie blanche', *Poétique*, no. 5, 1971

Select bibliography

'Living on: Border Lines' in *Deconstruction and Criticism* (H. Bloom *et al.*), New York, 1979

Descombes, V. *L'Inconscient malgré lui*, Paris, 1977
    Modern French Philosophy, Cambridge, 1980

Douglas, M. *Implicit Meanings*, London, 1975
    (ed.) *Rules and Meanings*, London, 1973

Dummett, M. *Frege: Philosophy of Language*, London, 1973

Eagleton, T. *The Function of Criticism, From 'The Spectator' to Poststructuralism*, London, 1984

Eco, U. *A Theory of Semiotics*, Bloomington, 1976
    The Role of the Reader, London, 1981
    Semiotics and the Philosophy of Language, London, 1984

Felman, S. *La 'Folie' dans l'œuvre romanesque de Stendhal*, Paris, 1971
    La Folie et la chose littéraire, Paris, 1978

Foucault, M. *Les Mots et les choses*, Paris, 1966
    La Volonté de savoir, Paris, 1976

Frege, G. *The Philosophical Writings of Gottlob Frege*, Oxford, 1970

Freud, S. *Jokes and Their Relation to the Unconscious*, London, 1976

Frye, N. *Anatomy of Criticism*, New York, 1965
    Fables of Identity, New York, 1963

Genette, G. *Figures*, Paris, 1966
    Figures II, Paris, 1969
    Mimologiques, Paris, 1976

Ginzburg, C. 'Signes, Pistes, Traces', *Le Débat*, November 1980

Girard, R. *Mensonge romantique et vérité romanesque*, Paris, 1961

Goldmann, L. *Pour une sociologie du roman*, Paris, 1964

Gombrich, E. *Meditations on a Hobby Horse*, London, 1963

Goodman, N. *Languages of Art*, Indianapolis, 1976

Habermas, J. *Knowledge and Human Interests*, Boston, 1972

Hegel, G. *Äesthetik*, Stuttgart, 1928 (trans. Knox, Oxford, 1975)

Jakobson, R. *Problèmes de linguistique générale*, Paris, 1963

Jameson, F. *Marxism and Form*, Princeton, 1971

Jean, R. *La Poétique du désir*, Paris

Jeanneret, M. *La Lettre perdue*, Paris, 1978

Kanes, M. *Balzac's Comedy of Words*, Princeton, 1975

Kermode, F. *The Sense of an Ending*, Oxford, 1968
    Essays on Fiction 1971–82, London, 1983

Kristeva, J. *Semiotiké*, Paris, 1969
    Le Texte du roman, The Hague, 1970

Lacoue-Labarthe, P. 'Typographie' in *Mimesis. Des articulations* (Agacinski *et al.*)

Leach, E. *Culture and Communication*, Cambridge, 1976

Lentricchia, F. *After the New Criticism*, Chicago, 1980

Lukács, G. *Studies in European Realism*, New York, 1964
    History and Class Consciousness, London, 1971

Select bibliography

The Theory of the Novel, London, 1978

Lyotard, J.-F. *La Condition postmoderne*, Paris, 1979

Au juste, Paris, 1979

Le Différend, Paris, 1983

McCabe, C. *James Joyce and the Revolution of the Word*, London, 1978

Norris, C. *The Deconstructive Turn*, London, 1983

Nuttall, A. D. *A New Mimesis*, London, 1983

Peirce, C. S. *Collected Papers*, Cambridge, Mass., 1931–58

Poulet, G. *Les Métamorphoses du cercle*, Paris, 1961

Price, M. *Forms of Life, Character and Moral Imagination in Literature*, New Haven and London, 1983

Ricœur, P. *La Métaphore vive*, Paris, 1975

'Narrative Time', *Critical Inquiry*, vol. 7, no. 1, 1980

'Mimesis and Representation', *Annals of Scholairship*, vol. 11, no. 3, 1981

'On Interpretation', *Philosophy in France Today*, Cambridge, 1983

Robert, M. *Roman des origines et origines du roman*, Paris, 1972

Rorty, R. *Philosophy and The Mirror of Nature*, Princeton, 1980

Consequences of Pragmatism, Minneapolis, 1982

Ron, M. 'Free Indirect Discourse, Mimetic Language Games and the Subject of Fiction', *Poetics Today*, vol. 2, no. 2, 1981

Rousset, J. *Forme et signification*, Paris, 1962

Sartre, J.-P. *Qu'est-ce que la littérature?*, Paris, 1948

Les Mots, Paris, 1971

Searle, J. *Expression and Meaning*, Cambridge, 1979

Schütz, A. *Collected Papers*, The Hague, 1967

Simpson, D. *Irony and Authority in Romantic Poetry*, London, 1979

Sollers, P. *Logiques*, Paris, 1968

Starobinski, J. *Les Mots sous les mots: les anagrammes de Ferdinand de Saussure*, Paris, 1971

Stern, J. P. *On Realism*, London, 1973

Tanner, T. *Adultery in the Novel, Contract and Transgression*, Baltimore and London, 1979

Todorov, T. *Poétique de la prose*, Paris, 1971

Les Genres du discours, Paris, 1978

Théories du symbole, Paris, 1977

Vernant, J.-P. 'Image et apparence dans la théorie platonicienne de la mimesis', *Journal de psychologie*, April–June, 1975

Watt, I. *The Rise of the Novel*, London, 1970

Weber, S. *Unwrapping Balzac*, Toronto, 1979

Williams, R. *Marxism and Literature*, Oxford, 1977

Wilson, B. (ed.) *Rationality*, Oxford, 1974

Wittgenstein, L. *Philosophical Investigations*, Oxford, 1972

Wollheim, R. *Art and its Objects*, London, 1980

INDEX